PRIVATE ASSOCIATIONS IN THE ANCIENT GREEK WORLD

Private associations abounded in the ancient Greek world and beyond, and this volume provides the first large-scale study of the strategies of governance which they employed. Emphasis is placed on the values fostered by the regulations of associations, the complexities of the private–public divide (and that divide's impact on polis institutions) and the dynamics of regional and global networks and group identity. The attested links between rules and religious sanctions also illuminate the relationship between legal history and religion. Moreover, possible links between ancient associations and the early Christian churches will prove particularly valuable for scholars of the New Testament. The book concludes by using the regulations of associations to explore a novel and revealing aspect of the interaction between the Mediterranean world, India and China. This title is also available as Open Access on Cambridge Core.

VINCENT GABRIELSEN is Professor of Ancient History at the SAXO-Institute of the University of Copenhagen. He specialises in Greek and Hellenistic history and epigraphy and was Director of 'The Copenhagen Associations Project' and is now Director of 'The Rhodes Centennial Project'.

MARIO C. D. PAGANINI is a Postdoc Research Associate at the Austrian Academy of Sciences. He is an ancient historian and papyrologist with a particular interest in the socio-cultural history of Hellenistic and Roman Egypt.

T0384727

PRIVATE ASSOCIATIONS IN THE ANCIENT GREEK WORLD

Regulations and the Creation of Group Identity

EDITED BY

VINCENT GABRIELSEN

University of Copenhagen

MARIO C. D. PAGANINI

Austrian Academy of Sciences

CAMBRIDGE
UNIVERSITY PRESS

University Printing House, Cambridge CB2 8BS, United Kingdom

One Liberty Plaza, 20th Floor, New York, NY 10006, USA

477 Williamstown Road, Port Melbourne, VIC 3207, Australia

314–321, 3rd Floor, Plot 3, Splendor Forum, Jasola District Centre, New Delhi – 110025, India

103 Penang Road, #05–06/07, Visioncrest Commercial, Singapore 238467

Cambridge University Press is part of the Cambridge University Press & Assessment

It furthers the University's mission by disseminating knowledge in the pursuit of education, learning, and research at the highest international levels of excellence.

www.cambridge.org
Information on this title: www.cambridge.org/9781009281300

DOI: 10.1017/9781009281317

First published 2023
Reissued as Open Access, 2023

A catalogue record for this publication is available from the British Library.

ISBN 978-1-009-28130-0 Paperback

Contents

Tables

Contributors

DR ILIAS ARNAOUTOGLOU, Academy of Athens

PROF. JAN-MATHIEU CARBON, Queen's University at Kingston

DR BENEDIKT ECKHARDT, University of Edinburgh

DR KASPER G. EVERS, Independent Scholar, PhD from the University of Copenhagen

PROF. VINCENT GABRIELSEN, University of Copenhagen

PROF. NIKOS GIANNAKOPOULOS, National and Kapodistrian University of Athens

DR MICAELA LANGELLOTTI, University of Newcastle

DR MARIO C. D. PAGANINI, Austrian Academy of Sciences

DR STELLA SKALTSA, University of Copenhagen

PROF. NICOLAS TRAN, University of Poitiers

DR SOPHIA ZOUMBAKI, National Hellenic Research Foundation

Preface

We should like to thank all the authors in this volume for their hard work, perseverance and patience during the long and at times not so straightforward path towards publication. Before being submitted to review by the Press, the chapters in this volume had been object of independent peer-review by international specialists: we are very grateful to them for accepting our invitation to act as readers and for their invaluable contribution.

The idea for this volume originated in a conference organised by the editors at the Danish Institute at Athens in May 2014, as part of the research activities of the Copenhagen Associations Project, generously funded by two grants of the Carlsberg Foundation. We are very grateful for the support received.

Vincent Gabrielsen
Mario C. D. Paganini

Abbreviations

Abbreviations in the Bibliography follow those of *L'Année Philologique*; editions of Greek inscriptions follow the abbreviations of the *Supplementum Epigraphicum Graecum*; editions of papyri follow the abbreviations in the *Checklist of Editions of Greek, Latin, Demotic, and Coptic Papyri, Ostraca, and Tablets* (http://papyri.info/docs/checklist); references to literary works by ancient authors follow the abbreviations and standards of Liddell, Scott and Jones, *A Greek-English Lexicon* and of the *Oxford Classical Dictionary* (4th ed.).

In addition to the above-mentioned, the following abbreviations are employed:

AE:	*Année Épigraphique.*
AGRW:	Ascough et al. 2012.
APIS:	The Advanced Papyrological Information System (https://papyri.info/).
Arthash(astra):	Kangle 1965–72.
AvP:	Habicht, Ch. 1969. *Altertümer von Pergamon, Band 8/3: Die Inschriften des Asklepieions.* Berlin. De Gruyter.
CGRN:	Carbon, J.-M., Peels, S., and Pirenne-Delforge, V. 2017-. *A Collection of Greek Ritual Norms* (http://cgrn.ulg.ac.be/).
CIL:	*Corpus Inscriptionum Latinarum.*
GRA	I: Kloppenborg and Ascough 2011.
GRA	II: Harland 2014.
I.Aeg. Thrace:	Loukopoulou, L. D., Parissaki, M. G., Psoma, S., and Zournatzi, A. (eds.) 2005. Επιγραφές της Θράκης του Αιγαίου: μεταξύ των ποταμών Νέστου και Έβρου (Νομοί Ξάνθης, Ροδόπης και Έβρου). Athens. National Hellenic Research Foundation.

I.Halikarnassos:	McCabe, D. F. 1991. *Halikarnassos Inscriptions. Texts and List*. 'The Princeton Project on the Inscriptions of Anatolia', The Institute for Advanced Study, Princeton. Packard Humanities Institute CD #6.
I.Rhamnous:	Petrakos 1999b.
IED:	Minon, S. 2007. *Les inscriptions éléennes dialectales (VIe-IIe siècle avant J.-C.).* 2 vols. Geneva. Droz.
IScM:	Stoian, I. 1987. *Inscriptiones Daciae et Scythiae minoris antiquae. Series altera. Inscriptiones Scythiae minoris Graecae et Latinae, II: Tomis et territorium.* Bucharest.
NGSL:	Lupu 2005 (second edition 2009).
PAT:	Hillers, D. R., and Cussini, E. 1996. *Palmyrene Aramaic Texts*. Baltimore and London. The Johns Hopkins University Press.
SER:	Pugliese Carratelli, G. 'Supplemento Epigrafico Rodio', *ASAA* 30-2 (1952–54): 247–316.
Thera II:	Doumas. C. (ed.) 1980. *Thera and the Aegean World II. Proceedings of the Second International Congress, Santorini, Greece, August 1978*. London. Thera and the Aegean World (distributed by Aris and Phillips).

This title is part of the Cambridge University Press *Flip it Open* Open Access Books program and has been "flipped" from a traditional book to an Open Access book through the program.

Flip it Open sells books through regular channels, treating them at the outset in the same way as any other book; they are part of our library collections for Cambridge Core, and sell as hardbacks and ebooks. The one crucial difference is that we make an upfront commitment that when each of these books meets a set revenue threshold we make them available to everyone Open Access via Cambridge Core.

This paperback edition has been released as part of our Open Access commitment and we would like to use this as an opportunity to thank the libraries and other buyers who have helped us flip this and the other titles in the program to Open Access.

To see the full list of libraries that we know have contributed to *Flip it Open*, as well as the other titles in the program please visit http://www.cambridge.org/fio-acknowledgements

CHAPTER I

Associations' Regulations from the Ancient Greek World and Beyond

An Introduction

Vincent Gabrielsen and Mario C. D. Paganini

The Book's Subject and Aims

Private Associations in the Ancient Greek World investigates the rules and regulations produced by ancient private associations in an attempt to show why and how associations were creating a system of well-ordered groups within their communities. Regulations represent, in fact, an understudied aspect of ancient associative life: this book aims to fill this gap by approaching the well-known phenomenon of ancient associations from a new angle. It analyses the organisational structures, legislative mechanisms and features of associations, while at the same time investigating the potential models from – and interrelations with – the habits and strategies of political institutions. It also provides an assessment of the associations' impact on the broader socio-cultural and physical environment and of their role in local societies, thanks to the establishment of such regulations. The book explores the ideology, values, ideas and aspects of identity embedded in the regulations as ways adopted by associations to create a specific profile to present to the outside world, as well as to members (both existing and future).

Although regulations of associations received attention in the classic accounts on the subject,[1] this was generally done in connection with commentaries on specific individual inscriptions, particularly rich in detail concerning the organisational and administrative aspects of associations.[2] Later works were even less systematic. The same generally applies to the papyri too: treatment of the subject took the form of learned commentaries on individual Greek or Demotic texts, typically in connection with their

---

[1] Foucart 1873, Ziebarth 1896, Waltzing 1895–1900 and Poland 1909.

[2] For instance, the regulations of the *Iobacchoi* (*IG* II² 1368; *LSCG* 51 = *CAPInv.* 339, with Poland 1909: 67–8 and *passim*, cf. A59; Tod 1932: 71–93; Moretti 1986; Jaccottet 2011) or the *hieros nomos* from Philadelphia (Keil and von Premerstein 1914: 18–21 no 18; *TAM* V.3 1539; *Syll.*³ 985 = *CAPInv.* 348, with Weinreich 1919; Barton and Horsley 1981).

publication.[3] On the whole, none of these works on associations made the regulations the object of a systematic study, let alone sought to contextualise the historical significance of the phenomenon.[4] Some broader overarching issues were, however, addressed in connection with the Egyptian material: the main question was whether the rules, along with the system of governance they imply, represented an independent Egyptian tradition, which was adopted by the Greek-speakers in Egypt,[5] or a single, common Greek–Egyptian tradition, probably originating from Greece.[6] Furthermore, more recent studies on Egypt have aptly started to analyse associations' rules with a focus on issues of membership, social standing and personal connections in different localities during the Ptolemaic and Roman periods.[7] However, further issues remain to be addressed regarding the phenomenon not only within Graeco-Roman Egypt, but also outside of its boundaries.

The geographical focus of the investigation is the Greek-speaking Mediterranean, based on at least two reasons. First, the book is linked with the work done on the Inventory of Ancient Associations, an open-access online database of all known private associations attested in the Greek-speaking world from ca 500 BC to ca AD 300.[8] Second, the analysis aims at uncovering similarities as well as differences in a comparative outlook within a common cultural sphere: the chapters of this book, by various international specialists, study specific aspects of associations' regulations from selected regions of the Greek-speaking world. Furthermore, the investigation concentrates on the Hellenistic and Imperial times, as most of the evidence on the subject dates from those periods.

The approach adopted in this book is therefore cautiously selective. However, in order to provide a strong comparative perspective and to give

---

[3] For instance, Boak 1937a; Boak 1937b (on *P.Mich* V 243, 244, 245); Norsa 1937 (on *PSI* XII 1265); de Cenival 1972: 3–10 (on *P.Lille Dem.* I 29) and 103–7 (on *P.Berlin Dem.* 3115); Arlt and Monson 2013 (= *P.Bagnall* 42 = *P.Standford Green Dem. inv.* 21).

[4] Close attempts in this direction are de Cenival 1972 (although providing a comprehensive and detailed study of all the Demotic material on the subject available at the time, this work fails to provide a larger historical analysis of the phenomenon in all its complexity and potentiality) and Schnöckel 2006 (re-edition of a 1956 doctoral dissertation, focusing on the regulations from the Tebtynis *grapheion* in early Roman Egypt). On the other hand, Muszynski 1977 is a descriptive work with limited scope.

[5] Roberts, Skeat and Nock 1936: 72–7; Muszynski 1977: 160–1.

[6] Boak 1937b: 219–20; Muhs 2001: 5.

[7] See, for instance, Muhs 2001; Monson 2007; Venticinque 2010.

[8] See https://ancientassociations.ku.dk/; each association recorded in the online Inventory of Ancient Associations is referred to by its unique identifier (*CAPInv.* #). This work was an international collaboration between forty specialists of various regions of antiquity and the principal outcome of the Copenhagen Association Project, generously funded by the Carlsberg Foundation.

a taste of the global character of the phenomenon of private associations (even in their legislative habits), we thought it important to include two case studies of associations operating outside our main area of enquiry (both geographically and temporally) with two different approaches: one follows within the path of tradition and looks at the associations of the Roman West, namely, at Ostia, whereas the other provides a new and unconventional perspective by bringing into the picture associations from ancient and medieval Asia, namely, from India and China. Thus, the content coverage, though selective, is ample, as it reaches beyond Greece and Asia Minor and includes Egypt, Ostia and the East.[9] By the same token, the book encompasses different (socio-political) local realities and source material of a different nature. This obviously results in a great variety of contexts and the reader should not expect absolute uniformity. Although potentially confusing or discouraging at first, such diversity represents the biggest value of this analysis: it allows the reader to better appreciate the world of associations and their normative attitudes in all their richness, while anchoring them in the specificities of their various local societies, from which they cannot be abstracted. Such a wide-ranging comparative approach produces a new perspective, which challenges us to cross the confines of traditional scholarly attitudes – for instance, the Hellenocentric view of the polis – in favour of a broader outlook.

Thanks to its comparative efforts, it is hoped that the book may be of interest to a wider readership, not only to specialists of associations and to those interested in the social, legal, administrative and religious histories of the Greek and Roman worlds, but also to historians and specialists of other periods and geographical areas. As a matter of fact, the comparative results gained in the volume encourage us all to have an open mind and be aware of the broader perspective, considering relevant developments of social phenomena outside of the confines of one's specialisation. Through the comprehensive and comparative analysis of different aspects of rules of associations, through the focus on the legal and institutional workings of non-state entities, on their regulation of space and on their interaction and reciprocal dialogue with local realities (both public and private), this volume aspires to make a new, independent – albeit perhaps modest – contribution to the field.

---

[9] Despite our best efforts, we were unable to include a systematic treatment uniquely devoted to the rich Demotic material. However, the Demotic regulations are exploited in various chapters of the volume (for instance, in Chapter 3 by Eckhardt, Chapter 6 by Arnaoutoglou, Chapter 8 by Langellotti and Chapter 10 by Evers) in connection with the larger analysis of specific aspects of normative behaviours by associations.

The chapters of this book adopt a threefold approach for their inquiries into the world of associations' regulations: a descriptive approach (by presenting the main aspects of organisational life and its ideology, beliefs, principles and values), a comparative approach (by relating associations' norms and procedures with those known to apply in other local institutional environments) and a contextualising approach (by investigating the wider role played by associations in their society thanks to their self-presentation as normative micro-systems). The last two approaches in particular have never before been applied to the topic of ancient associations.

What Is a Private Association?

Answering this question means identifying the clear object of investigation of the present volume. Both constituent elements of this notion need to be addressed: first, despite the intrinsic difficulties of providing universally valid and univocal definitions for ancient realities, we shall try to explain how we can identify an ancient association; second, we shall clarify what we mean by the term 'private'. It should be stated clearly that such an interest in a definition of the term is a modern scholarly concern: the ancients never spelt out of what they considered an association. However, the need for such a definition is no trivial matter, as it is fundamental for the selection of the material, in the interest of a stronger validity of research outputs. In this respect, we adopt a rather restrictive approach – often stricter than others – in order to identify a private association with some certainty: there is in fact a set of criteria that needs to be met.[10]

We understand an association to be a group of individuals gathering together as a body with some sense of self-identity (often expressed with general terms for 'association', such as *koinon, thiasos, synodos, collegium* and *corpus*, as well as with specific collective proper names, which encompass a variety of possible elements, from names of deities or activities to place names – also in combination), some form of organised structure (with more or less elaborate or codified regulations concerning membership and organisation) and some desire for a durable existence. They met in meetings or assemblies on more or less regular occasions for the most disparate reasons and with the most varied purposes and often behaved in

---

[10] For a lengthier discussion of the criteria defining private associations, see Gabrielsen and Thomsen 2015 and https://ancientassociations.ku.dk/CAPI/intro-criteria.php. See also Harland 2009: 26–35.

their dealings as a corporate body would. The terms employed (by associations themselves and by others) in the ancient sources to identify these realities are various but they mostly recall an idea of 'being, gathering, performing, possessing something together, as a community' – from the Greek term *koinon* to the Latin word *collegium*, for instance – thus showing how important the value of communality and, to some extent, some aspects of communal life were for associations' identity.[11] As associations' regulations clearly show, their members, besides being clearly defined vis-à-vis non-members (through criteria decided by themselves), were (expected to be) characterised by a relatively high degree of bonding, intimacy, solidarity, commitment and social cohesion.[12] Conversely, by the term 'private' we mean that associations were neither state-run institutions nor organisations established by the state: they were formed and managed by private individuals, with private funds and with self-government; they were not established as constituent parts of the constitutional features of the political communities where they were active. However, their private nature does not mean that they did not play any role in the public life of their communities; quite the opposite: they were not directly determined and run by the state but were very much embedded in, open to and projected towards the life of their local communities, which they in fact greatly influenced and by which they were influenced.

At the same time, private associations were quite distinct from other private groups, equally positioned outside of the constitutional spectrum of political or administrative institutions but characterised by a fundamentally different nature. These groups can be generically arranged under three headings: 'informal groups', 'ad hoc groups' and partnerships.

1. 'Informal groups' are a loosely knit type. Members' entrance/exit is often not only largely unregulated by formal rules but probably also undefined: individuals can join or leave the group without needing approval or notifying the other members. Likewise, formal meetings at which all members assemble might not occur at all. Additionally, even if some have a continuous (rather than temporary) existence, all groups belonging to this kind typically do not display any of the fundamental features that usually indicate a specific collective identity, such as a

---

[11] One should, however, note that some degree of polysemy existed: for instance, the Greek word *koinon* was employed to define a great range of disparate entities, from (private) associations to political communities such as federations or leagues.

[12] See Harland 2005: 493 for justified scepticism towards the view that, unlike Christian groups, associations lacked a developed sense of community.

collective proper name (for instance, the *Eikadeis*) and/or general designations for their group as a whole, such as the Greek terms *koinon*, *orgeones*, *thiasotai/thiasos*, *eranistai/eranos*, and so on. Demades and his friends in late fourth-century BC Athens are an example of such an informal group: high-profile people involved in politics, the navy and the grain trade, who shared common financial interests, helped each other and adopted concerted strategies for their own (economic) advantages.[13]

2. 'Ad hoc groups' were formed for the specific performance of a limited and specific task and did not extend their sphere of interest or sometimes even active existence beyond that occasion. These could include the so-called ad hoc cult groups or those age groups not embedded in the political constitution of the hosting community but, for instance, organised for a specific festival, event or ceremony. Although some had some form of collective identity and names, as well as potential rules of entry and exit, they do not display any other signs of more complex formal organisation (developed internal organisation, property, extended duration, etc.). An example of this may be the so-called *Thyadai*: a group of women who were active in the performance of rituals connected to the cult of Dionysus at Delphi.[14]

3. In partnerships (especially business partnerships), members are clearly defined, closely knit and probably also intimate, but by virtue of a written or unwritten legal contract between them. Besides stating (a) the purpose of their union, which is the group's *raison d'être*, this contract specifies (b) the duties and privileges of each member and (c) the duration of the group's existence, typically a (short) period of time that coincides with the completion of the stated purpose. After this time, the validity of the contract binding the members is dissolved. The holding of common property may result in added complications, as this would in fact have to be sold and its price redistributed amongst the former members when the partnership ended. The contractual character of partnerships and the nature of their activities give rise to certain legal requirements that the members have to meet in their dealings, especially vis-à-vis third parties: for this reason, partnerships might use one or more features of collective identity, such as a proper name. Partnerships, therefore, bear a resemblance to our associations. However, the majority of partnerships' fundamental features, not least their predetermined time of expiry, set them

[13] See Gabrielsen 2015.
[14] The term *thiasos*, if it was ever applied to the *Thyadai*, would most probably have meant simply worshippers. See e.g. [Plut.] *Moralia* 293d and 365a, with McInerney 1997: esp. 269 and 272.

apart from associations proper. An example of a partnership is the consortium of 'those gathering under the poplar tree' at Athens: a group of individuals who collectively purchased from the state the right to collect the *pentekoste* (the 2 per cent *ad valorem* tax) in 402/1 BC.[15]

Hybrid forms – between 'informal groups', 'ad hoc groups', partnerships and private associations proper – arguably existed. So far, they have largely remained unidentified. For analytical purposes, it is therefore preferable to regard them as theoretically distinct.[16] On the one hand, associations proper had regulations that stretched beyond the practical and somewhat narrow arrangements of the partnership; partnerships had contracts; on the other hand, mere groups needed nothing of the kind, because they could manage simply with an informal 'common understanding' among participants.

Traditional scholarship has tended to divide private associations into different types, giving them various general labels: trade/craft associations, professional associations, cult associations, religious associations and the like. This was done for practical reasons, in an attempt to give some structure to a complex phenomenon, which could often prove itself too confusing and too unsystematic for modern minds. Influenced – unconsciously or not – by the world of medieval and modern professional guilds and religious confraternities, historians have generally considered these types as fundamentally different sorts of organisations categorised on the basis of the alleged individual nature and main *raison d'être* of such associations. In many cases, such identification was mainly or solely based on the association's name, because little beyond that is often known from the sources: a group named *Apolloniastai*, for instance, would be labelled a 'cult association' and their existence would be linked to the worship of the god Apollo, whereas a weavers' club would be defined as a professional association, the activities of which were essentially believed to serve the purpose of facilitating their trade. However, things are more complex: although associations' names certainly advertised an image of the group and did have a meaning in connection with (one of) the characters that the group decided to project to the outer world at the time when the association chose its name, virtually nothing certain can be deduced from associations' names concerning their actual nature, activities, motives and

---

[15] And. 1.133–4. See Gabrielsen 2016b: 94–5.
[16] Associations and groups are treated indiscriminately in the essays collected in Fröhlich and Hamon 2013a. For the reason stated, 'Gruppenreligionen' in Rüpke 2007 may also be regarded as too vague a concept, not differentiating sufficiently between associations and other kinds of groups.

agenda – one of the first scholars of ancient associations had already remarked that 'the name of an association does not have to signify its purpose'.[17] As a matter of fact, the idea itself that an association had one sole nature or central purpose – together with our ability to identify it – is questionable: in those cases in which we know more about the activities and existence of an association, at a closer look we often see that the association's aims and interests were various and stretched beyond the confines of what its name or assigned 'type' might suggest.[18] The traditional division of ancient associations into types has therefore fallen short and is being rightly challenged.[19] Although convenient for the sake of classification and often also maintained in more recent scholarship (even in some of the chapters of this volume), in our view such a division is misleading and historically imprecise; therefore, it should be employed without dogmatic value and with caution – or, better still, it should be avoided altogether.

A recent trend in the field of ancient history has provided a new theoretical framework for the study of associations: the concept of networks. Interest in phenomena and realities beyond or outside the traditional poleis and the elements encompassed in their constitutional framework has gained momentum and has triggered the development of this different methodology for the purpose. One of its aims is to uncover and map out those – often complex – interrelations between various agents operating outside of the traditional categories of the political establishment: these relations are not always adequately visible through the lens of formal institutions or traditional descriptive categories; conversely, they become more clearly perceivable with a network approach. Therefore, such a method intends to highlight and interpret those agents that have been largely ignored in traditional scholarship but potentially did exert a distinct influence on historical change.[20] In fact, a steadily growing number of studies seek to understand and explain historical processes of various kinds by using the concept of network as their basic tool of analysis and network theory as the framework of their fundamental assumptions.

---

[17] 'Der Name einer Gennossenschaft braucht aber doch nicht ihren Zweck anzudeuten' (Poland 1909: 6). The contemporary Freemasonry is a further example in point: in spite of its name, the association neither gathers nor caters for stonemasons or builders (anymore).
[18] A variety of purposes for associations is also maintained by van Minnen 1987, Harland 2003: 55–87, Gibbs 2011, and Verboven 2011.
[19] See Gabrielsen 2001: esp. 218–19; Harland 2003: 28–53; Arnaoutoglou 2011a.
[20] See the essays in Malkin, Constantakopoulou and Panagopoulou 2009 and in Taylor and Vlassopoulos 2015a.

Some strive to retrieve the broader but dynamically evolving patterns of interrelations – cultural, technical, economic, and so on – formed through the circulation and use of artefacts over a wider geographical space.[21] Other studies explore the web of connections established by and between political communities (e.g. mother-cities and their colonies; leagues and confederations).[22] Highly promising steps have also been taken in the analysis of networks of cults and in the study of amphictyonies, which have shown rich potential in this respect too.[23] Finally, other studies focus on those networks that are generally described as social and economic networks, because they primarily reflect the organisational choices and connectivity strategies of individuals (rather than of political or large religious entities).[24] Associations are positioned within the frame of social, religious and economic networks.

The Regulations of Private Associations

The need to regulate the practicalities of internal organisation and the desire to set some principles for associations' life as a group prompted them to establish regulations. This is the data set that is the main object of investigation of this book: regulations were drawn up in various forms and are preserved both in inscriptions and in papyri, virtually covering the entire time span of antiquity (and beyond). In this respect, the reader should not expect absolute uniformity in the character and typologies in which associations' regulations could be clad, not only as differences could exist depending on place but also because the same association could adopt a variety of legal instruments – at the same moment or over a longer period of time – in order to formally record their dispositions. Furthermore, unwritten customs and traditions also existed and formed – an equally important – part of the system of regulations of associations: although these left no trace in our evidence and therefore cannot be assessed, they should neither be forgotten nor underestimated in their value.

Typologies and formats of the regulations of associations varied (see Table 1.1): they included decrees and contractual agreements, as well as

---

[21] Osborne 2009; Fenn and Römer-Strehl 2013. On network theory, in particular: Rutherford 2009, plus the works cited in Taylor and Vlassopoulos 2015b: 10–15 and in Davies 2015.

[22] Colonies: Malkin 2011 (also with some attention to cults). Leagues: Constantakopoulou 2015.

[23] On networks of cults: Bowden 2009; Davies 2009; see also Eidinow 2011 and Rutherford 2013. On amphictyonies: Hornblower 2009: 39; Malkin 2011: 224; Davies 2015: 252 n. 35.

[24] Granovetter 1983; Terpstra 2013; Taylor and Vlassopoulos 2015a; Bramoullé, Galeotti and Rogers 2016.

unilateral dispositions such as endowments or foundations, testamentary wills and sacred laws or orders. Furthermore, besides fully formed, self-contained and formal charters, dispositions on different matters and procedures of the association's life could also form part of other documents by associations, from honorific decrees to administrative decisions. Therefore, the body of associations' regulations often had the character of a corpus or a collection rather than of a single normative text: composed of various dispositions contained in and scattered over different documents, these regulations were often drawn up over the course of the association's lifetime, could be added one to another and also adapted to changing circumstances and needs. As established in relevant dispositions appended to associations' texts, the binding validity and force of these regulations was secured by their publicity, accessibility and preservation: associations made sure that members had access to these documents, which were often set up on stone on the association's premises as well as recorded on more perishable materials (tablets and papyrus) to be stored in the association's archives.[25] The best known examples of regulations by an association include the rules of the *Iobacchoi*, the name carried by the members of a second-century AD Athenian association which formally called itself 'the *Bakcheion*',[26] and the regulations of associations from Pharaonic, Ptolemaic and Roman Egypt, written in Demotic and Greek. There are some twenty sets of such regulations, often rich in details, the earliest of which dates to the early fourth century BC; they are commonly referred to by modern scholarship as *nomoi*, 'laws', from the name given to them in the Greek papyri.[27]

For reasons of practicality and theoretical analysis, one may draw a general distinction between two kinds or aspects of these regulations: on the one hand, we find rules relating to administrative matters and procedures; on the other hand, there are rules that focus on members' conduct. For instance, to the former belong rules establishing the

---

[25] The *Koragoi* of Mantinea, for instance, in all likelihood had their own archive where association's records were kept: *IG* V.2 265, l. 46 = *CAPInv.* 428 (see discussion by Zoumbaki in Chapter 7). See also the *synodos* of landowners of Psenemphaia in the Egyptian Delta (*CAPInv.* 1441): *I.Prose* 49, l. 54 (5 BC). On archival practices in antiquity, see, for instance, the papers in Faraguna 2013.

[26] *IG* II² 1368; *LSCG* 51 (AD 164/5) = *CAPInv.* 339. On the *Bakcheion* and their rules see also Chapter 2 by Giannakopoulos, Chapter 3 by Eckhardt and Chapter 6 by Arnaoutoglou.

[27] On Demotic regulations see de Cenival 1972. The earliest example of association regulations from Egypt (IV cent. BC) is de Cenival 1988 – evidence for associations is, however, older: see, for instance, de Cenival 1986, an account of an association of mortuary priests from the sixth century BC. On the regulations of associations from early Roman Egypt, see also the discussion by Langellotti in Chapter 8.

number, methods, frequency and length of appointment of associations' officials, the regulations about formal decision-making and voting procedures during assemblies and the dispositions about the handling of funds, including the penalties in case of non-compliance. Regulations requiring that members did not drink too much during associations' banquets, did not insult fellow members or sleep with other members' wives belong to the latter. Concerning the regulation of administrative matters, associations were acting as an independent organisation similar to a political community: in this respect, the character of their regulations resembles that of the laws of the state. On the other hand, by establishing rules of conduct, associations appear to be inclined to perform as a 'social' entity: in this respect, they share this trait with no other collective of classical antiquity.[28] Strictly speaking, it is only the first that may be immediately associated with the concept of governance, while the second may be largely characterised as behavioural, because it chiefly seeks to provide a code of good conduct: manners, politeness, propriety, courtesy, piety, decorum and so on. In other words, what modern scholarship tends to call civility.[29] To the extent that our evidence permits it, the chapters in this volume address both of these aspects.

It is true that in many cases these two kinds of norms not only coexisted side by side (the rules of an association may contain regulations on administrative matters and on members' behaviour) but were also mixed: rules about governance expected the compliance of specific behaviours by the members. For instance, regulations about proper conduct during assemblies or association meetings seem to be concerned as much with civility as with the smooth and effective completion of the business on the meeting's agenda.[30] Dispositions concerning the reasons for the award of honours and the type of recognition granted to members and non-members blend issues of governance with issues of decorum and proper behaviour. By establishing honorary awards to associations' officials who performed their duties in an exemplary manner and by allowing them to set up their honorary monument at a (most) conspicuous place on the association's

---

[28] The philosophical schools cannot be used as an objection to this, since they most probably were organised as associations themselves: Haake 2015.

[29] These rules of good conduct should be understood in a broad perspective, encompassing also, for instance, the so-called religious rules that codified the performance of rites and regulated worship. Piety, devotion and observance of traditions for the good relationship with the divine were in fact part of the proper behaviour fostered by associations.

[30] On this point, see Arnaoutouglou in Chapter 6 and Eckhardt in Chapter 3.

premises, for instance, associations were at the same time setting the expected conduct in office, regulating procedures for granting honours and codifying the management of space.[31] Moreover, in certain cases even regulations of a religious nature (for instance, rules on purity, on the timely and proper performance of cultic rites and celebrations or concerning the duties of the group's cultic personnel) equally belong to the sphere of the general administration and to that of reverent or pious behaviour. This is even more the case if one considers how important religion was for nearly all associations and how religious concerns shaped the organisation of many associations. Cult and religion played a significant role also in the definition and regulation of space by associations.[32] However, the main objective that the regulations on governance and those on conduct aimed at regulating was different in essence: therefore, such a distinction appears helpful, at least from an analytical point of view. In fact, there are instances in which the rules were solely concerned with the behaviour of associations' members, such as those detailed in the *hieros nomos* of Dionysios from Philadelphia (on which more below) or those found in the Demotic papyri with the *nomoi* of associations.[33] Furthermore, the rules of conduct include two elements, which are even further from the rules of governance and from the ideological model offered by the polis: mutual assistance among members, which sometimes is extended to the friends of members,[34] and the dispositions regarding the treatment of deceased members, which range from communal funerals and/or 'associational burial' to post-mortuary honours and commemorative celebrations.[35] In particular, the first – mutual assistance – underlines the value of *philanthropia* that is cherished by many associations. If the polis honoured good behaviour, associations seem to have demanded it – although they also honoured particularly generous acts by distinguished members.

The ways in which the regulations were validated or officially set up varied: they were often linked to the typology of documents in which the regulations were contained. It is generally assumed that regulations were formulated and validated by the members themselves: this is indeed one

---

[31] E.g. the *koinon ton thiasoton* in *IG* II² 1263 (*CAPInv.* 263; Piraeus, 300/299 BC) and *hoi Sarapiastai* in *IG* XII Suppl. 365 (*CAPInv.* 17; Thasos, II cent. BC).

[32] The importance of religion within associations is underlined in several chapters of this volume; see, for instance, Chapter 4 by Carbon, Chapter 5 by Skaltsa (in particular for the definition of space), Chapter 7 by Zoumbaki, Chapter 8 by Langellotti and Chapter 9 by Tran.

[33] See also Monson 2006.

[34] E.g. *IG* II² 1275, ll. 7–9 (Piraeus, 325–275 BC), concerning a *thiasos* (*CAPInv.* 266).

[35] E.g. *IG* XII.1 155 d I, ll. 38–95 (Rhodes, II cent. BC = *CAPInv.* 10).

of the principal criteria identifying as 'private' a specific association.[36] An external imposition of the norms (especially by a political authority) would compromise the association's independent private nature. However, in a number of instances an association's charter – in part, at least – was drawn up and validated by its founder(s) at the inception of the organisation: in this case, the membership's involvement is confined to their commitment to follow the rules. In some cases, the original document incorporating the rules and regulations may formally take the form of a testament. One well-preserved specimen is the testament of Epikteta from Thera, which forms the legal foundation for the establishment of the *koinon tou andreiou ton syngenon*.[37] In other cases, the document may somewhat resemble a Great Rhetra, which was drawn up by the founder on the instructions of a divine authority and enshrined in the association's place of assembly in a monumentalised form. An illustrative example of this *may* be the rules (literally 'ordinances' or 'commandments': *paraggelmata*) of the *hieros nomos* of Dionysios from Philadelphia in Lydia: it was certainly so at least in the eyes of Dionysios, drafter of the rules; however, it is uncertain whether Dionysios' wish to attract cult followers did lead to the formation of an association proper.[38] A clause ensuring the regulations' validity for eternity and strictly prohibiting alterations to any of its parts is often present.[39] Yet, the pre-existence of a 'founding charter' (in testamentary or other form) does not at all preclude the simultaneous existence of a second set of rules, which may be validated, modified, reaffirmed or renewed by the entire membership, as the case may be.[40]

Once regulations were in place, it was necessary to make sure that they were followed. Therefore, their enforcement often occupies an important position within the regulations' dispositions: it is no surprise that all the chapters of this volume address this issue. In fact, although members agreed to abide by the rules set in the association's regulations, the extant documents contain (often detailed) clauses about what is to be done in cases of transgression. The analysis of this aspect has important

---

[36] On voting and decisional practices of private associations in Ptolemaic and early Roman Egypt, for instance, see Paganini 2016.

[37] *IG* XII.3 330 (210-195 BC = *CAPInv.* 1645). Worse preserved is a specimen from Halicarnassus: Isager 2014 (*CAPInv.* 840). See also discussion by Skaltsa in Chapter 5.

[38] *CAPInv.* 348. See also discussion by Carbon in Chapter 4.

[39] E.g. Isager 2014: no 2A (*CAPInv.* 840).

[40] One clear example of this is the Rhodian second-century BC *Haliadan kai Haliastan koinon* (*CAPInv.* 10): the association possessed a double set of 'laws', one 'unmovable' (ὁ νόμος ὁ ἀκίνητος: *IG* XII.1 155 d.III, ll. 103–4) and the other 'current' (ὁ νόμος ὡς κεῖται: *ibid.* l. 93), which may be the object of changes.

consequences regarding the values behind associations' regulations and their interplay with local societies. Only a few of these important matters are highlighted here. The venue where the enforcement is said to take place is of consequence: associations could decide to deal with the matter inside or outside the association's purview. Furthermore, a question of authority arises: if matters were dealt with within the associations, those empowered with the right of execution could be the whole membership or a part thereof, such as individual members chosen for the purpose or designated officials. If matters were delegated outside of the association, the enforcement could be exercised within the judicial system of the association's community (e.g. courts of law or local representatives of the political authority) or could be entrusted to one or more divine powers. Finally, one may question the effectiveness of the intended enforcement: most scholars assume that enforcement was indeed effective and that for this reason members usually complied.[41] This may well have been true in most cases but a more definite answer to the question is to be found only in the careful analysis of associations' documents other than the regulations proper: the existence of punitive measures and sanctions in the regulations, which are characteristically normative, is per se not adequate proof of the rules' effectiveness. An investigation of the ultimate means, which an association could use in case of persistent non-compliance towards the internal punitive measures, would in fact illustrate the attitude by associations regarding collaboration with, reliance on or avoidance of external courts of law. However, it is only in very few cases that the evidence at our disposal is sufficient enough to allow some meaningful conclusions on associations' actual attitudes in case of dispute and on the range of mechanisms adopted by them to make sure that members complied with the rules' requirements. It appears that associations preferred procedures for internal dispute resolution, spanning from mediation, peer pressure, threats, fines, physical coercion, confinement to temporal expulsion; the involvement of external judicial systems seems to have been endured when everything else failed, as *extrema ratio* only.[42] Besides the desire for

---

[41] For instance, Monson 2006; Venticinque 2010: 284; Broekaert 2011.

[42] The evidence from Egypt is particularly instructive in this respect: on the systems of (internal) dispute resolution of private associations in Ptolemaic Egypt see, for instance, Paganini in press b. For an example of the use of state courts by associations from fourth-century Athens, see *IG* II² 1258 (*CAPInv.* 341): some members of the *Eikadeis* were prosecuted for false testimony in a dispute about the association's property. On the unique case of direct evidence for the actual imposition of fines by an association see the late third- or early second-century BC Greek ostraca from Maresha (Idumaea) published by Ecker and Eckhardt 2018.

maintaining a public image of friendly and unproblematic behaviour amongst members, by demanding to keep possible problems internal and to avoid resorting to state courts, associations expected members to display particular loyalty, a high sense of community and a developed feeling of trust. Members were urged to have confidence in the association's channels for dispute resolution and ultimately to put the group's collective good and reputation before their personal issues. In this respect, associations seem to have adopted the values and behaviour of the family.[43]

The analysis of these various aspects relating to associations' regulations brings to the fore the question of whether they had a real significance. Because regulations constituted their institutional hallmark, associations strove to have them in place as much as possible in order to signal something specific about the group's habitus, to use a term borrowed from sociological studies. However, it is unlikely that these regulations and their enforcement clauses were simply rhetorical, with no significant value. Systematic failure or reluctance by associations to enforce them would have undermined the association's credibility and produced a detrimental image, as the group cladded itself in empty procedures followed by no one: regulations were real and were therefore enforced, as far as possible. On a further level, one may wonder whether in some cases these regulations were substituting for or ranking higher than those of the political community. The main issue consequent on this is whether private associations were proposing laws and values, which were new, different, concomitant, additional or opposed to those of their socio-political communities. These are vast issues and not all of them can be answered, as our sources do not permit us to draw definite conclusions in all cases. However, the chapters in this book illustrate to what extent associations' regulations had a real significance and how they may relate to and interact with the values of their wider societies.

The regulations of associations reflected adherence to a specific ideology, beliefs and sets of principles and values. Generally speaking, those rules of governance (regulating the membership as a group) are intimately linked to values of efficiency, accountability, transparency, righteousness, egalitarianism (or at least the cherishing of a participatory culture) and respect for tradition – including religious practice. The rules of conduct (directed towards the individual member), conversely, foster values of reciprocity, compassion, trust, philanthropy, civility in an attempt to make each member useful, both directly to the group and indirectly to outsiders,

---

[43] See the insightful discussion of this aspect in Harland 2005.

because these values may ultimately become embedded in a person's nature. The key notion that all these features implicitly but forcefully support is that of 'good order' to establish associations as 'well-ordered groups'. By regulating both governance and members' behaviour, by allowing different sections of society into their membership and by highlighting the importance of norms of conduct, associations tended to reach out to, manage and somehow 'control' all facets of their membership: rather than mirroring political communities proper, such a holistic approach recalls the philosophers' state utopias, which encompassed polis and society in a homogeneous unit.[44] Associations were therefore providing a model of community in addition to that of the polis and were engraining sets of values parallel and in some cases complementary to those of the political communities. In this respect, with this book we hope to stimulate further debate on the issue of whether associations were creating something new.

The associations of antiquity, precisely thanks to their rules and regulations and to their desire to be – or at least to appear as – well-ordered groups, became the carriers into much later periods of values, procedures and modes of collective behaviour, as the following example indicates. An extraordinary document, written in Syriac and found in a late ninth-century AD collection of materials by Gabriel, the bishop of Bashra, attests to the continuing transmission of a long tradition. Entitled 'Concerning the ordering and regulation of associations of the crafts called NN', the document offered itself as a blueprint for incipient associations.[45] Probably originating in the late Sassanian or early Arab period as the rules of a particular association, the document, after having been cleared of the specifics connecting it to its parent association, was turned into a prototype to be used by any association wishing to provide regulations to its members. The rules on governance and on conduct coexist here in perfect harmony. However, what makes this document really extraordinary is that it simultaneously embraces two aspects, one looking to the future and the other to the past. In fact, on the one hand, this text perpetuates a specific and still cherished associational culture, as its purpose as a 'blueprint' makes clear. On the other hand, it links the historical roots of that culture to a distant past: as commentators have noticed, there are clear similarities

---

[44] See Hansen 1991: 61–4.
[45] Kaufhold 1976. In his review of Kaufhold, Degen 1977: 147 called the document *ein hochinteressantes und meines Wissens einzig dastehendes Dokument*: 'a highly interesting and to my knowledge unique document'. See Brock 2009 (English tr. and brief commentary) and also discussion by Evers in Chapter 10.

to the rules and regulations of the Graeco-Roman associations, particularly to those of the *Iobacchoi*.[46]

The Meaning of 'Well-Ordered'

The regulations and the other various documents produced by associations are not theoretical or abstract in nature: they do not analyse the ideals that informed associations' behaviour but are rather concerned with the application of these ideals and their specific factual results. Associations created documents in order to respond to practical needs, by setting expected procedures, granting honours for specific behaviour and providing solutions to current requirements. Therefore, the general principle of 'good order', which underpins the life of associations, is uncovered by a process of induction, so to speak, from the specific factual content of the regulations' various dispositions and of other documents produced by associations, in particular honorific decrees. The characteristics expected from members – which also correspond to those praised and rewarded by associations – encompassed moral, religious, social and financial virtues: excellence (ἀριστεία), virtue (ἀρετή), piety (εὐσέβεια), favour (εὔνοια), benevolence (φιλανθρωπία), intimacy (οἰκειότης), friendliness (φιλοφροσύνη), love for what is good (φιλαγαθία), concern for good reputation (φιλοδοξία), distinction (λαμπρότης), generosity (μεγαλοψυχία), usefulness (εὐχρηστία), quality of being a benefactor (εὐεργεσία), love for social distinction that comes from one's munificence (φιλοτιμία), liberality (ἀφειδία).[47] Ultimately, a member of an association should strive to be 'good' (καλὸς καὶ ἀγαθός) – and behave accordingly.[48] Associations' regulations did exactly this: they ensured that members were 'good' by requiring them to act in a specific manner towards each other and by striving to mould themselves as well-ordered groups.

The idea of 'well-ordered' employed here embraces both the moral concept of good behaviour, linked to obedience to regulations, and the modern notions of legal and institutional order, linked to procedural efficiency. As appears clear in their regulations and honorific decrees, associations strove to be well-ordered both by running their common affairs in an orderly fashion (with the help of clear, efficient and codified

[46] Brock 2009: 55–6.
[47] Cf. *I.Délos* 1520 (*CAPInv.* 9), *I.Prose* 40 (*CAPInv.* 38) and *IGR* III 209–10 (*CAPInv.* 1969).
[48] *I.Délos* 1520, l. 18 (*CAPInv.* 9); *IG* XII.1 155 d I, l. 9 (*CAPInv.* 10); *P.Mich.* V 244, l. 4 (*CAPInv.* 1409).

measures to that effect) and by gathering people with a moral imperative towards proper and excellent behaviour (who thus were expected to follow the rules). As a matter of fact, the former was only possible because of the latter: practical order was the direct and tangible result of a moral principle.

The various dispositions in their regulations exemplify how much associations cared to establish order and on which different aspects they put particular emphasis: it is clear that the self-presentation as well-ordered groups was therefore no trivial matter in the associations' agenda. Beyond an interest for the (important) practical advantages of efficiency, associations had an added desire to be well-ordered because such a thing necessarily implied that the members were well-mannered, honest, trustworthy and respectable people – and as a corollary, that the association as a whole was too. The fundamental consequence of this is that associations thus created a specific profile within their local societies, with its associated social and economic advantages.

Associations' Role within Local Society

It should never be forgotten that associations were very much local realities: they were inextricably embedded in their local society, from which they cannot be abstracted. Therefore, they must be analysed in their socio-political and geographical settings: local phenomena and dynamics greatly influenced associations, which adapted themselves on the basis of their surrounding circumstances and could behave differently depending on their location and period. In this respect, one ought to have an open-minded approach: one should not necessarily expect uniformity but rather a variety of different scenarios. Despite the initial potential bewilderment that one may have at the prospect of having to deal with a number of different contexts, this variety constitutes the interesting part of the analysis, as it showcases the vivacity, the dynamic character and the multifaceted essence of the ancient world.

Associations played a fundamental role in society as active agents on a variety of levels: they were in fact contributing to the life of their local communities on a wide spectrum, from economic to cultural and religious aspects. This was made possible by the specific social profile that they established, thanks to their nature – or, at all events, their self-portrayal – as well-ordered and respectable groups. It was exactly the fact that they were being perceived in this way, both as a whole group and as single members, that allowed them to have scope of action by creating bonds of trust and esteem with other local institutions and individuals.[49]

First and foremost, associations had an important impact on local economic life: this is probably the most extensively studied feature of private associations and therefore also the most familiar topic to be treated when focusing on them. Although we do not intend to underplay this important aspect, the economy per se is not the central concern of this volume. Recent scholarship has uncovered a variety of details concerning the associations' role in the ancient economy. In particular, through the employment of a larger theoretical scheme that incorporates the concept of 'social capital', some studies attempted to interpret the broader economic ramifications of associations' regulations, more specifically, inside as well as outside of associations themselves: the reader should refer to these for a fuller analysis.[50] For our purposes here, it suffices to say that associations as groups could provide the setting for the facilitation of specific aspects in the organisation of a specific branch of a trade or profession. They often allowed the creation of a network that diminished transaction costs, eased trade and provided social and human capital; in some cases they represented platforms of cooperation with the state and could provide the framework for the mobilisation of foreign capital and for a freer business participation of agents whose action would have been otherwise more restricted (for instance, non-citizens in the Greek poleis). Associations could also act as substantial consumers of marketed goods and services, thus boosting the local market. In addition, they could provide employment. Single individuals also reaped different economic advantages by being members of associations. They could build networks of trust and create commercial alliances; they had at their disposal preferential channels for the availability of ready capital when necessary; they could have considerable advantage from the sharing of information, know-how and potential risks. As a matter of fact, although it is fairly impossible to quantify with certainty, the members of those associations that left a trace

---

[49] Standard work on the concept of 'trust' and 'trust networks', especially for their economic implications, is Tilly 2005. Related to it is the concept of 'social capital', developed in sociology and institutional economics: see, for instance, Coleman 1988 and Burt 2005, with Ogilvie 2004. For a theoretical treatment of esteem and social recognition, including its economic implications, see, for instance, Brennan and Pettit 2004.

[50] See, for instance, van Minnen 1987; van Nijf 1997; Gabrielsen 2001; Monson 2006; Gabrielsen 2007; Liu 2009; Broekaert 2011; Gibbs 2011; Tran 2011; Verboven 2011; Venticinque 2013; Gibbs 2015; Venticinque 2015; Gabrielsen 2016b; Langellotti 2016b; Venticinque 2016: esp. 35–66; Gabrielsen in press.

in our evidence were usually individuals who had at their disposal some means and time, which they were willing to spend in the setting of associational life.[51]

Beyond the economy, associations contributed to the local life of their communities on a number of other levels. For instance, they often were in charge of the performance of some religious tasks or activities and provided services that others did not (for instance, in funerary practices); in some cases they could uphold the continuation of rites, which would otherwise have been discontinued, or could introduce new ones. They could also create the opportunity for the establishment of somewhat formalised social interaction between sections of the population for which full integration was not an option (for instance, foreigners in the Greek poleis). Furthermore, they could provide scope of action for those who could otherwise not have been able to contribute to their communities in the same way (for instance, women and slaves). Conversely, they could also operate as means for social distinction and as a way of separation from others. Their influence could also extend to the setting or diffusion of artistic trends and architectural typologies, as well as to the make-up of local topography.[52] Depending on the contingent situation, associations adopted a variety of different strategies and developed approaches and solutions in order to achieve their agenda: this wide-ranging sphere of action, which associations enjoyed, led to various degrees of impact on the most disparate facets of their societies.

On a deeper and more fundamental level, the input associations gave to their local communities may have also gone beyond the more tangible and practical matters discussed so far. In fact, by accepting and being subjected to the operation of specific regulations, which embodied particular principles, associations' members internalised such values, made them their own – with various degrees of willingness and awareness – and exported them to some degree to their larger communities. In this way, associations could potentially become not inconsiderable influencers of society values. However, as said, associations (and their values) were at the same time also affected by the society in which they were active.

[51] See also the discussion by Giannakopoulos in Chapter 2 and by Langellotti in Chapter 8; see further Gabrielsen and Paganini in Chapter 11.
[52] For an example of this, for instance, in the villages of Hellenistic Egypt, see Paganini 2020b. See also the discussion by Skaltsa in Chapter 5.

Overview of the Chapters

The first four chapters after this Introduction focus on various broader aspects of the regulatory behaviours of associations, namely, admission and financial survival, participation in associations' life, religious concerns and normative attitudes towards physical space.

Chapter 2 by N. Giannakopoulos analyses the practice (often modelled on those of the hosting communities) by associations to vet admissions, regulate entrance-fees and secure financial contributions by the members, all important procedures to maintain associations' purported egalitarian, well-ordered and prosperous profile. However, in certain cases, deviations which could prima facie seem to undermine the egalitarian character and immediate income of associations were contemplated: this was done in accordance with a well-planned attitude, which sometimes included practices long abandoned by the local political counterparts, to achieve greater advantages and respectability than by following standard norms.

B. Eckhardt in Chapter 3 explores the normative attempts by ancient associations in the Greco-Roman world to regulate the obligatory participation by members in associations' activities and their implications for the relationship between associations and local societies. The practice was widespread among associations in time and place: associations relied on members' participation for their existence; finding ways to 'encourage' their presence was of vital importance and formed a constituent part of associations' regulatory practices.

Chapter 4 by J.-M. Carbon deals with normative concerns regulating the religious sphere, in particular concerning purity: through norms on purity, associations aimed at maintaining good order and propriety within the group, while at the same time attempted to expand their network of followers, for instance by regulating access to sanctuaries and behaviour for a wider community of worshippers. With precise technical display of epigraphical finesse, case studies (mainly from Asia Minor) showcase the wide spectrum of characteristics of these norms, which could mirror traditional civic practices or be more stringent, and the ways in which associations asserted and regulated (as well as enforced) them.

Chapter 5 turns our attention to a different aspect ingrained in the topic of regulations. Using modern sociological definitions of space, S. Skaltsa seeks to explain the ways in which associations created space and constructed their own identity through well-defined physical as well as social space. A major outcome of the chapter is to show how spatial arrangements were as much part of an association's self-perception and self-presentation as the composition and activities of its membership. The empirical basis of this analysis consists of the epigraphic dossier of three 'founders' of associations: Epikteta from Thera, Poseidonios from Halicarnassus and Diomedon from Cos.

Chapters 6–9 allow us to turn our attention to defined geographical areas of the ancient world, with specific case studies centred on associations from Athens, Mantinea, Egypt and Ostia.

Chapter 6 by I. Arnaoutoglou investigates the attention to and regulation of orderly behaviour in the world of the so-called cult associations of Athens, from the late fourth century BC to the late second century AD. In this respect, the opposition of the two concepts of *thorybos*, 'clamour, tumult, confusion', and of *eusthateia*, 'tranquillity, quiet conduct', is presented and it is argued that Athenian associations shifted from allowing the former to stressing the latter as a response to Roman attitudes of diffidence towards possible unrest caused by associations.

S. Zoumbaki in Chapter 7 devotes her study to associations in Mantinea and their regulatory dispositions, in which specific values allowed the creation of an image of well-ordered and respectable institutions, in order to establish interactions with local society, in particular with local elites. Thanks to the adoption of specific strategies and sets of conduct, associations claimed a specific scope of action and role in public life within fields no longer monopolised by civic institutions, such as in the case of specific aspects of traditional religious life and of women's participation. In so doing, they complemented polis institutions in the public life of their communities, while all agents involved (associations, polis and local elites) reaped full advantage from the practice.

The values embedded in the regulations by associations of early Roman Egypt, together with their relation to the values of the local communities and the provincial administration, and their attempt to present themselves as well-ordered and respectable institutions are investigated in Chapter 8 by M. Langellotti. Traditional ethical values fostered by associations continued to be successfully mobilised and adapted to conform with the new values of local societies and of political contingencies. Thanks to regulations, associations established a successful model of order that guaranteed their existence, also in the face of changed socio-economic circumstances.

Chapter 9 by N. Tran presents associations in Ostia in the second and third centuries AD, which had their regulations primarily kept in their own archives and thus often lost to us. However, the set of their regulations transpires from associations' *alba* 'membership lists' and honorific texts: they testify the spread and wide-ranging dispositions for the uphold-ing of a ruled environment, including vetting of admissions, expulsion of unworthy members and the regulation of activities, contributions, votes and appointments. These rules characterised the very existence of associ-ations, which thus presented themselves as well-ordered, respectable and socially integrated institutions; just as they defined themselves as *ordines*, imitating the public sphere.

Chapter 10 broadens up the horizon of our investigation. Adopting a comparative approach with Greco-Roman associations, K. G. Evers brings into the analysis evidence of regulatory practices by associations from India and China, showing the communal Eurasian and thus global character of the phenomenon. Despite different inputs from diverse socio-political realities, Roman, Indian and Chinese associations with members sharing the same profession in fact developed parallel institutional traditions and independently adopted regulations (with comparable content, values and practices) to answer similar circumstances.

Chapter 11 provides some concluding remarks on the role and position of private associations in the societies of the ancient world, bringing together the various issues analysed in detail in the preceding chapters of the book.

Table 1.1. *Tentative list of associations' regulations and of texts with clear references to regulations from the ancient Greek-speaking world (VI cent. BC–IV cent. AD)*

CAPInv.	Association's Name	Date	Source	Provenance	Physical format and text type	Language	Terminology	Notes
1584	*platiwoinoi*	f. VI BC	*SEG* 30:380	Tiryns, Argolis	blocks on wall; list of dispositions	Greek	(Argaean)	N/A
538	N/A	VI–V BC	*SEG* 11:244	Sicyon, Peloponnese	bronze tablet; dispositions for the use of a dining hall, with list of members	Greek	N/A	Uncertain whether this was a private association.
1964	*Labyadai*	VI–IV BC	*CID* I 9	Delphi, Phocis	stele; decree	Greek	*thesmos* 'precept'	Uncertain whether this was a private association.
1047	*Molpoi*	VI–II BC (?)	*I.Milet* I.3 133	Miletus, Ionia	stele; decree	Greek	N/A	Uncertain whether this was a private association.
1687	N/A	391/0 BC	de Cenival 1988: 39–42	Memphis (?), Egypt	papyrus; list of dispositions	Demotic Egyptian	N/A	Uncertain whether this was a private association.
337	*Diataleis*	s. IV BC	*IG* II² 1267	Athens, Attica	stele; decree (fragmentary)	Greek	*nomos* 'law'	Uncertain whether this was a private association.
230	*Orgeones*	330–323 BC	*IG* II² 1361	Piraeus, Attica	stele; decree (?)	Greek	*nomos* 'law'	
266	*Thiasotai*	325–275 BC	*IG* II² 1275	Piraeus, Attica	stele; decree (?)	Greek	*nomos* 'law'	

Table 1.1. (*cont.*)

CAPInv.	Association's Name	Date	Source	Provenance	Physical format and text type	Language	Terminology	Notes
109	*Orgeones* of Heracles in Kome	late IV BC	ASAA 2006: 534 no 10	Kome, Lemnos	stele; security boundary stone	Greek	*grammateion orgeionikon* 'register/contract of the *orgeones*'	The association's financial activities were regulated by a *grammateion*.
1919	N/A (Diomedon's foundation)	IV/III BC	*IG* XII.4 1 348	Cos	stele; unilateral dispositions (foundation)	Greek	*ta syntetagmena* 'the orders'	Uncertain whether this was a private association.
858	*eranos*	IV–III BC	*IG* XII.7 58	Arcesine, Amorgos	slab; boundary stone	Greek	*nomos* 'law'	Reference to the association's *nomos*.
264	*Thiasotai*	299 BC	*IG* II² 1271	Piraeus, Attica	stele; honorific decree	Greek	*nomos* 'law'	Reference to the association's *nomos*.
830	N/A (Poseidonios' foundation)	285–240 (?) BC	*LSAM* 72	Halicarnassus, Caria	stele; endowment and decree by Poseidonios and his descendants	Greek	N/A	Uncertain whether this was a private association.
563	*Th[i]asotai*	273/2 BC	*IG* II² 1278	Athens, Attica	stele; honorific decree	Greek	*nomos* 'law'	Possible reference to the association's *nomos*.
269	*Koinon* of the *thiasotai*	258/7 BC	*IG* II² 1298	Athens, Attica	stele; list of members and decree	Greek	N/A	
1812	N/A	mid III BC	Decourt and Tziafalias 2012	Larisa, Thessaly	stele; sacred law	Greek	N/A	Uncertain whether this was a private association.
1691	N/A	250–210 BC	*P.Bagnall* 42	Tebtynis, Ars., Egypt	papyrus; (contractual) agreement (?)	Demotic Egyptian	N/A	

Table 1.1. (*cont.*)

CAPInv.	Association's Name	Date	Source	Provenance	Physical format and text type	Language	Terminology	Notes
1808	*Basaidai*	250–200 BC	*SEG* 36:548	Metropolis, Thessaly	stele; (communal) dispositions	Greek	*syntheke* 'agreement'	Uncertain whether this was a private association.
304	*Koinon* of the *eranistai*	s. III BC	*IG* II² 1291	Athens, Attica	stele; honorific decree	Greek	*no]moi koinoi* 'common laws'	Reference to the association's *nomoi*.
1688	N/A	245/4 or 244/3 BC	Vittman 2011	Arsinoites, Egypt	papyrus; (contractual) agreement (?)	Demotic Egyptian	N/A	
281	*Koinon* (of the *Thiasotai*)	245/4 and 2444/3	*SEG* 59:155; *SEG* 44:60	Salamis, Attica	stelae; honorific decrees	Greek	*nomoi* 'laws'	References to the association's *nomoi*.
1657	*Basilistai*	243–197 (?) BC	Wörrle 2015	Limyra, Lycia	stele; decree (?) with list of members	Greek	N/A	
232	(Thracian) *orgeones*	241/0 BC and 240/39 BC	*IG* II² 1283 and 1284	Piraeus, Attica	stele; decree (*IG* II² 1283); honorific decree (*IG* II² 1284)	Greek	*nomoi* 'laws'	Reference to the association's *nomoi* in *IG* II² 1284.
1689	The association of the temple of Horus-Behedet	223 BC, 17 Mar–15 Apr	de Cenival 1972: 3–10	Pisais, Ars., Egypt (from cartonnage from Ghoran)	papyrus; (contractual) agreement	Demotic	*hp.w* 'laws'	
754	N/A (*thiasos*?)	221 BC, 26 Feb	*P.Enteux.* 20	Alexandrou Nesos, Ars., Egypt (from cartonnage from Magdola)	papyrus; petition to the King	Greek	*thiasitikos nomos* 'law of the *thiasos*'	Reference to the association's *nomos*.

Table 1.1. (*cont.*)

CAPInv.	Association's Name	Date	Source	Provenance	Physical format and text type	Language	Terminology	Notes
1645	The *koinon* of the relatives	210–195 BC	*IG* XII.3 330 = Wittenburg 1990	Thera	statue pedestal; Epikteta's testament and decree of the *koinon*	Greek	*nomos* 'law'	
539	*Thiasotai*	III BC	*I.Kalchedon* 13	Chalcedon, Bithynia	stele; list of dispositions	Greek	N/A	
861	*Hierourgoi* of Athena Itonia	III BC	*IG* XII.7 241	Minoa, Amorgos	stele; honorific decree	Greek	*nomos* 'law'	Reference to the group's *nomos*. Uncertain whether this was a private association.
1707	N/A	III–I BC	*P.Cair.* II 30654 (dem.)	Pathyris	papyrus; (contractual) agreement (?) (fragmentary)	Demotic Egyptian	N/A	
235	*Dionysiastai*	185–175 BC	*IG* II² 1325 and 1326	Piraeus, Attica	stelae; honorific decrees	Greek	*nomos* 'law'	Several references to the association's *nomos*.
361	*Koinon* of the *orgeones*	183–174 BC	*IG* II² 1328	Piraeus, Attica	stele; two decrees	Greek	N/A	
1686	N/A	early II BC	Arlt and Monson 2010	Bakchias (?) Ars., Egypt	papyrus; (contractual) agreement (?)	Demotic Egyptian	N/A	
1655	*Koinon* of the coppersmiths	mid II BC	*SEG* 58:1640	Tlos or Xanthos, Lycia	stele; Symmasis' endowment and decree (?) by the *koinon*	Greek	N/A	
1186	(*Bakchikos thiasos*)	II BC	*I.Kallatis* 47	Callatis, Euxine coast, Thrace	stele; sacred regulations	Greek	N/A	These regulations likely concern the *bakchikos thiasos* attested in other inscriptions.

Table 1.1. (*cont.*)

CAPInv.	Association's Name	Date	Source	Provenance	Physical format and text type	Language	Terminology	Notes
10	*Koinon* of the *Haliadai kai Haliastai*	II BC	*IG* XII.1 155 c IV + d I–III	Rhodes	stele; honorific decree	Greek	*nomos* 'law'	Reference to a 'current law' and to an 'unmovable' (i.e. unchangeable) law of the association.
17	*Sarapiastai*	II BC	*IG* XII Suppl. 365	Thasos	stele; decree	Greek	*nomos* 'law'	Reference to the association's *nomos*.
829	*Syggeneis*	ca 200 BC–AD 100 (?)	*I.Halikarnassos* 118	Halicarnassus, Caria	stele (?); dispositions (fragmentary)	Greek	N/A	Uncertain whether this was a private association.
1971	N/A	179 BC, 4 Feb–5 Mar	de Cenival 1972: 39–40, 215–18	Krokodilopolis, Ars., Egypt (found at Tebtynis)	papyrus; (contractual) agreement with list of members' contributions	Demotic Egyptian	[*mt.wt*] 'words, matters'	
1932	The association of the priests of Sobek Lord of Tebtynis	178 BC, 6 January	Bresciani 1994	Tebtynis, Ars., Egypt	papyrus; (contractual) agreement with list of members' contributions (two sets, one fragmentary)	Demotic Egyptian	*hp* 'law'	Six sets of the yearly regulations of the same association have been preserved.
921	N/A	168–164 BC	*SEG* 52:1197	Apollonia (?), Mysia	stele; list of dispositions	Greek	*nomos* 'law'	

Table 1.1. (*cont.*)

CAPInv.	Association's Name	Date	Source	Provenance	Physical format and text type	Language	Terminology	Notes
1932	The association of the priests of Sobek Lord of Tebtynis	157 BC, 27 Aug–25 Sep	de Cenival 1972: 45–51 and 218–19	Tebtynis, Ars., Egypt	papyrus; (contractual) agreement with list of members' contributions	Demotic Egyptian	*hp* 'law'	Six sets of the yearly regulations of the same association have been preserved.
1932	The association of the priests of Sobek Lord of Tebtynis	151 BC, 30 Oct	de Cenival 1972: 59–61 and 219–20	Tebtynis, Ars. (Egypt)	papyrus; (contractual) agreement with list of members' contributions	Demotic Egyptian	*hp* 'law'	Six sets of the yearly regulations of the same association have been preserved.
840	*Syggeneia*	150–100 BC	Isager 2014: 186–8, text A	Halicarnassus or Mylasa (?), Caria	block; unilateral dispositions (testament?)	Greek	ta *diatetagmena, ta epitetagmena* 'orders'	
845	*Heroistai*	150 BC–AD 100	*I.Mylasa* 423	Mylasa, Caria	stele; orders or testament (?) (fragmentary)	Greek		
9	*Koinon* of the Berytian *Poseidoniastai*	149/8 BC	*I.Délos* 1520	Delos	stele; honorific decree	Greek	*nomos* 'law'	Reference to a *nomos* of the association.
1932	The association of the priests of Sobek Lord of Tebtynis	147 BC, 3 Jan	de Cenival 1972: 63–8 and 221–2	Tebtynis, Ars., Egypt	papyrus; (contractual) agreement with list of members' contributions	Demotic Egyptian	*hp* 'law'	Six sets of the yearly regulations of the same association have been preserved.
1932	The association of the priests of Sobek Lord of Tebtynis	145 BC, 20 Sept	de Cenival 1972: 73–8 and 222–5	Tebtynis, Ars., Egypt	papyrus; (contractual) agreement with list of members' contributions	Demotic Egyptian	*hp* 'law'	Six sets of the yearly regulations of the same association have been preserved.

Table 1.1. (*cont.*)

CAPInv.	Association's Name	Date	Source	Provenance	Physical format and text type	Language	Terminology	Notes
1690	The association of [the processions and of the festivals?] in the Polemon district of the Arsinoites	137 BC, 1 May	de Cenival 1972: 83–91 and 225–7	Tebtynis, Ars., Egypt	papyrus; (contractual) agreement with list of members' contributions	Demotic Egyptian	*ḥp* 'law'	Association's name after Bresciani 1994: 53 n. 16.
1970	The association of [the companions?]	137 BC, 3 Jun	de Cenival 1972: 93–7 and 227–9	Tebtynis, Ars., Egypt	papyrus; (contractual) agreement with list of members' contributions	Demotic Egyptian	*ḥp* 'law'	Association's name after Bresciani 1994: 53 n. 16.
645	*Phratores*	137/6 BC	Marek, *Stadt* 1	Abonoteichos, Paphlagonia	stele; honorific decree	Greek	*nomos* 'law'	Reference to the association's *nomos*.
955	*Technitai* from Isthmus and Nemea	112 BC	*F.Delphes* III.2 70	Delphi, Phocis	blocks on wall; *senatus consultum*	Greek	*nomoi* 'laws'	Several references to the association's *nomoi*.
1480	The Association of Amon-Opet	109–108 BC	de Cenival 1972: 103–31	Thebes, Egypt	papyrus; dossier; (contractual) agreements	Demotic Egyptian	*mt.wt* 'words/ matters'	
142	*Koinon* (connected with the gymnasium)	II–I BC	*IG* XII.3 253	Anaphe	stele; list of dispositions (fragmentary)	Greek	N/A	

Table 1.1. (cont.)

CAPInv.	Association's Name	Date	Source	Provenance	Physical format and text type	Language	Terminology	Notes
176	*Koinon* of the *technitai* of Dionysus from Isthmos and Nemea, performing in Chalcis	II–I BC	*IG* XII.9 910	Chalcis, Euboea	statue base; honorific decrees	Greek	[*nomos*] 'law'	Reference to the association's *nomos* (supplied).
777	*Synthiasitai*	II–I BC	*C.Ptol.Sklav.* 92	Magdola, Ars., Egypt	papyrus; list of contributions; list of dispositions	Greek	N/A	The association's regulations may have been written in the missing part of the papyrus, before the list of contributions.
780	*Synodos*	II–I BC	*IG* V.2 264	Mantinea, Arcadia	plaque; decree (fragmentary)	Greek	*nomos* 'law'	References to the group's *nomos*. Uncertain whether this was a private association.
348	N/A (Dionysios' *oikos*)	II BC–I AD	*TAM* V.3 1539	Philadelphia, Lydia	stele; unilateral dispositions as divine instructions	Greek	*paraggelmata* 'commandments'	Uncertain whether this was a private association.
1292	*nekrotaphoi*	95 BC and 67 BC	*P.Ryl.* II 65	Oxyrhynchus (?), Egypt	papyrus; judicial sentence	Greek, Demotic	*Aigyptia syngraphe* 'Demotic contract'	Reference to an *Aigyptia syngraphe* entered by the members of the group, regulating the burial of corpses. This was either the group's rules or a contract of partnership.

Table 1.1. (cont.)

CAPInv.	Association's Name	Date	Source	Provenance	Physical format and text type	Language	Terminology	Notes
654	Synodos of Zeus Hypsistos	69–58 BC	P.Lond. VII 2193	Philadelpheia, Ars., Egypt	papyrus; (contractual) agreement	Greek	nomos 'law'	Reference to the nomos regulating finances. Uncertain whether this was a private association.
1684	Thiasos of the Dionysiastai	50 BC–AD 50	SEG 4:598	Teos, Ionia	stele; decree	Greek	nomos 'law'	
357	Koinon of the Heroistai of Diotimos, [Zenon,] and Pammenes	39/8 BC	IG II² 1339	Athens, Attica	stele; decree	Greek	N/A	
1963	The troop of the weavers of Coptos	30 BC, 19 Jan	Short Texts I 158	Coptos	stele; (contractual) agreement	Demotic Egyptian	ḥn.w 'agreements'	
1782	Hetairoi kai Sabbatistai	27 BC–AD 14	GRA II 152	Elaeousa Sebaste, Cilicia	stele; decree	Greek	N/A	
1514	N/A	I BC	BGU XIV 2372	Heracleopolite, Egypt	papyrus; (contractual) agreement (?) (fragmentary)	Greek	N/A	
627	N/A	AD 1–50	PAT 0991	Palmyra, Syria	stele; sacred law	Aramaic	N/A	Uncertain whether this was a private association.

32

Table 1.1. (*cont.*)

CAPInv.	Association's Name	Date	Source	Provenance	Physical format and text type	Language	Terminology	Notes
1408	N/A	AD 14–37	*P.Mich.* V 243	Tebtynis, Ars., Egypt	papyrus; dispositions undersigned by members	Greek	*nomos* 'law'	
1409	*Apolysimoi*	AD 43, 26 Aug	*P.Mich.* V 244	Tebtynis, Ars., Egypt	papyrus; decree, list of members and subscriptions	Greek	*cheirographon* 'document'	
1273	Shepherds	AD 45/6	*P.Mich.* II 123 *recto*, XVI l. 12	Tebtynis, Ars., Egypt	papyrus; entry in register of the record office	Greek	*nomos* 'law'	
1437	*Synodos theou*	AD 45/6	*P.Mich.* II 124 *recto*, II l. 23	Tebtynis, Ars., Egypt	papyrus; entry in register of the record office	Greek	*nomos* 'law'	
1430	*Synodos* of Psosneus the oil maker	AD 45–47	*P.Mich.* II 123 *recto*, VI l. 18	Tebtynis, Ars., Egypt	papyrus; entry in register of the record office	Greek	*nomos* 'law'	
1432	Builders	AD 45–47	*P.Mich.* II 123 *recto*, XVII l. 38	Tebtynis, Ars., Egypt	papyrus; entry in register of the record office	Greek	*nomos* 'law'	
1975	*Synodos* of Kroni...	AD 46, Jan	*P.Mich.* II 123 *recto*, IX l. 45	Tebtynis, Ars., Egypt	papyrus; entry in register of the record office	Greek	*nomos* 'law'	
1976	*Synodos* of Kronion, son of Kames	AD 46, Jan	*P.Mich.* II 123 *recto*, X l. 6	Tebtynis, Ars., Egypt	papyrus; entry in register of the record office	Greek	*nomos* 'law'	
1977	*Synodos* of Herakleios, son of Pichis, of the 'farmyard'	AD 46, 30 Jan	*P.Mich.* II 123 *recto*, XI l. 36	Tebtynis, Ars., Egypt	papyrus; entry in register of the record office	Greek	*nomos* 'law'	
1658	Salt merchants of Tebtynis	AD 47, 18 Aug	*P.Mich.* V 245	Tebtynis, Ars., Egypt	papyrus; decree with list of five members	Greek	N/A	It is possible that this constituted a partnership.

Table 1.1. (*cont.*)

CAPInv.	Association's Name	Date	Source	Provenance	Physical format and text type	Language	Terminology	Notes
349	*Synodos* of the *Herakliastai* in the Marshes	AD 90 (?)	*SEG* 31:122	Attica	stele; decree with unilateral dispositions of the chief-*eranistes*	Greek	N/A	
569	N/A	end I AD	*IG* II² 1346	Athens (?), Attica	stele; decree	Greek	N/A	Uncertain whether this was a private association.
1329	*Synodos* of the *hieronikai*	I AD	*I.Smyrna* 709	Smyrna, Ionia	stele; unilateral dispositions (endowment, fragmentary)	Greek	N/A	Uncertain whether this was a private association.
491	*Mystai* of the *phyle* of Zeus	I–II AD	*REG* 2 (1889): no 19	Amorion, Phrygia	stele; honorific decree	Greek	N/A	
1786	Those gathering Mobrenis, son of Rhondos, and those with him	I–II AD	Hagel-Tomaschitz, *Repertorium* Ada 3	Lamos, Cilicia	sarcophagus; funerary inscriptions, agreement	Greek	*homologon* 'agreement'	
1788	N/A	I–II AD	Hagel-Tomaschitz, *Repertorium* Ada 15	Lamos, Cilicia	tomb monument; funerary inscription, agreement	Greek	[*homologon*] 'agreement'	Uncertain whether this was a private association.
1791	*Koinon*	I–II AD	Hagel-Tomaschitz, *Repertorium* Dir 6	Lamos, Cilicia	tomb monument; funerary inscription, dispositions	Greek	N/A	Possibly the same association as *CAPInv.* 1793.

Table 1.1. (*cont.*)

CAPInv.	Association's Name	Date	Source	Provenance	Physical format and text type	Language	Terminology	Notes
1793	*Koinon*	I–II AD	Hagel-Tomaschitz, *Repertorium* Dir 7b	Lamos, Cilicia	tomb monument; funerary inscription, dispositions	Greek	N/A	Possibly the same association as *CAPInv.* 1791.
1795	N/A	I–II AD	Hagel-Tomaschitz, *Repertorium* Dir 9	Lamos, Cilicia	tomb monument; funerary inscription, dispositions	Greek	N/A	
1797	*Koinon*; Rhodon, son of Kydimasas, Selgian, and those with him	I–II AD	Hagel-Tomaschitz, *Repertorium* Dir 10	Lamos, Cilicia	tomb monument; funerary inscription, dispositions	Greek	N/A	
1798	N/A	I–II AD	Hagel-Tomaschitz, *Repertorium* Dir 11	Lamos, Cilicia	tomb monument; funerary inscription, dispositions	Greek	N/A	
1799	N/A	I–II AD	Hagel-Tomaschitz, AntK 25	Antiochia ad Cragum, Cilicia	marble slab; funerary inscription, dispositions	Greek	N/A	
1311	N/A	I/II AD	SEG 40:624	Gorgippia, northern coast of the Black Sea	stele; list of sacred regulations	Greek	N/A	Uncertain whether this was a private association.
1659	N/A	AD 117–38	*MDAI (A)* 32 (1907): 293–6 no 18	Pergamum, Mysia	stele; decree (?) (fragmentary)	Greek	N/A	
1050	*Oikos* of the *naukleroi*	AD 131	Ehrhardt and Günther 2013	Miletus, Ionia	marble block; letter of Emperor's Hadrian	Greek	*nomos* 'law'	Hadrian confirmed the *nomos* for the foundation of the association.

Table 1.1. (cont.)

CAPInv.	Association's Name	Date	Source	Provenance	Physical format and text type	Language	Terminology	Notes
991	Synodos thymelike peripolistike of the technitai hieronikai stephanitai of Dionysus	AD 134	SEG 56:1359	Alexandria Troas, Troad	marble slab; unilateral dispositions by Emperor Hadrian (Imperial letters)	Greek	nomoi 'laws'	
437	Thiasos of Amandos	mid II AD	IG IX.1² 670	Physcus, West Locris	stele; list of dispositions	Greek	nomos 'law'	
339	Bakcheion (Iobacchoi)	AD 164/5	IG II² 1368	Athens, Attica	column; decree	Greek	N/A	
308	Eranos	s. II AD	IG II² 1369	Mesogaia, Attica	stone (lost); list of dispositions	Greek	nomos 'law'	
306	Hieros doumos	AD 171/2	TAM V.1 536	Maionia, Lydia	stele; order (cult rule) presented as a dedication	Greek		Uncertain whether this was a private association.
1081	Corpus of the Heliopolitans	II AD	CIL X 1579	Puteoli, Campania	marble slab (boundary stone?); list of dispositions	Latin	lex et conventio 'law and agreement'	
1138	Symbiosis of the flax workers (?)	II AD (?)	I.Smyrna 218	Smyrna (?), Ionia	grave stone; dispositions for members' burial	Greek	N/A	
1787	The partners and associates with Neon son of Nous	II AD (?)	Hagel-Tomaschitz, Repertorium Ada 4	Lamos, Cilicia	funerary monument; list of dispositions	Greek	N/A	

Table 1.1. (*cont.*)

CAPInv.	Association's Name	Date	Source	Provenance	Physical format and text type	Language	Terminology	Notes
979	*Synodos* of the *heroiastai* of our children Epaminondas and Theokrine	late II AD	Roesch 1982: 136–8 no 16	Acraephia, Boeotia	pillar; funerary foundation	Greek	N/A	
476	*Thiasos*	II–III AD	*Corinth* 8.3 308	Corinth, Peloponnese	stele (?); dispositions (?) (fragmentary)	Greek	N/A	
747	*Eriphiastai*	II–III AD	Nigdelis 2010: 39 no 14	Thessalonica, Macedonia	plaque; decree (?)	Greek	N/A	Uncertain whether this was a private association.
907	*Symbiosis* of *philomikoi*	II–III AD	*TAM* V.3 1521	Philadelphia, Lydia	architrave; orders	Greek	N/A	Uncertain whether this was a private association.
143	*Semnotate ergasia* of the purple-dyers	II–III AD	*Altertümer von Hierapolis* 133; 227, 342; *AAT* 101: 305, no 23	Hierapolis, Phrygia	stelae; epitaphs, unilateral dispositions (funerary endowment)	Greek	N/A	Uncertain whether this was a private association.
170	*Ergasia thremmatike*	II–III AD	*Altertümer von Hierapolis* 227b	Hierapolis, Phrygia	stele; epitaph, unilateral dispositions (funerary endowment)	Greek	N/A	Uncertain whether this was a private association.
984	*Hiera gerousia* of the Saviour Asclepius	AD 212–50	*SEG* 32:459	Hyettus, Boeotia	stele; decree	Greek	N/A	

Table 1.1. (*cont.*)

CAPInv.	Association's Name	Date	Source	Provenance	Physical format and text type	Language	Terminology	Notes
804	N/A	end III AD	*IG* X.2 1 Suppl. 1048	Thessalonica, Macedonia	stele; dispositions (fragmentary)	Greek	N/A	
417	Wool merchants	AD 301	*I.Ephesos* VII.2 3803d	Hypaipa, Lydia	plaque; endowment	Greek	N/A	Endowment of vineyards and grape presses to the city and to six associations.
418	Linen weavers	AD 301	*I.Ephesos* VII.2 3803d	Hypaipa, Lydia	plaque; endowment	Greek	N/A	Endowment of vineyards and grape presses to the city and to six associations.

CHAPTER 2

Admission Procedures and Financial Contributions in Private Associations
Norms and Deviations

Nikolaos Giannakopoulos

Introduction

The self-perpetuity of Greek private associations and the continuous performance of their collective activities presupposed the ability both to admit new members and to draw regular contributions (that is to say, material support) from the existing ones. The diffuse evidence on the rules that regulated these essential aspects of the associations' internal functions has been thoroughly examined both in the pioneering works of the late nineteenth and early twentieth centuries and in more recent studies.[1] The modest purpose of this chapter is to offer some, it is hoped, fresh remarks on certain aspects of these rules that bear relevance to issues related to the purpose of this volume. Associative laws and regulations cannot be viewed exclusively as administrative measures. They constituted, *inter alia*, instruments through which particular associations were constructing themselves as credible and respectable networks composed of equally credible and respectable members. In this respect, those rules that provided for the admission of members and the fulfilment of their regular financial obligations created real and imaginary moments within the associative time that enabled the most vivid demonstration, (re)confirmation and reproduction of the fundamental qualitative features that defined the associative identity, both at the individual and at the collective level. Within this framework, the present chapter will investigate the values endorsed by these rules, the image of the associations that they promoted and their relation to the broader social and civic environment. Here, I will mainly focus on evidence from mainland Greece, the Aegean islands and Asia Minor, but the rich material from Egypt will be also taken into proper account, mainly for the sake of comparison. The first section of this

---

[1] Ziebarth 1896: 140–2 and 156–7; Poland 1909: 274–7, 299–300, 437, 492–4; Arnaoutoglou 2003: 96–101.

chapter deals with the rules regulating admission into the *orgeones* of Bendis. The second section focuses on the regular financial contributions imposed by associations in the Hellenistic period. The third section examines the evidence relating to the Imperial period. The final section gives a brief general assessment in the light of the network paradigm issues raised by the editors of this volume in Chapter 1.

The *Orgeones* of Bendis

The well-known decree of the *orgeones* of Bendis at Piraeus (*CAPInv.* 230), dated to 330–324 BC, may be considered as the first document that provides comprehensive information on the rules regulating admission to a private association.[2] Lines 20–5 establish a two-stage procedure that includes first the payment of a uniform entrance-fee for all aspiring members and the registering of the contributors' names on a stele and then a process of scrutiny.[3]

   The point that I would like to underline is that the decree itself provides us with a highly interesting but so far barely noticed clue regarding the potential audience to which these admission rules were addressed: it envisages the possibility of individual private sacrifices being offered not only by existing members but also by outsiders (the term *idiotes*, 'private individuals', that is to say, non-members, here is indicative) who, in so doing, were obliged to pay dues ranging from 1½ to 3 obols and, in addition, to hand over the skin and the thigh of the sacrificial offering to the priests and priestesses. This rule testifies to the existence of a circle of devotees who, despite their affiliation to Bendis, stood outside the association. The fact that they alone were subject to this sacrificial fee, as opposed to the members of the association who were declared immune, functioned as a material and symbolic mark of their exclusion.[4] In my

---

[2] *IG* II² 1361. On the various issues concerning the character of this association, see Wilhelm 1902: 132; Ferguson 1944: 98–9; Ferguson 1949: 156–7; Garland 1992: 111–13; Mikalson 1998: 140–1, 152–3 and 155; Jones 1999: 257; Ismard 2010: 265–70; Kloppenborg and Ascough 2011: 38; Steinhauer 2014: 34–5, 48 and 92–3. Arnaoutoglou 2015: 39–49. Gabrielsen 2016a: 141–6.

[3] On this admission procedure, see Foucart 1873: 10 and 12; Ferguson 1944: 99–100; Jones 1999: 257–60; Arnaoutoglou 2003: 98 (convincingly refuting Ferguson and Jones' view that before the decree's enactment membership to these *orgeones* was hereditary; I would simply add that the fragmentary clause at the beginning of the decree explicitly distinguishes between registered members and their descendants, so it cannot reflect previous rules for entering the association); Kloppenborg and Ascough 2011: 35–7.

[4] *IG* II² 1361, ll. 3–6. It could be argued that the phrase '*orgeones* participating at the sanctuary' used to describe the collective may demonstrate that there were individuals who were not viewed as *idiotai* but as *orgeones* who nonetheless did not participate at the sanctuary. But the emphasis on the

view, this was exactly the group of people at which the provisions recorded in lines 20–5 were mainly targeted. These *idiotai* were persons familiar with the sanctuary and the cult of Bendis, with the relevant rituals and certainly with the members of the association, the use of the same sanctuary providing space and opportunities for cultivating social bonds with them. Paulin Ismard has recently emphasised the existence of a cultic network centred on Bendis and Artemis all over Attica, and the persons in question here were probably somehow involved in this.[5] These outsiders – who were outsiders not to the cult of Bendis but to the group of its *orgeones* – were now encouraged to become full members of the association. Both the entrance-fee and the regular annual contribution of 2 drachmas paid by every member should be assessed against the background of the immunity enjoyed by the associates for their private sacrifices and the right to participate in the monthly common assemblies.[6] This indicates that the more these non-associate *idiotai* were devoted to Bendis and the more they were willing to show this devotion by offering private sacrifices, the more financially attractive their eventual full participation in the association became to them.

The examination of each newcomer by the *orgeones'* assembly also favoured the aforementioned *idiotai*. The use of the verb *dokimazein* (δοκιμάζειν), 'to scrutinise, examine', indicates that this process was envisaged as being structured on the model of similar civic institutions.[7] Although the decree of the *orgeones* did not refer to fixed questions addressed to the candidates, the evidence regarding those civic *dokimasiai*, 'examinations', on which we have detailed information (the *dokimasiai* of the Athenian ephebes before entering the demes, of the councillors and the magistrates), the manifestly cultic character of the *orgeones* and the information on associative *dokimasiai* from the Imperial period (discussed below) suggest that the questions posed concerned not only the moral qualities of the candidates but also their religious devotion, particularly to

---

sanctuary simply reflects the fact that this was the key element of the collective's identity (Gabrielsen 2016a: 145).

[5] Ismard 2010: 270–2. If the split between an association of *orgeones* based at Piraeus and one based at the *asty* had already taken place by the time the decree *IG* II² 1361 was passed (Gabrielsen 2016a: 142–5), the members of the second association may have also constituted a potential target group for the provisions under examination here. But there is no evidence to press this hypothesis further.

[6] *IG* II² 1361, ll. 17–20. Jones 1999: 257–60 conceived of these payments as a remedy for the lack of benefactions and endowments and as a means of dealing with the bad financial situation in which the *orgeones* found themselves. But such payments are very widespread in the world of private associations. They are not a particularity of the *orgeones* of Bendis, hence they need not be considered as indicative of financial problems.

[7] Ustinova 2005: 185 and Feyel 2009: 42–4.

Bendis.[8] In this respect, there can be no doubt that each candidate would have had to present his own credentials, and the individual sacrifices of the *idiotai* would surely have functioned as such.

Another point needs to be stressed. While the civic *dokimasia* was clearly an institution following popular election or appointment by lot (permitting the correction of what could be perceived as mistaken choices), the scrutiny of newcomers in the decree of the *orgeones* was technically not a confirmation of a prior choice made by the group – such a choice is not mentioned at all – but a deliberation on a candidate's application and an examination of his suitability, both conducted at the same time. In this respect, it could be argued that it was the payment of the entrance-fee and the registering on the stele that functioned as the equivalent to the civic election or appointment by lot. This symbolic statement on the part of the aspiring member about his willingness to share the association's cause was the preliminary stage of the admission procedure, to be followed and validated by the approval of the collective. Compared to the analogous civic process, this associative one was clearly more time-saving and convenient, both for the candidates and for the members of the controlling assembly.

But these differences concerned issues of procedure. In every other significant way the admission rules enacted by the *orgeones* of Bendis fit in perfectly with the overall tendency of private associations to be integrated into the public sphere.[9] In this respect, scrutiny did not only serve the purpose of ensuring the suitability of new members. It also turned admission into a prize, elevating in this way the prestige both of the group (presented as a respectable and privileged organised body) and of its individual members who, in order to achieve participation, were to be examined as thoroughly as the Athenian citizens and magistrates were. The very fact that the approval of the association was granted in the standard democratic and egalitarian way of an individual vote, exactly as the Athenian judges voted individually in the scrutiny of civic magistrates, underlines this point.[10]

---

[8] See Arnaoutoglou 2003: 98 and Feyel 2009: 25–6 and 115–80.

[9] See, *inter alia*, van Nijf 1997 (for professional associations); Arnaoutoglou 2003: 21–2 and 154–5 (for democratic Athens); Suys 2005: 214; Gabrielsen 2007; Fröhlich and Hamon 2013b: 14–26. Arnaoutoglou 2015: 49 (on the *orgeones* of Bendis).

[10] Feyel 2009: 176–9. As noted by Arnaoutoglou 2003: 99, scrutiny is not attested in other private associations of the Late Classical and Hellenistic periods. However, since our documentation does not include general regulations, such as the decree of the *orgeones* of Bendis, but decisions responding to specific needs of the issuing bodies, this lack of evidence should not be necessarily taken as evidence of absence. In fact, the regulations set up by Diomedon for the familial association

Money Contributions and Entrance-Fees in the Hellenistic Period

Besides the decree of the *orgeones* of Bendis, entrance-fees (Table 2.1) are also attested in a decree of the *thiasotai* of Artemis in Athens in 248/7 BC (*CAPInv.* 269). This group decided to erect a stele recording the names of their members, and newcomers were to be registered after the payment of the required *argyrion*, 'money'.[11] As the reference to this rule is incidental, the amount is not specified: it was obviously regulated by the law of the group mentioned in the same phrase. Regular financial contributions are attested in the second-century BC *Haliadan* and *Haliastan koinon* at Rhodes (*CAPInv.* 10), which charged each member 3 obols, payable at every meeting, for the purchase of a crown to be given as a posthumous honour to their leader Dionysodoros from Alexandria.[12] Moreover, in 57/6 BC, an association of Athenian *Heroistai* (*CAPInv.* 357) decreed that even those members who were absent from Attica had to pay half the contribution of 6 drachmas imposed on every associate, while those present in Attica but not attending had to pay the whole sum, termed φορά.[13] To this evidence should be added various references to immunities granted by associations from Athens, Delos, Rhodes and Maroneia to those of their members who acted as benefactors.[14]

Commenting on the status of *asymbolos*, 'exempt from contributions', awarded to Telestas by the Rhodian *Adoniastai* (*CAPInv.* 1612), Durrbach

he founded on Hellenistic Cos prescribed a process of examination for allowing *nothoi*, 'illegitimate children', to participate in the sacred rites. Probably this examination aimed at certificating that these *nothoi* were indeed sons of existing members: see *IG* XII.4 1 348 D, ll. 146–9 (bibliography and discussion in *CAPInv.* 1919). Moreover, *dokimasia* is consistently present in the epigraphical record of the Imperial period (see below).

[11] *IG* II² 1298, ll. 16–20. On the interpretation of this clause as referring to entrance-fees and not just dues (as Kloppenborg and Ascough 2011: 114 understand it), see Arnaoutoglou 2003: 99 n. 32. On the status of the members of this group and its relation with the *thiasotai* of a goddess who issued an honorific decree followed by a list of members in 237/6 BC (*IG* II² 1297; *CAPInv.* 268), see Mikalson 1998: 149; Ismard 2010: 353; Kloppenborg and Ascough 2011: 113 and 135; Arnaoutoglou 2011b: 28–39; *CAPInv.* 269. Entrance-fees are also mentioned in a Demotic inscription with the regulations of an association of weavers at Coptos (*CAPInv.* 1963): each newcomer pays 90 deben.

[12] *IG* XII.1 155 d, ll. 22–3. See Foucart 1873: 43. On the context of this decision and the way it was implemented, see Gabrielsen 1994: 143–7.

[13] *IG* II² 1339. On the character of this association, which seems to have celebrated the cult of Zenon, Pammenes and Diotimos from Marathon, see Geagan 1992; Baslez 2004: 107 and 115; Baslez 2006: 166; Ismard 2010: 362; Kloppenborg and Ascough 2011: 218–19. On regulating compulsory participation in associations, see Eckhardt in Chapter 3.

[14] For a detailed treatment, see Poland 1909: 437 and 492–4. The rules of several Egyptian associations also imposed regular membership fees. See Table 2.1.

Table 2.1 *Evidence on entrance-fees and regular contributions (indirect evidence, e.g. mentions of immunities, is not included)*

CAPInv.	Association	Entrance-fees	Regular contributions	Location	Date
1687	Unknown name		Monthly: unspecified sum	Memphis	391/0 BC
230	*Orgeones* (of Bendis)	Unknown sum	Annual: 2 drachmas for sacrifice	Piraeus	330–324 BC
269	*koinon ton thiasoton* (of Artemis)	Unspecified sum		Athens	248/7 BC
1689	Association of the temple of Horus–Behedet		Monthly: 1 kite	Pisais (Arsinoites)	223 BC
1686	Unknown		Unspecified sum	Arsinoites	192–100 BC
1971	Those of the association of …		2 deben	Krokodilon polis (Arsinoites)	179 BC
1932	The association of the Priests of Soknebtynis		Monthly: unspecified sum	Tebtynis (Arsinoites)	178–145 BC
1690	The association of …		Monthly: 5 deben	Arsinoites	137 BC
1970	Those of the association of (the companions?)		Monthly: 5 deben	Arsinoites	137 BC
10	*Haliadan and Haliastan koinon*		Three obols at every meeting for the purchase of a crown	Rhodes	II cent. BC
357	*To koinon ton Heroiston*		Phora of 6 drachmas	Athens	57/6 BC
1963	The troop/crowd of the weavers of Coptos	90 deben		Coptos	30 BC
1408	Unknown name		Monthly: 12 drachmas for banquets	Tebtynis (Arsinoites)	AD 14–37
1325	*He hiera synodos ton peri ton Breisea Dionyson techneiton kai myston*	Unspecified sum; possible reduce for *patromystai*		Smyrna	AD 80–83

			Phora for ekdoseis (unspecified sum)	Paiania (Attica)	Early II cent. AD
349	*Synodos ton Herakliaston en Limnais*	sons of members: 16½ minas of pork; others: 33 minas of pork			
1653	*Hymnodoi* of Augustus and Rome	Sons of members: 15 denarii to the gods and 7 denarii to each actual member + *choreion*, receiving a 50 per cent return; others: 100 denarii for sacrifices, 30 denarii to the gods and 15 denarii to each actual member.		Pergamum	AD 127–138
339	*Bakcheion (Iobacchoi)*	Sons of members: 25 denarii; brothers of members: 50 denarii; others: 50 denarii + libation	*Phora* for wine (unspecified sum)	Athens	AD 164/5
1659	Unknown name	Sons of members for over 5 years: 50 denarii; others: the whole sum (not specified)		Pergamum	II cent. AD
1912, 1939 and 1952	Worldwide association of Dionysiac artists	100 denarii (beg. of the 3rd cent.); 250 denarii (after c. AD 250)			III cent. AD
984	*Hiera Gerousia tou Soteros Asklepiou*	Sons of members: no entrance-fee; other relatives: 50 denarii; outsiders: 100 denarii		Hyettus (Boeotia)	After AD 212

45

and Radet observed, using the only available parallel at the time – the civic *ateleia πασῶν τῶν συμβολῶν πορευομένοις εἰς τὰ Ἰτώνια*, 'exemption from all contributions for those travelling to the festival of Athena Itonia', given to Kleophantos of Arkesine and his relatives – that the honorand was exempted not from monthly subscriptions but from payments for festivals, sacrifices and common meals.[15] This connection between regularly required payments and sacrifices has been noted by several scholars.[16] The point I would like to stress is that it was the official public discourse of the associations themselves, as expressed in their decrees, which perceived and recorded these 'membership fees' as being an integral part of and a prerequisite for the groups' common activities. Civic parallels do exist. We now know that in Hellenistic Amorgos two more benefactors besides Kleophantos are attested to have financially supported the festival of Itonia, proclaiming that the participants were to be *asymboloi* or *ateleis ton symbolon*, 'exempt from contributions'.[17] Moving to a purely associative context, we find the Dionysiac artists in Cyprus (*CAPInv.* 1033) establishing a perpetual *asymbolos* festival in honour of their benefactor Isidoros: the association defined this event as one directly financed by the common treasury and not by individual contributions, as was normally expected to be done.[18] The decree of the Tyrian merchants at Delos (*CAPInv.* 12) awarding to Patron the status of *asymbolos* and *aleitourgetos*, 'exempt from compulsory services (to the association)', recorded these privileges as being valid at every meeting of the association.[19] A second-century BC decree issued by the Maroneian *therapeutai* (*CAPInv.* 937) declared the former priest Sokles to be

---

[15] Durrbach and Radet 1886: 260–1 (for the same inscription, see *I.Rhod.Per.* 12). For Kleophantos, see *IG* XII.7 22, ll. 27–9. In the technical vocabulary of Greek corporate bodies, *symbole* denotes contributions imposed on the existing members. See Giannakopoulos 2013: 16–18.

[16] Poland 1909: 494; Aneziri 2003: 182 n. 65.

[17] *IG* XII.7 241 (Epinomides); *IG* XII Suppl. 330 (Agathinos). See Gauthier 1980: 206–7.

[18] Le Guen 2001: I 308–10 no 66. See Aneziri 2003: 182.

[19] *I.Délos* 1519, ll. 43–5. As far as the associative *leitourgiai* are concerned, we are in no position to know whether they were imposed only on the wealthiest associates or, as Foucart 1873: 44 has suggested, on all the members by some sort of rotation. Based on what we know of the civic *leitourgiai*, it could be argued that the associative ones were also imposed only on the wealthiest members. However, as we shall see below, the regular associative *eisphorai* and *symbolai* were paid by all the associates and, in this respect, they were manifestly different from their civic counterparts. Hence, in principle there is no reason to deny the possibility of associative *leitourgiai* being imposed on all the members. Admittedly, there is no evidence to support either of these hypotheses. In any case, the formulation of the decree for Marcus Minatius (see below n. 25) demonstrates that the *leitourgoi* of private associations were required to provide both personal work and financial support. In fact, the terms *leitourgoi* and *leitourgia* could denote the officials of associations. See *SEG* 41:74, ll. 27–8 (*Serapiastai* at Rhamnous; *CAPInv.* 350) and *SEG* 33:639, ll. 14–15 (*Sabaziastai* at Rhodes; *CAPInv.* 2111). Hence *aleitourgesia* may refer to exemption from assuming such posts.

aleitourgetos kai aneisphoros pases eisphoras, 'exempt from compulsory services and from all dues', but at the same time emphasised the fact that the honorand was nonetheless entitled to take part in all the common affairs of the association.[20] Already in the late fourth century BC the *chous* (wine-contribution for banquets) from which Kalliades and Lysimachides – members of the *orgeones* of Amynos, Asclepius and Dexion (*CAPInv.* 229) – enjoyed *ateleia* was recorded as being applied to both of the association's temples (*en amphoin toin hieroin*).[21] The decree of the *orgeones* of Bendis (*CAPInv.* 230) explicitly ordered that the members' annual payments of 2 drachmas, described with the verbs δίδωμι, 'to give', and συμβάλλω, 'to collect', were to be given to the religious officials, the *hieropoioi*, that is to say, to finance a collective sacrifice, as opposed to the individual ones mentioned at the beginning of the decree.[22] Finally, the *phora*, 'tribute', of 6 drachmas to which the Athenian *Heroistai* (*CAPInv.* 357) were subject was also defined as a means to finance a communal event, as is indicated by the clause prescribing that the absent members should nonetheless pay, but without receiving their due share.[23]

Admittedly, entrance-fees in particular and perhaps also the aforementioned *symbolai*, 'contributions', could produce a surplus that could potentially have been used to meet various irregular expenses.[24] However, this does not change the fact that, whenever the associative contributions and immunities are placed in a meaningful context by the associations themselves, they are advertised not as general subscriptions to be deposited in

[20] *I.Aeg.Thrace* E183.
[21] *IG* II² 1252+999, ll. 11–12. On this association see Ferguson 1944: 86–91; Mikalson 1998: 145–6; Jones 1999: 254–6; Ismard 2010: 257–9; Kloppenborg and Ascough 2011: 43–7; Steinhauer 2014: 30–2.
[22] *IG* II² 1361, ll. 17–20. See recently Arnaoutoglou 2015: 43–4.
[23] *IG* II² 1339, ll. 9–15. See Steinhauer 2014: 46. Based on the mention of the term *eranos* in the relevant clause, Foucart 1873: 42–3 argued that this was a monthly contribution.
[24] *P.Tebt.* I 118 (*CAPInv.* 1213) demonstrates that the common treasury could benefit from the surplus of contributions imposed for communal events such as banquets and feasts (see Arlt and Monson 2010: 121). It has been argued that the *Heroistai* and the *eranistai* from Paiania provided friendly loans to the associates (Raubitschek 1981: 97; Baslez 2006: 166–8; but see Arnaoutoglou 2003: 70–87 on the use of the term *eranos* for various kinds of associations), but if they did so, there is no evidence regarding the source of the money used for that purpose. Although Hellenistic associations frequently provided in various ways for the burial of their members (e.g. *IG* II² 1323 = *CAPInv.* 274; *IG* II² 1327 = *CAPInv.* 361; *IG* II² 1277 = *CAPInv.* 267; *IG* XII.9 1151 = *CAPInv.* 86; Marchand 2015 on Boeotia; Gabrielsen 1997: 123–5 on Rhodes; Maillot 2013: 207–10 on Cos; see also *P.Enteux.* 20 = *CAPInv.* 754, *P.Ryl.* IV 580 = *CAPInv.* 671 and *P.Ryl.* IV 590 = *CAPInv.* 674; discussion in van Nijf 1997: 50–3 and Steinhauer 2014: 113–18), there is no direct evidence linking entrance-fees or regular contributions with this practice. In fact, the purchase of a burial plot could be financed through the means of an irregular *epidosis*, 'collection' (Gabrielsen 1997: 125).

the common fund but rather as regularly levied payments in connection with and attached to the realisation of specific associative events.[25]

The significance of this connection lies in the fact that these events had a well-defined spatial and temporal dimension, establishing a clear notion of a well-ordered associative space and time.[26] *Symbolai* may thus be seen as the result of rules that, by regulating access to this associative universe, articulated the reciprocal rights and duties both of the group vis-à-vis its members and of the members vis-à-vis the group. On the one hand, we find associative decisions that create, control, manage and offer material infrastructures, building space and opportunities, fixed in time, for the collective expression of religious piety. Within this framework the associations emerged as agents eager to publicly declare the transparent way in which they exploited the financial resources drawn from their members: contributions were always linked with pre-defined expenses of the collective.[27] On the other hand, we find that the members were entitled to make use of this associative space and time upon payments that were, at least implicitly, justified not only by reference to the contributors' status as associates but also – and in a much more emphatic way – in terms of their

---

[25] In this respect, the case of the *orgeones* of Bendis is highly indicative: they were more than willing to relieve themselves of the obligation to pay a *telos* 'dues', when they sacrificed as individuals. But this was not the case when the *orgeones* functioned as participants in a collective sacrifice organised by the group itself. To the aforementioned examples of immunities from contributions should be added the decree of the Berytian merchants at Delos (*CAPInv.* 9), awarding to the banker Marcus Minatius the right to be *aleitourgetos pases ascholias kai dapanes pases*, 'exempt from all obligations and costs' (*I.Délos* 1520, ll. 48–9). Moving to Rhodes, we find the *eranistai* of Adonis (*CAPInv.* 1612) honouring two more benefactors besides Telestas as *asymboloi*, granting them *ateleia* as well. See Pugliese Carratelli 1939/40: 147 no 1 for Sosikles and Demetrios. Five other Rhodian associations are equally known to have awarded an *ateleia* from all charges. See *IG* XII.1 155 (*CAPInv.* 10) and Maiuri 1925: no 46 (*CAPInv.* 2060; see also Gabrielsen 1994); *IG* XII.1 867 (*CAPInv.* 1821); Pugliese Carratelli 1939/40: 153 no 11 (*CAPInv.* 2049).

[26] As Arnaoutoglou 2003: 22 has eloquently remarked, associations 'set a rhythm of life for their members'. On regulations of space by associations, see Skaltsa in Chapter 5. The connection between members' financial contributions and associative space and time is highlighted in the rules of an association of worshippers of Zeus *Hypsistos* from Philadelpheia in Egypt (*P.Lond.* VII 2193 = *CAPInv.* 654): these rules prescribe monthly banquets in Zeus's sanctuary for all the *syneisphoroi*, 'contributing members'. The same connection is unsurprisingly manifest in records of extraordinary payments destined to support the associations' infrastructure or the realisation of communal events. For example, a third-century BC decree of the *Amphieraistai* of Rhamnous (*I.Rhamnous* 167 = *CAPInv.* 356) advertised the association's decision to invite its members to contribute at will to the rebuilding of certain parts of the sanctuary. Likewise, a decree issued by a Dionysiac *thiasos* at Hellenistic Teos (*SEG* 4:598 = *CAPInv.* 1684) referred to money given by the members for a festival in honour of the priestess Hediste, which seems to have been also financed by an endowment founded by the priestess. For a fragmentary decree concerning the organisation of an *epaggelia*, 'promise', by a Coan *thiasos*, see *IG* XII.4 1 125 (*CAPInv.* 1883).

[27] References to the accountability of associative officials (*IG* II² 1292 = *CAPInv.* 351; *Agora* 16 161 = *CAPInv.* 227) may be seen in the same light.

actual or anticipated presence in the various collective activities. Individual participation in the collective was not limited only to deliberating in the decision-making processes regarding the establishment of common events but also extended to an active involvement in bearing the cost of the execution of these decisions and the realisation of these events. Viewed in this light, *symbolai*, 'contributions', and *eisphorai*, 'dues', were envisaged as multi-functional tools of internal governance: they not only enabled the association to present itself as an independent, self-financing entity following rules that obeyed the principle of transparency, but they also promoted within the group a specific concept of membership based on commitment to constant active participation in all the different temporal and spatial aspects of associative life, which ensured the reproduction of the group as a living organism. The specific way in which the associates' contributions were formalised, conceptualised and publicised expressed both the durable character of the ties that brought them together and the intensity of the association's internal functions as a well-structured network of members.[28]

It may, in a certain sense, seem natural to draw a similarity with analogous civic institutions and practices. The various mechanisms relating to the accountability of civic officials also highlighted the significance of financial transparency as a key element for the normal functioning of the city.[29] Paying taxes, justified in terms of civic suzerainty and property-rights on the various goods and resources that the citizens used, was a central element of citizen status.[30] As noted above, in demanding regular contributions private associations also acted as owners of communal space and time, that is to say, as micro-cities, while the payment of *symbolai* and *eisphorai* was a crucial element of the fundamentally participatory associative identity as well. Moreover, taxes as means of financing specific purposes and activities were levied by the Greek cities as well.[31] However, there was a noteworthy difference that deserves some comment. Civic taxes were levied in proportion to property (as in the case of the Athenian *eisphora*) or to the extent to which each individual used the civic facilities and resources or proceeded to engage in commercial transactions

---

[28] On durability and intensity as features of social networks and private associations, see Arnaoutoglou 2011b: 43–4, Arnaoutoglou 2011a: 273–4 and Harland 2013a: 120. For contributions to Athenian demes as factors 'reinforcing collective identity', see Whitehead 1986: 151.
[29] Fröhlich 2004.
[30] See Chankowski 2007: 303–6; Liddel 2007: 210–307 (262–82 for financial obligations).
[31] Gabrielsen 2013: 335–7.

(as in the case of the percentage or *ad valorem* taxes).[32] Not all the citizens were called upon to pay the same taxes and not all the citizens liable to the same tax paid the same amount of money. However, associative *symbolai* and *eisphorai* demanded a fixed uniform sum from all.[33] In this respect, they were much closer to the various payments and offerings demanded by all those who, as private individuals, consulted oracles, were initiated in mysteries and performed sacrifices.[34] It seems that these religious 'taxes' had a much greater influence on the way associations regulated their members' financial obligations than the concepts defining civic taxation. This uniformity of regular associative *symbolai* may, as a practice, seem, proportionately, to have been a heavier burden on the poor than on the rich, but in reality it worked the other way around. A wealthy Athenian citizen could boast about properly paying his *eisphora*, turning compulsion into an act of euergetism and highlighting his superiority and excellence within the citizen-body.[35] Regular associative *symbolai* and *eisphorai* left no room for such claims. They reflected equality, not internal hierarchy. It was mainly the extraordinary collections of funds that could permit the display of individual superiority, in terms of higher voluntary contributions.[36]

Although associative euergetism did not operate within the framework of regularly levied contributions, it exercised a considerable impact on associative 'fiscal' rules: the immunities awarded as honours in response to

---

[32] See Chankowski 2007: 307–19. On the Athenian *eisphora*, see Rhodes 1982: 1–13; Gabrielsen 1987; Christ 2007a: 146–8.

[33] Possible exceptions may be observed in late Hellenistic Egypt. The accounts of two associations record individual contributions of different amounts, which are sometimes called *symbolai*. They also refer to *asymboloi* members: see *SB* III 7182 (*CAPInv.* 856) and *P.Tebt.* III.2 894 (*CAPInv.* 863). It is not entirely clear, however, what kind of payments was included in these lists. As it is well known, the regulations of Egyptian associations prescribed additional payments from those members occupying associative offices (de Cenival 1972: 207–8; Monson 2006). In fact, the regulations in question (see Table 2.1) often drew a sharp difference between monthly contributions and 'fees of office'; this difference was explicitly expressed even in lists of members and payments such as *P.Prague Dem.* 1 (*CAPInv.* 1690), where we find officials contributing strikingly higher sums than ordinary members. It appears that the concept of proportional 'taxation' was not unknown to Egyptian associations. It was institutionalised but functioned in relation not to income or property but to possession of associative offices. See also below n. 74.

[34] On these payments, see Sokolowski 1954: 153–9.   [35] Liddel 2007: 276.

[36] Hence, two lists of contributors to *thiasoi* (or a single one?) at Hellenistic Knidos (I. *Knidos* 39 and 23), with sums ranging from 3 to 5 drachmas and from 5 to 300 drachmas, respectively, seem to have recorded extraordinary *epaggeliai*, 'promises (of money)' (cf. *I.Knidos* 39, l. 29). See *CAPInv.* 836 and 839. It should be noted, however, that the aforementioned list of contributors to the *Amphieraistai* of Rhamnous (n. 26 above) recorded only names and not the donated sums of money. In this particular case, possible unequal contributions did not result in a publicly recorded expression of individual superiority.

benefactions actually constituted deviations from universal associative norms and created internal hierarchies.[37] A comparison with the similar tactics adopted by the polis illustrates this point. While private associations known to have offered immunities honoured their own members in this way, their hosting cities normally did not treat immunities as honours for their own citizens. Admittedly, Demosthenes' speech *Against Leptines* is a valuable testimony of the honorary immunities awarded to Athenian citizens, but the Athenian orator makes it absolutely clear that these fiscal exemptions concerned only specific non-military liturgies and not regularly levied *eisphorai*.[38] Athenian tribes are also known to have rarely honoured some of their members with exemptions, but again these concerned liturgies.[39] Hence, although this Athenian practice may be considered as a parallel to the aforementioned exemptions from associative *leitourgiai*, 'compulsory services', it can hardly be viewed as such to the exemptions from the regular associative *symbolai/eisphorai* or to the *ateleia* from the regular contribution to a collective banquet given by the *orgeones* of Amynos, Asclepius and Dexion (*CAPInv.* 229) to two of their own co-associates.

Within this framework of deviations from standard associative rules as a form of honour, even the regulations regarding entrance-fees could be sometimes overlooked. In a second-century BC honorific decree issued by a Delian *synodos* (*CAPInv.* 859), the honorands were awarded several rather common honours, including the status of *aleitourgos*, but were also admitted into the association without having to pay the regular *eisodion*, 'entry fee'.[40] Although such exceptions do not seem to be as frequent as the immunities from *symbolai/eisphorai*, more impressive privileges at odds with normal admission procedures are also attested. A decree of a *synodos* of *geouchoi*, 'landowners', of Psenamosis (*CAPInv.* 38) in Ptolemaic Egypt admitted into the group the benefactor Paris, donor of a plot of land, declaring him *asymbolos*, *aleitourgetos* and *aneisphoros* but also awarding him the right to introduce three new members into the group without any

---

[37] On this aspect of associative euergetism, see Arnaoutoglou 2003: 147–53.

[38] Dem. 20.18, 20.26–8. According to the Athenian orator, such *ateleiai* had been awarded to Konon and Chabrias (Dem. 20.68–79). On this law, see Rhodes 1982: 13; Gauthier 1985: 112–13; Gabrielsen 1987: 15; Christ 2007a: 151–2. On exemptions, see also Hansen 1991: 114. Those given to orphans, archons, disabled persons and associations did not have an honorific character.

[39] Evidence for fiscal exemptions given by tribes and demes in Migeotte 2010: 59–60 nn. 20–1. Among the eleven inscriptions cited, only three concern exemptions given as honours to members of the honouring parties (*IG* II² 1140, *IG* II² 1147 and *SEG* 23:78).

[40] *I.Délos* 1521, ll. 16–19. The honorands were also declared *aleitourgetoi*.

charge.[41] Similarly, the Athenian *Heroistai* (*CAPInv.* 357) gave to those who contributed 30 drachmas the right to introduce new members to the group.[42]

Clearly, the Athenian *Heroistai* went significantly further than the Egyptian *geouchoi*, giving to the same privilege a fixed, institutionalised form: the deviation from the traditional admission-rules was not a decision taken ad hoc in response to an individual's services, but a general rule applicable to all those meeting well-defined criteria. This practice potentially deprived the association of the ability to determine collectively who was going to enter the body, allowing this fundamental function to be exercised by generous contributors taking individual decisions that had a significant effect on the composition of the association. The nature of the group in question may partly explain this: it was devoted to the cult of three distinguished Athenian citizens from a single family of Marathon and was probably presided over by the son of one of these heroised figures.[43] At least some of those willing to contribute 30 drachmas were surely relatives of the deceased heroes. These persons were both able and willing to open the group to their clients and personal connections and to promote even further a cult likely to enhance their own influence in the city.[44] Hence, the fundamental equality of the associates, materially expressed in their uniform contributions, was combined with a possibility of internal hierarchisation. There were of course methods that, if adopted, could effectively counterbalance this institutionalised superiority of certain individuals within the association. In AD 64, the *Gerousia* of Akmonia gave to a certain Demades the right to introduce an *asymbolos* member to the body, but his choice was subsequently sanctioned by vote.[45] Whether a similar approval was also envisaged in the decree of the *Heroistai* cannot be established, as the stele breaks off at that point and the whole context is not entirely clear.

---

[41] *I.Prose* 40, ll. 31–4. For a detailed analysis of this inscription, see Paganin in press a.

[42] *IG* II² 1339, ll. 15–18: ὁμ[οί]ως δὲ ἔδοξ]ε ἐμβιβάζειν ἐξεῖναι τοῖς [τε]λοῦσιν ἔραν]ον δραχμῶν τριάκοντα κα[ὶ]| – – – – – ων ἐξ δραχμῶν καὶ μὴ π . . . See the translation of this section in Kloppenborg and Ascough 2011: 218 and Arnaoutoglou 2003: 99 n. 34, who speaks of an entrance-fee.

[43] See n. 13 above.

[44] See Ismard 2010: 362, who rightly remarks that the location of the stele erected by these *Heroistai*, i.e. the sanctuary of Athena in the centre of the *asty*, 'town', indicates that this particular group sought to give an as widely public as possible dimension to the memory of its associative heroes.

[45] Giannakopoulos 2013: 18–23 on *SEG* 56:1489.

The Imperial Period

A group of inscriptions dated to the second and third centuries AD allows us to follow the evolution of the associative rules under examination here and to trace various kinds of combinations. These inscriptions include:

a. A decree issued by the *Herakliastai* at Limnai from Paiania (*CAPInv.* 349), regulating various issues of the group's function.[46]
b. The well-known law of the *Iobacchoi* (*CAPInv.* 339).[47]
c. A decree of the Sacred *Gerousia* of Asclepius at Hyettus in Boeotia (*CAPInv.* 984) engraved on a stele, which also recorded two donations of small estates and a list of members.[48]
d. The foundation charter of a second-century AD association of *eranistai* from Paiania (*CAPInv.* 308).[49]

The offerings of wheat flour ordained in l. 36 of the decree of the *Herakliastai* (διδότωσαν δὲ τὴν σιμίδαλιν πάντες τῇ δημοσίᾳ χοίνικι [.], 'all shall give the wheat flour according to the measure of the public choenix …'), have to be combined with the feast days to which the preceding lines 30–3 refer.[50] The *phorai*, 'dues', mentioned in lines 42–3 are explicitly defined as means of financing the *ekdoseis*, 'outgoings', made by the treasurer of the body (τὰς δὲ φορὰς καταφέριν τῷ ταμίᾳ ἐπάναγκες ἰς τὰς ἐγδόσις, 'it is compulsory to hand over the dues to the treasurer for the expenses').[51] Likewise, the participation of the *Iobacchoi* in the various meetings of the group depended on the payment of a well-defined *phora* for the purchase of wine, non-compliance bringing exclusion.[52] In both

---

[46] *SEG* 31:122. See also the bibliography and the discussion in Kloppenborg and Ascough 2011: no 50.

[47] *IG* II² 1368. The vast bibliography on the *Iobacchoi* is assembled in Jaccotett 2003: II no 5 and Kloppenborg and Ascough 2011: no 51. As far as the admission rules are concerned see, *inter alia*, the recent treatment in Ebel 2004: 144–6.

[48] *IG* VII 2808. [49] *IG* II² 1369. Bibliography in Kloppenborg and Ascough 2011: no 49.

[50] On these feast days, see Lupu 2005: 187.

[51] Raubitschek 1981: 97 thought that these *ekdoseis* refer to loans made by the *eranos* to its members, while Lupu 2005: 189 prefers to see them as contracts signed by the association for the provision of sacrificial victims and wood. Accepting this interpretation would mean that the contributions given by the associates to the *tamias* would have been used by the latter in order to pay the contractors. A Rhodian association (*CAPInv.* 2032) is attested to have honoured a benefactor for giving money to a bank account (ἔνθημα) opened by the association so as to finance contracts (ἔγδοσις) let out for works in the collective's buildings. See *IG* XII.1 937, ll. 10–11 with Bogaert 1968: 215–16 and Fraser 1972a: 116–17.

[52] *IG* II² 1368, ll. 42–9. See Ebel 2004: 145–6. It was perhaps from this contribution that the secretary appointed by the *tamias*, 'treasurer', was exempted (*IG* II² 1368, ll. 155–60). Another similar exemption concerns the *ateleia* and *aleitourgesia*, 'exemption from dues and compulsory services', awarded to a lifelong priest, either upon entering the association or upon assuming the

these cases, the prescribed *phorai* have to be understood as payments in cash, though the exact amount is not given. As in the Hellenistic period, private associations continued to link associative 'taxes' with the notions of active participation and financial transparency,[53] the members' contributions being explicitly attached to specific associative events and activities.[54]

The major change has to do with the place occupied by the principle of heredity in the admission rules. However, it should be stressed that there was no uniformity. In certain cases, family lineage allowed for lower entrance-fees. Thus, any member of the *Herakliastai* wishing to introduce his son was obliged to contribute 16½ minas of pork, while other individuals wishing to enter the association were bound to contribute 33 minas of pork.[55] According to the law of the *Iobacchoi*, the members' sons were obliged to pay an entrance-fee of 25 denarii, while the fee for the members' brothers was fixed at 50 denarii, and those indicatively styled as *me apo patros*, 'not (receiving membership) from the father', had to pay 50 denarii and to offer a libation. Furthermore, sons of members were to pay half the regular monthly contribution of wine until they reached puberty.[56] However, in the case of the *Gerousia* of Hyettus, a filial relationship with a member brought a complete exception: if any member died, the *Gerousia* had to elect his replacement from among his sons, newcomers paying no entrance-fee at all. If the deceased member had no sons, one of his closest relatives was allowed to enter the body, subject to an admission-fee of

---

priesthood, by a Megarian *synodos* of *thiasotai* of Dionysus (*CAPInv.* 1527) in the second century AD. See Kloppenborg and Ascough 2011: 290–2 no 60 and SEG 61:323bis.

[53] Another relevant example comes from Egypt. The charter of a private association from Tebtynis (*P.Mich.*V 243, dated to AD 14–37; *CAPInv.* 1408) prescribed monthly dues of 12 drachmas for the organisation of a monthly banquet. Moreover, several documents with accounts of private associations bear headings that explicitly link individual contributions with expenses for common events. See n. 74 below. The contributions in wine recorded in *O.Theb.* 142 (accounts of the *synodos* of the god Amenothes; *CAPInv.* 1385) were certainly used for banquets and other events.

[54] Once again, there is no direct evidence of any link between these payments and the provision of cash for loans and funerals. Ebel 2004: 145–6 duly highlights the different use of membership fees between the *Iobacchoi* and the *cultores Dianae et Antinoi* from Lanuvium (*CIL* XIV 2112; see Bendlin 2011). Nevertheless, the Augustales of Cassandreia who provided 75 denarii for the burial of their co-associates κατὰ τὸ δόγμα, 'as per decree' (Juhel and Nigdelis 2015: 103–7; see also *AE* 1991 no 1424 on a *collegium urbanorum* giving 50 denarii for the burial of a member) are very likely to have included such a (regular?) contribution among the obligations assumed by their members.

[55] *SEG* 31:122, ll. 38–9. This was an entrance-fee in kind, presumably intended to provide for a communal meal (see Lupu 2005: 188, who remarks that the minas refer to the weight of the animal, and Kloppenborg and Ascough 2011: 239–40). The fact that the relevant clause immediately followed the one relating to the sacrificial victim offered to Heracles supports this conclusion. Thus, the contribution imposed upon each entering member ultimately functioned as another opportunity for organising an event to bring together the associates.

[56] *IG* II² 1368, ll. 37–41 and 53–5.

50 denarii. Finally, an outsider entering the body had to pay an entrance-fee amounting to 100 denarii.[57] It should also be noted that in an inscription regarding a Chalcidian *synodos* centred on the local gymnasium, certain new members were stated as having been enrolled ἀπὸ κληρονομιῶν, 'by hereditary right', other newcomers being admitted ἀπὸ ἡβητηρίας, 'chosen from among the former ephebes'.[58]

Diversity also characterises the institution of *dokimasia*, 'examination, scrutiny'. It was a necessary condition even for the sons of the *Iobacchoi*, as no one could enter the group unless his worthiness and suitability were tested by a process that involved an individual vote by each member.[59] But in the *Gerousia* of Hyettus, only those completely unrelated to the existing members were tested by the collective. This is a point worth emphasising. The association in question consisted of a small number of members, perhaps belonging to a circle of inter-related nuclear families.[60] The choice of the group's name was a deliberate strategic move aimed at placing this association on a par both with the respectable 'public' *gerousiai*, 'councils of the elders', widespread in Asia Minor but sporadically attested on the Greek mainland, and, rather more directly, with organised groups of elders in the Peloponnese, affiliated with important local deities and mythical figures.[61] Clearly, this small religious association envisaged itself as a highly esteemed family organ devoted to an important local cult.[62] Hence, it was only natural that descent was conceived as an indisputable proof of a

---

[57] *IG* VII 2808 B, ll. 1–12. For a brief analysis of these clauses, see Oliver 1941: 29–30; Roesch 1982: 159; Van Rossum 1988: 66–8.

[58] *IG* XII.9 916. See Giannakopoulos 2012: 212–16. An inscription from Smyrna (*I.Smyrna* 731; *CAPInv.* 1325), dated around AD 80, lists new members of a Dionysiac association, probably a local branch of the oecumenical association, who had paid the entrance-fee, but also refers to *patromystai*, 'sons of members', who might had paid a lower fee. On entrance-fees to the worldwide association, see Table 2.1. The 850 denarii paid by a high-priest (*Pap.Agon.* 3, l. 15 = *CAPInv.* 1912) may not correspond to the fee normally demanded from newcomers. Regular contributions are implied by Hadrian's decision that members awarded with Roman citizenship should continue to fulfill their financial obligations to the *synodos*. See SEG 56:1359 (*CAPInv.* 991).

[59] *IG* II² 1368, ll. 35–7 and 53–5. Recent discussion in Ebel 2004: 144. As already noted, an individual vote was well in accordance with the Athenian civic traditions; the connection of the *Iobacchoi* with the sphere of Athenian civic politics has been recently emphasised by Suys 2005: 205 and 213

[60] See on this point Roesch 1982: 158–9, who bases his conclusions on the names included in the members' list.

[61] See Giannakopoulos 2008: 43–56, 289, 300–2 and 424–7. The difference between the *Gerousia* of Hyettus and the 'civic' ones is amply demonstrated by Van Rossum 1988: 66–8 contra Oliver 1941: 30. On 'The Argive *gerontes* descended from Danaos and Hypermestra' in Argos and 'The sacred *gerontes* of Upesia descended from Kresphontes' in Messene, see now Spawforth 2012: 169–79 with further bibliography. Similar tactics were adopted by professional groups in Philadelphia and Saittai, called *phylai*, 'tribes' (van Nijf 1997: 184).

[62] Roesch 1982: 157–60.

newcomer's moral qualities; that is why, while relatives of members were simply elected, scrutiny was restricted to those completely unrelated to the existing members.[63]

Conversely, family lineage appears to play no formal role in the admission rules of the *eranistai* from Paiania, an association explicitly formed on the basis of the bonds of friendship that united the original members.[64] The recruitment of new ones was the result of a process that, as in the case of the *Iobacchoi*, equated selection with the testing (note again the use of the verb *dokimazein*) of the moral quality and piousness of the candidates.[65] Admittedly, this examination was not performed by an assembly of the collective but delegated to a group of officials.[66] However, most of them were appointed by lot. Moreover, the parallel cases of the *Iobacchoi* and the *Herakliastai* of Paiania indicate that the basis for allotment was broad enough to include all the associates.[67] Consequently, it is quite safe to conclude that the *dokimasia* of new *eranistai* retained its traditional democratic character.[68] One cannot escape noticing that Athenian private associations still valued and preserved democratic procedures associated with the Classical Athenian democracy, such as sortition from among all the members of the community, even at a time when the host polis had abandoned them.[69]

The following clause in the foundation charter of the *eranistai* prescribed that the *eranos* should be increased by means of generosities (*philotimiai*). This has been viewed as a reference to outsiders promising

[63] The difference in the vocabulary is in this respect highly indicative. The *Gerousia* 'elects' (ἕληται) sons of members, but an outsider is 'tested' (δοκιμα|[σθ]ῇ). See *IG* VII 2808 B, ll. 5–10. It should be noted that in the familial association established by Diomedon on Cos (above n. 10), a process of *dokimasia* concerned only the *nothoi*, 'illegitimate sons'.

[64] See Arnaoutoglou 2003: 129. Sokolowski 1969: 104–5 argued that this association assumed the cost of its members' burials.

[65] *IG* II² 1369 ll. 31–8. On the common points between the *Iobacchoi* and the *eranistai* from Paiania in respect of the examination of new members, see Arnaoutoglou 2003: 99 and Kloppenborg and Ascough 2011: 231 and 234.

[66] A point already noted by Poland 1909: 276 and Feyel 2009: 374.

[67] For the *Iobacchoi*, see *IG* II² 1368, ll. 125–7: magistrates appointed by lot from among all the members. For the *Herakliastai* see also *SEG* 31:122, ll. 22–9: executive posts filled by lot from among all the members when those appointed refused to serve.

[68] On the democratic character of sortition, see indicatively Demont 2003: 39–44 and Taylor 2007.

[69] Magistrates and councillors were not allotted in Imperial Athens. Moreover, not all the citizens were eligible for these posts. See Geagan 1967: 3–5, 17–19, 75–6; Oliver 1970: 57–61; Sartre 1991: 221–2; Muñiz Grijalvo 2005: 271–2 on priesthoods. This contrast may invite us to rethink the implications of the whole relation between private associations and the imperial Greek polis, the first being perhaps more 'democratic' than the second in terms of organisation and function. In this respect, the associations' size and social composition need also to be taken into account. But this is a topic that cannot be treated here.

to provide contributions and hence achieve membership of the association.[70] However, it is equally probable that the clause on the *philotimiai*
referred not to an additional admission rule but to contributions given by
the existing *eranistai*, which were consequently viewed as means to increase
the funds available in the common treasury and to enhance the overall
situation of the association.[71] In this respect, the aforementioned clause
may have constituted an open call to all the *eranistai* to function as
associative *euergetai*. The important point is that, whether referring to
newcomers' entrance-fees or to members' contributions, the clause in
question prescribed no standard amount of money. At the same time,
however, voluntarism, an integral part of any *philotimia*, took the form of
compliance with a formal rule integrated in the *nomos*, 'law', of the
eranistai. This reflects the basic concept which characterises the *eranos* in
question: *philia*, 'friendship'. If we view associative payments not only
instrumentally, as sources of income, but also sociologically, as proofs of
devotion, we can see how commitment to a group based on a *philia* that
was stressed as being voluntary was conceptualised as an obligation that
could not be measured in terms of fixed sums of money.[72] Instead, it
demanded – just like a civic *epidosis*, 'collection of donations'– the best
possible of what a *philos*, 'friend', could offer, irrespective of his family
origin.[73] In fact, the provision in question prevented the potential
exclusion of poorer *philoi*, 'friends', while it encouraged wealthier ones to
contribute as much as they wished or could afford.[74]

---

[70] *IG* II² 1369, ll. 39–40: αὐξανέτω δ[ὲ] | ὁ ἔρανος ἐπιφιλοτειμίαις, 'may the *eranos* be increased by
means of generous acts'. On the interpretation of this clause, see Robert 1979: 159; Kloppenborg
and Ascough 2011: 233.

[71] For parallels of a similar use of the verb αὔξειν, 'to increase, augment', or its derivatives in an
associative context, see *IG* II² 1297 l. 5–6 (a donation of a stele 'increases' the *koinon*) and *IG* II²
1343, l. 18 (a treasurer 'increases' the common fund) and l. 40 (those who will imitate the honorand
will 'increase' the *synodos*).

[72] Arnaoutoglou 1998b: 70 rightly remarks that the individual will of the original members was
highlighted as the sole driving force for the creation of the association.

[73] Thus, although friendship in the ancient world was a bond conceived to be passed on from one
generation to the next, the *eranos* in question prescribed no reduced payments for sons of members.
On altruism and spontaneous generosity between equals as a feature of friendship, see Konstan
1997: 51–82.

[74] A *nomos*, 'law', issued by the *thiasos Amandou* at Physcus (*IG* IX.1².3 670 = *CAPInv.* 437; see also
Kloppenborg and Ascough 2011: 292–4 no 61) fixed the members' financial contributions at the
rate of 14 obols and no less. Although this stipulation was obviously targeted against those not
paying their entire share, it also left room for those willing to contribute more. Unequal individual
contributions are mentioned in several Egyptian papyri of the Imperial period as well. *P.Mich.*
V 246 (AD 25–56; *CAPInv.* 1276) records contributions to the *synodos tou Harpochratou* in
Tebtynis, with amounts ranging from 10 to 24 silver drachmas. *P.Lund* IV 11 (AD 169/70;
CAPInv. 1860) includes a λόγος δ[απάν]ης στολισμ[οῦ] θεῶν Διο[σ]κ[ο]ύρων, 'account of the

It has been widely held that in every period the associates' descendants and relatives constituted an important source from which new members were admitted.[75] This is, after all, quite a natural aspect of all such groups, generated by the various mechanisms of socialisation that characterise them. But there was an important novelty in the Imperial period that should be highlighted: it was only now that the privileged treatment of the existing members' relatives was formally integrated into sets of rules prescribing reduced entrance-fees. Are we to see these rules as means of materially facilitating the continuous presence of certain already tested families in the respective associations? A positive answer would presuppose that the reduced entrance-fees represented a significant financial benefit, but, although this may be at least partly true in the case of the sons of poorer associates, it is not necessarily so in the case of those of wealthier ones. Conversely, there can be no doubt that these lower entrance-fees carried an important symbolic significance: they formally linked the perpetuation of the collective's function and respectability with the expectation that the descendants of its members would carry on what was envisaged as a family tradition and duty.[76] Admittedly, this was in accordance with the general social and political climate of the Imperial period, similar tendencies towards a regularisation of the continuing presence of certain families through lower entrance-fees being observed in certain illustrious semi-public bodies, like the *hymnodoi*, 'choral singers', of Augustus and the goddess Roma at Pergamum (*CAPInv.* 1653), and, more importantly, but in a rather different way, in the civic councils as well.[77]

---

expense for the vestment ritual of the gods Dioscuri', with payments varying from 20 drachmas (3 contributors) to 100 drachmas (6 contributors), including 10 contributions of 60 drachmas and 1 of 80 drachmas (it remains uncertain whether this was an organised religious association). *P.Athen.* 41 (first cent. AD; *CAPInv.* 1440), labelled as ἔκθεσις οἰνικῶν συνόδου ὀνηλατῶν τῶν ἕως Φαρμοῦθ(ι) ιγ, 'list of the expenses for the wine of the *synodos* of donkey-drivers up until 13 Pharmouthi', also records different payments for wine, apparently made during a period of time (a year?) until the 13th of the month Pharmouthi. The headings of these documents raise the possibility that they did not include (only?) regular membership fees, but other payments as well, such as fees of office (see above n. 33) or contributions destined to cover specific needs, perhaps levied in accordance with individual associative status (at least two of the contributors in *P.Mich.* V 246 were officials titled *kleisiarchai*). The heading of the accounts of an association of sacred victors (λόγος τῶν δεδωκότω[ν......] ἱερονικῶν) is equally inconclusive as to the nature of the payments included: *P.Oslo* III 144 (AD 272–275; *CAPInv.* 1381).

[75] Poland 1909: 275–6 and 299–300; Arnaoutoglou 2003: 35–6 and 63 (references to Isaeus 2 (*On the Estate of Menekles*) 14 and Isaeus 9 (*On the Estate of Astyphilos*) 30); Harland 2013a: 19.
[76] Cf. Arnaoutoglou 2003: 96.
[77] On the *hymnodoi*, see *I.Pergamon* 374 D, ll. 13–19. Price 1984: 90 observes that this was an exclusively elite association with extremely high entrance-fees, which, however, were considerably lower for the old members' sons. Similar provisions are included in two other Pergamene documents (Hepding 1907: 293–6 nos 18–19) regulating admission into associations (*CAPInv.*

This emphasis on the conservative values of family tradition, which were widely recognised in contemporary civic discourse, may be seen as another reflection of the tendency on the part of associations to gain respectability by emulating models drawn from political institutions.[78] It also highlights another factor frequently mentioned by recent scholarship: the extent to which private associations functioned as loci of relationships, complementary but not alternative to the ones fostered within family and kinship units.[79] We may thus observe the integration of informal family networks within a wider formal network provided by the associative structures and activities. Also of particular interest is the precise form that the privileged treatment of the associates' descendants took and its implications. As is well known, by receiving larger portions of food and higher sums of money in public banquets and distributions, councillors and gerousiasts were publicly viewed as persons of high civic status. In an inverse but similar way, the reduced entrance-fees paid by the associates' descendants undoubtedly gave the existing members a sense of superior identity, highlighting what was perceived as their and the entire collective's elevated status vis-à-vis the outside world.[80]

Nevertheless, the rules favouring hereditary membership did not challenge the control exercised by the entire collective, at least at the final stage of the admission procedures. The *dokimasia* functioned as a weapon in the hands of the *Iobacchoi*, which they could potentially use to rule out any unsuitable future member. Even in the *Gerousia* at Hyettus, which was restricted in number and orientated towards specific families, it was the body that chose who among the deceased's sons or relatives were to be

1659), which may be identified as the local *gerousia* and the council (Van Rossum 1988: 68–77 and 239–40; Ventroux 2017: 114). In the first case, sons of presumably ex-members who had participated in the association for at least five years paid 50 denarii as an entrance-fee. However, if a son entered the association while his father was also a member or if his father had been an associate for less than five years, the newcomer paid the whole entrance-fee, the amount of which is not preserved on the stone. In the well-documented Bithynian case, a reduced *decurionatus honorarius*, 'honorary office of decurion', is not attested, only the determination of the *censores*, 'censors', to select first and foremost the descendants of 'honourable families'. See Sherwin-White 1966: 721–2; Fernoux 2004: 142–5; Bekker-Nielsen 2008; 67; Madsen 2009: 36–8; Fernoux 2011: 350.

[78] On family tradition in the civic discourse, see Gauthier 1985: 58 and Fernoux 2007.

[79] Bendlin 2011: 252–3 with further bibliography.

[80] Ebel 2004: 144; however, her conclusion that the reduced entrance-fees conveyed the message that the admission of outsiders was undesirable is rather problematic (see my remarks in the last paragraph of this section).

admitted.[81] Poland found this curious.[82] In fact it was not: although family lineage obviously mattered, priority was given to the collective, self-defined and self-advertised to the outside world as a union of equal members sharing an honorific status achieved after a thorough examination.[83]

Moreover, the increased significance of the hereditary principle in the Imperial period did not lead to the transformation of associations into exclusively family groups. On the contrary, every association on which we have adequate information envisaged the admittance of outsiders as well. The higher entrance-fees demanded from them show how this admittance was conceptualised: these persons might not have been the heirs of a long-standing commitment to the common cause, but they were willing (and required) to counterbalance this lack by offering more and by exhibiting their *eunoia*, 'good-will', and *philotimia*, 'zeal, generosity', so as to acquire full membership on an equal footing. In this way, not only could the accepting body's decision be legitimised but a not insignificant sense of personal superiority and psychological satisfaction could also be offered to these newcomers, (self-) perceived as having achieved admission on their personal merit, as associative small-scale *euergetai*.

Final Remarks

Due to restraints of space, I have consciously avoided so far discussing a crucial topic – namely, whether the level of the fees set by associations could actually deter candidates from applying for membership. However, certain methodological remarks are necessary. The evidence presented above raises the question of how expensive participation in private associations was and how rich associates had to be. In this respect, several factors should be taken into account. As noted above, the various financial obligations imposed by associations could have worked as an additional informal selection mechanism, potentially discouraging or even excluding poor outsiders from attempting to become members. Moreover, the rules

---

[81] The formulation of the relevant section in *IG* VII 2808 B, ll. 1–10 clearly demonstrates that no precedence was given to the first-born or to the closest relative. The choice of the newcomer, if more than one candidate existed, was in the hands of the body as a whole.

[82] Poland 1909: 300.

[83] Undergoing a process of *dokimasia* was required for all the newcomers in the already mentioned Pergamene association *CAPInv.* 1659, even for the sons of old members. *I.Smyrna* 218 contains a particularly interesting – in fact the only – mention of *dokimasia* in a professional association: the *symbiosis ton syppinadon* (probably workers of flax) granted burial in the association's grave chamber to members who had undergone examination (*CAPInv.* 1138).

prescribing the regular payment of membership fees could have driven existing members facing economic difficulties out of an association. Finally, not all associations were equally burdensome. Obviously, the very existence of entrance- and membership-fees suggests that the members of the associations mentioned in this chapter were persons with adequate means, willing to invest a portion of their income in achieving and maintaining their associative status.[84] Conversely, rather subjective factors such as a strong desire to be part of an association could potentially lead persons of rather modest means to acquire and sustain membership. One cannot escape noticing that any attempt to quantify all this is extremely difficult. It demands a lengthy analysis, taking into consideration factors such as wages, net output and subsistence levels, which are by definition highly uncertain and probably quite variable in space and time. The value of such an enterprise is indisputable but lies beyond the scope of the present investigation.

In terms of content, procedures and symbolic messages, the rules of private associations on admission and regular financial contributions displayed a tendency not only to respond to vital internal needs but also to construct in various ways a respectable collective identity, perceived as such both by the members and the outside world. A creative and flexible use of civic models highlighted the notions of transparency in the exploitation of financial resources and of responsible active involvement in common affairs; the principles of participation and equality were combined with – but not undermined by – a sense of hierarchy, created by 'legitimate' deviations from standard rules that took the form of individual immunities, rights to introduce new members and, in the Imperial period, reduced entrance-fees for the members' relatives. Two points should be stressed. First, the egalitarian principle of a newcomer's examination by the collective remained formally and officially valid even in the Imperial period, in accordance with various democratic survivals in the civic sphere, which coexisted with – but were not eliminated by – widespread tendencies towards oligarchisation.[85] Second, while the reduced entrance-fees levied on the existing members' relatives functioned as marks of a superior status enjoyed by the associates and their families as well, the higher entrance-fees for other newcomers may be equally seen as mechanisms through which the admission of an individual with no family tradition was experienced by all the parties involved as an honourable distinction.

---

[84] Monson 2006: 224–8 on the members of Egyptian religious associations in the Fayyum.
[85] See indicatively Pleket 1998: 206–12 and van Nijf and Alston 2011: 9–14. See also above n. 69.

The *orgeones* of Bendis recruited new members from a wider network of people who had already integrated the cult of Bendis into their individual set of religious beliefs and practices. Other cult associations, as well as the *eranistai* from Paiania, also viewed individuals integrated into networks based on kinship, personal contacts and friendship as potential new members and took steps to formally encourage their admission. In this respect, private associations may be viewed as formally organised networks of members that depended on wider informal networks of related people and volunteers in order to ensure their perpetuity in time.

At a different level, the concepts of transparency, respectability, participation, egalitarianism and hierarchy, being widely accepted social and civic values, formed 'ties' that brought each individual association into contact with other similar structures and with the polis itself. Admittedly, these conceptual 'ties' were abstract and imaginary, in the sense that they involved a movement of ideas and practices, not official contacts and interpersonal relations.[86] But they may be seen as complementing the more formal bonds between private associations and public institutions and the people who controlled them, demonstrated by the place occupied by the former in the award of honours and in various public ceremonies.[87] This aspect of the associative admission and 'fiscal' rules enables us – and presumably the inhabitants of the Greek cities as well – to regard private associations as well-structured *koinoniai*, 'communities', forming part of a wider, diverse and plural *politike koinonia*, 'political community'.[88]

---

[86] On the concept of ties linking different nodes that form parts of a network and its applicability in ancient history, see Malkin, Constantakopoulou and Panagopoulou 2007; Rutherford 2007: 26–7; Vlassopoulos 2007b: 12–13.

[87] See, *inter alia*, van Nijf 1997: 73–206 and Harland 2013a: 71–139.

[88] On the use of these Aristotelian concepts within the framework of a network analysis, see Vlassopoulos 2007a: 71–96. Cf. Ustinova 2005: 189.

CHAPTER 3

Regulations on Absence and Obligatory Participation in Ancient Associations

Benedikt Eckhardt

Introduction

One of the most often repeated facts about ancient associations seems to be that they were imitating the state. Even a cursory reading of scholarly literature reveals a number of concise definitions. Associations were 'cités en miniature', 'mirror-images of the city on an organizational level', they 'posed as little republic[s]' – the list could be continued.[1] And the main insight is of course correct. The designations for officials, the delineation of sacred space, the formulae of honorific decrees, voting procedures – all these elements were regularly taken over by associations from the model provided by their respective cities.

But there are practical limits to the self-fashioning as a little republic. They become obvious when the very people who have built and sustained the association through their attendance at meetings and their payment of membership fees decide to stay home this month, to eat sacrificial meat somewhere else or to simply spend more time with other people. Real republics did not have to fear that citizenship and its benefits would lose their appeal. They could feel a need to encourage active participation, as is particularly evident when cities like Athens (in the late fifth century BC) or Iasos (in the late fourth century BC) introduced financial remuneration for participation in civic assemblies.[2] But such measures were dictated by political ideology; they were not essential for a city's survival. Associations, in contrast, could run out of members and hence cease to exist.[3] Far from offering financial rewards for participation, they therefore resorted to much stricter policies. In a number of cases from all over the

---

[1] Quotations from Arnaoutoglou 1998b: 75; Baslez 2006: 157; Gabrielsen 2007: 189. I thank the editors and the anonymous reviewers for their helpful suggestions and Kimberley Czajkowski for correcting my English.

[2] On Athens, see Podes 1993; on Iasos, Gauthier 1990.

[3] On financial regulations by associations see Giannakopoulos in Chapter 2.

ancient world, we have epigraphical evidence for fines on non-participation in the activities of an association. My aim is to present and compare the relevant regulations, to study their implications and to look for parallel phenomena outside of associations, in order to show how this specific set of rules contributed to the relationship between associations and society.

Regulations on Absence

The following discussion focusses on the regulations themselves. Preference is given to Greek regulations, but evidence from other regions is also collected. This may enable us to understand how the same set of regulations could serve different purposes in varying circumstances.

The Greek World

Around 330 BC, the *orgeones* of Bendis issued a set of rules concerning the maintenance of their sanctuary in the Piraeus.[4] Members were supposed to meet on the second day of each month to discuss their affairs. In the month Thargelion, each member had to give to the ἱεροποιοί, 'sacrificers', two drachmas for the sacrifice, before the sixteenth day – that is to say, three days before the Bendideia. 'Whoever is in Athens and in good health but does not contribute, owes two drachmas, sacred to the goddess' (ll. 19–20). We should expect a penalising aspect; the two drachmas would then have to be an additional charge added to the normal contribution. It may also be argued that members who did not pay could not participate in the festival but were later expected to contribute, the penalising aspect being that they had to finance an activity they had not been a part of. Either way, the penalty would be modest compared with other regulations: if someone sacrifices beside the altar, he or she owes 50 drachmas. Possible exculpations for absence are given implicitly: if someone is not currently in Athens or hindered by illness, no additional charge applies.

The fragmentary inscription does not seem to have contained similar regulations for the regular assemblies. It specifically connects obligatory participation only with the religious festival, not with the necessities of internal decision-making. Given that the Bendideia were a civic festival where the association would probably be expected to play a part, this focus

---

[4] *IG* II² 1361 = *GRA* I 4. See also Arnaoutoglou in Chapter 6.

seems significant.[5] While necessarily phrased as an obligation of individual members to the association, our earliest regulation on attendance may in fact be read as reflecting the association's obligation to the city. The fact that both readings would have been possible at the same time illuminates a general point about such inscriptions. None of the extant 'laws' of associations regulates everything that could possibly be regulated; the rules they include were selected out of a range of possible options, presumably with a view to the communicative dimensions of stone inscriptions. By choosing this particular regulation, the *orgeones* not only bound their members to an obligation they had accepted upon entering the association. They also made clear to the interested public (namely, the visitors of the sanctuary) that they did indeed intend to be a reliable institution of Athenian civic cult. Seen from this angle, legitimation and obligation are two sides of the same coin.

There are two additional inscriptions from Athens, both from much later periods, that use very similar terminology. The first is a decision by 'the *Heroistai* of Diotimos, Zenon (?) and Pammenes' dated to 57/6 BC.[6] The text is heavily mutilated. According to the accepted reconstruction, the decision explicitly concerned the income of the association:

```
5               ἔδοξεν τῶ[ι κοι]-
        [νῶι τῶν Ἡρ]οϊστῶν, προνοηθῆναι τῆς [προσ]-
        [όδου ὅπω]ς οἱ ἀποδημοῦντες τῶν Ἡ[ροϊσ]-
        [τῶν καθ' ὁν]δηποτεοῦν τρόπον διδῶ[σι εἰς]
        [τὴν θυσίαν?] δραχμὰς τρεῖς, οἱ δὲ ἐπιδη[μοῦν]-
10      [τες καὶ] μὴ παραγινόμενοι ἐπάναγκ[ες]
        [ἀποδιδῶ]σι τὴν φορὰν τὰς ἓξ δραχμ[ὰς ἐ]-
        [ὰν καὶ μή? λάβ]ωσιν τὰ μέρη· ἐὰν δὲ μὴ διδ[ῶσι]
        [τὴν φοράν, ἔ]δοξεν μὴ μετέχειν αὐτο[ὺς]
        [τοῦ ἐράν]ου ἐὰν μή τινι συμβῆι διὰ πέ[ν]-
15      [θος ἢ διὰ ἀ]σθένειαν ἀπολειφθῆναι.
```

The association of *Heroistai* has decided to provide for the income, so that those of the *Heroistai* who are away in one way or other contribute three drachmas to the sacrifice (?), but those who are home and do not come are obliged to pay the fee, the six drachmas, even if they do not (?) receive the portions (of the sacrifice). But if they do not pay the fee, it has been decided

[5] On the Bendideia, see Parker 1996a: 173–5. *IG* II² 1283 (240/39 BC) refers to a civic law (τῆς πόλεως νόμος) that obligated the Thracians to participate in a procession to the Piraeus, where they would then be hosted by the *orgeones*.
[6] *IG* II² 1339 = *GRA* I 46.

that they do not have a part in the club, except if someone stayed away because of grief or illness.

Several parts of this reconstruction are insecure.[7] In particular, the type of meeting and the consequences for those who do not pay are open to question. While θυσία in line 9 is plausibly restored in light of the μέρη mentioned in line 12, the procedure regarding the portions is not entirely clear. A less rigid rule could also be envisaged if the μή (which causes this line's restoration to be longer than the others) drops out: people might not be present, but still receive ἀποφόρητα, 'portions delivered home', for their payment. The definite article before φόρα seems to suggest that 6 drachmas was the normal fee for the sacrifice.[8] People who are away pay half the sum; whether or not they received leftovers or ἀποφόρητα is not stated (practicalities might stand in the way). The only actual penalty then seems to be the rule on exclusion (μὴ μετέχειν) from the association (or possibly 'the sanctuary'),[9] and it is this rule that is mitigated by the possible exculpations. Its connection to the sacrifice is not quite clear, as 'the fee' could have been paid earlier; the regulation may be of a more general nature: those who do not pay (an act that demands physical presence) are out unless they had good reasons not to show up in person.

In spite of these insecurities, it is clear that the regulations are concerned neither with equality at the banquets nor with assistance for members who are ill or in grief.[10] The situation is similar to the procedure established for

---

[7] The number of letters missing at both margins is unclear. Pittakes 1842: 520 calculated at 0–3 letters missing at the left margin and up to 8 missing at the right, which results in a very different restoration that does not always give a suitable sense. Cf. also Keil 1855: 37–41 for a different restoration based on similar premises.

[8] Kloppenborg and Ascough in *GRA* I (p. 219) assume that these were 'penalties on those who did not attend'.

[9] The term *eranos* is a rather arbitrary supplement both here and in l. 17: τοῖς τε[λ]οῦσιν ἔραν]ον. It seems to be based on the term ἀρχερανιστής, 'head of the *eranos*', in l. 4, but this designation for leadership can be found in many *thiasoi vel sim.*; it is not at all tied to *eranos* as a group designation (cf. Arnaoutoglou 1994). Compare *SEG* 43:59 (Rhamnous, ca. 41/0 BC), ll. 4–5: [τὰ ὀνόματα τῶν] μετεχόντων τῆς συν[όδου] 'the names of those who participate in the *synodos*', but the leader is called ἀρχερανιστής and the members ἐρανισταί. We may therefore opt for θίασος, σύνοδος, κοινόν or perhaps ἱερόν, 'shrine', if the association owned a sanctuary (cf. *IG* II² 1361, l. 22: μετεῖναι αὐτῶι τοῦ ἱεροῦ; *I.Kyme* 37, ll. 13–14: παρ᾽ [ἐκ]άστου τῶν μετεχόντω[ν] | τῶν ἱ[ερῶ]ν).

[10] The first interpretation is offered by Baslez 2006: 162, the second by Ismard 2010: 356. Baslez 2006: 163 n. 45 also thinks that οἱ ἐπιδημοῦντες, 'those staying in town', and οἱ παραγινόμενοι, 'those present', are two distinct categories of potential participants, namely, people living in Athens and people living abroad but passing through. She points to ethnic merchant-associations on Delos, where compatriots passing through could be allowed to participate in the meetings without having to pay a membership fee, and postulates a similar situation for our *Heroistai*. But although some members of the family of Zenon and Pammenes did have administrative positions on Delos, the context of the *Heroistai*-association seems to be purely local. The plain sense of the text is a

the *orgeones* almost 300 years earlier. Money is collected for a specific event; handing over the money is only possible in person; rules are therefore made to regulate the membership status of those who could not make the payment because they were away, ill or in grief. The *orgeones* had the same rule for being away and being ill (no payment necessary); the *Heroistai* made those who were away pay half the sum (presumably in advance). Those who were ill or in grief might also have had to pay later; the regulation only protects them from being expelled.

Both *orgeones* and *Heroistai* seem to have introduced these rules in an attempt to (re)organise their general financial situation. In both cases, practicalities may be partly responsible for the focus on a particular sacrifice – presumably the most expensive (and hence most vulnerable) activity of both associations. However, we have argued for an additional communicative dimension in the case of the *orgeones*, and the same considerations may well apply to the *Heroistai* (about whom we do not have any further information). Again, one aspect of the regulation may be a claim to reliability. No civic cult was involved, but the display of reliability might well be directed at the founder(s) of the association, who might have stipulated that members carry out Heroic sacrifice for a deceased.[11] Recourse to an established language of obligation and exculpation would have enhanced the donors' trust in the association and encouraged future investment.

The remaining text from Athens is the famous rule of the *Iobacchoi* probably issued in AD 164/5.[12] Their long inscription contains two regulations on absence. The first one concerns active participation (ἕκαστος ἢ λέγων ἢ ποιῶν ἢ φιλοτειμούμενος, 'each saying or doing or acting eagerly') in the monthly meetings and the collection of the contribution (φόρα) for wine. If someone 'does not fulfil' (μὴ πληροῖ) these obligations,

> he shall be excluded from the *stibas* and those who are recorded in the decree shall have the power (to do so), with the exception of a journey, grief, illness or if someone who should be admitted to the *stibas* is forced (to remain absent) by very urgent reasons, with the priests acting as judges. (ll. 48–53)

---

regulation for the irregular case that ἐπιδημοῦντες are not παραγινόμενοι – that they are in Athens, but do not come.

[11] For such constellations and their impact on the formulation of inscriptions, see the discussion of an example from Lydia by Jones 2008.

[12] *IG* II² 1368 = *GRA* I 51. On the date, see Ameling 1985.

This regulation is more developed than the ones we have seen, as it not only defines terms of active participation as opposed to mere physical presence, but allows for possible cases of urgency that may be defined on a case-by-case basis. It is nevertheless noteworthy that the possible exculpations remain the same ones we have already encountered. The motivation behind the regulation seems to be financial, as μὴ πληροῖ most likely refers to the financial contribution. However, the problem of a member who does not pay is dealt with later in the same inscription: 'None of the *Iobacchoi* who have not paid for the (meeting on the) ninth day and the yearly festival shall be allowed to come to the *stibas* until judgement has been made over him [*sic*] by the priests, whether he shall pay or come' (ll. 67–72). It is tempting to see this apparent redundancy as an indication that μὴ πληροῖ refers more broadly to physical and active presence in the meetings, but a different formulation might then be expected. The second regulation is rather a specification with regard to procedure in the cases of absence mentioned above.

Stibas can refer to a building, an association or a meeting. In this case, it certainly needs to be distinguished from the administrative meetings (*agorai*) that could be convened for the purpose of internal jurisdiction. For these, another regulation on absence was in place: 'If one of the *Iobacchoi*, knowing that an obligatory assembly is convened for this purpose, does not join the meeting, he shall pay to the treasury 50 light drachmas' (ll. 96–9). Failure to pay results in exclusion from the *Bakcheion* until the payment is made. No exceptions are named in this case. The penalty is not severe, but certainly considerable: 50 light drachmas were probably equivalent to a little more than 8 denarii; other offences, like insulting or hitting other members, were already available for 4. So there seems to be a distinction between regulations for the *stibas* and regulations for an *agora*, where the internal administration of the association was taking place. One could be excluded from the first (without a financial penalty), but not from the second, where non-participation was subject to a comparatively high monetary fine. Similarly, excuses could be made regarding the *stibas*, but not regarding the *agora*. So what was the *stibas*? The similarity to the regulations set up by the *Heroistai* needs to be considered. There, the regulation mitigated by possible exculpations excluded the respective persons from either the association or the sanctuary. *Stibas* could mean both things, but for both, the *Iobacchoi* use the term Βακχεῖον. The terminological ambiguity hardly permits definite answers, but it seems to be a better option to take *stibas* as a designation for festive meetings, which would have been more attractive than the assemblies that actually kept the association intact as an organisation.[13]

It would seem that despite the similarity in terminology, the *Iobacchoi*'s rules on obligatory participation follow a different pattern from those we have seen so far. There is nothing to suggest that the *Iobacchoi* were involved in the civic cult of Dionysus in any way. Assuming that they were not and that the *stibas* was a festival specific to the association, there does not seem to be an external communicative dimension to this inscription.[14] Not paying the membership fee in time simply resulted in exclusion from what would have been seen as the fun part of associational life – you do not get what you do not pay for. In contrast, non-participation in the administrative meetings endangered the association's internal processes and therefore led to an actual penalty. In this case, the concern is indeed with the functionality of associative democracy. While one might attempt to somehow connect this difference in focus with the changed legal environment of the Roman imperial period, it seems more likely that associations had always been concerned with safeguarding their internal procedures – it was just not an aspect that was usually selected for inclusion in stone inscriptions, which were at least in part designed to present a specific image of the association to outsiders. The exceptionally detailed regulations of the *Iobacchoi*, apparently written up for internal use only, thus make visible an aspect of associative life that was unlikely to be represented in other epigraphical contexts.

Outside of Athens, Greece offers only one further example. In Locrian Physcus, the νόμος, 'law', of the *thiasos* of Amandos has survived in an inscription dated to the mid-second century AD.[15] The members of this Dionysiac association were called maenads and cowherds; their regular contribution was '14 obols and not less' (ll. 5–6). After a regulation against attacking or abusing other members, the texts include a two-stage regulation on absence. 'One who does not come to the meeting (σύνοδος) although he is at home (ἐπιδημοῦντα)' has to pay 4 drachmas, like someone who attacks another member (ll. 13–15). But 'one who does not come to the mountain has to pay five drachmas to the treasury' (ll. 16–17), with no possible excuse mentioned. Some of the terminology is known from the Athenian examples. As in the (roughly contemporary) case of the *Iobacchoi*, a clear distinction is made between the regular

---

[13] For this meaning of *stibas*, cf. also Jaccottet 2011: 417–18.
[14] The inscription was found in the *Iobacchoi*'s own building, on which see Schäfer 2002.
[15] *IG* IX.1².3 670 = *GRA* I 61.

meetings and a religious event, in this case the procession to the mountain (ὀρειβασία). The penalty is considerable in both cases, but higher in the latter: non-participation in the festival leads to a fine that is more than twice as high as the membership fee. The regulations ensure not only regular financial contributions, but also active participation in the religious activities of the group. The bidirectional understanding of such regulations established above might well elucidate this case as well, but to put it into context, we would need to know more (or rather: anything at all) about Amandos and the environment in which this association operated.

There are hardly any νόμος-inscriptions from the rest of the Greek world. The one regulation on absence from Asia Minor is a special case. In an inscription from the mid-second century BC found in the theatre of Iasos, the Dionysiac artists of Ionia and the Hellespont decided to honour the city of Iasos by sending eight representatives of the association in order to organise choruses and participate in contests.

> If someone of those chosen by the multitude does not come to Iasos or does not participate in the contests, he shall pay to the association of Dionysiac artists 1,000 Antiochene drachmas, sacred and unalienable for the god, except the one who was hindered by illness or bad weather. To him, exemption from the penalty shall be given if he presents his defence in front of the multitude, bringing clear evidence, and is acquitted by a vote according to the law.[16]

The Dionysiac artists, the *technitai* (τεχνῖται), were a special case of private association, not easily comparable to the local groups discussed so far. Members who did not come to Iasos threatened the diplomatic credibility of a κοινόν that acted like an independent state in many ways. The obvious parallel would not be local associations, but delegates in inter-state diplomatic affairs.[17] The text is nevertheless interesting for the unusual details it provides on the administrative side of exemptions (a trial and a vote). It also demonstrates again the plausibility of understanding such regulations and their epigraphic publication at least in part as directed at the outside world. The *technitai* clearly wanted to show how seriously they took their obligation towards the Iasians and offered them insights not only into the obligations they put on their members, but also into the internal procedures that ensured compliance.

---

[16] *I.Iasos* 152, ll. 19–25.   [17] On these, see below.

The East and Rome

Much closer parallels to the Athenian texts discussed above can be found in the regulations of Egyptian associations, particularly in the Demotic statutes of the Ptolemaic period. The nature of these groups is still debated, because the regulations seem to have been contractual agreements valid for only one year, after which most members apparently left the association, to be replaced by others.[18] While the type of group is therefore still open to question, a number of regulations are strikingly similar to those of Greek private associations, including the ones on absence. In a papyrus from Qus dated to 223 BC, it is stated that if someone from the 'association of the temple of Horus' does not come to the assembly although it is proven that he could have come, he has to pay half a *kite* (the normal membership fee being 1 *kite*).[19] No financial interest seems to be at stake, because the collection of the fees is regulated separately – if someone does not bring his contribution, he has to pay 2 *kite*. Similarly, in some statutes of the second century BC, the context seems to be mere sociability: whoever does not come to drink beer with the others has to pay 50 *deben*, unless he has a good excuse.[20] In several almost identical regulations, both failure to deliver the necessary contributions and non-participation in the main cultic events are fined with 25 *deben* (and a curse by the gods), exemptions being made – as in the first example from Qus – for those who are ill, in prison or in a legal dispute with the royal treasury.[21] The same exemptions are valid for those who do not escort a deceased member (or a member whose close relatives have died) to the necropolis, although the fine is lower (5 *deben*).[22]

---

[18] Seidl 1962: 152–5 thought that these were priestly liturgies to be fulfilled by the male adults of a village; this remains a plausible view. Cf. Lüddeckens 1968: 198–201. Against this, Monson 2005 points to some associations with lesser (but still considerable) fluctuation and to the internal magistracies that do not mirror the temple hierarchies; these are valid points, but the problem of membership fluctuation (as well as the unusual competencies of leaders to interfere with the members' private dealings) still needs to be explained.

[19] *P.Lille dem.* 29, l. 6 = de Cenival 1972: 3–10.

[20] *P.Vogl. dem.* 77 A, l. 27 = Bresciani 1994: 'Quello di noi che si rifiuterà di riunirsi in seduta con noialtri, eccetto che (abbia la giustificazione) di dover fare una cosa (irrinunciabile), e (si rifiuterà) di bere birra con noi, la sua ammenda sarà 50 deben e sarà perseguibile legalmente per fargli assolvere il suo obbligo'. Cf. *P.Cair.* II 30606, l. 24 = de Cenival 1972: 45–51. The associations seem to be identical; cf. Muhs 2001: 7; Monson 2005: 184.

[21] E.g. *P.Hamburg* 1, l. 9–11 (150 BC) = de Cenival 1972: 59–61; cf. *P.Lille dem.* 29, l. 8 (reconstructed from *P.Hamburg* 1); *P.Cair.* II 31179, ll. 10, 12–13 (147 BC) = de Cenival 1972: 63–8; *P.Cair.* II 30605 (145 BC), ll. 9–10, 12 = de Cenival 1972: 73–8.

[22] E.g. *P.Cair.* II 30606, l. 14; 31179, ll. 14–15; 30605, l. 13; cf. *P.Lille dem.* 29, ll. 18–19 (half a *kite*).

In all these regulations, the fine for not attending a meeting is not very high compared to others. It is much more expensive to insult a superior or to wrongly accuse someone of being a leper. Special regulations concern the absence from a procession in honour of the gods (in the statute from Qus, the price is 1 *kite* and being cursed by the god), from internal juridical proceedings or from funerals carried out by members of the association for their relatives. This is a set of rather different circumstances. The first one clearly relates to religion and the stated main purpose of the group, which may have entailed an obligation not only to the gods but to village society as a whole. This would connect these rules to what we have seen in Hellenistic Athens. However, the other two sets of circumstances (legal proceedings and funerals) pertain to social relations within the group, an aspect emphasised even further by the omnipresent obligation to keep internal quarrels internal. As non-monumental forms of documentation, the papyri may better reflect such concerns, which are – as noted above – only occasionally visible in inscriptions.

The parallels between the Egyptian papyri and Greek associational laws are obvious, and Greek influence has often been postulated.[23] However, the Demotic laws follow a consistent pattern, the earliest fragmentary example of which dates to 387 BC. It may already have contained a regulation on absence from funerals and a possible exemption in case someone had not received the invitation.[24] The question of influence (and its direction) is a complicated one.[25] We may be on safer grounds in the case of three well-known Greek documents from early Roman Tebtynis.[26] They contain the internal laws of professional associations; some elements are known from the Demotic tradition of associations, others only have Greek parallels. The first unknown association states that 'if anyone receives notice of a meeting and does not attend, let him be fined one drachma in the village, but in the city four drachmas'. Four drachmas is also the penalty for not attending the funeral of a member.[27]

---

[23] E.g. Boak 1937b: 220: '... that the freedom of voluntary association and the contractual basis of such association was introduced into Egypt under Greek influence'. Against this view, see already Seidl 1962: 152–3; but cf. Muhs 2001: 5: 'a single common tradition, probably deriving from Greece'.

[24] *P.Bibl. Nationale* E 241 A, l. 7 = de Cenival 1988 (p. 44 on the regulation on absence).

[25] Less so for some of the Greek regulations from Egypt, like *P.Lond.* VII 2193 (69–58 BC). This papyrus also contains a clause on obligatory participation in meetings (ll. 11–12), but no fines and no exemptions. On the question of Greek and Egyptian traditions, see now Paganini 2017.

[26] See also Langellotti in Chapter 8.

[27] *P.Mich.* V 243, ll. 4, 11–12 (AD 14–37); APIS translation.

The local salt-merchants may not have formed a durable association, but a partnership for one year. But they also had clear ideas about obligatory participation : 'It is a condition that they shall drink regularly on the 25th of each month each one a *chous* of beer [——] in the village one drachma, outside four drachmas, and in the metropolis eight drachmas.'²⁸ On first sight, these rules appear to further refine the distinction, well known from Greece, between absence of ἀποδημοῦντες, 'those away from town', and ἐπιδημοῦντες, 'those in town', but from a third example it emerges that in Tebtynis, it was not the members, but the meetings that could be in different places.²⁹ The rather high fine for not attending a meeting in the metropolis was a way to deal with two contradictory interests: the likely importance of such meetings for economic and possibly legal purposes and the unwillingness of members to travel the 14 miles from Tebtynis to the city in order to attend them.

These three documents have recently been used to show how professional associations could bring together potential partners in business and foster solidarity against outsiders, be they other merchants or representatives of the state. Since these advantages depended on direct interaction, such associations had to insist on physical presence during the meetings.³⁰ It is evidently plausible to assume that private networks based on trust (and not, like cities, on kinship relations) had to devise mechanisms for constantly renewing that trust.³¹ Still, the economic context cannot be the whole story. Rules on obligatory participation can be found already in the Demotic documents and in Greek associations that do not seem to have been professional networks. The problem is thus a more general one, relevant to all forms of private or semi-public organisation.

Apart from Egypt, two possible regulations on absence are known from the Near East, and Greek influence has been claimed for both. The 'rule of the community' from Qumran reveals the organisation of the *yaḥad*, a movement with several cells active in Judea in the late Hellenistic and early

---

²⁸ *P.Mich.* V 245, ll. 34–7 (AD 47); APIS translation. There is not enough space to insert anything like the detailed introduction from *P.Mich.* V 243 ('if anyone receives notice . . .'). As the text of ll. 35–6 now runs, it is unintelligible: ἐάν τε πλερετιν, ἐάν τε λι[[ ] στάσεος. We might supply something like [ἀπο]στάσε{ω}ς in the sense of 'distance' (from village, metropolis, etc.), but the remaining text still does not make adequate sense. For the categorisation of the group as a partnership and not an association, see Gabrielsen 2016b: 92–5.
²⁹ *P.Mich.* V 244, ll. 7–9, 16–17 (AD 43).   ³⁰ Broekaert 2011: 247.
³¹ On associations as trust networks, see Monson 2006; Gabrielsen 2016b. If the salt-merchants are seen as a consortium rather than an association, the purpose of their meetings may primarily have been to regularly 'check the progress of their work against the terms of their agreement', as Gabrielsen 2016b: 93 points out.

Roman periods. One of the rules on internal discipline has been understood as a regulation against absence during voting procedures:

> ... and the same punishment applies to the man who goes away at a session of the Many, aimlessly and wantonly up to three times at a session, he shall be fined for ten days, but if they should hold a vote and he goes away, then he shall be fined for thirty days.[32]

Fines could not be paid in money, because when entering the *yaḥad*, members had to give up their private possessions; offenders were rather excluded from the common meal for a certain period. In general, the *yaḥad* could be more demanding of its members than Greek associations, because membership implied a break with mainstream society and joining a new 'people'. A Greek organisational model has nevertheless been postulated not least for the regulation on absence, but, as the meaning of the text is not entirely clear, it is of limited value in this debate.[33]

A close similarity to Greek forms of associations has also been postulated for the Palmyrene *marzeḥa*. Relevant for our purposes are the regulations of a group that calls itself 'the priests of Belastor and Baalshamin'.[34] According to its first editor, one partially preserved line of the fragmentary inscription contains a regulation on absence, introduced by 'someone who goes abroad'.[35] This supposedly shows that the group was a *thiasos* built according to a Greek model (incorporating a regulation on 'those away from town'), but nothing in the text clearly speaks in favour of identifying the group with anything other than a priestly college. More importantly, the interpretation of the fragmentary line has not been accepted in more recent editions.

Finally, two Latin texts deserve to be highlighted. The earliest statute of a *collegium* comes from the time of Augustus and concerns a *collegium aquae*, possibly an association of fullers.[36] The nature and status of the

---

[32] 1QS 7.10–12: *wkn lʾš hnpṭr bmwšb hrbym | ʾšr lwʾ bʿṣh wḥnm ʿd šlwš pʿmym ʿl mwšb ʾḥd wnʿnš ʾšrt ymym wʾm yzqpw | wnpṭr wnʿnš šlwšym ywm.* The translation is by Weinfeld 1986: 29, who also compares this regulation to those of other associations. However, the translation of *yzqpw* with 'hold a vote' is questionable (*zqp* means 'to erect' or perhaps 'to rise').

[33] On the general comparison between other associations and the *yaḥad*, cf. Gillihan 2012 and, for a similar approach with a different result, Eckhardt 2017b.

[34] *PAT* 0991; Teixidor 1981.

[35] Teixidor reads l. 19 as *wmn mn dy ʾzl* and translates 'et autre que celui qui est en voyage', taking the last letters to derive from *mēzal.* McLaughlin 2001: 51–3 and Kaizer 2002: 168–9 refuse to give an interpretation of this very fragmentary line.

[36] *CIL* VI 10298. The inscription has long been lost and the text relies on a copy preserved in the collection made by Francesco Barberini in the seventeenth century; cf. Rudorff 1850: 203–6. On the identification with fullers, cf. Mommsen 1850: 346–7. A more recent discussion of the group's status is offered by Moschetta 2005, who compares its *lex* with municipal laws.

group are not quite clear. The frequent use of the future imperative mirrors public laws and has been taken as evidence for a more public than private nature of the group, but the tendency to build 'little republics' by copying formulae makes such conclusions rather difficult. The first part of the heavily reconstructed inscription deals with an oath to be taken by magistrates and with assemblies. 'If someone announces that it is necessary for him to go more than 120 miles away for the state or for some controversy, the judgement about this matter shall lie with the magistrates. If he announces it after the time, he shall pay a fine of 50 asses' (ll. 8–9).[37] The person in view here is probably a member who should be present at the assembly, but it could also be a magistrate who is expected to swear the oath on a certain occasion. The sum is not extraordinarily high, given that 500 asses have to be paid for some other offenses, but it is also not the lowest sum mentioned (which is 1 as). According to a possible but by no means certain reconstruction, the text gives further details on procedure: if someone has ordered a *nuntius*, 'messenger', to excuse him in time, but the *nuntius* fails to do so, he shall pay the fine himself (l. 11).[38] This would again point to detailed and thoughtful regulations on absence in this *collegium*, but as the reconstructions are unsupported by parallels, they need to be treated with such caution that no argument can be based on them.

The second text, of a much later date, comes from Simitthus in Africa Proconsularis.[39] The group in question was originally thought to be a *collegium funeraticium*, but is actually a municipal *curia*.[40] Still, many regulations are similar to those of private associations, including regulations on absence. After several rules concerning officials, the *magister* and the *quaestor*, it is said that 'if he does not come to the assembly although he is present, he will have to give a *congius* (of wine)' (ll. B 6–7). The payment is not high compared to the honorary sums to be paid by future office holders, which could amount to two or three amphorae (16 and 24 *congii*, respectively). It therefore seems unlikely that it refers to the *magister* or the *quaestor*, as earlier commentators have assumed. The inscription also

---

[37] Ll. 8–9: *[si quis nuntiabit necesse sibi esse i]re peregre longius p(assuum) CXX rei p(ublicae) e<t> (l)itis causa magistrorum | [de ea re iudicium esto. si post tempus nuntiabit ei multa] esto a(ssium) L.* The *res publica* might also be the *collegium* itself.

[38] Ll. 11–12: *[nuntius quem quis ita se excusare iusserit tempore ius]to si non denuntiarit ipsius multam sufferto | [aut q(uantae) p(ecuniae) quis ita multatus erit t(antae) p(ecuniae) ei in nuntium ex hac] lege actio esto.*

[39] *CIL* VIII 14683 (AD 185).

[40] Cf. Schmidt 1890. The ensuing debate about the supposed 'degeneration' of *curiae* into clubs need not concern us here.

contains rules for attending funerals. 'If one of the relatives has died within the distance of 6 miles', absence at the funeral is fined with 2 denarii, 5 for dead parents (ll. C 6–9). Surprisingly, the text goes on with a regulation against not attending the funeral of one's own parents, a rather unusual interdependence of the membership role and private life. There is no regulation for the funerals of members; perhaps in these cases, participation was a self-evident necessity.

Special Cases: Endowments and Benefactors

The practical reasons for implementing regulations on absence in the groups discussed so far could be twofold: ensuring the economic survival of the association when physical presence was equivalent to paying the membership fee or (more common) ensuring participation in administrative, social and cultic operations, thus safeguarding the functioning of the group as a tight social network. The situation was obviously different in the case of endowments. When the association had to offer something for free, there was no need for penalties that might ensure participation. Rules were rather needed that could limit the number of people demanding their share of the cake. While the case of the *Heroistai* has reminded us of the interest a donor might have in an association's regulations on absence, at least some associations based on endowments did not punish absence, perhaps because it was actually advantageous to those who were present. In most cases, the necessity of being present for receiving one's share would go without saying,[41] but occasionally, such associations – or the respective donors – did formulate normative statements on obligatory participation.

A few examples may suffice to illustrate this general rule. The Roman *collegium* of Asclepius and Hygieia had received a building and 50,000 sesterces from Salvia Marcellina; from that sum, *sportulae*, 'handouts', as well as bread and wine were to be distributed among the members, whose number was limited to sixty.[42] Only those present at the meetings were entitled to these distributions, with two notable exceptions that are by now familiar: 'The *sportulae* of bread and wine of those who do not come to the banquet on the above-mentioned days shall be sold and (the money) shall

---

[41] It could be mentioned as a matter of course; cf. *CIL* VI 33885 (Rome, time of Hadrian): distributions among those *qui ad tetrastylum epulati fuerint*, 'who will have come to feast by the tetrastyle' (ll. 11, 13, etc.).

[42] *CIL* VI 10234 (Rome, AD 153). Cf. Liu 2008 on endowments of *collegia*.

be distributed among the participants, except the *sportulae* of those who are overseas or hindered by severe illness.'[43] In this case, the exceptions are relevant not for avoiding punishment, but for receiving one's share. In other cases, the policy seems to have been less lenient. In Amorion in Phrygia, an interesting but also difficult text from the first century AD records some regulations of a group called φυλῆς Διὸς μύσται, '*mystai* of Zeus's tribe'.[44] The *mystai* care for the tomb of the deceased Kyrilla during the Mithrakana festival and have received a vineyard from her father as an endowment. The group seems to have come into existence for this purpose.[45] A regulation on obligatory participation was incorporated into its foundation document that has unfortunately been preserved only fragmentarily; it presumably went along the line of 'whoever does not come shall have no part in the interest generated from the vineyard' (ll. B 17–21).

Benefaction and endowments also influenced regulations on absence in another way, for special rules were occasionally in place for donors who could not be expected to show up. In Egyptian Psenamosis, a *synodos* of fellow farmers honoured their benefactor Paris in a rather detailed inscription.[46] Paris, who had given some land to the association for building a gymnasium, receives various honours, including the title 'priest for life'. He is nevertheless exempted from the – implicit – obligation to be present during meals: 'And he shall receive double shares (of food). But if he is not present, it shall be sent to him, and during the feast, he shall be crowned with a special crown by the association.'[47] A similar situation may be envisaged in the case of a loyalist association from the environment of Pergamum.[48] During the meetings, the association honoured with crowns members of the Attalid dynasty as well as local governors who were certainly not present. In such cases, the association clearly could not make any demands; no ordinary member could expect such special treatment.

---

[43] Ll. 16–17: . . . *ea condicione qua in conventu placuit universis ut diebus s(upra) s(criptis) ii qui ad epulandum non convenissent sportulae et pane et vinu | eorum venirent et praesentibus divideretur excepto eorum qui trans mare erunt vel qui perpetua valetudine detinetur.*

[44] Ramsay 1889: 17–23 no 1; Laum 1914 no 175–6. The status of the group (association or actual φυλή?) is discussed by Kunnert 2012: 26–28; Eckhardt 2016: 163.

[45] *I.Prose* 40 = *I.Delta* I 446 (first century BC). On this text, see Paganini in press a.

[46] Ll. A 13–14: τ[οῖ]ς συνεστῶ[σιν] ἀπὸ ἄρτι [μ]ύσταις.

[47] L. 41–2: . . . καὶ λαμβάνειν διπλᾶ μέρη· ἐὰν δὲ μὴ παρῆι, πέμπεσθαι αὐτῶι, στεφανοῦ|σθαι δὲ καὶ κατὰ πόσιν διαφέροντι στεφάνωι ὑπὸ τοῦ κοινοῦ.

[48] *SEG* 52:1197 (between 168 and 164 BC); cf. Müller and Wörrle 2002.

Contextualising Obligatory Participation

It has become clear from this overview that associations and groups all over
the ancient world tended towards regulating obligatory participation.
While the meaning, function and communicative dimension of such
regulations varied according to circumstances, their practicalities appear
almost standardised. This is especially true for the rather fixed set of
exemption clauses. These in particular raise the question of how the
regulations of associations relate to the general normative universe of
ancient cities. Where were people obliged to be present under threat of
punishment and what were accepted excuses? Due to the availability of
comparative evidence, discussion in this section will be focussed on the
Greek world.

Numerous situations can of course be envisaged where the physical
presence of individuals was legally demanded. A person summoned to
court was obviously obliged to attend, although in fourth-century Athens
one could delay proceedings by swearing an oath, accepted excuses being
illness, absence due to civil service and, according to one scholion, death in
the family.[49] In the context of inter-state diplomacy, the persons chosen by
the respective cities to serve as delegates or judges could be obliged to be
present under threat of punishment; the only recorded excuse was illness,
again to be proven by an oath.[50] These regulations contain the grounds for
exemption by now familiar to us, but the context – temporary duties
incumbent on individuals – is very different from associations.

When it comes to participation in collective action, the most obvious
societal sphere to be taken into consideration would be the civic assemblies. While the evidence sometimes adduced for compulsory voting in
ancient Athens is weak, Aristotle has a comment on some unspecified
constitutions that require people to register for participation in assemblies
or courts and impose heavy fines on them when they do not come.[51]
Aristotle regards this as oligarchic manipulations of a formally democratic
system, designed to scare off the poor. This would be a possible context for

---

[49] Lipsius 1905: 901–2; Schol. vet. Dem. 21,84 (281a).
[50] *IG* IV².1 68, l. 94 (Epidauros, 302 BC); IG V.2 357, l. 53–4 = Thür/Taeuber 1994, no 17 (treaty
between Sikyon and Stymphalos, 303–300 BC). I thank Kaja Harter for making me aware of
these regulations.
[51] Arist. *Pol.* 1297a.16–28. The history of compulsory voting is traced back to Classical Athens by
Malkopoulou 2015: 49–54. But the chasing of citizens to the Pnyx, carried out by Scythian slaves
with a red-dyed rope (Ar. *Ach.* 22) can hardly be taken as evidence for formally regulated
obligatory participation.

association inscriptions; we might even say that the oligarchs envisaged by Aristotle run their cities like private associations, imposing similar rules. However, as neither the reality behind Aristotle's schematic discussion nor the formal rules of obligation and exemption are known in any detail, we turn to a more promising field for comparisons: civic religion.

It has often been claimed that participation in Greek civic cults was obligatory, but on closer look this claim has turned out to be difficult to prove.[52] In the Greek world, an important exception concerns young men (νέοι) or boys (παῖδες), who were regularly obligated to participate in festivals.[53] A couple of examples may illustrate the relevant regulations. In Coresia on Ceos, a civic festival in the early third century BC included a torch-race and other gymnastic shows to be performed by the young men.[54] 'But he among the youth who is not present although he could shall be liable to pay as a penalty up to one drachma' (ll. 25–26). Young men were also addressed when the city of Delphi instituted a relay torch-race as part of the Eumeneia-festival and decided that the ten λαμπαδισταί, 'torch-race runners', should be chosen by the leaders of the φυλαί, 'tribes'; if they did not nominate runners, they had to pay 10 staters to the city.[55] 'If, after the leaders have written down those in the (right) age, someone does not want to obey although he could, he is liable to pay the leader and the other λαμπαδισταί 10 staters privately (that is to say, from his own resources?) during the festival' (ll. 16–18).[56] If he claimed to be either unable to run or older than the records indicated, he had to prove this through an oath (ἐξομοσάσθω), as in the cases of interstate diplomacy mentioned above. In the late second century BC, the city of Aigiale on Amorgos received an endowment by a certain Kritolaos in order to commemorate his deceased son, including an ἀγών, 'contest', with a torch-race.[57] 'In order that the torch-race may take place with boys (παῖδες) and men (ἄνδρες), the gymnasiarch shall take care of it, ordering it as seems good to him, and forcing all the youth to run, as far as they have the designated age' (ll. 84–6). Young men could thus be forced (ἐπανα[γ]κάζων), while no such language is used with regard to adults.

---

[52] Most of the relevant data is discussed by Krauter 2004.   [53] Cf. Ziebarth 1914: 41–4.

[54] *IG* XII.5 647.   [55] *CID* 167 (160/59 BC).

[56] Ll. 16–18: εἰ δέ τ[ι]ς, τῶν ἀγεμόνων καταγραψάντων τοὺς ἐν ἁλικίαι, μὴ | θέλοι πειθαρχεῖν δυνατὸς ὤν, πράκτιμο[ς ἔ]στω τῶι ἀγεμόνι καὶ τοῖς ἄλλοις λαμπαδισταῖς ἀ[ρ]|γυρίου δέκα στατήρων ἰδίαι καὶ ἐν ταῖς ἱερ[ο]μηνίαις. *CID* translates ἰδίαι as 'sur ses biens personnels'; contrast Jones 1987: 82: 'Not to the state, but "privately" to the ἀγεμών and the other *lampadistai*'.

[57] *IG* XII.7 515.

Since the νέοι were often organised in corporate bodies along the same lines as associations, it was probably not very difficult to get hold of them.[58] Children were a different matter, because their participation depended on the agreement of their fathers. In a fragmentary regulation from Eretria for a procession in honour of Asclepius (late fourth or early third century BC), a list of boys and girls is created.[59] Two lines end with 'if he/she is not present' and 'if he/she does not send' (ll. 11–16). According to Wilhelm's restoration, the text also included a rule on exemption due to πένθος οἰκεῖον, 'mourning in the family'.[60] We have already seen πένθος οἰκεῖον as grounds for exemption in the inscriptions of the *Heroistai* and the *Iobacchoi* from Athens, and it has an exact parallel in a later text from Stratonicea (that Wilhelm referred to): in the second century AD, it was decided that thirty boys of high birth were to be chosen, whose daily task was to sing a hymn to Zeus and Hecate.[61] Exceptions were made 'if some of them are not healthy or are held back due to mourning in the family'.[62] Otherwise, the fathers were obliged to provide the chosen hymn-singers and were punished for not doing so. The distinction obviously relates to legal maturity; we can compare the ephebarchic law of Amphipolis, where parents or guardians have to pay the fine for the non-attendance of ephebes during lessons.[63]

Some other constellations seem less pertinent and may be mentioned here only briefly. Cities could obligate their citizens, or at least the owners of houses and workshops, to build inscribed altars in front of their houses during a procession, as can be learned from the regulations concerning the Eisiteria festival of Magnesia on the Meander.[64] The inscription contains a reference to potential consequences of non-conformity: 'if someone does not do so, it shall not be good for him (μὴ ἄμεινον αὐτῶι εἶναι)'. This is not necessarily evidence for the city's inability to enforce 'real' penalties, but it is also less concrete than the rules of associations. In Cos, certain groups in society could be obligated to sacrifice on festivals as a corollary

---

[58] On the organisation of νέοι, cf. the different perspectives offered by Dreyer 2004; van Bremen 2013.

[59] *IG* XII.9 194.   [60] L. 28: – – πέν]θο[υς] οἰκε[ίου – – (without context).

[61] *I.Stratonikeia* 1101.

[62] Ll. 13–14: ... ἐ]άν τινες αὐτῶν μὴ ὦσι ὑγιεῖς ἢ πένθι | οἰκείῳ κατέχωνται ...

[63] Text in Lazaridou 2015; this regulation ll. 11–14.

[64] *LSAM* 33, ll. 86–9. In a similar manner, the city of Teos could obligate each of its συμμορίαι, the civic subdivisions, to 'build on its own place next to the altar of the συμμορία one altar of King Antiochos (III) and his sister Queen Laodice and to perform the sacrifice on it': *SEG* 41:1003 II = Ma 2005: no 18.

effect to the Coan custom to sell the civic priesthoods.[65] Among these groups are newly married couples, as well as professional groups.[66] This is obligatory participation phrased in purely monetary terms; it may well have done without physical presence. Finally, we should not underestimate the potential of cults to demand participation without enforceable regulations. The confession inscription by Gaius Antonius Apellas from Blaundos, who 'was punished by the god often and for a long time, because he did not want to come and take part in the mystery, although he had been summoned', is a case in point.[67] It is impossible to know whether there was a law made by humans that demanded participation or if Apellas just deduced a divine law from the empirical evidence (that he had been punished by the god).

From the comparative evidence gathered so far, the information on absence regulations in Greek associations can be fleshed out a bit further. It is interesting to note that absence due to mourning is epigraphically allowed for in just two cases: association members and children. This might be a mere coincidence, especially if the regulation on mourning were to be connected not with social obligations at home, but with impurity. However, it does suggest that the associations' demands would be perceived as unusual. It is also interesting to note that in the case of appointed judges and delegates, illness had to be proven by taking an oath. This offers a window into one of the practical problems left untouched by the rules and regulations of associations: How were other members to judge whether or not someone had actually been ill? The Egyptian associations vaguely refer to 'proof' against a person, and the Greek sources offer little more than the unusual case of the Dionysiac *technitai*, who demand clear evidence of some sort. We may perhaps surmise that following procedures established in official contexts, association members who claimed to have been ill had to take an oath.

However, the most important insight is that the evidence for obligatory participation of adults in civic cults is very meagre indeed. This makes the rules of associations especially interesting, but it also raises the question of how realistic it was that someone who did not come actually saw themselves obliged to pay a fine. The question as such is not limited to regulations on absence: while we have much evidence for associations threatening to exact fines for this or that violation of the law, how exactly

[65] Cf. on the evidence Wiemer 2003: 293–300.
[66] Maillot 2013: 215–20 argues against their organisation as voluntary associations.
[67] Petzl 1994: 126 no 108 (first/second century AD).

this worked in practice almost always eludes us.[68] The normal mechanisms of internal jurisdiction do not seem very helpful in this case, as they demand physical presence. We therefore have to briefly consider other possibilities, especially cooperation with the state.

In Ptolemaic Egypt, the laws of associations could become the subject of legal disputes before the royal authorities – if the ταφικόν, 'burial indemnity', for a deceased had not been paid or, in one case, if the common economic agreements were not adhered to.[69] But these were exceptional cases that associations would try to avoid, for instance by demanding that members resort to internal jurisdiction and giving wide-ranging competences to their leaders. If someone did not pay the membership fee, the financial administrator could come to his house and take surety for it, resistance leading to another fine; in another case from the Roman period, the president was allowed to seize a disobedient member on the street and 'hand him over', presumably to state authorities (because contracts had been violated).[70] These cases seem to show that, at least in the conditions that determined associative life in Egypt, membership roles could extend beyond the narrow confines of a monthly assembly, and we can imagine that these associations had their ways to ensure participation as well.

There is no similar evidence for associations outside Egypt. The lack of papyri goes some way towards an explanation, but it is also possible that the relationship to the state was somewhat different in Greece. Cooperation with state authorities may occasionally have been possible,[71] but the attested cases concern either public associations or the financial interests of the city. Thus, the σύνοδος of the priests of Asclepius in Mantinea involved the civic official ἐπιγνώμας into their affairs, who was responsible for monitoring the proper implementation of a particular decree, but this was not a private group.[72] Private associations might also offer incentives for state authorities to safeguard the upholding of regulations, but the occasions where this could happen were basically limited to problems of grave care.[73] The Dionysiac *technitai* are, again, a special case.

---

[68] Three ostraca from Maresha published by Ecker and Eckhardt 2018 are the first pieces of evidence for the actual exaction of fines by an association, but they do not say what the offence was.

[69] *P.Enteux.* 21 and 20; *P.Ryl.* II 65; cf. Gibbs 2011: 295 n. 16.

[70] *P.Cair.* II 30605, ll. 7–8; 30606, ll. 7–8; 31179, ll. 8–9; *P.Hamburg* 1, ll. 6–7 etc.; *P.Mich.* V 245, ll. 41–2. On taking surety, cf. San Nicolò 1927: 291–2.

[71] San Nicolò 1927: 293–4 argues that the contractual nature of Greek associations enabled them to get support from state authorities, but no case is known from Greece.

[72] *IG* V.2 269 (first century AD). But cf. Zoumbaki in Chapter 7.

[73] A good example is *IG* VII 2725 (Akraiphia; second century AD; cf. Roesch 1982: 136–8). A woman called Pythis had founded an association of *Heroastai* commemorating her children. Fines were due

In one of the letters by Hadrian found at Alexandria Troas, they receive imperial backup for claims against unwilling members: 'Those who contribute according to the laws of the σύνοδος, even if they stop working or become Roman citizens, shall remain obliged to these laws.'[74] This was a powerful tool, but one that no normal association could hope to acquire. For them, a more likely fate was the one suffered by the *collegium Iovis Cerneni* in Alburnus Maior that published its dissolution in AD 167 because the number of members had declined from fifty-four to seventeen, one *magister* had disappeared and 'for such a long time no one has wanted to come together on the days that have been stipulated in the statute or to pay the burial indemnities or the dues'.[75]

Conclusion

In English scholarly literature, the groups that this volume is interested in are often labelled 'voluntary associations'. The term has been criticised for being anachronistic and not very precise, given that social pressures of various kinds are likely to have determined membership in associations in a number of individual cases.[76] However, with this caveat in mind, it is certainly legitimate to use the term 'voluntary' in order to distinguish these groups from civic subdivisions or age classes. What this chapter has highlighted, however, is the fact that associations in their rules and regulations did not present participation in their activities as voluntary at all. They rather demanded participation and tried to find – or pretended to have – ways to punish those who did not fulfil this basic obligation of membership.

These regulations on obligatory participation do not find many parallels outside the world of associations. True, at least in Greece, both the rules on exemption and the likely procedure in cases of legitimate absence are known from other contexts, and it seems possible to argue that they were in fact one of the elements associations took over from the state in their attempt to build a 'little republic'. However, while magisterial titles or

---

if someone opened the grave chamber or damaged the inscription; in both cases, 2,000 denarii were to be given to the σύνοδος and 2,500 to the city, without a formal lawsuit. This is how one could raise the likelihood of cooperation between associations and the state.

[74] *SEG* 56:1359, ll. 51–2 (AD 134): οἱ κατὰ τοὺς τῆς συνόδου νόμους συνβάλλοντες, κα[ὶ] ἂν παύσωνται ἀσκοῦντες κἂν Ῥωμαῖοι γένωνται | ἐκείνοις τοῖς νόμοις ἐνεχέσθωσαν, καθ' οὓς συμβεβλήκασιν.

[75] *CIL* III p. 924, ll. 15–17 = *IDRTabCerD* I.

[76] Harland 2009: 28. The same objections have been raised with regard to modern associations; cf. Amis and Stern 1974: 91–2.

voting procedures could easily be transferred from one context to another, regulations on absence were different. By entering an association, or at least one that had drafted regulations of this kind, people submitted themselves to a rigid social order that they did not know from normal experience outside of their membership role. They had to accept obligatory presence as a general demand that was not tied to specific offices or one-time events. If we want to draw the analogy to civic cult, the members of associations accepted being treated like the young men who could be obligated to participate in torch-races or like the children who had to sing hymns to Zeus and Hecate in Stratonicea. They entered a world of well-ordered parallel societies.

For associations, such rules fulfilled several functions, all of which highlight the limits of imitating city structures. At least in some associations, one aspect was certainly economic survival. Ensuring the physical presence of members was the only way to ensure a steady income. However, we have also seen cases where the financial aspects are treated separately from non-participation in social activities. Soft factors must therefore be integrated into the explanation. If associations are seen as trust-networks, regular face-to-face interaction may well have been deemed a necessity for establishing and maintaining that trust. The main religious events were particularly important in this regard because of the shared emotional experience they offered, which may be another reason why non-participation in these events is sometimes subject to a higher fine. We have also noted repeatedly that inscriptions can communicate an image of a group to outsiders. In the competition for new members and benefactors, it was helpful to convey the impression that the group was capable of collective action and devoted to its cause. Donors could rest assured that the regular announcement of their merits would take place in front of a proper crowd. The rules of exemption may be accorded a double role here: on the one hand, their practical ambiguity (what counts as an illness?) left some room for testing out the boundaries of trust. On the other hand, as they were taken over from civic contexts and were perhaps familiar to outsiders from highly obligatory and very hierarchical events such as civic processions and the torch-races of young men, they could reinforce the impression of seriousness and reliability.

For most purposes, the cities themselves did not need to establish similar rules. Here, what associations wanted to achieve through regulations on absence and obligatory participation (economic survival, trust, respect) could normally be taken for granted. It is thus no surprise to find regulations on absence much more clearly spelled out in private associations, even though they appear in so many other ways as 'little republics'. We have seen that absence was basically regulated along the same lines in many associations, even beyond the Greek world. The physical presence of members was in many ways vital for the existence of associations, more important perhaps than refraining from personal insults. And yet the fines were often not very high compared to others. This rather lenient punishment, combined with the rules on exemption, can perhaps be interpreted as a way to offer those who had been absent for whatever reason a way back into the association. For all the rigid statements in these regulations can barely obscure the fact that most associations had very little leverage if a member decided to test the boundaries and stay home. Like all newly emerging little republics, private associations were always in danger of becoming failed states.

CHAPTER 4

The Place of Purity
Groups and Associations, Authority and Sanctuaries[*]

Jan-Mathieu Carbon

This chapter proposes to look in some detail at a few evocative cases, primarily from the Hellenistic and Roman periods, where associations or other groups, such as bands of worshippers, were especially concerned with purity or where they published inscribed rules of purity.[1] Limited in number partly due to the vicissitudes of epigraphic preservation, partly due to the geographic and chronological specificities of this material – post-Classical Asia Minor and the Aegean – other factors may also explain their scarcity and warrant further investigation.

Leading such an investigation entails probing the often-murky background and motivations for the publication of inscriptions regulating cult practice. These have traditionally been called 'sacred laws' – a questionable designation, since the documents are not always laws, nor 'sacred' in and of themselves. A newer proposal is to view such inscriptions as representative of 'ritual norms'. These are a heterogeneous group of inscribed documents that defined, prescribed and/or codified norms for Greek ritual practices, such as purification.[2] The context for the passing of such rules is not often explicitly defined and, indeed, this is usually the case with rules of purity.

---

[*] The writing of this chapter formed a part of my work as a member of the Copenhagen Associations Project (CAP) during 2015–16, an opportunity for which I continue to be deeply thankful. I am also grateful to the anonymous peer reviewers for their constructive remarks as well as to the editors for their diligence and extensive patience. Edward Harris kindly provided useful guidance and feedback. As always, Stella Skaltsa provided acute comments on my work, from which I greatly benefitted. The chapter was revised and partly updated in 2018 and 2019.

[1] A subject not discussed in the excellent recent survey and legal classification of 'sacred laws' in Harris 2015, but see esp. 70–1 on rules of associations (and cf. now the online appendices to this article by Harris with Carbon at https://journals.openedition.org/kernos/2299).

[2] On the question of the terminology and criteria for identifying cultic regulations, see recently Carbon and Pirenne-Delforge 2012; Zimmermann 2016; Petrovic 2017. Cf. also Harris 2015: esp. 58–60, who attractively distinguishes between laws or decrees *regarding* sacred matters and other more informal rules or summaries of formal rules, preferring to call the latter 'signs'. After the volumes of Sokolowski (*LSAM*; *LSCG Suppl.*; *LSCG*) and Lupu (*NGSL*), for a new online collection of 'sacred laws', see now *CGRN*.

In confronting the difficult question of context, the relevant cases adduced here are particularly instructive for apprehending the identity and the authority of the groups in question. One can outline a relatively broad spectrum of groups and associations: those that were identified with a specific sanctuary but do not seem to have been fully in control of it (Section 1); others that expounded purity regulations for sanctuaries that they evidently controlled but where entry was open to other worshippers (Section 2); and finally, cults that were founded by private individuals, whether for their families or for a wider audience, which also enacted rules concerning purity (Section 3).

These case studies thus frame a wider investigation, aimed at addressing the question of why associations and other groups would promulgate rules of purity in the first place. Purity was a fundamental type of order, an indispensable aspect of the definition of any sacred space or cultic community. Proper religious conduct or piety included abstaining (cf. ἀγνεία, 'purity', and related concepts) from sources of pollution, a *sine qua non* for maintaining a successful relationship with the gods (being ἀγνός, 'pure', καθαρός, 'clean', ὅσιος, 'pious, holy' and the like).[3] As this applied in society at large, so it did too in a smaller religious group or within an associational cult site. Many chapters in the present volume ably and amply underscore the importance of maintaining good order in assembled masses of people, such as associations. Concerns of this sort were administrative, logistical, even hygienic, but could also include ethical factors or those of religious decorum.

On fundamental level, then, it can be assumed that associations with direct ties to a cult or to a sanctuary would naturally wish to maintain it in a 'well-ordered' fashion, notably with regard to purity. Where sanctuaries are concerned, it is immediately apparent that associations sought in any eventuality to safeguard the sacrality of this space. For instance, associations in Attica regularly stipulated in lease agreements that a person renting their property treat it not just as normal land, but 'as sacred' (ὡς ἱερός).[4]

---

[3] On ἀγνεία and the concepts of purity/impurity in the ancient Greek world, see Parker 1996b and cf. also now Parker 2018b, revisiting both old and new evidence. On the term ὅσιος and the framing of an adequate relationship with the gods, see Peels 2016: esp. 168–206 (ch. 6) with regard to ritual norms and purity.

[4] Cf. *LSCG* 47 (*CAPInv.* 242; 306/5 BC), ll. 5–7, χρῆσθαι... ὡς ἱερῶι; *IG* II² 2501 (*CAPInv.* 243; late fourth cent. BC), ll. 4 (restored) and 15–16, ὡς ἱερ⟨ῶ⟩ι. On this, see Parker 1996b: 162, also adducing a later 'law concerning precincts' from Athens, which notably forbade birth and death, both dangerous sources of pollution.

Implicit in this requirement was also the essential preservation of the purity of the space.

But why did purity in particular matter to some groups? In what cases did this subject become an overt preoccupation? Beyond a general concern for maintaining pious conduct and the integrity of sacred space, such questions are normally difficult to answer fully in the absence of other evidence, though the rationale of the rules can occasionally become clear. Some progress can be made by looking at the circumstances of the development of such rules, where these can be identified, and at exactly how they were articulated. Did they precisely correspond with norms of purity at large or with ones in the local area of the community in question? Or were they different – for instance, more flexible or more stringent? In this regard, comparing purity rules in their local and wider context can be particularly illuminating (see Sections 2 and 3). Some rules articulated by groups can be recognised as inclusive or pragmatic, while others were apparently more strict or moralistic. Qualifying the rules of purity in this way can to some degree help evaluate their motivations. These can further be tied with the overall characteristics of the group, be it one generally welcoming outsiders in its sanctuary or one possessing more selective criteria of admission.

Making a sacred space accessible to worshippers, whether a select or a wider group, created a risk of impurity that needed to be carefully managed. In many if not most cases, associations and groups must have relied on existing, traditional rules of purity, whether recorded by the city and community or not. In other, more distinctive cases, regulations of purity became an intrinsic part of the definition of the cultic community and the organisation of its sacred space. The subject of purity rules therefore forms an interesting focus for apprehending how associations considered and managed sacred space as well as for illuminating the profile of the associations in their local and wider context.

The *Bacchoi* at Cnidus

Ensuring the purity of a sanctuary, if this was not a private cult site in any sense of the term, may be presumed to have been the remit either of the *polis* or of the sanctuary itself and its officials. In late Classical or early Hellenistic Cnidus, a group of *Bacchoi* made a petition to the city council and its *prostatai*, 'leaders'. These worshippers of Dionysus formed a cultic group that was sufficiently well organised to make a collective action in front of the civic authorities, though whether they were formally an association – with a charter, rules, fixed membership or the like – remains unclear. The concern of the *Bacchoi* was apparently that many other worshippers were camping in the sanctuary, thus rendering it not only insalubrious but, worse, impure. Indeed, it must be stressed that the concern of the *Bacchoi* was not merely a logistical or hygienic one, but rather, as the resulting decree of the city makes explicitly clear, 'that the sanctuary remain pure' (ὅπω[ς] | ἀγνεύηται τὸ [ἱαρὸ]|ν, ll. 4–6). The petition of the *Bacchoi*, though now lost to us, will almost certainly have framed their complaint in religious terms, specifically pointing to the necessary purity (ἀγνεία) of the sanctuary of Dionysus.

The city acted on the recommendation of the *Bacchoi* and passed a decree forbidding camping altogether and very probably imposing penalties to that effect, which are now missing in the fragmentary lines concluding the stele (cf. ll. 12–13). The fragmentary inscription recording this decree is normally presented and restored as follows:[5]

> ἔδοξε Κνιδίοι[ς, γν]|ώμα προστατᾶ[ν]· | περὶ ὧν τοὶ Βάκ[χοι] | ἐπῆλθον· ὅπω[ς] | ἀγνεύηται τὸ [ἱαρὸ]|ν τοῦ Διονύσ[ου το]|ῦ Βάκχου, μὴ ἐ[ξῆ|μ]εν καταλύε[ν ἐν | τῶ]ι ἱαρῶι τῶν [Βάκ|χ]ων μ]ηδένα, μή[τε | ἄρσ]ενα μή[τε θή|λεια]ν· εἰ δέ κ[ά τις]| καταλ]ύηι – – – – –

> It was decided by the Cnidians, on the proposal of the *prostatai*, regarding the matters for which the *Bacchoi* approached (the civic authorities): so that the sanctuary of Dionysus Bacchus remain pure, no one is to be allowed to camp in the sanctuary [of the *Bacchoi*], neither male nor [female]. If [anyone] should make camp [... (then) ...]

A crux of the text occurs in lines 8–10: [ἐν | τῶ]ι ἱαρῶι τῶν [Βάκ|χ]ων μ]ηδένα. This widely accepted restoration would either – highly paradoxically – restrict the prohibition of camping only to the *Bacchoi* themselves ('none of the *Bacchoi* is to camp . . .') or would – much more naturally, and

---

[5] *I.Knidos* 160 (*CAPInv.* 838). Note that, from autopsy as well as the recently published photograph (*I.Knidos* II, p. 118), the stone clearly reads τῶν and not τῶμ in l. 9 (the latter being a possibility considered by its editor W. Blümel in *I.Knidos*, notably on the basis of a squeeze in the *IG* archives consulted by K. Hallof). The left hasta of the letter is straight and vertical; part of the right vertical hasta seems to be visible at the break; by contrast, mu has angular hastae in this inscription. Reading τῶν rather than τῶμ may lend further support to my suggestion below, because the dental nu, rather than an assimilated labial mu, would tend to anticipate a different word than [Βάκχων]. For a balanced discussion of the arguments for and against the associational character of the group in question, see Jaccottet 2003: II 257–8 no 154. Some other groups of *Bacchoi* included in the Inventory of Ancient Associations are similarly problematic: cf. e.g. *MDAI(A)* 27 (1902): 94 no 86, l. 3 (*CAPInv.* 913; 158 BC); but contrast the much more fully developed *Iobacchoi* of Athens (AD 164/5), who owned a *Bakcheion* and participated in both private and – apparently – civic rituals: *IG* II² 1368 / Jaccottet 2003: II 27–35 no 4 / *AGRW* 7 (*CAPInv.* 339).

as translated here – suggest ownership of the sanctuary by the *Bacchoi*. Yet the latter reading also begs the question: why, if they owned or controlled the sanctuary, did the *Bacchoi* either bother or need to ask the city to intervene in the matter of the purity of their sacred space? We could perhaps imagine that they attempted to pass rules regarding purity in the sanctuary and that these proved to be ineffective, possibly for want of tangible sanctions. The *Bacchoi* would then, in a surprising display of their lack of competence, have approached the city to lend its authority to the regulation of their sanctuary.[6]

While that reconstruction remains possible, there is an alternative: this is to view the completely uncertain restoration τῶν [Βάκ|χων] as inherently problematic. A fairly simple solution, for example, might be to restore the passage in question as τῶν [θυόν|των μ]ηδένα. This reading would entail that 'none of those offering a sacrifice' – essentially any worshipper – 'is to camp in the sanctuary'. While some inscribed rules granted those who offered sacrifices the right to feast and linger overnight, others restricted camping altogether.[7] This seems to me to be the case here at Cnidus, where

---

[6] An analogy might be sought in the case of the priests of Sarapis and Isis who obtained a decree from the council of elders in Seleucid Laodicea-by-the-Sea regarding the application of a civic law to their private sanctuary (*IGLS* IV 1261, 174 BC). That the concern of the priests was framed in terms of private property, is repeatedly made clear in the text (ἰδιόκτητον, line 10; ἡ κτῆσις αὐτῶν, ll. 16–17). On this document, see the detailed discussion of Sosin 2005. Yet this is essentially a different situation from the one at Cnidus: the private petition at Laodicea sought to make a pre-existing law concerning the dedication of statues apply to a privately owned sanctuary; any regulation made by the priests themselves in this regard would potentially have conflicted with the laws of the city. For a different emphasis on why the priests would not turn away dedicants, namely, because of their piety, see Sosin 2005: 139. In the case of the *Bacchoi*, piety certainly fuelled their anxiety about unclean campers, but would not explain why they would have permitted such visitors to set up camp in their own private sanctuary in the first place. On the possible legal precedents for the petition of the *Bacchoi*, see further below.

[7] Most clearly, cf. the interdictions of camping in all sacred areas stipulated by Antiochus III and Zeuxis to Seleucid troops (*I.Labraunda* 46, 203 BC, ll. 8–9: μήτε ἐν τοῖ[ς ἱεροῖς | τόπ]οις καταλύετε; cf. also *I.Amyzon* 10; for these texts, see also Ma 1999: 304–5 no 15 and 294–5 no 6, respectively). A similar rule may have been enacted at Olympia already ca. 500 BC concerning Epidamnian, Lybian and Cretan pilgrims to the sanctuary (*IED* 8, l. 6: αἱ δέ τις σταθμείοι ἐν τίαροῖ, EN[–] κτλ.). The immediately following lines, if directly connected with this lacunose passage, evoke fines not only for the pasturing of animals (ὁ νομε⟨ύ⟩ς) but also, it would seem, for lodging outside of the expected or prescribed guesthouse (τὸν ξενεῶνα, δαρχμάν κ' ἀποτίνοι). For analogous rules concerning access to and purity in the sanctuary at Olympia (ca. 520–500 BC), see also *IED* 3 / *CGRN* 4 (case of a foreigner, ξένος), *IED* 4 / *CGRN* 5 (a θεαρός, 'visitor', having sex in the sanctuary). Conversely, other ritual norms grant the right to camp, but only to those who have performed a sacrifice: *SEG* 36:1221 (Xanthos), ll. 11–14: μηδ' ἐν ταῖς | στοιαῖς καταλύειν | μηθένα ἀλλ' ἢ τοὺς | θύοντας; or *SEG* 57:1674 / *CGRN* 129 (Patara, ca. 300–200 BC), ll. 7–8: μηδὲ καταλύειν | ἐν τῶι τεμένει πλὴν τῶν θυόντων. Camping in these cases was thus restricted to the specific category of worshippers who had sacrificed; these were allowed to stay and feast, others were not. To be distinguished from the above-mentioned cases are others that required camping and thus enforced consumption of meat on the spot (cf. e.g. *LSCG* 82 / *CGRN* 33, Elateia, fifth cent. BC, ll.

'neither a male nor a [female]' worshipper, not just the *Bacchoi*, is to be allowed to remain overnight in the sanctuary and potentially pollute it.

What might have been the source of impurity that so worried the *Bacchoi*? Urination and defecation were possible forms of pollution in the ancient Greek world, though they rarely if at all warrant any mention in the available evidence.[8] It was perhaps simply expected that one did one's business outside the sanctuary.[9] Since the purpose of the Cnidian decree is framed in terms of necessary abstention (ἁγνεία) and explicitly excludes both genders, the background of the petition of the *Bacchoi* suggests that campers were not just dirtying the sanctuary, but succumbing to that most natural of night-time proclivities: sex. Together with birth and death, as well as the shedding of blood and, much more rarely, the consumption of certain foods, intercourse was envisaged as one of the principal vectors of pollution in the ancient Greek world.

This new reading would also have the advantage of clearing up the question of the authority over the sanctuary at Cnidus: it belonged to the city and was controlled by it. Archaeological and epigraphical evidence for the sanctuary of Dionysus at Cnidus remains rather slim, but it is apparent that the city – as is also expected from other Greek cities – controlled the local festival of Dionysus, the Dionysia, from at least the early Hellenistic through the Roman periods.[10] Nevertheless, the *Bacchoi* formed an important group: their name echoed the epithet of the god and they probably

---

3–4: θύοντα | σκανεν; *IG* XII.4 1 293 / *LSCG* 168, Cos, late second cent. BC, with its repeated injunction θυόντωι δὲ καὶ σκανοπαγείσθων).

[8] For guidelines concerning urination and defecation, see already Hes. *Op.* 727–32. But these say nothing about religion or sanctuaries in particular, recommending instead the discretion of night-time and of a well-enclosed courtyard (ἐυερκέος αὐλῆς). On this subject, see especially the comments of Parker 1996b: 293 and Parker 2018b: 26 ('excrement is almost never mentioned in Greek religious laws, it is of no interest or concern').

[9] One of the only relevant inscribed rules is *SEG* 56:890 (Nymphaeum, fifth cent. BC), which advises: μὴ χέσες· ἱερόν, 'do not defecate: sacred'. The irregular shape of the reused block in this case may suggest that it was affixed as a reminder (a sign) for a small or private sanctuary that was not otherwise immediately obvious (hence the need to include the word ἱερόν *in fine*). Note also that no notion of purity is invoked nor are any sanctions mentioned. The interdiction against urination in the peristyle of the sanctuary of the new inscription from Marmarini, Decourt and Tziafalias 2015 / Bouchon and Decourt 2017 (ca. 250–150 BC), face B (I), ll. 80–81, is remarkable but no doubt to be attributed in large part to the uniqueness of the document itself and the foreign cult it defines.

[10] For the usual identification of the temple with the late Byzantine church 'C', see Blümel at *I.Knidos* 160, with refs. For the Dionysia, cf. *I.Knidos* 231, ll. 20–5 (decree of Smyrna from late third or second cent. BC, in which, pending authorisation – παρακ[α]λεῖν Κνιδίου[ς] – crowns are to be proclaimed in the theatre during the Dionysia, [πα]ρ' αὐτοῖς ἐν τῶι θεάτρωι Διονυσίων τῶι ἀγῶνι. . .; for direct parallels, cf. *I.Kaunos* 17, second cent. BC, ll. 38–40), *I.Knidos* 606 (first cent. BC), ll. 12–13 (proclamation by the herald of the council during the Dionysia), *I.Knidos* 74 (first–second cent. AD) and *IG* XII.3 322 + Suppl. p. 282 (Thera, second cent. BC), ll. 1–18.

had a substantial degree of involvement in the sanctuary, taking it upon themselves, we might envision, to perform and maintain the cult in collaboration with the – probably civic – priest.[11] What is more, it should be noted that their petition to the polis worked: the city listened to their concerns and deemed them valid; the stele publicising the decree is the material manifestation of this. The sanctuary continued, as usual, to be allowed to receive visitors for sacrifices, but none of these – *Bacchoi* included – was allowed to stay overnight.

In other words, we seem to have here the case of a group that was closely connected with a sanctuary and had a role to play within it, but which did not properly control it. The *Bacchoi* were most probably not a fully formalised association.[12] As a recognised interest-group, they were generally concerned with maintaining the sanctuary as a 'well-ordered' space, but not fully empowered to do so. As a group with a manifestly religious vocation and cultic function, they notably focussed on preserving the indispensable purity (ἁγνεία) of the sanctuary, an emphasis which facilitated a successful appeal to the civic authorities.

Though the sanctions of the decree from Cnidus are not preserved after lines 12–13 and therefore remain unclear to us, the text nonetheless demonstrates that the city took matters in hand. These sanctions may have included concrete penalties or fines for those contravening the rule and illegally camping in the sanctuary of Dionysus. Reference may also have been made to general norms of purity, whether codified or not, which were espoused by the city. Transgressing such rules would have carried either a concrete penalty – for instance, requiring a ritual process purifying the sanctuary as a whole – or a seemingly less tangible, but nonetheless

---

[11] For a probable priest of Dionysus, see *I.Knidos* 113 (ca. 200–150 BC). Since this is a familial monument, it remains unclear whether he was a civic official or not, though given the civic importance of the cult (see n. 10, above), that he was a public priest is highly likely.

[12] A similar uncertainty hovers over other groups of Dionysiac worshippers, such as *mystai*. In the present study, a particularly intriguing case is the metrical and casuistic purity regulation consecrated by (. . .)tes the son of Menander who calls himself ὁ θεοφάντης: *I.Smyrna* 728 / *LSAM* 84 / *GRA* II 140 (*CAPInv.* 1337; second or third cent. AD). In this text, Dionysus is called Βρόμιος (l. 2) and we also find the mention of Bacchic festivals (ἐν Βακχείοις, l. 12). Though the initiative of the official in promulgating the rules is noteworthy, likely indicating an independent or private sanctuary where multiple gods might have been worshipped (τέμενος and ναοί, l. 2; cf. also plural altars in l. 10), we cannot ascertain any further information about the contextual framework of this cult. The provenance of the inscription is regrettably uncertain and, though a group of *mystai* are mentioned in l. 18, the formal character of the group as an association is far from evident. The purity rules present several standard and stringent delays of abstention regarding impurity: forty days in the case of exposition of a child or an abortion/miscarriage, ca. ten days (a 'third of the month') from the death of a relative, etc. On these delays of ἁγνεία, see further below.

more oppressive one – for instance, being considered impious (ἀσεβής) and incurring the anger of the gods.[13]

A subcategory of the 'sacred laws' alluded to previously – texts that prescribe ritual norms or regulate religious behaviour in some way – consists of what might be called casuistic purity regulations. From the Archaic to the early Hellenistic periods especially, these regulations take the form of extensively detailed laws, enacted by the polis, which seek to define different cases of impurity and their recommended solutions.[14] The formulary of these laws is organised on a case-by-case basis – 'if such-and-such happens, then do the following', hence the designation 'casuistic'. For example, in the laws of the city of Cos concerning purity, codified in ca. 240 BC, but at least in part probably belonging to an earlier tradition or model, priestly personnel were explicitly prevented from entering a house in which a person had died. The period of abstention (ἁγνεία) in this regard was to last five days after the body was carried out for burial; if any priestesses or priests contravened the rules, then a purification with water poured from a golden vessel and a sprinkling of grain was required.[15]

The importance of civic authority in these kinds of regulations becomes less perceptible – if at all – in the epigraphic evidence from the late Hellenistic and Roman periods. This should not be taken to mean that the laws of the city that were already enacted did not remain in effect – they demonstrably did, in the case of Cos, for instance[16] – only that the regulations published in later periods are generally of a different sort. The style of these later texts is also more practical and to the point. It now

---

[13] For an example of both, see the law (νόμος, e.g. l. 19) concerning the purity of the sanctuary of Electryone, enacted by a decree of Ialysos, *IG* XII.1 677 / *CGRN* 90 (ca. 350-300 BC), ll. 27–30: ὅ,τι δέ κά τις παρὰ τὸν νόμον | ποιήσηι, τό τε ἱερὸν καὶ τὸ τέμενος | καθαιρέτω καὶ ἐπιρεζέτω, ἢ ἔνοχος ἔστω τᾶι ἀσεβείαι. On impiety, see notably Delli Pizzi 2011.

[14] For epigraphic purity regulations, see the still unsurpassed discussion of Parker 1996b: i.a. 144–6, 176–8, 332–56. For early, but regrettably more fragmentary cases, see e.g. *IG* IV 1607 / *LSCG* 56 / *CGRN* 3 (Cleonae, ca. 525 BC; a civic context is nearly certain, see ll. 15–16). Two notable early Hellenistic examples include the famous 'Cathartic Law' of Cyrene, Dobias-Lalou 2000: 297–309 / *CGRN* 99 (ca. 325–300 BC), and the inscription from Cos, *IG* XII.4 1 332 / *CGRN* 148 (ca. 240 BC; see n. 15 below). Both sets of laws are notably interesting in their claims to a deeper form of religious authority or tradition: in the case of Cyrene, they are presented as an oracle of Apollo (cf. l. 1); in that of Cos, they are explicitly said to be sacred (ἱεροὶ νόμοι – here indeed 'sacred laws' properly speaking) and expounded by the official interpreters of religious matters (ἐξαγηταί).

[15] *IG* XII.4 1 332 / *CGRN* 148 (Cos, ca. 250 BC), ll. 23–4 and 29–30: μηδὲ ἐς οἰκίαν [ἐσέρπεν ἐν ὁποίαι κα ἄνθρωπος ἀποθά]νηι ἁμερᾶν πέντε ἀφ' ἇς κα ἁμέ||[ρας ὁ νεκρὸς ἐξενιχθῆι ... αἰ δέ τί κα τῶν] | ἄλλων συμβᾶι, ἀπὸ χρυσίου καὶ π[ροσπερμείας.

[16] On Cos, reference to the purity laws for priests and priestesses (*IG* XII.4 1 332 / *CGRN* 148, cf. n. 15 above) is clearly made some centuries later in a contract for the sale of the priesthood of Nike (*IG* XII.4 1 330 / *CGRN* 163, first cent. BC, ll. 12–14): καὶ ἁγνευέσθω | [ὅσ]ων καὶ τοῖς λοιποῖς ἱερεῦσι ποτιτέτακται ἁ|[γν]εύεσθαι.

involves inscribing a series of rules, for instance on a legible stele or a pillar, which should be observed by worshippers wishing to enter a sanctuary.[17] As a representative example of this later form of casuistic purity regulation, we might take the following regulation inscribed on the entrance to the temple of Artemis Chitone near the agora at Miletus:[18]

[καθαροὺς εἰσι|ένα]ι εἰς τὸν νε|[ὼ] τῆς Ἀρτέμι|δος τῆς Κιθώνη[ς], | [ἀ]πὸ μὲν κήδε[ο]ς | [καὶ] γυναικὸς [τ]ε|[κούση]ς[19] καὶ κυνὸς | [τε]το[κυ]ίας τ[ρ]ι|[τα]ίου[ς] λουσα|[μ]ένους, ἀπὸ [δὲ | τῶ]ν λοιπῶν [αὐ|θημ]ερὸν λουσα|μέν[ους.]

[Enter as pure individuals] into the temple of Artemis Chitone: from a funerary ritual [and] from a woman [having given birth] and from a bitch [having given birth], on the third day, having washed; and from the rest (that is to say other causes of impurity), on the same day, having washed.

Though the beginning is partly missing, the text is essentially preserved.[20] It is relatively clear that the regulation was simply addressed to worshippers and probably did not include any preamble concerning its source. In other words, the authority behind the regulation was left implicit. Moreover, no form of sanction for any contravention of the rules is stipulated at Miletus. In other rules, some form of sanction could occasionally be mentioned, but this usually took the form of a curse (or a blessing, which also implies its reverse: again, a curse).[21] We never find fines or other tangible penalties associated with this later form of casuistic purity regulation.

Typically, these rules apply to any and all who wish to enter the sanctuary (εἰσιέναι, εἰσπορεύεσθαι, *vel sim.*). The form that they take is again set of cases, defining purity – the words καθαρός or ἁγνεία are often invoked, though they may also be left implicit – from (ἀπό) a specific

[17] See now Petrovic and Petrovic 2018 for a helpful review of these inscriptions. For such texts as 'signs', cf. again Harris 2015: esp. 58–60.

[18] *Milet* I.7 202 / *LSAM* 51 / *CGRN* 214, ca. 75 BC to 1 BC.

[19] The long-standing restoration may be maintained, though [τ]ε|[τοκυία]ς might alternatively be envisaged. To my knowledge, in the case of purity rules, the aorist participle is only used in *I.Pergamon* 255 / *LSAM* 12 / *CGRN* 212, l. 7: καὶ τεκούσης γυναικὸς δευτεραῖο(ι) (see below, Section 2, on this text from Pergamum). The perfect τετοκυῖα is somewhat more widely found: *I.Pergamon* 264 / *LSAM* 14, *IG* XII Suppl. 126 / *LSCG* 124 / *CGRN* 181, *LSCG Suppl.* 54 / *CGRN* 217, *LSCG Suppl.* 119 / *CGRN* 144.

[20] As the edition in *I.Milet* I.7 202 informs us, the inscription was incised on a narrow anta-block, probably originally belonging to the temple itself. From the photograph, some erosion is perceptible above the extant text on the block, suggesting that only one or at most a few lines are now missing above. Unless we were to assume that further text was inscribed on another anta-block originally situated above this block, the inscription should be treated as essentially complete.

[21] For an early example, see the conclusion of the rules concerning the sanctuary of Meter Gallesia at Metropolis (*I.Ephesos* 3401 / *LSAM* 29 / *CGRN* 71, fourth cent. BC): ὃς δ᾽ [ἂν] ἀδικήι|[σηι,] μὴ εἵλως αὐ|[τῶι ἡ] Μήτηρ [ἡ] Γαλ[λησί]α.

source of impurity, followed by a delay during which one must abstain from entry into the sanctuary and/or by a set of purificatory requirements, normally washing from the head down or other forms of ablution. Each scenario is either listed on a case-by-case basis or a group of cases may be treated under the same rubric in the regulation.

From the Hellenistic period onward, then, the inscribing of rules of purity, rather than emanating directly from the city or another form of political authority, was often left to the discretion and the initiative of sanctuaries and their officials, of private individuals or of other groups, notably associations. A related observation must be made. This type of evidence is more or less confined to the eastern Aegean and Asia Minor, with only a few cases from mainland Greece,[22] and one example coming from Ptolemais in Egypt.[23] Prima facie, this geographical distribution need not be surprising or significant in and of itself, since a large proportion of the Hellenistic and Roman epigraphical sources comes from these areas of the ancient Greek world. A recent discussion, however, has sought to argue that these purity regulations all or nearly all pertain to foreign cults, more specifically Egyptian or Near Eastern forms of worship, whence they must have developed in Greek communities.[24] Without denying that several of these regulations do indeed relate to such cults, it should be said that the question of the 'origins' of specific purity rules remains difficult to answer. Particularly cautioning any hasty judgement is the fact that the norms underpinning these casuistic regulations match the aforementioned purity laws of the city and thus seem to derive from much the same traditional sources.[25] Moreover, as we shall see immediately below for the Attalid Kingdom, many of the cults that are concerned by such rules are far from straightforwardly explained as 'Near Eastern' or as having any connection

---

[22] Apart from the inscription for a West-Semitic cult found at Marmarini near Larissa in Thessaly (Decourt and Tziaphalias 2015 / Bouchon and Decourt 2017 / *CGRN* 225, ca. 250–150 BC), two other cases are regulations for the sanctuary (of Despoina?) at Lycosura (*NGSL* 8 / *CGRN* 189, second cent. BC) and for the sanctuary of the Egyptian gods at Megalopolis (*NGSL* 7 / *CGRN* 155, ca. 200 BC).

[23] For the case from Ptolemais, written on a conical cone of basalt, see *LSCG Suppl.* 119 / *CGRN* 144 (first cent. BC); the context or authority of this regulation has not been clearly identified.

[24] Petrovic and Petrovic 2018.

[25] Note, for instance, the abstention (ἀγνεύεσθαι) from sex for the night preceding the sacrifice to Zeus Polieus on Cos, which the ἱαροποιός chosen as a sacrificer (σφαγεύς) must respect (*IG* XII.4 1 278, ca. 350 BC, ll. 41–43). This sort of abstention is typical of casuistic purity regulations and does not have any perceptibly 'foreign' aspect here. In fact, regulations concerning purity can usually be seen as striking some form of compromise between traditional norms and local trends, an assessment that is partially discussed below, but still warrants further study than is possible here.

to Egyptian practices.[26] For all of their diversity in terms of provenance, content and context, the regulations present a coherent picture of the need to avoid the spread of impurity in a community, by restricting the entry of impure individuals into sacred space.

Pergamum and the Attalid Kingdom

A particularly intriguing case study for examining the purity rules of associations in their local context is Pergamum and the wider area of the Attalid kingdom. Here, we find a series of conspicuous examples where the different sources of authority behind the promulgation of purity rules are particularly clear. One inscription, from the sanctuary of Athena Nikephoros on the Acropolis of the city of Pergamum, forms an apt starting point.[27] It has been thought to date to the period after 133 BC, but on the basis of its letterforms, could alternatively be dated to the late Attalid period:[28]

Διονύσιος Μηνοφίλ[ου] | ἱερονομήσα[[ντε]]ς τῶι δήμ[ωι]. | ἁγνευέτωσαν δὲ
καὶ εἰσίτωσαν εἰς τὸν τῆς θεο[ῦ ἱερὸν] | οἵ τε πολῖται καὶ οἱ ἄλλοι πάντες
ἀπὸ μὲν τῆς ἰδίας γ[υναι]|κὸς καὶ τοῦ ἰδίου ἀνδρὸς αὐθήμερον, ἀπὸ δὲ
ἀλλοτρίας κ[αὶ] | ἀλλοτρίου δευτεραῖοι λουσάμενοι, ὡσαύτως δὲ καὶ ἀπὸ |
κήδους καὶ τεκούσης γυναικὸς δευτεραῖο⟨ι⟩· ἀπὸ δὲ τάφου | καὶ ἐκφορᾶ[ς]
περιρα⟨ν⟩άμενοι καὶ διελθόντες τὴν πύλην, κα|θ' ἣν τὰ ἁγιστήρια τίθεται,
καθαροὶ ἔστωσαν αὐθήμερον. κτλ.

Dionysios son of Menophilos, having served as *hieronomos* for the people.
Let both citizens and all others abstain and enter into the [sanctuary] of the
goddess, from (sex with) one's own wife and one's own husband, on the
same day, from (sex with) another woman and another man, on the next
day, having washed; and in the same way (that is to say having washed)
from a death and from a woman having given birth, on the second day;

---

[26] It could instead be argued that, where Egyptian or Near Eastern cults implanted in Greek communities were concerned, rules of purity needed spelling out *in Greek terms* due to the novelty of the cults in question. Codification could be undertaken for a variety of reasons, the inauguration of the cult being one of them (see n. 25 above on the sacrifice to Zeus Polieus and below for other 'foundations').

[27] *I.Pergamon* 255 / *LSAM* 12 / *CGRN* 212. Given its findspot, the stele must originally have been erected close to the Nikephorion, which Kohl 2002 identifies with the known temple of Athena on the Acropolis of Pergamum, and near the gate leading to the upper city/citadel. At the end of l. 3, the common restoration is [ναόν], which certainly remains possible, as in the case of Artemis Chitone at Miletus, discussed above; [ἱερόν] is the suggestion of *CGRN*, noting that a reference to the sanctuary in general also occurs in l. 21 of the text.

[28] For the earlier date, specifically in the reign of Eumenes II (197– 159 BC) or shortly after, see Kohl 2002; Müller 2003.

from a tomb and from a funeral, having washed themselves all around and gone through the gate, where the vessels for lustration are placed, let them be pure on the same day. (Two decrees of Pergamum are also quoted)

The inscription is tripartite, forming a dossier of regulations on the sanctuary and the cult of Athena Nikephoros. A heading in larger letters (ll. 1–2) states that the stele was inscribed at the initiative of Dionysios, son of Menophilos, who served as an annual *hieronomos* or 'sanctuary-warden' for the city of Pergamum.[29] The first document inscribed on the stele (ll. 3–9) and quoted above, a list of purity regulations and entry requirements for the sanctuary, contrasts with the other two included below it, which are official documents, namely, decrees of the city of Pergamum. As presented on the stele, the rules of purity may represent an excerpt from a written document that was available to Dionysios: in this regard, note the beginning of the text in line 3, ἀγνευέτωσαν δὲ . . ., where the conjunction δὲ, presupposing an earlier clause, may thus imply a quotation. But, as far as we can tell, these rules derive from no other source of authority than that of recorded tradition, expounded by Dionysios in his role and his office as *hieronomos*.[30] It is without doubt in this capacity also that Dionysios undertook to reinscribe the two excerpts from decrees of the city of Pergamum below the purity rules. Both decrees seek to regulate the fees for those sacrificing in the sanctuary of Athena.

Dionysios' stele provides eloquent confirmation of the idea that, in the Hellenistic period, cities did not habitually inscribe casuistic purity regulations relating to specific sanctuaries: this was left to the occasional initiative of cult officials or other agents. General rules of the city remained

[29] The *hieronomoi* at Pergamum were apparently a board of civic officials responsible for administering sanctuaries and cult in the city. On these officials, see *I.Pergamon* 246 (ca. 138–133 BC), ll. 20–1: *hieronomoi* responsible for a sacrifice for Attalus III and the resulting feast. For the role of *hieronomoi* in Attalid territory, see *CIG* 3562 / *LSAM* 16 / *CGRN* 108 (Gambreion, third cent. BC; a law for the Gambreiotai passed under a probably identical *hieronomos* and *stephanephoros*) and *TAM* V.2 1253 (155/4 BC, attributed to Hierocaesarea in Lydia; a dedication to Artemis by οἱ ἐγ Δοαρρήνης ἱερόδουλο[ι] in honour of a beneficent *hieronomos*). For *hieronomoi* specifically attached to the cult of Athena in Pergamum, though only occurring in a later period, cf. *I.Pergamon* 161 (post-Attalid, probably first cent. BC on the basis of its letterforms), ll. B11–14 (τοὺς ἱε[ρο]|νόμους τῆς Ἀθηνᾶς, paying for the setting up of a stele 'from the funds' of the goddess) and the restorations proposed at *I.Pergamon* 474 (ca. 88–86 BC). In the case of Dionysios son of Menophilos, it is interesting that the stone-cutter made a mistake in his title: ἱερονομήσα⟦ντε⟧ς, erasing three letters (still visible), to correct this to the singular participle ἱερονομήσας rather than the probably expected plural denoting a board of civic or sanctuary officials. At any rate, τῶι δήμ[ωι] makes it clear that Dionysios, acting alone in this case and apart from any other members of his board, did so in an official capacity for the city.

[30] Cf. also now Parker 2018a: 182, 'we see here the distinction between (recorded) tradition and ψηφίσματα'.

in effect and would be consulted, but as in the case of the *Bacchoi* in Cnidus, groups or individuals needed to act in order to publicise or expand purity rules and encourage good behaviour. The need for such individual initiative remained current in Pergamum. One of the other major cults of the city, that of Asclepius, was also the recipient of two sets of cultic rules, which doubtless again derived from relatively long-standing tradition, but were only inscribed, as far as we know, in the second century AD. As the dedicatory formula concluding one of the texts makes clear, the rules were again inscribed at the behest of a *hieronomos*, one (. . .) Claudius Glykon.[31]

How do these rules erected by civic and religious officials compare with those set up by private groups? Two inscriptions from the Attalid kingdom, in the period ca. 250–150 BC, may be adduced. One particularly intriguing albeit only potential case comes from Maionia in Lydia. The text is officially dated to the reign of Attalus II (147/6 BC):[32]

βασιλεύοντος Ἀττά[λου] | ἔτους τρεισκαιδεκάτου. | ἀγαθῆι τύχηι ἔστησαν | τὴν στήλην Λ[– – ca.8 – – | – – ca.9 – –] οἱ ΕΜΦΥΣΗ[. .]ΧΗ[. . . .], ἀγνεύειν δὲ | ἀπὸ μὲν κ[ή]δους ὁμαίμ|ου πεμπταῖον, τοῦ δὲ ἄλ|λου τριταῖον, ἀπὸ δὲ γυναι|κὸς εἰς τὸν περιωρισμέ{νο}|νον τόπον τοῦ

---

[31] *AvP* VIII.3 161 (mid-second cent. AD; see also Lupu, *NGSL* p. 61, von Ehrenheim 2015: 224–7 no 7, Renberg 2017: 194–5), with ll. 35–6 for the concluding formula: [. ca.2 . Κ]λώδιος Γλύκων | [ἱερ]ονομῶν ἀνέθηκεν. The abbreviated *praenomen* of the full name is missing. Among various sacrificial and other ritual prescriptions, cf. ll. 11–14 for the rules concerning purity: ἀγνευέτω δὲ ὁ | [εἰσπορευ]όμενος εἰς τὸ ἐγκοιμητήριον ἀπό τε τῶν προειρημέ[νων πάν]των καὶ ἀφροδισίων καὶ αἰγείου κρέως καὶ τυροῦ κα[ὶ | . . ca.7 . .]ΙΑΜΙΔΟΣ τριταῖος; for the latter case, the photograph reveals that in ΙΑΜΙΔΟΣ only the bottom of the first supposed *iota* is visible: this is thus very likely to be read as [κ]υαμίδος, 'from beans' (cf. *LSJ* s.v. κυαμίδες and i.a. ἀ[πὸ] κυάμων in a regulation perhaps belonging to an Asklepieion in Rhodes, *LSCG Suppl.* 108, first cent. AD). Other rules would therefore have been mentioned earlier (ἀπό τε τῶν προειρημέ[νων πάν]των). See further ll. 18–19, where it is stated that the same purity rules applied to the 'small' incubation chamber: εἰς δὲ τὸ μικρὸν ἐγκοιμητήριον | [ὁ εἰσιὼν ἁγ]νείαν ἁγνευέτω τὴν αὐτήν. Another, somewhat later and more fragmentary regulation concerning the Asklepieion and its ἐγκοιμητήρια is *I.Pergamon* 264 / *LSAM* 14 (late second cent. AD, with the discussion of Wörrle at *AvP* VIII.3 161, p. 180 n. 66), which specifies different rules for entry in an unclear context (perhaps for the sanctuary generally, ἱερόν, rather than the ἐγκοιμητήριον and its incubation-rituals, which are then mentioned from ll. 4ff.): [εἰσπορευέσ]θω εἰς [τὸ ἱερὸν τοῦ Ἀσκληπιοῦ ἁγνεύων ἀπό . . . ἡμέ]ρας δέκα, ἀπὸ δὲ ⟨τ⟩ετοκ[υίας (καὶ τρεφούσης?) ἡμ|έρας . . ., ἀπὸ δ' ἀφροδ]εισίων λουσάμενος. The first scenario envisaged, entailing a delay of ten days, is perhaps a funerary ritual or abortion/miscarriage; the second, probably involving successful childbirth, would entail the same or a shorter delay. For a commendable effort to eliminate the restorations in this text, without yielding much progress, however, see now Renberg 2017: 196–7. On the specific practices and rules of abstinence and purification surrounding the rites of incubation, see now von Ehrenheim 2015: esp. 23–43; Renberg 2017: 242–4.

[32] *TAM* V.1 530 / *LSAM* 18 / *CGRN* 211. For the *editio princeps*, with full details concerning the provenance (reused in a house) and with a facsimile, cf. Keil and von Premerstein 1911: 82–3 no 167.

Μητρῴου | τῆι αὐτῆι λουσάμενον εἰσ|πορεύεσθαι· ἑταίρα τριτ|αία, περιαγνισαμένη καθὼ|ς εἴθισται.

In the thirteenth year of King Attalus. With good fortune, they set up the stele [. . .] the men [. . .] and to keep pure from the death of a blood relative, (until) the fifth day, from that of another (that is to say a non-relative), the third day, from (sex with) a woman, into the place of the Metroion which is demarcated by boundaries, on the same day, having washed, one is to enter. A *hetaira* (can enter) on the third day, having purified herself all around as is customary.

Conforming to the expected pattern, the polis seems to be absent here. The first editors of the inscription, Keil and von Premerstein, already noted that while identifying the group responsible for erecting the stele containing these rules of purity represents a substantial problem, the traces following the lacuna in lines 4–5 are suggestive of a possible subject for the third-person plural verb ἔστησαν, 'they set up', in line 3. This intervening lacuna is rather large, however, and may perhaps have contained other names or nouns. Following it, we find what seems to be a definitive article, οἱ, and some other traces. Keil and von Premerstein tentatively suggested the restoration οἱ ἐμ Φυση [ὀρ]χη[σταί], thinking of an association of dancers at an unknown place called Physa or Physe.[33] While this bold proposal has not been retained in most of the succeeding editions, we might suppose that Keil and von Premerstein were on the right track. An alternative restoration, for instance, could be οἱ ἐμφυση||[ταί], involving a group of pipe-blowers.[34] The role of flute or brass musicians as performers in the cult of the Mother goddess, alongside players of percussion instruments such as tambourines and cymbals, is well known.[35] If this reasoning is correct, some or all of the musicians involved in the cult of Meter regulated by this stele may have temporarily joined forces or (less likely) formed a more permanent association, seeking to regulate the cult. If such a group could claim authority over the sanctuary, at least in matters of purity, it might suggest that this cult-site was not owned or controlled by the political community at Maionia. But we could just as easily be dealing

[33] An alternative proposal by Keil and von Premerstein would make this clause anticipate the one directly following it. This would seek to bar entry to individuals who were sick with emphysema: [μὴ εἰσίτωσαν] οἱ ἐμφύση||[μα ἔ]χ[οντες], ἁγνεύειν δὲ . . .

[34] Cf. *LSJ* s.v. ἐμφυσητής, φυσητήρ (II), φυσητήριον; note e.g. Ar. *V.* 1219: αὐλητρὶς ἐνεφύσησε.

[35] See particularly, Roller 1999: 110 ('The *tympanon*, the most common instrument of the Graeco-Roman Kybele, does not appear in Phrygian representations of the goddess' but rather the lyre and especially the flute; for the *tympanon* appearing only in later depictions, as a Greek addition, see pp. 136–7, 148). The *Homeric Hymn to Meter* also mentions flutes (αὐλοί) alongside κρόταλα, 'castanets', and *tympana* (see again Roller 1999: 122–3; cp. 149–55, 232 n. 278).

with the private initiative of a group of individuals involved in a civic cult, not a fixed group of authoritative officials.

We are on much more secure ground with another set of ritual norms, which were manifestly enacted by a small cultic association. These are the rules of the *Asklepiastai* at Yaylakale in Pergamene territory (the Yüntdağ, ca. 30 km southeast of Pergamum).[36] One stele found there testifies to the fact that a certain Demetrios, *phrourarchos* or commander of the Attalid garrison in this area, founded a sanctuary of Asclepius and gathered the first *Asklepiastai* at this relatively remote site in the first half of the second century BC.[37] Another stele discovered near the same site, though its beginning is missing, contains rules of purity for entering the sanctuary and, much more fragmentarily, the dormitory for incubation which was situated beside it:[38]

[– – ἀγ]ν̣[εύεσ]|θαι τ̣ὸ[ν εἰ]σ̣πορευ̣|ό̣μενον ὑγίας ἔν̣|ε̣[κ]εν̣ εἰς τὸ ἱερόν· |
ἀπὸ μὲν τῶν ἀφρο̣|δισιακῶν̣, κατὰ κε̣|φαλῆς λου̣σάμε̣|νον, ἀπὸ ν̣εκροῦ δὲ |
κ̣αὶ ἀπὸ ἐκφο̣ρᾶς (?) | δευτεραῖο̣ν̣ καὶ | ἀπὸ διαφθορᾶς τ̣ὸ | αὐτό· ἐὰν δέ τις |
ἐπέλθῃ ἐπὶ τὸ πα̣|ρὰ τὸ ἱερὸν ἐγ̣κοιμη̣|τήριον, [. . .]Α[.]Ο̣Υ – – – – – –

... The one going into the sanctuary is to keep pure for the sake of good health: from sexual matters, washing from the head down (that is to say on the same day); from a corpse and from a funeral (?), (enter) on the second day and from an abortion/miscarriage, the same. If anyone visits the place of incubation beside the sanctuary, ...

Though this inscription is much more difficult to decipher than the other stele, its editor, Müller, expressed no doubt that it constitutes a part of the same dossier for the cult that was created by the *phrourarchos* Demetrios and the 'first *Asklepiastai*'.[39] This association will therefore have issued

---

[36] Müller 2010 (ca. 250–150 BC); see also von Ehrenheim 2015: 227–8 no 8, Renberg 2017: 242–3. For more details on the context of this find and the new sanctuary founded, see Skaltsa in Chapter 5.

[37] Müller 2010: 427–38 (*SEG* 60:1332), ll. 1–5: ἐπὶ Δημητρίου φρου|ράρχου, τοῦ κτίσαν|τος τὸ ἱερόν· ἀγαθῇ | τύχῃ· συνῆλθον οἱ πρ|ῶτοι Ἀσκληπιασταί. A list of fifteen names follows. For a privately founded sanctuary of Asclepius at Thuburbo Maius in North Africa, which published purity rules in Latin, see Renberg 2017: 626–7.

[38] Müller 2010: 440–7 (*SEG* 60:1333). *In fine*, we might have expected the regulation to say that the same rules applied to the ἐνκοιμητήριον (cf. *AvP* VIII.3 161, ll. 18–19, cited above n. 31). But the apparent trace of a genitive at the end of l. 15 seems to introduce the consideration of other sources of impurity. Accordingly, then, a possible restoration at the end of l. 15 could be [ἀπὸ τ]ά̣[φ]ο̣υ | [καὶ ἐκφορᾶς…], as in *I.Pergamon* 255 cited above, though this variation from νεκροῦ in l. 8 of the text from Yaylakale might also be viewed as surprising. On incubation in sanctuaries of Asclepius, see again n. 31 above.

[39] Müller 2010: 447: '(…) dass nicht nur der Stein, auf dem die Lex sacra aufgezeichnet ist, nach Material und ursprünglichen Dimensionen mit der Stele übereinstimmt, die die Liste der

rules concerning the purity expected of worshippers visiting the new sanctuary of Asclepius or seeking incubation there.

In terms of content and normative characteristics, the purity rules closely parallel those found in the city and the area of Pergamum that we looked at earlier. After sex, entry into the sanctuary is allowed on the same day, having washed from the head down: this is essentially the same prescription as one finds in the inscription from Maionia quoted above and in the sanctuary of Asclepius at Pergamum (*I.Pergamon* 264, n. 31 above), but also very widely elsewhere.[40] Sex between man and wife was similarly allowed on the same day as entry into the sanctuary of Athena Nikephoros in Pergamum (quoted above). Yet the cults in the city seem on occasion somewhat more restrictive: in the sanctuary of Athena, waiting until the next day (δευτεραῖοι, counting inclusively it would seem) was necessary after sex with someone who was not one's spouse; until the third day (τριταῖος) after any form of sexual intercourse before visiting the incubation chambers of the Pergamene Asklepieion (*AvP III* 161, n. 31 above). Still, the match with the rules from Pergamum is particularly apparent when it comes to the other categories of impurity mentioned by the *Asklepiastai* at Yaylakale. From contact with a deceased individual, as well as with a woman who had aborted or miscarried, the delay was only until the next day (δευτεραῖον, still counting inclusively). These delays are nearly identical with those recorded for the cult of Athena Nikephoros. At the Nikephorion, entry was permitted on the next day following the death of an individual, whether a relative or not (ἀπὸ κήδους... δευτεραῖο⟨ι⟩), and even on the same day from attendance at a funeral or at a tomb. At the Nikephorion again, abstaining the same amount of time was required after exposure to a woman who had given birth (ἀπὸ... τεκούσης γυναικός), while at Yaylakale, this delay applied to contact with an abortion or miscarriage.

In general, then, the regulations expounded by the association of the *Asklepiastai* at Yaylakale closely match those found in their immediate

---

Gründungsmitglieder des Asklepiastensvereins trägt, sondern auch die Beschriftung beider Monumente in Größe und formaler Gestaltung identisch ist.'

[40] For the widespread notion that one could enter on the same day after sexual intercourse, though often only after having washed from the head down: cf. Dobias-Lalou 2000: 297–309 / *CGRN* 99 (Cyrene, ca. 325-300 BC); *IG* XII.1 789 / *LSCG* 139 (Lindos, ca. AD 117–38); *I.Lindos* II 487 / *LSCG Suppl.* 91 / Petrovic and Petrovic 2018 (ca. AD 225); Decourt and Tziafalias 2015 / Bouchon and Decourt 2017 / *CGRN* 225 (Marmarini near Larisa, ca. 250–150 BC), face B (I), line 27; *NGSL* 7 / *CGRN* 155 (Megalopolis, ca. 200 BC); as well as in the recently published second cent. BC text from Thyateira, Malay and Petzl 2017: 25–30 no 1, with further commentary in Parker 2018a.

regional context. On the other stele, no ethnics are recorded for the names of the members of the 'first *Asklepiastai*'. Though it is probable that some of the members were foreign soldiers, it is not impossible that at least a few of them were Pergamene or Mysian.[41] At any rate, it is likely that these men will have had some occasion to visit the Attalid capital and its famous sanctuaries, such as the Nikephorion and the Asklepieion. In other words, the rules most probably derive from those that Demetrios the *phrourachos* or other members of the group had commonly observed in practice at Pergamum. Though parallels with the Asklepieion of Pergamum might be thought the most suggestive,[42] it is perhaps especially the sanctuary of Athena on the Acropolis, close to where the garrison was located in the upper city and its arsenal, which seems to have influenced the purity rules of the 'first *Asklepiastai*'.[43] The *phrourachos* and his garrison at Yaylakale wished to found a cult-group and new sanctuary and thus closely modelled it on these Pergamene structures and their cultic framework.

The periods of abstention known from Pergamum were considerably generous. Other cults, as we have already glimpsed and shall see further below, would often require an abstention of several days, usually around ten after the death of a relative, somewhat less, such as five, for that of another individual,[44] and typically of ten days in the case of contact with an abortion or miscarriage (forty days for the woman concerned). The rules articulated by the association at Yaylakale were of a similarly mild character, attributable to their Pergamene models but also with a view towards inclusivity. Indeed, the rules at Yaylakale expressly emphasised their function: not only was purity required ([ἁγ]ν[εύεσ]θαι, ll. 1–2, if we accept this probable restoration), but the avowed purpose of the regulation

---

[41] For a thorough and cautious discussion of the names of the leader and the members, see Müller 2010: 429–35.

[42] For conscious modelling of the structures of the *Asklepiastai* on the Asklepieion located near the city, cf. the conclusions of Müller 2010 and also Renberg 2017: 243 ('almost certainly was directly influenced by practices at the more prominent Asklepieion, instead of representing a separate tradition'). For this sanctuary, see also Radt 1999: 220–42.

[43] For the building of the arsenal, the upper city/citadel and its palaces, see Radt 1999: 63–78. Note also that the offerings to Athena Nikephoros could (but apparently not always) involve sacrifices 'on the *akra*', where tariffs would need to be paid to the gatekeeper of the citadel (*I.Pergamon* 255 / *LSAM* 12 / *CGRN* 212, ll. 26–7: τῶν δ᾽ ἐν τῆι ἄκραι θυομένων καὶ πυλω|ρῶι τῆς ἄκρας βοὸς κτλ.).

[44] For example, purity rules from neighbouring Lydia, to the south of Pergamum and Mysia, are different. The text from Maionia quoted above is relatively generous, but not as much: four full days of abstention are required for the death of a relative, two for that of another individual. The new text from Thyateira in Lydia (see n. 40 above) is even more strict: nine days were prescribed in the case of a relative, three or less in other cases.

was to foster good health (ὑγίας ἔνεκεν, ll. 3–4). This was a particularly apt goal for an Asklepieion, of course, a cult site whose purpose was to serve as a place for the worship of the god of healing (and perhaps of Ὑγία/Hygieia herself, the personification of Good Health and one of the daughters of Asclepius, often found associated with the god). In the view of the 'first *Asklepiastai*', purity (ἁγνεία) was thus a precondition for good health (ὑγία). This helped to rationalise the need for rules of purity and served to advertise their beneficial function by publishing the stele containing them.[45]

In their remote Attalid garrison, the 'first *Asklepiastai*' thus recreated elements of the Pergamene community, by founding a small local Asklepieion to honour the god, but also to consolidate their own identity, to invite worshippers from nearby villages and to host incubation rituals. The 'well-ordered society' developed in this case replicated on a smaller scale the civic and religious structures of Pergamum, being stimulated by an Attalid official and his soldiers for the inclusive benefit of a local community.[46] In particular, the rules of purity published by the group underscored all of these features: they were modelled on the rules of the major sanctuaries, maintained their short or 'generous' delays of ἁγνεία and at the same time advertised good health (ὑγία) to promote access to the sanctuary.

From Families to 'Associations in the Making'

From the beginning of the Hellenistic period, familial associations become more conspicuous in the epigraphical evidence. By this designation, one may refer to cults that were privately established for the benefit of a restricted kinship group, normally the immediate family of the founder.[47] The membership of such groups was by definition exclusive: male relatives

---

[45] It should therefore be clear that, without denying that economic factors had a role to play in the development of this sanctuary by the *Asklepiastai*, I cannot readily agree with the view of Eckhardt 2017b: 417, who claims that 'the sanctuary was modeled closely on the famous Asklepieion of Pergamum – a smaller copy of a major sanctuary could thus serve as a source of income', citing (but also simplifying) Müller 2010: 446 in support of this view, 'auf regelrechten Kurbetrieb ausgerichtet'. Yaylakale was primarily a sanctuary, providing a model for a cultic community, not merely a remote mountain spa.

[46] For the importance of the cult of Asclepius to the Attalid rulers, which the *phrourarchos* Demetrios served as a minor official, see esp. *IG* IV².1 60 (191 BC, reign of Eumenes II) or *I.Pergamon* 246 (Attalus III).

[47] See Carbon and Pirenne-Delforge 2013 and now Campanelli 2016; on the misleading term 'foundation' often applied to these documents, see also Harris 2015: 71–7. On the construction and use of space by familial associations, see Skaltsa in Chapter 5.

by marriage were sometimes accepted; bastards might be included with some provisos; occasionally a wider familial circle might be defined.[48] Most of these groups constituted a completely different type of association from the *Asklepiastai* at Yaylakale, in that they sought less publicity or visibility, a fact reflected for instance in not having a well-defined name.[49]

An interesting though unique case of a familial association which published rules of purity comes from the deme of Isthmus on Cos:[50]

[ἱερὸν ἔστω τόδε] τὸ τέ[μενος καὶ τὸ] | ἱερὸν Ἀρτέμιτο[ς . . . .]ας καὶ
Διὸς Ἱκ[ε]||σίου καὶ Θεῶν Πατρώιων· ἀνέθηκε δὲ | Πυθίων Στασίλα καὶ ἁ
ἱέρεια [[. . . .]] παιδ|ίον ὧι ὄνομα Μακαρῖνος ἐλεύθερον ἱε|ρὸν τᾶς θεοῦ,
ὅπως ἐπιμέληται τοῦ ἱερο[ῦ] | καὶ τῶν συνθυόντων πάντων, διακονῶν |
καὶ ὑπηρετῶν ὅσσῳ κα δῆ ἐν τῶι ἱερῶι· | ἐπιμελέσθω καὶ Μακαρῖνος καὶ
τῶν ἄλλων | ἱερῶν καὶ βεβάλων καθάπερ καὶ ἐν τᾶι ἱερᾶι δέλ|τωι
γέγραπται, καὶ τῶν λοιπῶν ὧγ καταλεί|πει Πυθίων καὶ ἁ ἱέρεια· τοῖς δὲ
ἐπιμελομέ|νοις καὶ συναύξουσι τὸ ἱερόν, εὖ αὐτοῖς | ἔη καὶ αὐτοῖς καὶ
τέκνοις εἰς τὸν ἀεὶ χρόνον· | ἁγνὸν εἰσπορεύεσθαι – τὸ δὲ ἱερὸν ἔστω |
τῶν υἱῶν πάντων κοινόν – ἀπὸ λεχοῦς καὶ | ἐγ δια⟨φθ⟩ορᾶς ἀμέρας δέκα,
ἀπὸ γυναικὸς τρεῖ[ς].

[. . . this] precinct [and sanctuary] is to be sacred to Artemis [. . .] and Zeus Hikesios and the Ancestral Gods. Pythion son of Stasilas and the priestess [. . .] dedicated a slave, whose name is Makarinos, to be free (and) sacred to the goddess, so that he takes care of the sanctuary and of all those who make sacrifices together and provides services and also performs any other tasks that are necessary in the sanctuary. Makarinos is also to take care of other matters, whether sacred or secular, as is written on the sacred tablet, and of the other things that Pythion and the priestess bequeath. May good things happen to those who take good care of the sanctuary and augment it, both to themselves and to their children for all time. Enter pure – the temple is to be common to all the sons – from childbirth and after an abortion/ miscarriage, ten days; from (sex with) a woman (or wife?), three.

This consecration of a cult by Pythion and a nameless priestess (perhaps his wife), albeit much briefer, shares many resemblances with the much

[48] Male in-laws and bastards: cf. Carbon and Pirenne-Delforge 2013: 80–3. For the familial circle of Epikteta, see n. 49 below.

[49] An exception is the dossier of Epikteta, where the association was named τὸ κοινὸν τοῦ ἀνδρείου τῶν συγγενῶν, 'the community of the male group of relatives': cf. *IG* XII.3 330 / *LSCG* 135 / *CGRN* 152 (ca. 210–195 BC; *CAPInv.* 1645); for the list of members of the familial group, which also includes women, see ll. 81–106. The designations occasionally given for the groups of Poseidonios at Halicarnassus (e.g. Ποσειδώνιος καὶ οἱ ἔκγονοι οἱ ἐκ Ποσειδωνίου καὶ οἱ εἰληφόντες ἐξ αὐτοῦ: Carbon and Pirenne-Delforge 2013: Appendix; *CAPInv.* 830) and of Diomedon on Cos (τοὶ ἐγ Διομέδοντος καὶ ἀεὶ τοὶ ἐξ αὐτῶν γενόμενοι, see below with n. 51) are polymorphous and not formalised associational names.

[50] *IG* XII.4 1 349 / *LSCG* 171 / *CGRN* 162 (ca. 200–150 BC).

more detailed cultic dossier of Diomedon on the same island of Cos.[51] In both cases, a sanctuary is consecrated to a group of deities – at least in part ancestral, though the epithet of Artemis in the case of Pythion remains mysterious[52] – and a slave is associated with this consecration to take care of the sanctuary. Doubtless we would have further details about the cult if the 'sacred tablet' mentioned in lines 10–11 or details concerning the bequests, probably testamentary, of Pythion and the priestess (τῶν λοιπῶν ὧγ καταλείπει, ll. 11–12), were preserved.

The conclusion of the stele is particularly interesting for our purposes: it clearly begins to mention rules for entrance into the sanctuary in line 15 (ἁγνὸν εἰσπορεύεσθαι...), but these are interrupted by the interjected phrase τὸ δὲ ἱερὸν ἔστω | τῶν υἱῶν πάντων κοινόν. This is to be taken to mean that the sanctuary (*to hieron*) is held in collective ownership by the sons of Pythion. A cultic community of *synthyontes pantes* is also vaguely alluded to in line 7 (τῶν συνθυόντων πάντων): this is most naturally interpreted as constituting the immediate family or the descendants of Pythion (and perhaps the priestess).[53] The question that can be raised, however, is whether the interjected clause in line 15 has a purpose: does it seek to define those who may enter (εἰσπορεύεσθαι) the sanctuary, is it simply misplaced or is there another reason for its placement? In the first view, the clause concerning the ownership of the sanctuary clarified that only the sons of Pythion had privileged access to it. But in fact, it cannot be just the sons of Pythion who were granted access to the sanctuary: the priestess and the slave Makarinos needed to enter it and we might presume that female family members, at least, could also do so.

A further alternative might be that access to the sanctuary was not strictly limited to the familial group of Pythion. As they are often expressed in inscriptions affixed to sanctuaries open to visitors, the purity rules published on Pythion's stele could be taken to imply that the *hieron* inaugurated by him was in fact open to members of the general public: by agreeing to respect their prescriptions, access to the sanctuary would be permitted. Anyone could then become part of the *synthyontes pantes* during one of the celebrations envisaged. But the clause appended, presumably out of fear of the property becoming alienated, quickly clarified that ownership and control of the sanctuary remained in the hands of

---

[51] Diomedon: *IG* XII.4 1 348 / *LSCG* 177 / *CGRN* 96 (*CAPInv.* 1919; ca. 325–275 BC). That dossier, however, does not include any rules concerning purity.

[52] For a detailed discussion of the deities forming the focus of Pythion's cult, see Campanelli 2016: 143–4.

[53] As stressed and further elucidated by Campanelli 2016: 154–6; 170.

Python's sons (in perpetuity, one assumes). Such an idea would also go some way towards explaining why this is the only case of a 'familial cult' which does not appear to have had strict rules of membership and also why, again uniquely among similar groups, it enacted purity regulations for entry into its sanctuary.

As we have seen, however, the evidence provided by this relatively brief stele is hardly complete. It seems to have served as a sign for worshippers and as a reminder of some essential aspects. Other documents, a 'sacred tablet' and likely a testament, would have provided a much fuller view of this familial group and the sanctuary that it consecrated. Any definitive conclusions should therefore be resisted, though it remains highly probable that the rules of purity were aimed at other worshippers coming to visit the sanctuary consecrated by Python.

Indeed, what we can affirm is that the purity rules defined by Python and his family readily match others known elsewhere in the epigraphic evidence from across the eastern Aegean and Asia Minor. A delay of ten days is specified before entry after childbed or an abortion/miscarriage. This matches some of the delays stipulated in the regulation of an unknown cult at Eresos and also seems to agree with a regulation for the cult of Despoina at Lycosura, though that text is quite lacunose.[54] At Eresos, the delay of ten days was aimed at a man who entered into contact with a woman who had miscarried; but ten days was also the required *hagneia* for a woman who had given birth (only three days for a man). As a result, it remains somewhat unclear if women were also concerned by the purity rules enacted by Python. Apparently more demanding was the requirement to abstain three days from the sanctuary after sex with one's wife (ἀπὸ γυναικός; or does this mean 'any woman' here?). As we saw earlier, ablutions might be required after sex, but entry into the sanctuary would usually be permitted on the same day, after no delay. Yet the delay of three days in fact closely corresponds to other, stricter norms found elsewhere: in the *enkoimeterion*, 'dormitory', of the Asklepieion at

---

[54] Eresos: *IG* XII Suppl. 126 / *LSCG* 124 / *CGRN* 181 (second cent. BC). There, ten days is the delay for a person entering into contact with a woman who has aborted/miscarried (forty days for the woman concerned); ten days for a woman having given birth (three days for another individual entering into contact with her). Despoina at Lycosura: *NGSL* 8 / *CGRN* 189 (second cent. BC). Cf. also the delay of ten days after an unknown cause of impurity mentioned in the regulation of the Asklepieion at Pergamum, *I.Pergamon* 264 / *LSAM* 14, cited above n. 31.

Pergamum, as we have already seen, but also in the sanctuary of Syrian gods on Delos and in the sanctuary of Meter Gallesia at Metropolis.[55]

To broaden this understanding of Pythion's cult on Cos, instructive comparisons and contrasts may briefly be drawn with two famous epigraphic dossiers. The first is the cult of Men Tyrannos privately founded by Xanthos, probably a slave or a freedman, at Laurion, at a date that remains debated, but probably lies somewhere in the first century BC or AD.[56] The details of the cult, originating from Anatolia – Xanthos is notably called Λύκιος, 'Lycian' – are known from a pair of stelae. These are nearly identical in their formulary, though not entirely so. The narrower of the two (text B), functioning more as a sign, includes only a brief summary of the rules that were discussed more extensively in the lengthier document (text A). The cult elaborated by Xanthos following a command of the god (αἱρετίσαντος τοῦ θεοῦ) does not explicitly aim at creating an association; rather, it confers pride of place on the founder as the principal participant or agent in the cult. Xanthos, while living, is to be present at all sacrifices (μηθένα θυσιάζειν ἄνε[υ] τοῦ καθειδρυσαμένου τὸ ἱερόν, A, ll. 7–8; cf. B, ll. 11–13) and any violence, perhaps especially against him, is proscribed.[57] Upon anything undermining Xanthos' role as founder of the cult, such as his death, illness or emigration, no one is to have any right to the sanctuary, unless Xanthos himself confers it.[58] Therefore, by contrast with Pythion, the cult was not familial and Xanthos had apparently not yet thought of a precise successor.

Xanthos also enacted elaborate rules concerning sacrifices and purity. The cult was open to any participant who chose to follow these guidelines. In the context of the sacrifices, Xanthos in fact grants the opportunity for anyone to gather a temporary or ad hoc cult group (A, l. 21: τοὺς. . .

---

[55] Intercourse with one's own wife required a two-day ἁγνεία (or three days counting inclusively) at Pergamum: see above n. 31 on *AvP* VIII.3 161, ll. 11–14; Delos: *I.Délos* 2530 / *LSCG Suppl.* 54 / *CGRN* 217 (second cent. BC); and Metropolis: *I.Ephesos* 3401 / *LSAM* 29 / *CGRN* 71 (fourth cent. BC).

[56] Text A: *IG* II² 1366 / *LSCG* 55; Text B: *IG* II² 1365. This is a case that has already stimulated a large bibliography and ample commentary, to which little justice can be done in this short overview. For useful references and a summary of the evidence, see *GRA* I 53. Strangely, it is also only on the briefer stele B that we find the exclusion of murderers from the cult, ll. 21–2: ἀνδροφόνον μηδὲ περὶ τὸν τόπον. On the continued concern for pollution from homicide, see Harris 2018, with further refs.

[57] This appears to be the aim of the clause in Text A, ll. 8–9: ἐὰν δέ τις βιάσηται, ἀπρόσδεκτος | ἡ θυσία παρὰ τοῦ θεοῦ (cp. text B, ll. 13–15). When anyone acts violently – perhaps especially towards Xanthos/the founder as the implicit object of the verb – the sacrifice is de facto to be considered invalid.

[58] Text A, ll. 12–14 (cf. B, ll. 27–9): ἐὰν δέ τινα | ἀνθρώπινα πάσχῃ ἢ ἀσθενήσῃ ἢ ἀποδημήσῃ που, μηθένα ἀνθρώ|πων ἐξουσίαν ἔχειν, ἐὰν μὴ ᾧ ἂν αὐτὸς παραδῶι.

βουλομένους ἔρανον συνάγειν) for the purposes of celebrating the god and holding a sacrificial feast; these groups might even wish to camp at the cult-site to continue their night-time feast (cf. also ll. 24–5: ἐὰν κατακλιθῶσιν οἱ ἐρανισταί...). There is little evidence that such groups would go on to form durative cult associations, though this of course remains possible.[59] In terms of rules concerning purity, we find some general precepts. On a basic level, Xanthos was concerned that nothing impure be brought forward to the cult-site and its altar: καὶ [μηθένα] ἀκάθαρτον προσάγειν (A, ll. 2–3; cf. B, 8–9). Such a rule was presumably designed to prevent the sacrificial offering of animals or foodstuffs viewed as impure in the cult (pork and garlic are specifically mentioned in the text; perhaps porcine products, such as leather, which might be brought into the sanctuary, would also be concerned by this interdiction). Another rule was presented as a blessing: that the god would be merciful to those who worshipped him with a simple soul. This is tantamount to the fundamental requirement that the worshipper's mind be pure, which is explicitly found in entry regulations for sanctuaries from the Hellenistic period onward.[60] The moral sense of these rules is further underlined in other clauses containing stringent sanctions, notably against any interference in the cult.[61] All of this is coupled with practical cases of impurity such as we have looked at here. On both stelae, specific causes of impurity such as garlic, pork and sex are said to be remediable simply by washing from the head down. Impurity resulting from the eating of pork is found in one other purity regulation, appropriately from a sanctuary focussed on Near Eastern rituals.[62] Other standard causes of impurity, but apparently only

---

[59] One intriguing possibility for such a group is the ἐρανισταί known from *IG* II² 2940 (second [rather than fourth] cent. BC) at Laurion, who apparently preceded Xanthos' cult and may have made a dedication to Men Tyrannos; the reading of the name of the deity has been questioned, however (for a helpful summary of the debate, see *CAPInv.* 311).

[60] Text A, ll. 11–12: καὶ εὐείλατος γένοιτο ὁ θεὸς τοῖς θεραπεύουσιν ἁπλῆ τῆ ψυχῆ (cf. B, ll. 25–6); repeated *in fine*, l. 26: καὶ εὐείλατος γένοιτο τοῖς ἁπλῶς προσπορευομένοι[ς]. On this widespread concept of purity of the mind in Greek religious thought, see now Petrovic and Petrovic 2016.

[61] Cf. the stipulation that those who enquired excessively into the affairs of the god or interfered with them would be guilty of an insurmountable offence to the god (Text A, ll. 14–16; cf. also B, 29–32): ὃς ἂν δὲ πολυ|πραγμονήσῃ τὰ τοῦ θεοῦ ἢ περιεργάσηται, ἁμαρτίαν ὀφειλέτω Μηνὶ | Τυράννωι, ἣν οὐ μὴ δύνηται ἐξειλάσασθαι.

[62] The sanctuary of the Syrian gods on Delos: *I.Délos* 2530 / *LSCG Suppl.* 54 / *CGRN* 217 (second cent. BC). Similarly, after ingestion of pork (ἀπὸ ὑείου), only washing is required and entry is permitted on the same day. In the context of Near Eastern rituals and the interdiction to sacrifice swine, mention must be made of the new stele from Marmarini/Larisa (ca. 250–150 BC), which perhaps emanated from an association or a group of initiates: for the *editio princeps*, Decourt and Tziaphalias 2015; see now Bouchon and Decourt 2017 / *CGRN* 225 for an improved text. For the hypothesis of an association, see Carbon 2016; against this view and with an extensive discussion of the purity rules, see Parker and Scullion 2016: 256–66.

for women, are treated with severe but normative periods of abstention: menstruation (seven days and washing), contact with a corpse (ten days) and abortion or miscarriage (forty days).[63]

The second interesting case for comparison is the much-discussed stele from Philadelphia in Lydia, which can only very briefly be treated here.[64] Debate continues to be sparked regarding the precise characteristics and background of the cult, as well as the interpretation of the text (about a third of the lines is missing to the right). The rules outlined in the text are presented as a written account of the divine commands ([παραγγέλμα]τα, ll. 3–4; παραγγέλ[ματα], l. 12) that were given to a certain Dionysios by Zeus, in a dream. On one view, the outcome of this divine inspiration was that Dionysios opened his own house (π[ρόσοδον διδόν]τ' εἰς τὸν ἑαυτοῦ οἶκον, l. 5), in which altars of large variety of gods have been constructed (ll. 6–12), to any worshipper, be they male or female, free or slave (ll. 5–6). Periodic sacrifices are also mentioned (l. 55), which would no doubt have served to gather together a community of worshippers. However, it has been questioned whether the stele actually reflects an attempt at inviting participants beyond the οἶκος, 'house', of Dionysios or whether it primarily concerns an existing cultic community (such as his kinship group and the slaves of his household).[65]

At any rate, the injunctions that Zeus made to Dionysios involve the performance of 'abstentions, purifications and (probably) mysteries, according to the ancestral customs as well as to what is now written on the stele' (τούς τε ἁ]|γνισμοὺς καὶ τοὺς καθαρμοὺς κ[αὶ τὰ μυστήρια

---

[63] See Text A, ll. 3–8; B, ll. 8–11 and 18–25. That women are primarily concerned by these three rules is made clear by the use of feminine ordinal adjectives on stele B: ἑβ⟨δ⟩ομαία⟨ν⟩, δεκατ⟨αί⟩αν, τετταρακοσταίαν. The delays are conventional and, though often found of 'foreign' cults, these are spread across the ancient Greek world: for instance, menstruation requires seven days also in the text from Marmarini (n. above), face B (I), ll. 27–8, also in the sanctuary of the Egyptian gods at Megalopolis (*NGSL* 7 / *CGRN* 155, ca. 200 BC) and in the unknown cult at Ptolemais (*LSCG Suppl.* 119 / *CGRN* 144, first cent. BC).

[64] *TAM* V.3 1539 / *LSAM* 20 / *CGRN* 191 / *GRA* II 117 (ca. 125–75 BC; see also *CAPInv.* 348). For a recent and highly successful attempt at situating the cult in a local (Lydian) as well as a wider legal context, see now de Hoz 2017.

[65] Stowers 1998 makes a case for seeing Dionysios' rules as those of a household cult, though this still begs the question of why they were published in the first place (he himself comments 294: 'What is most peculiar about this cult is that rules of the *oikos* which were normally unwritten and more implicit than explicit have been set up in writing'). This view has been recently followed by Hurtado 2016: 174, who concludes that 'there is no indication that Dionysios even sought to recruit followers from beyond his own household'. Both of these views, however, would require questioning the restoration π[ρόσοδον διδόν]|τ' εἰς τὸν ἑαυτοῦ οἶκον in ll. 4–5 as well as the purpose of the datives that follow ἀνδρά[σι καὶ γυναιξὶν] | ἐλευθέροις καὶ οἰκέταις, since these imply that Dionysios granted access to his house as part of the cult that was being developed.

ἐπι]|τελεῖν κατά τε τὰ πάτρια καὶ ὡς νῦν [γέγραπται], ll. 12–14).[66] Indeed, the bulk of the inscribed text (ὡς νῦν [γέγραπται]) contains precepts of purity that have a strong ethical dimension: for instance, worshippers entering the house are to swear an oath not to avail themselves of any magic or poison (ll. 14–19); instead of rules concerning the temporary impurity caused by an abortion or miscarriage, taking the oath required forsaking the use of any form of contraceptive (ll. 20–1); instead of lax rules concerning sexual intercourse, Dionysios promotes the virtue of marriage, strictly forbidding the 'corruption' of married women and of those who are not yet married by men (ll. 25–31) – while tacitly allowing for other, non-married partners or ἑταίραι – and by recommending the exclusive company of one's spouse for women (ll. 35–44).[67] Both men and women who fail in this regard are to be barred from entering (ll. 31–2). The guidelines and the outcomes of transgression are more severe for women, who are to be deemed impure and to spread this impurity to their kin (ll. 37–8: [μεμιασμέ]|νην καὶ μύσο[υ]ς ἐμφυλίου πλή[ρ]η), in addition to being barred from the cult.[68] Peer denunciation is to be the mechanism of enforcement (ll. 28–31), as well as the use of the stele itself as a touchstone (during prayers and the required oath-rituals, ll. 56–60), but in general the sanctions consists of threats of divine punishment (ll.

---

[66] The commonly accepted restoration κ[αὶ τὰ μυστήρια] in l. 13 is somewhat gratuitous, since no other aspect of the text explicitly mentions initiations; cf. however l. 41, which perhaps suggests this sense, though it could also refer to the contemplation of other rituals, such as sacrifices or those concerning the statues involved in the cult.

[67] Hurtado 2016: 174, wondering 'why there is no mention of prostitutes or courtesans', follows Stowers in thinking that 'the particular concern is actually about disruptive sexual activities *among the members of the household*, and so the inscription does not address what sexual activities a man may engage in with other kinds of individuals outside the household'. But the rules have a strictly moral purpose: sex is not being regulated per se, but 'corruption' by a man is defined in the cases where the woman, whether free or slave, is already married or if a child or unmarried girl is concerned, ll. 25–8: ἄνδρα παρὰ | τὴν) ἑαυτοῦ γυναῖκα ἀλλοτρίαν ἢ [ἐλευθέραν ἢ] | δούλην ἄνδρα ἔχουσαν μὴ φθερε[ῖν μηδὲ παῖδα μη|δὲ] παρθένον μηδὲ ἑτέρωι συμβου[λεύσειν]. In other words, male sex with (by definition unmarried) prostitutes and courtesans was not mentioned because it was tacitly accepted; see also below.

[68] Stowers 1998: 299 affirms that he 'see[s] no reason why normal practices of purification would not have taken care of an adulterous woman's impurity, even if the stele treats such pollution as especially severe'. It depends what one means by 'normal practices of purification'. For example, it is difficult to imagine that merely washing from the head down could have cleansed the woman or her kin, which would be contaminated as a result of her actions, from the severe pollution outlined by Dionysios. As elsewhere in Lydia, confession and the expectation of divine intervention might have been necessary; the oath required of participants in the cult, using the stele as a touchstone, could have served in this capacity; see de Hoz 2017: 101–2.

43–6, 48–50) while, conversely, blessings are formulated for those who respect and obey the commands (ll. 46–8, compare 50–4).

In other words, instead of a series of cases of impurity that could be readily resolved, whether through washing or delays in participation, the precepts outlined by Dionysios in this stele are detailed moral principles that hold dire consequences when contravened. This is not to say that some standard cases of abstention (ἁγνεία) and their correspondingly necessary purifications (καθαρμοί) would not have been covered implicitly by Dionysios' rules. This in fact seems to be what is alluded to by traditional practice in lines 12–14: ἁγνισμοί and καθαρμοί... κατά τε τὰ πάτρια.[69] To take the case of sexual relations, in addition to the ἁγνεία expected of men after sex with one's wife (ἀπὸ γυναικός) or after visiting a courtesan (ἑταίρα), Dionysios' stele makes explicit the parameters of these sexual relations: they are absolutely not to concern married women or those not yet married (children, maidens). It is probable that adultery was always implicitly proscribed, even by other purity regulations that seem to take a broader view of sexual relations, as ἀφροδίσια 'sexual dealings', for instance.[70] But in the case of women, the stele is still more strict: some form of ἁγνεία would still be expected after relations with one's husband,[71] but this was the only partner allowed for married women. This forms a marked contrast with some of the rules broaching the possibility of ἀφροδίσια even for women,[72] but it matches some other purity rules, for example, a text from Lindos that emphasises the licit character of sexual relations when discussing the necessary ἁγνεία in such a case; illicit sex is not mentioned at all, presumably because it was excluded and resulted in a more serious form of impurity.[73] In other words, Dionysios' rules supplement standard ritual practice and reshape existing ethical standards, by

---

[69] As perceptively remarked by Stowers 1998: 297–8 (such rules of purity 'are missing from the inscription').

[70] For ἀφροδίσια *vel sim.*, see *AvP* VIII.3 161 (n. 31) and the text from Yaylakale quoted and discussed above (Section 2). See Parker 1996b: 94–100 on the connection between sexual morality and purity.

[71] Purification after sex in the case of a woman is specifically mentioned in the text from Ptolemais (*LSCG Suppl.* 119 / *CGRN* 144, first cent. BC, l. 14: [ἀπ'] ἀνδρός, β΄, μυρσίνην δὲ [οἴσει (?)]).

[72] Note especially the possibility of sex, both for men and women, with partners who were not one's own spouse, in text from the Nikephorion at Pergamum (*I.Pergamon* 255 / *LSAM* 12 / *CGRN* 212), quoted above: ἀπὸ ... τῆς ἰδίας γ[υναι]κός... vs. ἀπὸ... ἀλλοτρίας; ἀπὸ ... τοῦ ἰδίου ἀνδρός vs. ἀπὸ... ἀλλοτρίου.

[73] *IG* XII.1 789 / *LSCG* 139 (Lindos, ca. AD 117–138), l. 14: ἀπὸ συνουσίας νομ[ί]μου κτλ. For συνουσία vs. κοινή (any intercourse), see also the inscription from Lindos in Petrovic and Petrovic 2018 (ca. AD 225).

adding rigid and much weightier moral requirements for participants in the cult housed in his οἶκος.[74]

In all of these cases, from Pythion to Xanthos and Dionysios, it is unclear if the intention of the founder of the cult was to create a group such as a durable association. None of the texts envisages the formal structure of an association, with a name and a well-defined membership, for instance. While these dossiers may potentially present primordial snapshots of associations in the making, what can clearly be discerned is that they represent private, individual efforts to inaugurate cults with doors at least partly open to the outside world. Pythion has founded a sanctuary that will belong to his sons, but which may well have accepted outsiders, who must respect some basic guidelines of purity. Xanthos instigates a cult where he is the founder but where anyone may freely gather, following some detailed guidelines for sacrifice and purification. Dionysios invites both genders, free individuals and slaves, but is more demanding, explicitly requiring that men, and women especially, abstain completely from deviant behaviour that is deemed impure. In these individual acts, then, the rules concerning purity play a fundamental role in regulating access to the sanctuary and the cult: the delays of ἁγνεία proposed by Pythion are relatively standard and strict, but are few in number and quite briefly presented at the conclusion of the stele, which seems to have functioned as a sign demarcating the sanctuary for worshippers; those expounded by Xanthos are of similar character, but are presented in a more detailed fashion and also include moral precepts, whether on the lengthier stele (text A) or on the sign for worshippers (text B). Finally, the case of Dionysios is different, since the strict rules he presented seem to have been aimed not just at safeguarding the purity of the sanctuary, but at shaping the moral character of worshippers in his οἶκος. All of these acts may represent attempts at a transition from private or familial worship to a cult that aimed to become more open to the public. The intended process is relatively clear given the *publication* of the inscribed documents for each cult, though it is not sure if this transformation became fully realised in each case.

Conclusion

Groups that were particularly concerned with purity form a disparate array. We have looked at one, the *Bacchoi* at Cnidus, which was concerned

---

[74] *Contra*, see Stowers 1998: 293 criticising the idea of 'supposedly elevated moral rules' and Harland in *GRA* II 117, pp. 190–2, who asserts that these rules are 'not unusual', except perhaps in their emphatic character.

to maintain standards of purity in a sanctuary but which did not have the authority or power to do so (Section 1). It is likely that many other cult groups and even associations, which partook in civic sanctuaries rather than possessing their own cult sites, were faced with similar problems. More clearly an association, the *Asklepiastai* at Yaylakale recreated the rules of the major sanctuaries of Pergamum for the use and benefit of worshippers in the countryside (Section 2). Finally, we analysed a series of private cults that expounded rules of purity, probably as part of a process of opening their doors to a wider community (Section 3). In the case of the *Asklepiastai* and the private cults of Pythion and Xanthos, it is no coincidence that we are dealing with the act of inaugurating a cult. One of the main strategies employed for addressing new and potential worshippers and for defining the sacred space used by the cult was the publication of casuistic rules of purity. Enacting rules of purity of this sort can thus be seen as a mechanism for fostering participation beyond the core group of the association or the family, while at the same time maintaining religious (and moral) standards expected of a sanctuary.

More distinctive is the case of Dionysios at Philadelphia, which in fact required that worshippers abstain *permanently* from certain acts, such as adultery, and, in the case of women, from sex outside of marriage. This was not just the casuistic type of ἁγνεία necessitating a temporary absence from the sanctuary, therefore, but a sort of 'categorical imperative' that was imposed on potential worshippers. Yet even such ideas were far from new. We might, for instance, recall a similar view aired as part of the accusations made against Androtion, in the speech written by Demosthenes in 356/5 BC.

ἐγὼ μὲν γὰρ οἴομαι δεῖν τὸν εἰς ἱέρ' εἰσιόντα καὶ χερνίβων καὶ κανῶν ἁψόμενον, καὶ τῆς πρὸς τοὺς θεοὺς ἐπιμελείας προστάτην ἐσόμενον οὐχὶ προειρημένον ἡμερῶν ἀριθμὸν ἁγνεύειν, ἀλλὰ τὸν βίον ἡγνευκέναι τοιούτων ἐπιτηδευμάτων οἷα τούτῳ βεβίωται.

In my opinion, the man who enters temples, touches lustral water and sacred baskets and intends to take responsibility for looking after the gods, should not only keep himself pure for a prescribed number of days, but keep his entire life pure from the kind of activities that this man has practiced during his life.[75]

Some impure deeds were severe enough that they could be viewed as beyond the remedy of time or mere purification by washing. In fact,

---

[75] Dem. 22 (*Against Androtion*) 78, as translated by Harris 2008.

casuistic purity rules could also include clauses that issued similar moral pronouncements. A prime example is a much later text from Lindos, recently reedited, which concluded a list of ἁγνεῖαι with the statement: 'from illicit acts one is never pure' (ἀπὸ τῶν παρανόμων οὐδέποτε καθαρός).[76] Xanthos in his rules also emphasised the moral dimension of purity, advising worshippers to approach or perform the cult 'with a simple soul'.[77]

While moral commands could thus be part of the entry rules for all worshippers, some of the difference between the casuistic rules of the *Asklepiastai*, Pythion and Xanthos, on the one hand, and the strict purity rules of Dionysios, on the other, can be explained in terms of whom these rules addressed.[78] The casuistic rules applied to any and all worshippers in sanctuaries that were open to a wide participation. In such cases, there could be a core group or association, but the cultic community was potentially much wider. The rules of Dionysios, by contrast, were more demanding and find closer analogies in rules for membership in an association. One celebrated Athenian inscription, containing the foundational rules (literally, 'a law of friendship', θεσμὸν φιλίης, l. 28) for a community calling itself an *eranos*, provides an evocative parallel.[79] The rules begin immediately with a stipulation of what an ideal member would be: no one is to be admitted to the group without a formal examination or *dokimasia* performed by the officials of the group.[80] This, of course, imitates some structures of the Athenian state, where the *dokimasia* was held to scrutinise the legitimacy of officials, whether they possessed citizenship and met all the requirements to hold a specific office.[81] But there is

---

[76] See now Petrovic and Petrovic 2018 (ca. AD 225), l. 20. But these παράνομα 'acts against the norms' do not seem to have concerned the distinction between sexual relations with one's spouse and those with another partner (see n. 73).

[77] Cf. n. 60 above. See again Petrovic and Petrovic 2016 on the long-standing moral aspects of purity, as well as several of the essays in Carbon and Peels 2018.

[78] Cf. e.g. Eckhardt 2017b: 417: 'While internal activities of associations were normally exclusive, their sanctuaries (qua being sanctuaries) were not'.

[79] IG II² 1369 / GRA I 49 (CAPInv. 308; end of second cent. AD), from the Mesogeia, probably the deme of Paiania. On this text, see also Arnaoutoglou in Chapter 6. This group has been related to SEG 31:122, the σύνοδος τῶν Ἡρακλιαστῶν ἐν Λίμναις found in the same area one century earlier (ca. AD 90), though unconvincingly as Arnaoutoglou 2003: 83–4 rightly argues.

[80] Ll. 31–6: [μη]δενὶ ἐξέστω ἰσι[έν]αι ἰς τὴν σεμνοτάτην | σύνοδον τῶν ἐρανιστῶν πρὶν ἂν δοκι[μασθῆ εἴ ἐστι ἁ[γν]ὸς καὶ εὐσεβὴς καὶ ἀγ|α[θ]ός· δοκιμα[ζέ]τω δὲ ὁ προστάτης [καὶ | ὁ] ἀρχιερανιστὴς καὶ ὁ γ[ρ]αμματεὺς κα[ὶ | οἱ] ταμίαι καὶ σύνδικοι.

[81] Other examples of a process of *dokimasia* for admission to associations are known, though the particulars of the examination remain murky: cf. already the *orgeones* of Bendis, IG II² 1361 / GRA I 4 (CAPInv. 230; ca. 350–300 BC), who allude to a *dokimasia* for new members, when they clearly sought to increase their membership (ll. 20–3); cf. also I.Smyrna 218 + vol. II2 p. 371 (CAPInv. 1138; first–second cent. AD), apparently requiring *dokimasia* to obtain a resting place in the burial

a fundamental difference in the case of this *eranos*: the *dokimasia* is not one of the legitimacy, but instead concerns the character of the prospective new member into an assembly that presents itself as 'most revered' or 'holy' (ἰς τὴν σεμνοτάτην | σύνοδον τῶν ἐρανιστῶν) and that was probably focussed on the cult of a hero.[82] The prospective member must first and foremost be ἁ[γν]ός, that is to say, chaste and abstemious with regard to known sources of impurity; the other criteria listed are piety (εὐσεβής) and general goodness of character (ἀγα[θ]ός; this adjective might also refer to 'good birth').[83] The rules then went on to discuss further, but related, practicalities: if anyone caused fights or disturbances, they would be expelled from the *eranos* and subject to a fine.[84] Only one who was not *hagnos, eusebes* and *agathos* would be at the source of such chaos in the sanctuary or risk shedding blood in the 'most holy assembly'.

Purity, piety and good morality were the requirements for membership in this Athenian association, as they were for participation in the cult of Dionysios at Philadelphia. A process of *dokimasia* was undertaken to test for these characteristics in the Athenian *eranos*, just as, in the *oikos* of Dionysios, oaths would be required of participants in good, ethical standing. The purity rules of Dionysios, though they do not explicitly claim this purpose, should therefore be thought of as analogous to membership rules for admission into an association. A recent study by Kloppenborg concluded that the moral principles that constituted criteria of admission in

plot; see also the commentary at *GRA* I 49. For a *krisis* of familial legitimacy, see the procedure by which bastards (*nothoi*) could become members of the cultic family of Diomedon, *IG* XII.4 1 348 / *LSCG* 177 / *CGRN* 96 (*CAPInv.* 1919), ll. 146–9; cf. also *MDAI(A)* 32 (1907): 293 no 18 for the *dokimasia* of fathers and their sons to enter into the membership of a *systema* at Pergamum, though the associational character of the group is unclear and it may be the *gerousia* (*CAPInv.* 1659; second cent. AD); similar rules concerning the replacement of members in *IG* VII 2808 (Hyettos, ca. AD 212–250), probably relating to the sacred and political *gerousia* of the community rather than a private association *stricto sensu* (*pace* Marchand in *CAPInv.* 984). On admission procedures codified by associations, see Giannakopoulos in Chapter 2.

[82] For the superlative σεμνοτάτη, see the commentary at *GRA* I 49. A heroic cult is implied by ll. 38–9, where the official called ὁμολείτωρ is appointed as responsible for the *heroon* for life: ὁμολείτωρ δὲ ἔ[[ι]]στω δ[ιὰ] βίου αὐτο[ῦ] | ὁ ἐπὶ ἡρώου καταλιφθείς. That this was the tomb of the founder of the group (Sokolowski, *LSCG* 53) is possible, but far from clear.

[83] The closest analogy is perhaps provided by the *dokimasia* in the cult of the *Iobacchoi, IG* II² 1368 / Jaccottet 2003: II 27–35 no 4 / *AGRW* 7 (*CAPInv.* 339), ll. 35–7: δοκιμασθῇ ὑπὸ τῶν ἰοβάκχων ψήφῳ, εἰ ἄξιος φαίνοιτο καὶ ἐπιτήδειος | τῷ Βακχείῳ. This suggests that new members were assessed only for their worthiness or goodness (ἄξιος cf. perhaps ἀγαθός) and their suitability to the *Bakcheion* (ἐπιτήδειος; and perhaps their serviceable or friendly disposition as potential benefactors). Yet this is also different: there were no overt criteria of religious rectitude, no connotations of purity or piety, in this case; though these may have been implicit to the constitution of the *Iobacchoi*, they were not explicitly expressed.

[84] Ll. 40–4: εἰ δέ τις μά|χας ἢ θορύβους κεινῶν φαίνοιτο, | ἐκβαλλέσθω τοῦ ἐράνου ζημιού|μενος [[ε]] Ἀττ[ι]καῖς κε΄ ἢ πληγαῖς αἰκ[[αικ]]ιζό|μενος ταῖς διπλαῖς πέ[[τ]]ρα κρίσεως.

associations 'not only served as a public advertisement of the propriety of the members, but functioned internally to create an ethos of trust and solidarity that no doubt served as an instrument of recruitment'.[85] What we have witnessed here, however, are quite varying strategies of advertising and potential recruitment: for instance, the *Asklepiastai* at Yaylakale promoted good health and simply recommended washing after *any* sexual activity; the precepts of Dionysios at Philadelphia on the same subject were, to say the least, much more strict and elaborately codified.

Rules of purity, though only occasionally apparent in the available evidence, constitute an interesting case study for evaluating how a cultic community chose to present and define itself. Such rules could be modelled on local practice or developed according to more widespread ethical and religious principles in the Greek world. The norms of purity functioned not only as a necessary precondition for the maintenance of good order, but could shape participation in the cultic community, whether this was formalised as an association or not. Purity regulations could be published to open and regulate access to a sanctuary for a wider group of worshippers, as well as to define admission and participation in a limited cultic group, like an association. Much like for sanctuaries generally, the rules of purity enabled groups to establish a difficult equilibrium between expanding their networks of worshippers and maintaining appropriate control over the cults themselves.

---

[85] Kloppenborg 2014: 226, speaking in particular of 'The Moralizing of Discourse' or 'the moralizing of association rules'. Given that morality was such a long-standing preoccupation in Greek society in general, I am not sure that to speak of a 'moralising' tendency is a good historical approach, however.

CHAPTER 5

Associations and Place
Regulating Meeting-Places and Sanctuaries*

Stella Skaltsa

The Spatial Turn and Associational Space

Associations were variably anchored in space and place.[1] Being active in different spheres of life, associations carved their own space into the urban fabric or in the countryside to accommodate their multifaceted activities. Associations were emplaced in civic, sacred and funerary space, enriching and expanding it through their dedicatory, honorific, religious and commemorative practices.[2] In these respects, their activities informed the built environment, which in turn framed social interaction.

This chapter sets out to explain the ways in which meeting-places of associations came into being, how the identity of associations was embedded in space and how these places were regulated. In particular, it draws on spatial theory, following a resurgence of interest by ancient historians in the 'spatial turn'. By this, one designates the study of space not as a mere physical form but as a social construct, which is being informed by and informs human behaviour.[3] The present objective is manifold: first, to address the importance of space in construing the group's identity; second, to assess the regulations that pertained to the management and/or use of associational space as a mechanism that informed the nature of the association in question (that is to say, its exclusivity or inclusivity).

* I am very grateful to Vincent Gabrielsen and Mat Carbon for fruitful discussions and their valuable comments. My thanks also extend to the anonymous reviewer for his/her thorough comments.

[1] According to geographers, the terms 'space' and 'place', though often used interchangeably, are interrelated, yet distinct from each other (Price 2013: 120). The literature on space and place as distinct concepts is massive; for an overview, see Price 2013.

[2] The sociologist Thomas Gieryn (2000: 466) has shown that all social life is 'emplaced'; in other words, social life exists in space. For the multifarious activities of associations, see for example Gabrielsen 2007 and 2017.

[3] The concept of space as a social construct has been taken up recently in ancient Greek as well as Roman history; see Scott 2013; De Angelis 2010. In the past decade, the notion of space and its importance in humanities has been thoroughly investigated by the Cluster 'Topoi' in Berlin, which produced a number of relevant publications, notably Paliou et al. 2014; Hofmann et al. 2017.

Social theorists and urban geographers have long pointed out that space is not static but the product of social interaction in that 'space can be shaped from the social meanings of people's lives'.[4] According to sociologists, place, as a concept, is characterised by three distinct features: a fixed geographical location, a material form and meaning – with all three features being closely interconnected to one another.[5] These features can readily apply to the meeting-places of associations. As physical entities, they provided a concrete locale where collective action unfolded. Through decision-making processes, the organisation of celebrations and other festivities that helped cement bonds of membership and togetherness, place took on specific meaning and became a point of reference for the collectivity.

Attachment to a specific place mattered a great deal, especially in societies witnessing an influx or outflow of people. Often a toponym or a geographical indication features as part of the official name of an association. In light of its name, an association appears tied to a specific city, area or even structure, on a physical just as much as on a perceptual level. Naming practices, thus, strongly suggest that attachment to a specific place was embedded in the identity of the group.[6] In the case of the Poseidoniasts on Delos, the adjectival ethnic 'Berytians' (Βηρύτιοι) features as one of the constituent elements of their official name.[7] The link with Beirut, the motherland, works on a mnemonic level, as the physical setting of their activities was far away from home, on the island of Delos in the Aegean. The association was well grounded on Delos as a trading society involved in maritime trade and seafaring, with its clubhouse being fully integrated into the urban fabric of the city, located in the heart of one of the residential quarters.[8] Yet, the notion of origin and the link with the mother city played an important role in the self-representation of the association, which was in turn embedded in the articulation of sacred space within the clubhouse.[9]

---

[4] Unwin 2000: 11. For an overview of the contribution of Henri Lefebvre and Michel Foucault to the concept of space as a social construct, see Warf and Arias 2009.

[5] Gieryn 2000; Price 2013; Cresswell 2015: 12–13.

[6] In the field of geography, Price designates attachment to a place as 'intimacy of place' (Price 2013: 125).

[7] *I.Délos* 1520. The full name of the association is τὸ ἐν Δήλωι κοινὸν Βηρυτίων Ποσειδωνιαστῶν ἐμπόρων καὶ ναυκλήρων καὶ ἐγδοχέων 'the *koinon* of the Berytian Poseidoniasts merchants and shippers and forwarding agents on Delos'.

[8] For the most comprehensive analysis of the use of space in the clubhouse of the *Poseidoniastai* on Delos see Trümper 2002, 2006, 2011.

[9] The clubhouse was dedicated to the *theoi patrioi* (*I.Délos* 1774) as indicated by the inscribed architrave of the peristyle. Already from the first building phase (153/2 BC) the clubhouse

For other associations, affiliation to a place was directly related to the physical setting. In a few instances, the meeting-place became a metonym for the association itself: the most characteristic example is that of the Athenian *Bakcheion*, denoting both an association as well as its meeting-place.[10] Moreover, spatial elements that were constituent parts of the name of an association certainly helped to distinguish between homonymous associations active in the same city. For instance, in Rhodes, where an abundance of associations co-existed in Hellenistic times, the reference to place seems to function on a multiple level: it demonstrates origin and/or place of action, while it can also reveal the interests of associations in a certain place, which often transcended the physical borders of a fixed locale.[11]

The objective of this chapter, however, is not to discuss the role of toponyms and other spatial features in the composition of the names of associations, despite the important insights into their self-representation which they can yield. Instead, this investigation focusses on the role of space as an element that grounded associations to a specific place, to a greater or lesser degree. By jointly discussing the membership profile of associations, their attachment to a specific meeting-place and the varied evidence about regulations that directly or indirectly pertained to the management and/or use of space, it will be demonstrated that the exclusivity or the inclusivity of the spaces corresponded with the exclusivity or the inclusivity of the association in question.

In most cases, the materiality of associational space largely escapes us. The multifarious activities of associations could be housed in a wide array of architectural forms. As a result, associational space as a physical entity does not necessarily present distinct architectural features (layout, articulation of space).[12] It is commonly accepted that, in the absence of

---

contained a shrine with two cult rooms for the *theoi patrioi* that flanked the west side of the courtyard as one entered the building. Additions and modifications in the shrine took place in later times (see Trümper 2002: 327–30).

[10] This is the case of the *Iobacchoi*: *IG* II² 1368 = *CAPInv.* 339. For the different meanings of the term *Bakcheion* – i.e. the association, the meeting-place and the festival – see Baslez 2004: 113.

[11] In a recently published inscription from Rhodes, four out of five associations bear a composite name with a reference to a place, e.g. Ἀσκλαπιασταὶ οἱ ἐν Σαλάκωι, Σωτηριασταὶ Φειδιανάκτειοι οἱ ἐν Φάναις, Ἀσκλαπιασταὶ Βουκοπῖδαι οἱ ἐν Αἰγιλείαι, [. . .]δαλιασταὶ οἱ ἐν Φάναις. For a thorough analysis, see Gabrielsen 2017: esp. 15 (text), 18, 20, 34–5.

[12] Bollmann 1998: 48–57 suggests some typological criteria for the identification of buildings used or frequented by associations, with a focus on architectural remains from the Italian peninsula and the Roman West. The topic has been extensively treated recently by Nielsen 2014, with a strong focus on the architectural setting of mystery groups and religious associations. Nielsen distinguishes three different spaces for the meeting of religious groups: a 'temple-type', a 'cave/grotto-type' and a

inscriptions found *in situ*, architectural remains can hardly be identified as meeting places of associations.[13] In cases of safely identified clubhouses, a combination of factors, from architectural features and the articulation of space to artefacts and other material remains, helps to considerably illuminate the organisation and the use of space.[14]

Inscriptions, however, can shed significant light onto issues directly related to the concept of space, understood less as a physical entity and more as a social and cultural one.[15] Indeed, the activities that took place within a space – such as rituals, assemblies and the like – can often be traced in the epigraphic record. Collective action took place at a specific locale: this constituted the setting for social interaction (physical space) and the product of social interaction (social space).

Here, my focus will be on the articulation of sacred space and the ways in which the latter was regulated. Drawing on associations whose *raisons d'être* differed substantially from one another, this chapter aims to elucidate differing attitudes towards the regulation of space. The analysis will focus first on three familial associations in the Aegean (Cos and Thera) and coastal Asia Minor (Halicarnassus) with a view to evaluate the degree of exclusivity in terms of membership profile and access to a place. The discussion will then move to NW Asia Minor in the Augustan period: an inscription from Cyme offers unique glimpses into a case of dislocation. The last part of the chapter will draw on material from Attica and the hinterland of Pergamum. It will be argued that regardless of the special interests an association had in a place, shrines managed by associations could be open to a wider community of worshippers, as this allowed the revival or the continuity of cult. In other words, bringing the 'spatial turn' into the study of associations, space is examined as a dynamic entity, often the object of close regulation. In light of

---

'banqueting/house-type' (Nielsen 2014: 241–53). However, her study fails to provide strict definitions of the groups under discussion, and in this respect it should remain open to what extent the architectural spaces discussed were indeed used and frequented by associations. Another recent study that discusses the architectural settings of associations is that of Steinhauer 2014: 110–40. Her observations are based on those cases where inscriptions can shed light on architectural remains.

[13] Trümper 2011: 51. In the case of Delos, Trümper has suggested identifying some buildings with clubhouses by comparing their layout and architectural articulation to the securely identified clubhouse of the *Poseidoniastai* in the island (Trümper 2006: 129–30).

[14] Trümper's analysis of the use of space in the clubhouse of the *Poseidoniastai* on Delos is exemplary in this regard. She points out that the clubhouse was designed to serve different functions from congregational and commercial to sacred and honorific, something that is reflected in the articulation of space (2006: 117–22; 2011: 53–8).

[15] For the concept of social space and the role of individuals and collectivities in using, producing and transforming natural space into social space, see an overview by Gans 2002.

the nature and content of rules that regulated space, it will be argued that the relationship of an association to place can inform us about the degree of exclusivity or inclusivity of the association in question.

Exclusive Spaces: Attachment to a Place

Three epigraphic dossiers, those of Diomedon on Cos (late fourth to first decades of the third century BC), Poseidonios in Halicarnassus (ca. 280–240 BC) and Epikteta on Thera (210–195 BC), respectively, are particularly illuminating with regard to the setting and built environment of meeting-places of associations, despite the absence of archaeological remains.[16] Diomedon's dossier consists of three different texts inscribed at different times, within the time span of a few decades between the late fourth and early third century BC.[17] Likewise, Poseidonios' dossier includes three different parts: an oracle given to Poseidonios (χρησμός, Laum 1914: II no 117, ll. 1–11), a pledge of properties from Poseidonios to his familial group (ὑποθήκη, ll. 12–22) and the decree of Poseidonios and the group (δόγμα, ll. 22–52). Epikteta's dossier, inscribed on the pedestal that once supported her statue and the statues of her two sons, contains her testament (*IG* XII.3 330, ll. 1–108) and the decree of the association (ll. 109–288), including its statutes (νόμος, l. 276).

The importance of these three groups for a study of associational space lies in the fact that they share features that are closely intertwined: a closed group (association), a locale fixed in space (meeting-place of the association) and performance of ritual activity (cult). As will be shown, the founders of the respective associations took concrete steps to regulate space, as this was vital not only or not always for the funding of the cult, but for the perpetuation of the association itself.

A consecrated area, *temenos* (τέμενος), dedicated to a god or a group of gods features in all three cases, while a designated funerary space is included in two instances (Thera and Halicarnassus). In Cos, the *temenos* was adjacent to other facilities such as guest houses with a garden and other

---

[16] All three texts were included by Laum 1914: II no 43 (Thera); no 45 (Cos); no 117 (Halicarnassus) in his monograph on endowments. These three texts have been discussed together by Kamps 1937, briefly by Parker 2010: 118–20 and Gherchanoc 2012: 159–68. Recently, Carbon and Pirenne-Delforge 2013 focussed on some specific aspects, such as the priestly officials; recently, a detailed analysis has been presented by Campanelli 2016. These three endowments have been recently discussed by Aneziri 2020: 16–18.

[17] Ross 1845: 45–54 no 311, the first editor, noted the different stonecutters, while Herzog 1928: 28–32 no 10, established the date of the dossier.

buildings (ξενῶνας τοὺς ἐν τῶι κάπωι; οἰκημάτια, *IG* XII.4 1 348, ll. 44–5), while in Halicarnassus the *temenos* probably encompassed a court-yard (αὐλή, Laum 1914: II no 117, l.17), a garden (κῆπον, l.17) and other unspecified facilities around the funerary monument (καὶ τὰ περὶ τὸ μνημεῖον, l.17), as the inscription informs us. Their exact location escapes us in all three cases. The pedestal inscribed with Epikteta's testament and the decree of the association was transported to Italy already by 1568.[18] Its original location is hence unknown. In the absence of funerary monu-ments from within the ancient city of Thera, the *temenos* of the Muses with the funerary monuments should have been located outside the city.[19] Likewise, the *temenos* of Heracles Diomedonteios in Cos should have been located in the outskirts of the city, as indicated by the findspot of the inscription.[20] More complicated is the picture with regard to the *temenos* consecrated by Poseidonios in Halicarnassus. Sara Campanelli envisages a rural setting for the *temenos*.[21] However, the inscription broken into pieces was built into a Turkish house not far away from the Mausolleion.[22] As the stele was found in Halicarnassus, we can assume with some caution that the *temenos* was laid out in Halicarnassus, and for this reason it was not felt necessary to further indicate its exact location, unlike the field that Poseidonios bequeathed to the association, the location of which was specified with precision.[23]

---

[18] Wittenburg 1990: 16–17.

[19] Conspicuous funerary monuments in the form of a temple-like structure are in fact attested in Thera, but concrete evidence is missing to identify any of them with the *Mouseion*, as for example the *Heroon* by the Evangelismos Church on the northern slope of the Sellada hill, not far away from the road that leads up to the city from the modern village of Kamari (*Thera* II: 240–51) or the *Heroon* at Echendra on the southern coast (*Thera* II: 251–4). See also Le Dinahet 2014: 353–6 and Caruso 2016: 341–5 on the architectural configuration of the *Heroon* by the Evangelismos Church.

[20] Cemeteries and funerary monuments have been located to the south and south-west of the city all the way to the *Asklepieion* (Tsouli 2013: 18–28). For example, the funerary monument of Charmylos, located in the area of Pyli, was part of a property consecrated to the Twelve Gods. For a discussion of this monument, see Campanelli 2016: 162–3.

[21] Campanelli 2016: 177–8. Her argument is based on the meaning of the term *aule*. She takes *aule* to stand for a farmstead and locates Poseidonios' *temenos* in the countryside by analogy to inscriptions from Mylasa, where αὐλή denotes a farm (Campanelli 2016: 176–7; cf. Robert 1945: 86–7). However, in Poseidonios' inscriptions, the term αὐλή is customarily translated as 'courtyard' (Carbon and Pirenne-Delforge 2013: 104). I prefer to translate αὐλή as an enclosed open-air space (Travlos 1986: 44), which can be part of a farm, a sanctuary or any other structure (Hellmann 1992: 59–61) in order to do justice to the architectural features of the word rather than its function, which might prove a contested issue.

[22] For the findspot, see Carbon and Pirenne-Delforge 2013: 101.

[23] This field is designated as being located in an area called Astypalaia and it is clearly demarcated with reference to adjacent properties belonging to different individuals.

Similarities and differences between these three epigraphic dossiers in terms of cult practice, financial management and use of space have been recently analysed at length by Campanelli.[24] Underlining the family-based character of the groups and their relation to landed properties and assets, she draws a distinction between real estate and sacred property. In doing so, she explains the different mechanisms employed in these three cases with regard to the management of revenue-bearing property and consequently the different financial means available for the financing of the cult. In the cases of Diomedon and Poseidonios, the meeting-place itself brought revenue to the association through leasing, unlike, for example, the meeting-place of the association of male relatives in Thera, which was protected against any sort of financial exploitation.[25]

The associations came into being at the initiative of individuals, in order to foster the cult of specific deities and/or deceased family members.[26] In all three cases, lineage, real or fictive, constitutes the underlying principle on which membership is based.[27] The association founded by Epikteta in Thera bears a full-fledged name – τὸ κοινὸν τοῦ ἀνδρείου τῶν συγγενῶν ('the association of the male relatives') – where all members are described as relatives, even though membership was drawn from three different families.[28] In the case of Diomedon, membership is based on descent from the male line of the family as well as on the sharing of the cult.[29]

---

[24] Campanelli 2016. Besides the three epigraphic dossiers, Campanelli expands her analysis to two more family cult foundations, those of Python (*IG* XII.4 1 349) and Charmylos (*IG* XII.4 1 355), both in Cos.

[25] In the case of Poseidonios, revenue for the financing of the cult derived from different resources, namely, from the leasing of the *temenos*, from the leasing of the field at a place called Astypalaia and from the rights of ploughing at a place called Taramptos; in the latter case, the association was entitled to half of the rights.

[26] Although I use the term 'association' to refer to all the three groups centred on ancestral or family cults for the sake of convenience and consistency, it should be noted that there are some noticeable differences between these three groups in terms of structure and organisation. In the case of Diomedon's dossier, descriptive terms such as *koinon*, which normally qualifies a group as an association, are missing (with similar concerns Kamps 1937: 154); the same can be said of Poseidonios' group, which does not have a formalised name (*thiasos* is only used to refer to the cult group during a specific year of celebrations: l. 45).

[27] On the composition of membership, see also Campanelli 2016: 148–53.

[28] *IG* XII.3 330; *CAPInv.* 1645. Wittenburg 1990: 63–6; Stavrianopoulou 2006: 292–302; see also Caruso 2016: 328–45. Epikteta founded the association in fulfilment of the request of her late husband, Phoinix, and late son, Andragoras (*IG* XII.3 330, ll. 16–26).

[29] *IG* XII.4 1 348, ll. 9–11, τοὶ ἐγ Διομέδοντος καὶ ἀεὶ τοὶ ἐξ αὐτῶν γενόμενοι; τοὶ τῶν ἱερῶν κοινωνεῦντες, ll. 7, 80–1, 87–8; τοὶ μετέχοντες τῶν ἱερῶν, ll. 52–3; cf. *CAPInv.* 1919. Unlike Paul 2013: 340 who considers the term *hiera* in the phrase τοὶ τῶν ἱερῶν κοινωνεῦντες as referring to the cult: Campanelli 2016: 149 and 156 proposes a more inclusive meaning, which includes not only the cult but also the sacred property and all sacred items dedicated in the sanctuary. She therefore claims that sharing extended to the physical space of the sanctuary (Campanelli 2016: 166 and 186).

Unlike Diomedon, Poseidonios is more inclusive when it comes to descendants, as both relatives from the male and female line are welcomed as well as those related by marriage to them.[30] Membership found its primary embodiment, when relatives and descendants – real or fictive – came together during the festivities that were held in honour of gods, founders and/or deceased family members.

In all three inscriptions under question (and especially in the case of Epikteta and Diomedon), the place of the group and its constituent components are among the first to be defined.[31] Celebrations were fixed in time, their duration was defined and the performance of rites and sacrifices was prescribed and regulated. Likewise, the meeting-place, where the association came together to partake in these festivities, was anchored in a specific locale, the use and management of which was strictly regulated. The cult was tied to a specific place and, conversely, the place demarcated the site for the performance of cultic and ritual activity. In all three cases, the meeting-place is not just any place, but in particular a shrine consecrated to a god or group of gods, a concrete locale for celebrations and ritual activity. A sacred precinct features in all three cases: a sanctuary of the Muses (*Mouseion*) in Thera, a *temenos* of Heracles Diomedonteios in Cos, a *temenos* consecrated to several gods in Halicarnassus (Zeus Patroos, Apollo who rules over Telemessos, the Moirai, the Mother of the Gods, the Agathos Daimon of Poseidonios and Gorgis and the Agathe Tyche of Poseidonios' parents).

Furthermore, a precinct with funerary monuments and a funerary monument is a key element of the cult site in Thera and in Halicarnassus, respectively. In Thera, within the *Mouseion* stood the *temenos* of the heroes (τὸ τέμενος τῶν ἡρώων) – a sacred precinct set aside for the funerary monuments (τὰ ἡρῷα) of Epikteta's husband and her two sons.[32] In Halicarnassus, the funerary monument of Poseidonios' parents is called *mnemeion*, a monument of memory; this term appropriately blends together function (tomb/monument) and symbolism (receptacle of memory).[33] It was surrounded by other unspecified structures, perhaps

[30] Carbon 2013 (new edition with commentary) ll. 12–13: καὶ οἱ ἐκ τούτων γινόμενοι, ἔκ τε τῶν ἀρσένων καὶ τῶν θηλειῶν, καὶ οἱ λαμβάνοντες ἐξ αὐτῶν; cf. *CAPInv.* 830.
[31] This would correspond to what geographers call 'place-making' (Price 2013).
[32] Wittenburg 1990: 139–47. On the *Mouseion* in Thera, see Caruso 2016: 341–5.
[33] On the term, see Guarducci 1974: 145; see also Chaniotis 2013: 27.

the altars of the other gods (τὰ περὶ τὸ μνημεῖον).[34] Though its location is not specified, by analogy to the case of Thera, it can be safely assumed that it was built within the precinct (*temenos*) that Poseidonios consecrated to the gods.[35] The funerary monuments in Thera and Halicarnassus did not stand in isolation but in an organic relationship to their surroundings, within an area consecrated to the god(s).

These funerary monuments underscore the role of memory as a mechanism for sustaining the identity of the association, being called a μνημεῖον or located in a *Mouseion*.[36] Memory of the deceased ancestors was enacted through ritual practice – a ceremony open only to members – and therefore acted as a unifying mechanism for the unity and social cohesion of the association. If this process of communication – the way one passes down the memory of the deceased – breaks off, then 'the consequence is forgetting', something that would jeopardise the identity of the association.[37] In Thera, in particular, the *Mouseion* provided the space for the association's annual gathering, a three-day celebration for the Muses[38] and in commemoration of the deceased members of Epikteta's family.[39] Epikteta had taken care to articulate the visual imagery of the sanctuary with statues of the Muses and of the heroised dead, that is to say, the deceased members of Epikteta's family. The interplay between the statues of the Muses – daughters of Mnemosyne – and statues of the deceased would have placed the latter on a level equal to the former. The visual space was thus loaded with semantics that helped evoke, accentuate and retain the memory of the heroised dead.

On Cos, conversely, as cult activity was not overtly directed at the commemoration of the founder, a funerary monument does not

---

[34] The phrase is interestingly paralleled in *MAMA* IV 171, a funerary inscription from Apollonia in Phrygia (first century BC or AD), alongside stoas. If juxtaposed to the more often attested phrase *ta peri ton theon*, then the *mnemeion* emerges as a nucleus of commemorative practice.

[35] For a similar view, see *CGRN* 104.

[36] On the power of collective memory, see Assmann 2011: 20, who has argued that 'remembrance is a matter of emotional ties, cultural shaping and a conscious reference to the past that overcomes the rupture between life and death'. On the connection of the Muses with the funerary sphere since Homer's time, see Caruso 2016: 37–40.

[37] Assmann 2011: 23.

[38] The inscription refers only to the cult of the Muses, while in other instances the Muses are worshipped together with Mnemosyne, their mother, e.g. in Camirus, *Tit.Cam.* 151.

[39] In Istros in the Black Sea, a *Mouseion* was built on private initiative, but there the *demos* was probably the recipient of an endowment of 300 gold staters for sacrifices to the Muses and for a gathering (*synodos*) (*IScM* I 1 and *SEG* 51:933, mid third cent. BC). See also Caruso 2016: 239–43. On account of another inscription from Istros that mentions a banquet (*synodos*) held in the gymnasium (cf. *BE* 1958 no 336), Caruso connects this *Mouseion* to a gymnasium. However, the inscription itself does not make any allusion to a gymnasium.

explicitly feature in the text. Instead, the unusual cultic epithet of
Heracles – Diomedonteios – alludes to an intimate personal connection
between the founder (Diomedon) and the deity (Heracles).[40] Although
Diomedon does not seem to have enjoyed a posthumous cult like Epikteta,
the infusion of a personal element in the cultic epithet of the god bears
constant witness to this privately founded cult of Heracles.[41]

A comparison of these three cases reveals a range of attitudes towards
space, in terms of management and use as well as accessibility. Relatives of
the deceased are normally responsible for the management of the property,
yet there are some noticeable differences from one case to another.

In Cos, the property and its assets (a slave and his descendants) were
overseen by 'those partaking in the sacrifices' (l. 7: τοὶ τῶν ἱερῶν
κοινωνεῦντες), a collective name denoting the members of this family-
based group. The property originally consisted of a *temenos*, consecrated to
Heracles Diomedonteios, guest houses within a garden (ξενῶνας τοὺς ἐν
τῶι κάπωι) and other buildings referred to as *oikemata* (οἰκήματα). At a
later stage, when the third text was inscribed, among the assets of the
group lands were included (τεμένη, l. 82) as well as an *oikia* in the *temenos*
(ll. 83–4), a *lesche* 'hall' (l. 84–5) and a *peripatos* 'covered walk' (l. 85). As
inferred by the inscription, the property generated income, which funded
the performance of cult activity and the upkeep of the facilities.[42]

A similar situation is also apparent in Halicarnassus. Poseidonios
bequeathed properties and resources in the form of a pledge (ὑποθήκη)
to his descendants, both from the male as well as the female line of descent
(ll. 13–14: τοῖς ἐκ τούτων γινομένοις, ἔκ τε τῶν ἀρσένων καὶ τῶν θηλειῶν,
καὶ τοῖς λαμβάνουσιν ἐξ αὐτῶν), in order to finance a familial cult centred
on members of his family and ancestral gods.[43] Only the eldest of
Poseidonios' descendants, who was also to serve as the priest, took over
the administration of the properties. Every year he was obliged to hand
over four gold coins of net value for the two-day performance of cult and
sacrifice.[44] In the decree passed by Poseidonios and his descendants, a
further provision, not envisaged in the original pledge, was taken. An
additional stipulation of the administration of the pledge was included in

---

[40] Cf. Carbon and Pirenne-Delforge 2013: 69 with nn. 20, 96.
[41] According to Kamps 1937: 156, a cult of the heroised Diomedon may have been introduced by later generations. Cf. Campanelli 2016: 139.
[42] For a detailed analysis of the property and its financial assets, see Campanelli 2016: 156–9.
[43] See above n. 25.
[44] According to Carbon 2013: 111, the χρυσοί of the inscription correspond to Ptolemaic staters, that is, 80 drachmas in total.

the decree with the aim of ensuring the financing of its annual gathering. More specifically, in cases in which the eldest of the descendants did not hand over the prescribed amount for the cult or was no longer willing to administer the pledge, then the pledged properties were to be held in common by the association (l. 28: εἶναι τὰ ὑποκείμενα κ[οι]νά). In this case, the financial administration of the pledge would be transferred to three *epimenioi*, appointed among members of the association (ll. 23–7, 28–30). They were responsible for farming out the land and the right of tillage as well as renting out the *temenos*.[45] From the stipulations included in the decree, it becomes apparent that the concerns of Poseidonios and the group were primarily of a financial nature. It was vital that the properties bequeathed by Poseidonios would produce revenues that would allow the organisation of the feast. Inextricably linked to a revenue-bearing property is the effective management of this property, which was placed on the shoulders of the association itself. It was in the group's interest to keep money flowing, which would fund the performance of ritual and would sustain its existence.

A different situation is observed in Thera. Although the *Mouseion* constituted the meeting-place of the association, ownership belonged to Epiteleia, the daughter of Epikteta. In other words, the association did not own the sanctuary; it was allowed to use the sanctuary for three days every year, when 210 drachmas would be handed over to the association on an annual basis for the celebration.[46] Nevertheless, the association was bound to the sanctuary in multiple ways. It was within this particular setting that members could come together for a common purpose – the three-day gathering – and thus reinstate their identity and strengthen their ties as relatives (συγγενεῖς) by sharing in common cultic and convivial activities. Moreover, as laid out in the testament of Epikteta, even if not enjoying ownership of the place, the association was instructed to act as its guardian under specific conditions (*IG* XII.3 330, ll. 52–4): the association had full power to act against anyone who would commit any sort of offence that would jeopardise the sanctuary and its monuments and by extension would put at risk the survival of the association. Thus, by appointing the

---

[45] Carbon 2013: 109–10 has shown that the ἐνηρόσιον ('rights of tillage') was probably related to the renting out or farming of sacred land, analogous to a relevant practice in Delos.

[46] Epikteta endowed the association of the male relatives with 3,000 drachmas; the group came into being thanks to her endowment. The 210 drachmas per year handed over to the association for the three-day celebration accrued from the interest on this capital.

association as an overseer to ensure the observance of these clauses, Epikteta took concrete steps to ensure its longevity.[47]

It seems that testamentary dispositions in Thera, as in Halicarnassus, possibly experienced potential problems with the continuous subsidy of the cult. For this reason, further provisions were taken to counter possible mismanagement in the long term. Even if space was well protected, as we will see further below, it was thanks to the regular flow of financial resources that the gathering of the association could become materialised. Indeed, both Epikteta's testament and the decree of the association went to great lengths to ensure the financial security of the dispositions. Alternate ways to annually hand over the amount of 210 drachmas to the *koinon* were envisaged by Epikteta. The *koinon* was entitled to the usufruct (καρπεία, l. 72) of designated lands up to the value of 210 drachmas (ll. 71–5). Otherwise, Epiteleia's successors had the option to transfer the initial capital of 3,000 drachmas that was bound to properties owned by Epikteta to another property (ll. 75–9). Likewise, the *koinon* appointed officials in charge of financial matters (the ἐπίσσοφος and ἀρτυτήρ) along with personnel commissioned to enhance the available funds (through the credit business: ἐγδανεισταί).[48]

So far, we have seen that Poseidonios' dossier placed emphasis on issues related to management of the property in order to ensure the subsidy of the cult, while Epikteta was also preoccupied with the annual remittance to the association of a fixed amount for the three-day celebration. However, Epikteta's dossier as well as that of Diomedon, unlike Poseidonios' dossier, went a step further in laying out stipulations that prevent any alienation of the meeting-place or any other inappropriate management or use of the place in question.

Diomedon's testamentary dispositions did not only regulate the protection of the property and the use of space but also laid out provisions for repair works. The inclusion of clauses that refer to repair works clearly demonstrate Diomedon's vision of the longevity of the association and the

---

[47] It seems that she succeeded, as a fragmentary inscription that dates to the late second or early first century BC attests to the *koinon* of the relatives: *IG* XII Suppl. 154, l. 11; cf. *CAPInv.* 1645. However, the attribution of this inscription to the *koinon* of the relatives founded by Epikteta has been a contested issue. Kamps 1937: 166–8 and Wittenburg 1990: 65 no 9 rejected Hiller von Gaertringen's attribution on the same grounds on which Hiller von Gaertringen 1914: 133–4 suggested this attribution, that is, on onomastics. Although the inscriptions are not contemporaneous – Epikteta's foundation dates one generation earlier – the overlap in the name of the association and in the members would speak in favour of one and the same association, especially in a small community like Thera.

[48] Wittenburg 1990: 103–9; Campanelli 2016: 179; *CAPInv.* 1645.

continuous use of space. Repair works had already been anticipated in the first inscription, and their funding was clearly laid out. There, it was stipulated that expenditure for the maintenance of the *oikemata* and the *temenos* was to be covered by the revenues from leasing (*IG* XII.4 1 348 III, ll. 47–51). In particular, income derived from renting out the garden (κῆπος) to the freedman, Libys, and his children, who were set free by Diomedon's consecration. They were obliged to pay the rent in the month prior to the annual feast in honour of Heracles (ll. 11–17). The financing of repair works was evidently still a matter of some worry in the early third century BC when the third text was inscribed on the pillar. In the third text, the efforts to define once again the potential source of funding for the refurbishment of the buildings and the maintenance of the *temenos*, this time in more detail, reveal concerns of what was considered the most appropriate use of space.[49] In particular, the rules sought to underscore the proper handling of finances for the benefit of the association and the importance of the upkeep of the place as essential prerequisites for the performance of cult activity.

Diomedon's dossier is particularly instructive in that it shows that the implementation of rules could prove a thorny issue and that self-appropriation by members posed a real threat. Space was not only carefully regulated but clarifications and complementary regulations had to be added to ensure the proper management and use of space as initially envisaged by Diomedon. Unlike Epikteta's dossier where these regulations were part of the testamentary dispositions and recorded as such in stone, in Diomedon's dossier direct resonances to the testament are made in regulations inscribed on the stone in later decades.[50] Diomedon's dossier is particularly instructive as to the ways in which the testament of the founder could be re-invoked to prevent future misuse. The third text in particular includes direct quotations of Diomedon's testament, an indication that it was in the association's interest to observe the stipulations laid out therein. At the same time, the testament as a legal document would offer a legal justification of the steps taken by the association in order to effectively protect its interests and, by extension, to ensure its longevity. It served to maintain its identity, which was intimately related to the

---

[49] Revenues accruing from the lease of the *temenos*, the garden and the guest houses were to be allocated, as was necessary, to the repair of these aforementioned structures, as well to the repair of the house (*oikia*) in the *temenos* (*IG* XII.4 1 348 III ll. 69–77).

[50] The third text uses first person singular forms (ll. 120, 155: ἀνέθηκα) as well as second person plural forms (l. 115 παρασκευᾶτε, l. 149: λαμβάνετε), as if Diomedon himself were speaking.

uninterrupted performance of cult and ritual once a year in the best possible conditions.

Originally, the regulations were concerned with prohibiting any appropriation (ἐξιδιάζεσθαι) of the *oikemata* and the *temenos*, as well as forbidding their sale and mortgage (ll. 43–7). In the early third century BC, Diomedon's descendants included three further prohibitions (ll. 80–6): to the members of the group (l. 81: τοῖς κοινωνοῦσι τῶν ἱερῶγ) it was prohibited (1) to cultivate the lands; (2) to dwell in the guest houses and the *oikia* in the *temenos*; and (3) to use the hall (λέσχη) in the sanctuary and the covered walk (περίπατος) as a storage facility, except during wartime. These further prohibitions help considerably to elucidate the content of the first prohibition in Diomedon's consecration (the first text), in other words, the content of the infinitive ἐξιδιάζεσθαι ('to appropriate for oneself').[51] In this regard, they should not be viewed as totally new prohibitions, but instead as further clarifications to the already existing regulations, with the aim of further ensuring their implementation.

In fact, some sort of alienation of property does seem to have occurred over the course of time: in the third inscription, we hear of individuals who owned houses in the sacred precinct.[52] Private possession of these *oikiai* would have taken place at a stage posterior to Diomedon's consecration, since they were originally and explicitly consecrated to Heracles Diomedonteios and thus constituted sacred property.[53] If this change in ownership is correct, then clarifying the question of what was meant by 'appropriation' would aim at preventing further misuse and mishandling of the property. The text, however, does not yield any direct evidence of possible disputes between the descendants of Diomedon over issues of property, albeit some hints of this alienation are perhaps perceptible. It is simply taken for granted that among the group, there were those who now possessed houses. In clarifying the content of 'appropriation', it seems that the concern now shifts from property management to the use of the properties. The text stipulates that both houses in question have to be

---

[51] *IG* XII.4 1 348 III Face C ll. 80–86: μὴ ἐξέσ|στω δὲ τοῖς κοινωνοῦσι τῶν ἱερῶγ [γε]|ωργεῖν τὰ τεμένη μηδ᾽ ἐν τοῖς ξε[νῶσι] | ἐνοικεῖν μηδ᾽ ἐν τῆι οἰκίαι τῆι ἐπὶ τ[οῦ τε]|μένευς μηδὲ ἀποθήκηι χρᾶσθαι τῆ[ι λέσ]|χηι τῆι ἐν τῶι ἱερῶι μηδὲ {ν} τῶι περιπάτωι | ἂμ μὴ πόλεμος ἦι.

[52] *IG* XII.4 1 348 III Face C ll. 104–5: οἱ τὰς οἰκίας ἐκτ[η]|μένοι, the men's house (ἀνδρεία οἰκία) and the women's house (γυναικεία οἰκία).

[53] This view has been put forward by Bosnakis and Hallof; cf. *CGRN* 96. Campanelli, following Dittenberger (*Syll.*³ 1106 n. 34), has envisaged a different scenario according to which 'the two houses had been inherited by some of Diomedon's descendants in their private capacity' (Campanelli 2016: 161).

made available for the celebration of weddings.[54] Furthermore, the men's house would also be made available during the festival of the group – the Herakleia – providing the venue to host the sacrifice and banquet to Heracles.[55] In other words, it is in the early third century BC that regulations about the use of specific buildings in the precinct were introduced for the first time. These apparently new regulations compelled the owners of these buildings to make available the listed property for common use at fixed times. Most important, in the time span of a few decades since Diomedon's consecration, his descendants took steps to lay out once again rules pertaining to the management of realty and, in addition, to dictate the way in which a number of buildings were to be used. Already in the second inscription it is regulated that the statues (ἀγάλματα) and votive offerings (ἀναθήματα) were to remain in the exact same place in the οἰκία where they stood (ll. 55–9). The following possible scenarios can readily be envisaged. Displacement and/or removal of statues and offerings was somehow anticipated or had occurred and it thus had to be prohibited. Alternatively, the space was becoming crowded with dedications, and for this reason the descendants of Diomedon wanted to ensure that the setting up of dedications in the future would not happen at the detriment of existing ones.[56]

Similar prohibitions towards the handling and use of space are to be found in Epikteta's testamentary dispositions, especially with regard to potential problems with the use of space. Epikteta laid out a number of regulations that aimed to preserve the integrity of the space and maintain its function. The prohibitions follow standard legal practice when it comes to the protection of property.[57] Specifically, the following is prohibited: (1) to sell the sanctuary and the *temenos* of the heroes along with the statues erected there; (2) to put it down as a mortgage; (3) to exchange it; (4) to alienate it; (5) to build up the *temenos* and (6) to use the sanctuary of the

[54] *IG* XII.4 1 348 III Face C ll. 104–8: καὶ οἱ τὰς οἰκίας ἐκτ[η]|μένοι τήν τε ἀνδρείαν καὶ τὴν γυναικ[εί]|αν παρεχόντω εἰς τοὺς γάμους τὰς οἰκ[ί]|ας παρεξελόμενοι οἰκήματα εἰς ἀπόθε|σιν τῶν σκευῶν.
[55] *IG* XII.4 1 348 III Face C ll. 108–11: ὁ δὲ τὴν ἀνδρείαν ἔχων|[π]αρεχέτω τὴν οἰκίαν καὶ εἰς τὴν θυσί|[αν κα]ὶ τὸν ξενισμὸν τοῦ Ἡρακλ[εῦς πάσας | τὰς ἡμ]έρας.
[56] In Greek sanctuaries, the display of offerings was sometimes a matter of regulation, at least when it came to areas that were prohibited from holding offerings, as happened in the *Asklepieion* in Rhodes (*SER* 1; cf. Harris 2015: 73). In other instances, overcrowding could also be a matter of concern, as can be seen in the privately owned sanctuary of Sarapis in Laodicea by the Sea (Sosin 2005).
[57] Similar stipulations, e.g. sale, mortgage, alteration, alienation, are attested in testaments for funerary monuments from Roman Asia Minor: see Harter-Uibopuu 2010: 257–61.

Muses in any other way.[58] The association was granted full power to act against anyone who would commit any of the above offences. Any trespass against these clauses would undermine the association itself. Failure to convene in the *Mouseion* would negate the original purpose that brought this association into being: a three-day celebration in honour of the Muses and the heroised dead.

The only exception allowed concerning further building in the *temenos* was the construction of a stoa (ll. 49–50). Its addition would have remarkably uplifted the sanctuary of the Muses, in that stoas were usually expected to be found in sanctuaries or public spaces frequented by many and on a regular basis.[59] Such an investment in the construction of a monumental structure was accordingly viewed as beneficial, facilitating the gathering of the association and its three-day festivities. It reveals the aspirations of the association and underlines its longevity. At its inception, the association already consisted of at least sixty members.[60]

As already noted in the case of Diomedon, the way in which space was to be used was well defined. Possible uses other than the ones prescribed are explicitly mentioned. In the last section of Diomedon's stele, we hear that weddings of impoverished male members of the family could be held right after the end of the feast.[61] A similar notable exception to the prescribed use of space is also noted in Epikteta's dossier, namely, the permission to celebrate in the *Mouseion* the wedding of members from Epiteleia's side of the family.[62] In Diomedon's dossier, details are also provided with regard to the buildings (ἀνδρεία οἰκία, γυναικεία οἰκία) that were to be used for the needs of the ceremony. In this case, different aspects of life pertaining to the group were consciously entwined; though the setting remained the same – the *Mouseion* in Thera, the *temenos* consecrated by Diomedon on Cos – the function of the space was expanded to encompass other activities, such as weddings. These activities, not necessarily related to ritual activity, sacrifice and dining in honour of the heroised dead, effectively demonstrate the course of life in the

---

[58] *IG* XII.3 330, ll. 41–51: μὴ ἐχέτω [δὲ ἐξου]|σίαν μηθεὶς μήτε ἀποδόσθαι τὸ Μουσεῖον [μή]|τε τὸ τέμενος τῶν ἡρώιων μηδὲ τῶν ἀγαλ|μάτων τῶν ἐν τῶι Μουσείωι μηδὲ τῶν ἐν | τῶι τεμένει τῶν ἡρώιων μηθὲν μήτε κατα|θέμεν μήτε διαλλάξασθαι μήτε ἐξαλλο|τριῶσαι τρόπωι μηθενὶ μηδὲ παρευρέσει | μηδεμιᾶι μηδὲ ἐνοικοδομῆσαι ἐν τῶι τε|μένει μηθέν, εἴ κα μή τις στοὰν οἰκοδομῆσαι | προαιρεῖται, μηδὲ χρῆσαι τὸ Μουσεῖον μηθενί, | εἴ κα μή τις τῶν ἐξ Ἐπιτελείας γάμον ποιῇ.
[59] Free-standing stoas were a frequent and almost indispensable feature in many Greek sanctuaries. On Greek stoas, see Coulton 1976; on stoas in sanctuaries in particular, see Hellmann 2006: 212–18.
[60] Stavrianopoulou 2006: 295. [61] *IG* XII.4 1 348, ll. 104–11.
[62] *IG* XII.3 330, l. 51: εἴ κα μή τις τῶν ἐξ Ἐπιτελείας γάμον ποιῇ.

microcosm of an association. It was fundamental for these groups to facilitate and participate in core events that marked the life of members and especially families, such as weddings. In this respect, the multitude of experiences in the same architectural setting further enhanced the attachment of the association to its specific locale and its sense of belonging. It formed a nexus for the group as a whole and especially for the expression of interrelated familial and cultic bonds.

To summarise, the founders – especially Epikteta and Diomedon – went into detail when defining the meeting-place of the association, prohibiting any mismanagement or use other than the one envisaged by them. In the detailed instructions of the three dossiers, space emerges as a dynamic concept whose physical articulation, use and management, was the object of careful regulation. The close regulation of space is intricately linked with the regulation of membership into the group. The founder envisaged that the identity of the association should be anchored to a specific place. This place sets the stage for the ritual activity that brings the association together. At the same time, place creates boundaries, explicitly materialised in terms of membership. Only members were allowed to take part in the annual celebration, and in this respect the ritual space was only open to members or to what Scott, discussing other instances, has called 'communities of permitted users'.[63] Only members could experience associational space as a sacred space or as a privileged space for 'family' members on certain occasions. By becoming a 'community of permitted users', members developed an intimate attachment to a place that, in turn, informed their identity as members of a familial association.

It can be noted that in all three cases the founders were fully aware of the inextricable link between the finances of the cult and the longevity of the association. The place where the association came together was the place where the ritual was performed. In other words, cult and association are grounded in a specific locale, explicitly spelled out in all three dossiers. Ritual was directed at different gods and/or ancestors, an aspect that further accentuates the uniqueness of an association, differentiating it from other groups.[64] The re-enactment of ritual activity once a year at a prescribed time imbued the place with special meaning: a sacred space as

---

[63] Scott 2013: 11.

[64] According to Assmann 2011: 23, there are two main factors that help sustain the cultural memory of a group; peculiarity and durability. The associations discussed in this section fulfil these two criteria.

well as a place of familial unity and ancestral commemoration.[65] The visual articulation of space with statues of the heroised dead, statues of deities and other votive offering further vested the space with special symbolism in this regard. Moreover, the founding act and/or the testamentary dispositions were monumentally displayed within the association's space in the form of a pedestal for statues (Thera), a pillar (Cos) or a stele (Halicarnassus), another prominent visual reminder of the role of the association in fostering a set of traditions within a specific locale.[66] Any dislocation would dramatically break this mnemonic link to place and would threaten the very existence of the association.

Identity and Dislocation from Space

Any circumstance that would prevent an association from gathering in its meeting-place could also potentially disrupt its activities and undermine its *raison d'être*. The *thiasitai* of Dionysus in Cyme were faced with such a reality in the early years of Augustus' reign.[67] A bilingual letter of the proconsul of Asia in Latin and partly in Greek (the stele is broken) sent to the local authorities in Cyme outlines the efforts of the *thiasitai* of Dionysus. They initiated a legal process to regain access to the sanctuary and resume control of its affairs.

The sanctuary had been mortgaged (ll. 13, 25–6) and ownership had passed to an individual (Lysias). The *thiasitai* approached Lysias to pay him back in their attempt to reclaim the sanctuary for themselves, but their claim was refuted. They therefore appealed to the proconsul through an intermediary, a citizen of Cyme (Apollonides, son of Lucius Norakeios). They claimed that they wanted to restore the cult (l. 15, *sacra*) to the god. Their claim found a legal footing in the edict of the consuls Augustus and Agrippa. Issued in 27 BC, the edict stipulated the restitution of public and sacred properties as well as dedications, which were subject to looting during the period of the civil wars (ll. 1–11). The proconsul therefore redirected the case to the local authorities to solve the issue. The *thiasitai* had the full support of the proconsul who, citing the legal precedent of the edict, was favourably disposed towards the restoration of the shrine to the

---

[65] As Mylonopoulos 2011: 57–9 has argued, two essential components of sacred space are architectural setting and the performance of ritual.

[66] Pedestal: H. 45.4 × L. 284.9 × W. 7.7–8.5 cm; pillar: H. 65 × W. 34 × Th. 24 cm; stele: H. 95.57 × L. 33.66–36.6 × Th. 12–12.7 cm.

[67] *IKyme* 17; *RDGE* no 61; Jaccottet 2003: no 104; Harland 2014: no 104; Dignas 2002: 121–6; see also *CAPInv.* 954.

god.[68] Although the outcome of the case is not recorded in the inscription, it can be safely guessed that it was resolved to the advantage of the *thiasitai*.[69]

For Pleket, this is a case of a public *thiasos* of Dionysus,[70] unlike Engelmann who takes the *thiasitai* to be a private association.[71] In my view, the scale tips towards the latter, for the *thiasitai*, even after being prohibited to access the shrine and perform the due rites to the god, retained a strong sense of identity and took corporate action by appealing to the proconsul through a representative. Before the unfortunate loss of the shrine, it seems that they used the shrine as a revenue-bearing property, probably for the subsidy of the cult, a practice attested in groups of *orgeones* in Athens or in the case of Diomedon and Poseidonios discussed above.[72] In Cyme too, it can be envisaged that the mortgage of the shrine brought to the *thiasitai* a steady income for the performance of cult; yet unfortunate events or mismanagement resulted in the loss of both income and access to the shrine. It was therefore vital for the *thiasitai* as a group to pull all their efforts together in order to reclaim the shrine. This shrine embodied the *locus* of their identity and their shared ritual experiences.

Inclusive Spaces: Opening up a Sanctuary to Non-Associates

In the cases presented above, it has been argued that place works as a formative element in the creation of the association's identity, creating a closed circle for ritual performance and cultic activity, which are both anchored in a specific locale. To maintain this exclusivity and to guarantee the longevity of the association, the administration and the use of space were closely regulated. However, these cases constitute only snapshots of a picture that is much more diverse and varied than they may otherwise suggest. The three cases of familial groups (Diomedon, Poseidonios and Epikteta) represent one end of the spectrum where both membership and attachment to a specific place have been shown to be exclusive. The richness of the evidence for associations, however, paints a picture with many different gradations between inclusivity and exclusivity.

---

[68] A telltale sign is that the proconsul explicitly pointed out that, if the sanctuary was restored to the god (*restituat deo fa\[num]*), he wanted the following to be inscribed in the sanctuary: 'Augustus restored it' (ll. 18–20: *Imp(erator) Caesar deivei f. Augustu[s] re[sti\tuit]*.

[69] Cf. also Oliver 1963: 121.   [70] Pleket 1958: 60. See also Oliver 1963: 121.

[71] Engelmann 1976: 54 and 57.

[72] On the *orgeones* and their leasing activities, see Papazarkadas 2011: ch. 4.3.

No matter how anchored an association was to a place, this attachment does not always suffice to demonstrate the inclusivity or exclusivity of the group or even how inclusive or exclusive this place would have been. In a number of cases, what appears to be inclusive or exclusive is the cult. This raises the question about the motivation or benefit of opening up the cult to non-associates. Moreover, if a certain degree of openness is attested for the cult, would different attitudes to the use and management of space be expected?

A law passed by the *orgeones* of Bendis in the last third of the fourth century BC underlines their involvement in the administration and management of the shrine.[73] The text contains regulations stipulating the financing of the repair of the shrine and the property (*oikia*) rented out by the *orgeones*. It also distinguishes between members and non-members and accordingly sets out different regulations for each group with regard to sacrifices to the goddess.[74] *Orgeones* who performed sacrifices to the goddess were exempted from any fees (l. 3 ἀτελεῖς), unlike a private individual (l. 4 ἰδιώτης) who had to abide by what the law prescribed. More specifically, in sacrifices performed by individuals, the goddess as well as the priest or priestess were entitled to perquisites that are clearly laid out in the text.[75] Apparently, then, non-*orgeones* were allowed to enter the shrine in their capacity as worshippers and make a sacrifice as long as they observed the relevant regulations.[76] This inclusivity of cult comes hand in hand with a wish by the *orgeones* for a broad-based membership or as stated in the inscription 'so that there may be as many *orgeones* of the *hieron* as possible' (ll. 20–1). As Vincent Gabrielsen has put it: 'shrine-participation (μετουσία) was the cardinal factor that drew the dividing line between members – "those who share in the *hieron*" (οἱ μέτεστιν τοῦ ἱεροῦ) – and non-members (ἰδιῶται)'. By passing this law, the *orgeones* made explicit the benefits of membership. The two sets of rules for sacrifices (one for members and one for non-members) can thus be considered an effective device for making membership attractive to non-members. By extension, a broad-based membership could augment the prestige of the cult. In the inscription, a 2 drachma contribution is mentioned for sacrifices on the occasion of the festival of the goddess.[77] If the finances of the festival came

---

[73] *IG* II² 1361.   [74] *IG* II² 1361, ll. 2–6.   [75] *IG* II² 1361, ll. 4–7.
[76] Gabrielsen 2016a: 145.
[77] Members were obliged to contribute 2 drachmas to the *hieropoioi* (ll. 17–19) before the 16th of Thargelion.

from membership contributions, then a broad-based membership would serve to more adequately maintain the cult.

The phrase '*orgeones* of the *hieron*' should not pass unnoticed. The identity of the *orgeones* is tied to their shrine and the activities performed therein.[78] In this regard, it was even more in their interest to keep the cult alive and to please the goddess in any way possible. It demonstrates that the significance of the place for creating and retaining identity did not diminish even if non-members had access to this place. The *orgeones* were not simply worshippers but managers of the affairs of the goddess.

The case of the *orgeones* of Bendis clearly shows that the openness of a cult, if properly regulated, could serve the interests of the association. Two more cases are particularly instructive in this respect, as they present features of inclusivity regarding the cult. In these two cases the cult is that of healing deities: Amphiaraus at Rhamnous in Attica and Asclepius at Yaylakale in Mysia.

The earliest of the two is that of the *Amphieraistai* in Rhamnous, an Attic deme and an important fort in north-eastern Attica.[79] The association came into being at the initiative of a soldier. As the prosopography of the membership demonstrates, members were predominantly fellow soldiers of the garrison.[80] As its name reveals, the association was centred around the cult of Amphiaraus, a healing hero, who also had a major shrine at neighbouring Oropos.[81] A sanctuary of Amphiaraus has been located a few hundred metres south of the fort at Rhamnous. By the time the association came into being, the sanctuary had gone into disuse and the cult had likely been discontinued.[82] By opening a subscription and thanks to generous contributions, the members of the association restored the sanctuary, while at the same time securing the subsidy of the cult in the form of an endowment.[83] In the inscription, it is stated explicitly that the *Amphieraistai* restored the sanctuary so that anyone who wished could participate in the cult.[84] Although membership in the association seems to have been restricted to soldiers and members, participation in the cult was open to non-associates. The primary preoccupation of the *Amphieraistai* was the revival and perpetuation of the cult. In this respect, a community of worshippers that would guarantee the performance of cult was of equal

---

[78] Gabrielsen 2016a: 144–5. [79] *I.Rhamnous* 167 = *CAPInv.* 356; Oetjen 2014: 160–2.

[80] For the prosopography see Petrakos 1999b: 167; Arnaoutoglou 2011b: 41; Skaltsa 2016: 83–6.

[81] For the cult see Petrakos 1999a: 319. [82] *I.Rhamnous* 167, ll. 2–6.

[83] *I.Rhamnous* 167, ll. 10–21.

[84] *I.Rhamnous* 167, ll. 8–10: ὅπως ἂν ἐπι|σκευασθέντων τούτων τῶι θεῶι ἔχωσι χρᾶσθαι κοινεῖ πάν|τες οἱ βουλόμενοι τῶι ἱερῶι.

importance to the subsidy of the cult, which the *Amphieraistai* sought to
guarantee. Without opening up the cult to non-associates, the efforts of
the *Amphieraistai*, an association predominantly consisting of soldiers,
would, following the removal of the garrison to another fort, be doomed
to failure. In this case, then, what was of paramount importance was to
regulate the financial backing of the cult and not necessarily issues of
accessibility or management of space.

A similar attitude with regard to the openness of the cult can be detected
in another instance of a healing cult, in the hinterland of the Pergamene
kingdom. On a plateau ca. 30 km to the south-east of Pergamum, in
Yaylakale, an association of *Asklepiastai* came into being under the initiative of Demetrios, a *phrourachos* (commander of a fortress) in the first half
of the second century BC.[85] The association was composed of fifteen
members, including the founder, with family ties noticeable among some
of the members.[86] Given the military office of Demetrios, the onomastics
of the members, as well as the strategic position of the location along the
route to NW Lydia, the *Asklepiastai* were probably members of the
garrison stationed there.[87] Unlike the *Amphieraistai* who restored a sanctuary fallen into disuse, Demetrios founded a new sanctuary (ἱερόν),
which, as the name of the association reveals, was dedicated to Asclepius.
It appears that the cult of healing deities, like Asclepius or Amphiaraus,
appealed to some degree to soldiers.[88]

The case of the *Asklepiastai* at Yaylakale becomes even more interesting
due to another inscription,[89] which was found in the neighbouring area of
Yala and which, as Müller has shown, should be read in conjunction with
the inscription attesting to the foundation of the shrine and the formation
of the *Asklepiastai*.[90] This inscription refers to rules for entry into a
sanctuary, to be identified with the one founded by Demetrios. The

[85] Ed. pr. Müller 2010: 427–40; *SEG* 60:1332. See also *CAPInv.* 857. Associations of *Asklepiastai* are
   sometimes found in state-administered sanctuaries of Asclepius, as can be inferred by the honorific
   decree for Alkibiades son of Herakleides from Thorikos set up by the *Asklepiastai* in Athens (*IG* II²
   1293 = *CAPInv.* 323); the stele containing the decree was found on the south slope of the Acropolis
   and has been attributed by Aleshire 1989: 68–70 to the nearby Athenian *Asklepieion*. For other
   attestations of *Asklepiastai*, see Müller 2010: 428 n. 1.
[86] Müller 2010: 435.   [87] Müller 2010: 428–40.
[88] The observation in Müller 2010: 437 that the cult of Asclepius was rather unusual among soldiers
   on account of the paucity of evidence may need to be revisited. In light of the inscription from
   Rhamnous discussed here (above), the epigraphic evidence shows that soldiers exhibited a certain
   interest in the cult of healing deities.
[89] Müller 2010: 440–7; *SEG* 60:1333.
[90] The survey conducted in the area where the stele was found revealed scarce architectural remains,
   but no other inscription came to light.

inscription is partly preserved; lines 1–12 regulate entry into the shrine (εἰς τὸ ἱερόν). All clauses refer to requirements pertaining to purity. In order to attain a satisfactory degree of purity, worshippers had to abstain from sexual intercourse and wash themselves thoroughly, stay away from a corpse and funeral for two days, and so on. The text also provides insights into the architectural setting of the sanctuary. As expected for a healing sanctuary, an incubation hall (ἐνκοιμητήριον) features in the text,[91] which stood in the vicinity of the sanctuary (ll. 13–14, παρὰ τὸ ἱερόν).[92] The sanctuary in Yaylakale was not only open to all those observing the purity regulations but was also equipped with the facilities needed for the development of the therapeutic aspect of the cult.[93]

The measures concerning purification resonate with regulations observed in other sanctuaries, most notably in the sanctuaries of Asclepius and Athena in Pergamum.[94] They therefore comply with practices attested in the capital of the Pergamene kingdom. It is, however, the authority laying out the rules that differs in this case: the founder of a private association. As a commander of the fort, Demetrios must have had close ties to the royal court. At any rate, he was acting as a representative of the royal power. By founding an association devoted to the cult of Asclepius, one of the major deities fostered by the Attalid rulers, he thus promoted a cult endorsed by the kings in the hinterland of the Pergamene territory, and at the same time he significantly enriched the religious life of members of the garrison as well as those living in the vicinity of the fort.[95]

The purity rules do not touch upon membership or management of space. In other words, these rules, though set out by the association and set up in a sanctuary founded by private initiative, do not aim at regulating membership but instead at opening up the cult to anyone who would observe them. Though membership of the association may have been fixed and internally controlled with a certain degree of exclusivity – namely, by being open only to members of the local garrison – a degree of inclusivity is therefore attested in the cult practice. And although the regulations aim at ensuring that worshippers have attained a state of purity before entering the sanctuary, their ultimate objective is nevertheless the health of the

---

[91] The building type of the *enkoimeterion* is far from standardised, see von Ehrenheim 2015: 79–86 with bibliography.

[92] Müller 2010: 446.   [93] See also Carbon in Chapter 4.

[94] Müller 2010: 446 notes the similarities with the regulations of the *Asklepieion* of Pergamum, while Carbon in Chapter 4 extends the comparison to the regulations of the sanctuary of Athena in Pergamum and offers an in-depth analysis of the purification measures.

[95] On the issue of cults endorsed both by the kings and the army, see Chaniotis 2002: 108–9.

worshipper (ll. 3–4: ὑγίας ἕνεκεν). Needless to say, worshippers would come to this sanctuary with a view to seeking healing from disease. The regulations would act as a reminder that cleanliness was required and certain sources of pollution had to be avoided. In light of the healing aspect of the cult (Asclepius) and the purity measures, it should not come as a surprise that in this case the regulations focus on health, a different virtue than the orderly behaviour or good order that might otherwise be expected of associations.[96] However, the phrase ὑγίας ἕνεκεν as such is quite exceptional, with no direct parallel in the corpus of purity regulations.[97] Inscriptions containing purity regulations were displayed in order to ensure ritual purity of the shrine in question.[98] In this respect, observance of regulations ensured that space would maintain its status that set it aside from other places: an unpolluted sacred space. In this case, however, observance of regulations had a dual objective, namely, to ensure the health of individual worshippers seeking help from the healing deity as well as the overall purity of sacred space.

Conclusions

The polis regulated the use of space in a range of places and institutions, from the agora and the gymnasium to the sanctuary, appointing civic or religious officials to attend to issues of propriety, upkeep of good order and avoidance of alienation, encroachment or misuse of space.[99] Regulations could take a wide array of material manifestations, from boundary stones demarcating the use of land to stelae bearing regulations pertaining to a number of issues such as purity measures, the exclusion of certain groups of people or opening and closing times.[100] As space preoccupied civic authorities, so its management and use raised concerns among associations too.

---

[96] See Gabrielsen and Paganini in Chapter 1.   [97] See also Müller 2010: 443.

[98] Lupu 2005: 14–21.

[99] For example, the law of the *astynomoi* in Pergamum, a second-century AD inscription that seems to have been passed during the reign of the Attalids, regulates issues ranging from water management to house planning (*OGIS* 483; for a commentary see Saba 2012).

[100] Different criteria of exclusion were applied depending on the space in question; in the case of the Athenian Agora, segregation could be exerted on the principle of gender (Just 1989: 105–25) and/ or political rights (Hansen 1976: 61–70), while in the case of a sanctuary of a mystery cult, such as the sanctuary of the Great Gods in Samothrace, non-initiates were not permitted access (*SEG* 12:395). Gymnasia were regulated by laws; two extant laws come from northern Greece: the gymnasiarchic law of Beroia (see Gauthier and Hatzopoulos 1993) and the ephebarchic law of Amphipolis (Lazaridou 2015 = *SEG* 65:420). The gymnasiarchic law forbids access to slaves, freedmen, the physically unfit (*apalaistroi*), male prostitutes, charlatans, drunkards and madmen.

It has been shown that familial associations with their orderly and closed membership created well-ordered spaces, going to great lengths to regulate the management and use of space. It has been argued that a primary reason for this is that space and the attachment to a place constituted a core feature of their identity. Exclusivity in the associations from Cos, Thera and Halicarnassus is perceptible in several features of the groups, from their membership profile (relatives, real or fictive) and cultic activity to the construction of space. The meeting-place as a physical space underlined a distinction between insiders (members) and outsiders (non-members), and in this respect it created a 'community of users'. Moreover, as a sacred space, it provided the locale for the cultivation of cognitive (memory) and social/emotional bonds between members through sharing in common traditions and cultic activity. Attachment to place fostered a sense of belonging, created physical and conceptual boundaries and embodied a special meaning ascribed to it by means of ritual and performance. In these respects, the meeting-places in Cos, Thera and Halicarnassus became mnemonic places, constructed to evoke memories and foster a specific identity, that of an associate who played tribute to real or fictive ancestors and worshipped certain gods.[101]

How much place was charged with emotional as well as material meaning for the identity of the association becomes manifest in cases of detachment from this space. Management of space, especially as a revenue-bearing property, entailed some risks, especially in cases in which the property was mortgaged. This happened with the shrine of Dionysus in Cyme: the *thiasitai* were expelled from the shrine by a certain Lysias who assumed ownership of the place. Yet despite the dislocation, it was the place itself as a sacred space that remained a point of reference for the group. It sought to reinstate its rights and reaffirm its identity by taking collective action to restore the sanctuary to the god.

Associations centred on the cult of healing deities, among others, show that sanctuaries managed by associations could be open to non-members. These cases present us with different attitudes to space and its regulation. The *orgeones* of Bendis had two sets of rules, one for members and one for

---

[101] Regulations pertaining to the prescribed use of space in relation to commemorative activities go back to the Archaic period. For instance, in late archaic Paros, a funeral pyre demarcated by boundary stones constituted a focus of commemorative activity for a phratry, which sought to retain the original function of this space by introducing a regulation that forbade the use of the area of the funeral pyre for private burials and funerary monuments (Matthaiou 2000–3; *SEG* 51:1071). Cf. also the boundary stone from Cymae that prohibits burial to the non-initiated to the Dionysiac mysteries: *LSCG Suppl.* 120; *SEG* 4:92.

non-members, when it came to sacrifices. In doing so, they underlined the benefits of membership, the latter open to whoever wanted to share in the cult. The *Amphieraistai* in Rhamnous and the *Asklepiastai* in Yaylakale restored or built shrines, not only for themselves, but also for the benefit of non-members who wished to partake in the cult. When studied together, the epigraphic evidence from these two sites outlines a fuller picture. Whereas the *Amphieraistai* took measures to ensure the subsidy of the cult, the *Asklepiastai* were more particularly concerned with the sanctity of space and its function as a place of healing – regulations are addressed to the community of worshippers, not only to members. Of prime concern was the health of the worshippers and, by extension, of the sanctuary as a community of worshippers, a virtue that could be achieved through the observance of purity measures.

Overall, the analysis offered here illustrates some aspects that pertain to the exclusivity or inclusivity of space. In the diverse body of evidence for ancient associations, we alternately find a looser or closer attachment to a place. For instance, groups of *orgeones* could meet just once a year and rent out their private property for the remainder.[102] The *Iobacchoi* in Athens, on the other hand, met on a regular basis in their *Backheion*, namely, monthly and on other specific occasions.[103] Still other groups were associated with a public sanctuary or a sanctuary open to the public.[104] For instance, three different associations are attested in the sanctuary of Pankrates in Athens in the third century BC.[105] Although their organisational structure and longevity escape us, this sanctuary apparently provided a fertile ground for the co-existence and interaction among these associations.

It has been argued that the control and ownership of the place, or lack thereof, as well as the type of place and its use (tomb, house, clubhouse or larger sanctuary), matter crucially. By looking closely at regulations and the attachments of associations to place, it has been suggested that we can shift emphasis from a focus on propriety and order to consider other important aspects of associations as well-ordered societies, such as their varying degrees of exclusivity and inclusivity or even the promotion of virtues like good health. Though archaeological remains of meeting-places of associations may continue to be elusive, the concept of space in the study of

---

[102] Papazarkadas 2011: 191–7.   [103] The *Iobacchoi* are discussed by Arnaoutoglou in Chapter 6.
[104] For the case of the *Bakchoi* in Cnidus, see Carbon in Chapter 4.
[105] The relevant inscriptions remain largely unpublished but references to *SEG* provide the names of the associations in question: *eranistai* (*SEG* 41:82 and 171); *koinon* of *thiasotai* (*SEG* 41:83); *orgeones* (*SEG* 41:84).

associations proves to be anything but static. Instead, intermittently contested and reinstated, it was being shaped by and at the same time was shaping the activities and experiences of the collectivity. Even in cases where an association became unmoored from its physical setting, place/space continued to inform the identity of the group. While the overall picture drawn from the epigraphic record is not uniform regarding the precise mechanisms involved in the regulation and use of space, nevertheless, space abidingly provided the locale for reunion, unity and cohesion among the collectivity.

CHAPTER 6

Greek thorybos, *Roman* eustatheia

The Normative Universe of Athenian Cult Associations[*]

Ilias Arnaoutoglou

In 330 BC, Demosthenes in his reply to the *graphe paranomon* brought by Aeschines six years earlier against the proposal of Ctesiphon to honour Demosthenes, launched a virulent attack on Aeschines, adducing a description of the activities of young Aeschines as follows:

> ἐν δὲ ταῖς ἡμέραις τοὺς καλοὺς θιάσους ἄγων διὰ τῶν ὁδῶν, τοὺς ἐστεφανωμένους τῷ μαράθῳ καὶ τῇ λεύκῃ, τοὺς ὄφεις τοὺς παρείας θλίβων καὶ ὑπὲρ τῆς κεφαλῆς αἰωρῶν, καὶ βοῶν 'εὐοῖ σαβοῖ,' καὶ ἐπορχούμενος 'ὑῆς ἄττης ἄττης ὑῆς,' ἔξαρχος καὶ προηγεμὼν καὶ κιττοφόρος καὶ λικνοφόρος καὶ τοιαῦθ᾽ ὑπὸ τῶν γρᾳδίων προσαγορευόμενος, μισθὸν λαμβάνων τούτων ἔνθρυπτα καὶ στρεπτοὺς καὶ νεήλατα, ἐφ᾽ οἷς τίς οὐκ ἂν ὡς ἀληθῶς αὐτὸν εὐδαιμονίσειε καὶ τὴν αὐτοῦ τύχην;

> By day you led brilliant bands of reveling worshipers through the streets. They wore crowns of fennel and white poplar as you clutched fat-headed snakes and swung them over your head. You would shout 'Euoi Saboi' and dance to the beat of 'Hyes Attes Attes Hyes' as the old hags would hail you as leader and guide, bearer-of-the-casket and bearer-of-the-winnow and so on. You were paid with soppy bread, twisted rolls and flat cakes. Enjoying all this, who would not regard himself and his lot in life as truly fortunate?[1]

Obviously, this is not the place to argue about the impact of the description on Demosthenes' rhetorical strategy.[2] The passage is significant in

---

[*] I wish to thank Mario C. D. Paganini and Vincent Gabrielsen for providing the opportunity to present and test my argument at the conference organised by them at Athens, as well as for their excellent editorial care. The anonymous referees helped with their useful remarks to improve parts of the chapter. All translations are mine unless indicated otherwise. Any remaining infelicities are my responsibility. An earlier version in Greek with a different focus was published in Arnaoutoglou 2016b.

[1] D. 18 (*On the Crown*) 260 as translated by Yunis 2005. See also D. 19 (*On the false embassy*) 199 (343/2 BC).

[2] See Dyck 1985: 46 on the role of details to lend credibility to the account provided by Demosthenes; Santamaría Álvarez 2010.

another, rather neglected, respect. It reflects the ambience created by these *kaloi thiasoi*, 'brilliant groups', an atmosphere of hustle and buzzes. It is exactly this sense of *thorybos* conveyed by the passage that interests me. Similar *thorybos* may be behind the decision of the deme of Piraeus to ban groups of worshippers convening outside the Thesmophorion in Piraeus, except on certain festival days.[3] *Thorybos* (that is, cheers, shouts, heckling and laughter) was an essential feature of social activity in the ancient Greek world. Quite apart the religious sphere, several scholars emphasised the role of *thorybos* in the working of Athenian democracy, in the assembly and in the lawcourts.[4] Judith Tacon claims that *thorybos* (that is, cases when speakers interrupt each other, *demos* interrupts speakers, *demos* allies with opposing speakers) was an integral feature of assembly debate and by extension of Athenian democracy. Anti-democracy theorists regarded it as negative. In the same vein, Robert Wallace notes that the Athenian *demos* felt no obligation to sit quietly and listen to talk they objected to; such conduct was a befitting feature of a monarchy, oligarchy or tyranny. *Thorybos* was some sort of a negative vote of the people. Melissa Schwartzberg regards *thorybos* as an acclamatory mechanism functioning simultaneously as a form of democratic participation in the deliberations and as an accountability mechanism. Similarly, Victor Bers and Adrian Lanni have pointed out the role of *thorybos* among *dikastai* in the lawcourts as well as among the audience.[5]

Nevertheless, *thorybos* heightens tension, which may develop either among the members of a group over, say, the ways of exploiting communal

---

[3] *IG* II² 1177, 3–12 (mid fourth century BC). Ziebarth 1896: 167 rejects the interpretation of the clause as a ban of forming associations; for earlier bibliography, see Arnaoutoglou 2003: 66 n. 110. See most recently a similar clause in *SEG* 57:1674, ll. 6–8 (= Schuler 2007: 134–5) (Lycia, Patara, second century BC): ἄλλωι δὲ μηθενὶ ἐξέστω συναγωγὴν | ποιεῖσθαι μηδὲ καταλύειν | ἐμ τῶι τεμένει πλὴν τῶν θυόντων 'it is not allowed to anyone else to congregate or to lodge in the sanctuary except those who sacrifice'. Compare the edict of the first Hungarian king St. Stephen (AD 1001) penalising inappropriate behaviour in Christian churches reported by Nemeth 1994: 59.

[4] *Thorybos* in the theatre: Dio Chrys. 32.74; in the *stadium*: Dio Chrys. 32.74; in the assemblies: Dio Chrys. 32.34; D. 6 (*Philippics* 2) 26; D. 19 (*On the false embassy*) 113; 122; Plu. *Phoc.* 24.5; Aesch. 1 (*Against Timarchus*) 1; in the lawcourts: Isoc. 15 (*Antidosis*) 272; X. *Apology of Socrates* 14–15; [D.] 57 (*Against Eubulides*) 50; Aesch. 1 (*Against Timarchus*) 174; Achilleus Tatius, *Leucippe et Clitophon* 7.9.1; 7.14.1. Ways to address occurrence of *thorybos*: Anaximenes, *Rhetorica ad Alexandrum* (M. Fuhrmann) 18.8. Bers 1985 defines 'dikastic *thorybos*' as 'any vocal expression that one or more jurymen (*dikastai*) direct to a litigant or other members of the jury panel' or in other words 'to any breach of dikastic silence, to well articulated utterances as well as to the indistinct roar the word normally implies' with reference to Pl. *Laws*, 876b, 949b; Aesch. 3 (*Against Ctesiphon*) 53 and 201. Punishment for *thorybos* in Syracuse: D.S. 13.91.4

[5] Tacon 2001: 181–6; Wallace 2004: 223–6 with reference to A. *Pers.* 591–4, Pr. 880, S. *Ant.* 690-2 and 757, Th. 8.66.1; Schwartzberg 2010: 17; Bers 1985; Lanni 1997; Villacèque 2013; Lanni 2012 underlines the importance of social status of litigants in raising the interest of the Athenian public.

property (*IG* II² 1289) or between two different groups.[6] Furthermore, tensions may result in conflicts, some of them resolved informally with mediation or arbitration, while some others will find their way into the formal ways of dispute resolution, that is to say into lawcourts;[7] the worst-case scenario is the conflict to turn into an open physical confrontation. Hence, the need arises to devise and to provide mechanisms and procedures to establish *eustatheia* – that is stability, steadiness – which in its turn will lead to *eukosmia,* the proper conduct in the premises of the association, something that will also reflect on the constantly constructed and projected image of the group.[8] At least in Roman times, it was thought that the best way to achieve this aim was by inscribing the rules of the group.[9] Be that as it may, the association of *thorybos* with Greece and *eustatheia* with Rome is certainly hyperbolic and sketchy, since there were definitely less noisy meetings of Greeks and livelier than average Roman gatherings.[10] The polarity *thorybos-eustatheia,* however, provides a hermeneutic scheme, perhaps not wholly satisfactory, to approach the normative universe of Athenian associations in the Hellenistic and Roman era.[11]

---

[6] Appeals to the unity or concord of the group, *IG* II² 1261 and 4985 with Baslez 2006: 158. Arbitration: *IG* II² 1289 with Papazarkadas 2011: 194–203.

[7] See *IG* II² 1258 and Is. frg. 35.26–27 (Thalheim). Inscription *F.Delphes* III.2 70 (Le Guen 2001: 98 no 12 and Aneziri 2003: C2) records a dispute between the Athenian and the Peloponnesian branches of the *peri ton Dionyson technitai* in the late second century BC that was finally resolved by the Romans in 112/1 BC.

[8] See Baslez 2006: 157–8. In the recently published ephebarchic law from Amphipolis (Lazaridou 2015) inscribed in 24/3 BC, ll. 36–51 concern *eukosmia* and ll. 127–8 prescribe the appropriate behaviour of ephebes during public performances. However, the concept of *akosmia* appears already in the fifth century BC; as far as it concerns religious ceremonies, see *CID* I 7B, ll. 12–13 (Delphi, ca. 425 BC), *IG* I³ 82, l. 25 (Athens, 421/0 BC), *Agora* 16 56, l. 32 (Athens, before mid fourth century BC), *IG* V 1390, l. 39 (Andania, 91 BC?) with Deshours 2006: 100 and Gawlinski 2012: 151, *I.Ilion* 5, l. 29 (Ilion?, second century AD?). For the opposition *thorybos-eustatheia,* see Philo, *Legatio ad Gaium,* 90: ὁ τῶν μὲν εἰς εὐστάθειαν καὶ εὐδαιμονίαν ἁπάντων κενώσας τὰς πόλεις, μεστὰς δὲ τῶν εἰς ταραχὰς καὶ θορύβους καὶ τὴν ἀνωτάτω βαρυδαιμονίαν ἀναφήνας … 'the one who stripped the cities of all that tends to stability and happiness and turned them into hotbeds of what makes for confusion and tumults and the height of misery' (tr. F. H. Colson). Note also the *thorybos*-related terminology in almost all the passages mentioning disturbances.

[9] This is best reflected in the Latin inscription *CIL* XIV 2112 (*ILS* 7212; *FIRA* I 49 and 175; *FIRA* I² 46; *FIRA* III² 35) from Lanuvium (AD 133–6) as reedited by Bendlin 2011. See also in *IG* II² 1368, ll. 15–16 the members of the *Bakcheion* shouting: εὐστάθειαν τῷ Βακχείῳ καὶ εὐκοσμίαν 'stability and decency to the *Backheion*'.

[10] D.H. 9.41.5; 10.41, *thorybos* and *akosmia* in a Roman assembly; Plu. *Cato Minor,* 26.2. The role of *thorybos* (clamour) in judicial proceedings is explored by Menard 2014.

[11] An anonymous reviewer pointed out that the term *eustatheia* is rarely used outside medical texts and the term *eukosmia* is therefore preferable. However, there is a considerable number of epigraphic texts in which *eustatheia* features prominently: e.g. *IAegThrace* E 205, ll. 29–31 (Maroneia, second/ first century BC), *IScM* I 54, ll. 34–8 (Istros, mid first century BC), *IOSPE* I² 82, ll. 86, 91, 94, 96, 100, 122, 132, 137–8, 141, 184 (Olbia, second-third century AD), *I.Olbia* 80, l. 86 (Olbia, mid-second century AD), *SEG* 48:948bis with *SEG* 57:727 (Olbia, ca. AD 220), *SEG* 49:1028b (Olbia,

In doing that I am going to refrain from any discussion of the rule attributed to Solon and reported in *Dig.* 47.22.4.[12] Current discussions on Athenian associations avoid a thorough examination of the legal aspect of their activities.[13] Following the three approaches to the normative world of ancient associations outlined by the editors in Chapter 1, I shall present, from a socio-legal perspective, the rules governing corporate activities in Athens from the late fourth century BC down to the late second century AD, in two chronologically distinct parts.[14] This approach is to a large extent dictated by the date of the available evidence. It will become clear, I hope, that in regulations of the Roman era there was a mutation of the normative world of Athenian associations; its main concern shifted to guaranteeing stability and proper conduct.[15] Following that, I shall explore the historical implications of the differentiated focus. Was the influence of the Roman authorities so decisive as to leave a permanent imprint on the modes of collective action? Was willingness to conform to precepts of *Romanitas* so great that it dictated the harmonisation or, some would say, the transfer of legal rules from the Italian peninsula to the Greek? And in this last respect we can point the finger to at least one major Athenian figure, who could have mediated, Claudius Herodes Atticus.

Rules and Regulations

Nine normative texts issued by Athenian cult associations survive, while several – mainly disciplinary – clauses are scattered among numerous honorary decrees.[16] Normative texts, that is to say, corporate decisions

late second century AD), *I.Milet* 1072 (AD 99/100). The term is also used to qualify the performance of the *agoranomia* in Imperial Ephesus (e.g. *I.Ephesos* 911–13, 916–17, 921, 926–9, 933, 935, 937; *I.Ephesos* 3010–13, 3015–16) or of other magistracies (e.g. *I.Ephesos* 3052; *IG* XII.2 243). The adjective *eustathes* qualifies even the *demos* of Side in *I.Side* 26 dated to AD 276? and an individual's life (*IG* XII.7 401 and 407, *TAM* V 3 1470, *I.Sardis* 55).

[12] Now in Leão and Rhodes 2015: 133 no 76a. I have expressed my doubts about its Solonian ancestry in its preserved form in Arnaoutoglou 2016a. According to Ziebarth 1896: 171, the disciplinary power of associations over their members rested upon *Dig.* 47.22.4.

[13] Recent studies tend to concentrate predominantly on their social impact and function; see Jones 1999, Ismard 2010, Steinhauer 2014.

[14] Similar regulations in Egyptian Demotic documents from 380 BC onwards are presented by de Cenival 1967/8; cf. de Cenival 1972. See Boak 1937b for a concise presentation of the relevant material from both Hellenistic and Roman Egypt's Demotic and Greek documents.

[15] See now the approach by Eckhardt 2017a, who regards associations in Roman Greece as a part of remembering strategies.

[16] Normative texts: *IG* II² 1361 (ca. 330–24 BC); 1275 (fourth/third century BC); *Agora* 16 161 (beg. of third century BC); *IG* II² 1283 (240/39 BC); 1328 (185/4 BC); 1339 (37/6 BC?); *SEG* 31:122 (ca. AD 94); *IG* II² 1368 (AD 164/5); 1369 (second half of second century AD). Decrees: *IG* II² 1263; 1273; 1292; 1297; *MDAI(A)* 66 (1941): 228 no 4. I have included texts containing both

introducing binding rules for their members (irrespective of any penal clause), are almost evenly spread in time. Five of them are dated between the late fourth and second century BC, while the remaining four are dated between the late first century BC and second century AD. The oldest, so far, is *IG* II² 1361, a fragmentary stele whose top and bottom are missing, dated ca. 330–324 BC.[17] It contains rules about sacrifices (portion to priests/priestesses, ban on *parabomia*, 'beside the altar' sacrifices, that is to say, outside the customary ritual), financial administration of the group's assets (land and water), enlisting new members and the necessary entrenchment clause (where the regulation is described as *nomos*). *Agora* 16 161 (beginning of the third century BC) records three decisions of an unknown group of *orgeones*; in the first, they regulate financial affairs (probably debts to the group) according to their older decisions (*archaia psephismata*), in the second decree sacral affairs are settled (date of sacrifice, kind of victim, portions), while from the third one only a few words survive. Inscription *IG* II² 1275 (late fourth or early third century BC) preserves the lower part of a stele on which the text of a *nomos* was inscribed; there survives only an exhortation to the next of kin of a deceased member to announce the death to the community and the fellows to attend the funeral as well as a stricture about solidarity.[18] The last six lines record an entrenchment clause, that is, terms of prosecution and sanction against the members who challenge the *nomos*. Inscription *IG* II² 1283 dated now to 240/39 BC contains regulations about the relation between the *orgeones* of the goddess Bendis in Piraeus and those in the city; according to it, the *orgeones* of the city will enjoy the same treatment during the procession, they will have priority in submitting requests to the *orgeones* of the Piraeus and they will have the right to join

---

rules of governance as well as rules of conduct as expounded by Gabrielsen and Paganini in Chapter 1.

[17] *IG* II² 1361, 13–15: [ἐὰ]ν δ[ἐ τι]ς [ε]ἴπ[ηι] ἢ ἐπιψηφίσηι παρὰ τόνδε τὸν νόμον, ὀφειλέτω (50) δραχμὰς τῆι | [θεῶι] ὅ τ[ε εἰπὼν καὶ] ὁ ἐπιψηφίσας καὶ μὴ μετέστω αὐτῶι τῶν κοινῶν. ἀναγράφειν δ|[ὲ αὐτὸν ὀφείλο]ντα τῆι θεῶι τοῦτο τὸ ἀργύριον εἰς τὴν στήλην τοὺς ἐπιμελητά[ς] 'and if anyone proposes or puts to vote (a proposal) against this law, he shall pay 50 drachmas to the goddess both the proposer and the one who puts to vote (such a proposal) and he shall not be allowed to take part in the common activities. The *epimeletai* shall inscribe his name as debtor of the goddess for this amount of money on a stele.' See the remarks about the use of the entrenchment clause in polis documents in Lewis 1974, Rhodes with Lewis 1997: 524 and Schwartzberg 2004. Date: Tracy 1995: 129. See also Giannakopoulos in Chapter 2.

[18] Similar clauses in *IG* II² 1368 and in Egypt, *P.Cair.* II 30606 (dem.) (157/6 BC), *P. Mich.* V 243, ll. 9–12 (Tebtynis, AD 14–37), *P. Mich.* V 244, ll. 16–18 (Tebtynis, AD 43). On Egyptian associations see also Langellotti in Chapter 8.

the group.[19] Inscription *IG* II² 1328 records two decisions, of which only the first one (ll. 4–20, passed in 183/2 BC) has a normative character; in particular, the decision clarified what priestesses ought to provide during the ceremonies and the mode of appointing an assistant to the priestesses.

Hellenistic Athenian normative texts, therefore, include principally clauses about cult activities, organisational corporate affairs and the exploitation of common property. Sometimes, but not always, rules are accompanied by sanctions.

Inscription *IG* II² 1339 dated to 37/6 BC forms in a sense a bridge between the Hellenistic and the Roman periods. It records the decision of a *koinon Heroiston* to take care of exacting the fees due by members, irrespective of whether they are abroad or in Athens. *SEG* 31:122, dated to ca. AD 94, appears as the decision of the chief-*eranistes*.[20] It begins with a disciplinary provision (penalty meted out on the member who starts a fight), settling financial affairs (use of a donated amount of money – *entheke* – and the penalties for abusing it, the provision of pork and wine, a clause on the conditions to lend the donated amount of money) and decisions affecting the organisation of the group (exercise of priestly duties, appointment of minor officials, penalty for the individual who does not wish to undertake the post of *pannychistes* or to serve until the end of the term, contributions for joining the group and accountability process). *IG* II² 1368 is probably the most cited corporate inscription and in certain respects unique. It is 163 lines long and is dated now to AD 164/5. The rules are the decisions (δόγματα) of the priest, the chief-*Bakchos*[21] and the *prostates*. They have received a vociferous and unanimous approval by the members of the association.[22] The rules, most often accompanied by

---

[19] The text of the inscription, despite the awkward syntax of ll. 8–9, is quite clear: the duty to perform the procession was dictated by the law of the polis. What is regulated in the decree is not the procession per se, but the participation and the subsequent treatment of the *orgeones* of the *asty*.

[20] ἔδοξεν τῷ ἀρχερανιστῇ ... τάδε δοκιμάτισαι 'it was resolved by the chief-*eranistes* ... these are his decisions'. The text does not allow any speculation about its ratification by the assembly of the *synodos'* members. Cf. Laubry and Zevi 2012: 334 *leges collegiorum* appear as decisions of the assembly of their members.

[21] For the office, see Turcan 2003: 56.

[22] ἐξ(εβόησαν)· τούτοις | ἀεὶ χρώμεθα ... ὅτῳ δοκεῖ | κύρια εἶναι τὰ ἀνεγνωσμένα δόγμα|τα καὶ ἐν στήλῃ ἀναγραφῆναι, ἀράτω | τὴν χεῖρα. πάντες ἐπῆραν 'they all shouted: "We will use them for ever. ... To whomever it seems good that the statutes that have been read out should be ratified and inscribed on a monument (stele) raise your hand". Everyone raised his hand' (tr. Ascough, Harland and Kloppenborg 2012: 13); see also in Athens *IG* II² 1343 (35/4 BC); *SEG* 43:864 (mid-second century AD) and *SEG* 30:82 (ca. AD 230). Expressions about voting by showing of hands and counting of votes on inscriptions, see *SEG* 57:1074 (Iasos, ca. 225 BC); *IG* XII.4 1 57 and 59 (Cos, second half of second century BC); *IG* XII.3 249 (Anaphe, first century BC); *IG* XII.9 906 (Chalkis, after AD 212) and Wilhelm 1921: 5–9.

penalties, settle affairs such as admission of new members[23] (scrutiny, fee, token as proof of membership, celebrations), members' discipline (behaviour during celebrations, fights, abuse and reproach, hubristic behaviour, wounds, fee-payment avoidance), magistrates' and members' duties and participation in the funeral of a deceased member.[24] *IG* II² 1369 (late second century AD) is the latest testimony of regulations in Athenian cult associations. It is designated as *nomos* and contains exclusively administrative rules pertaining to admissions, officials and expulsion as a penalty for those members who initiate a fight or disturbances.[25]

Offences[26]

Offences are outlined in any kind of corporate decision, be it a regulation or an honorary decree. In Athens, particular offences associated with

---

[23] See the use of the same words, *eukosmos* and *iselysion*, in *IG* II² 1368 and *I.Pergamon* 374 (AD 129–38). The latter term is attested also in *I.Smyrna* 731 (AD 80–3).

[24] References to verbal abuse (λοιδορία) and derivatives: *IG* IX.1².3 670, ll. 9 and 11 (Physkos-Lokris, mid-second century AD); resort to divine punishment, *TAM* V.1 251 and 269 (mod. Kula-Lydia, second-third century AD). See Spatharas 2006: 380 for the use of laughter as an aggressive weapon to hurt the pride of the opponent in many Athenian lawcourt speeches; something similar might have triggered outbursts of abuse and vituperation that could have escalated into physical violence among associates. For Egypt, see Boak 1937b: 217–18 with *SB* III 6319 *recto*, II ll. 44–7 (Magdola, Arsinoites, second-first century BC): ἂν τις ὑμῶν κακῶς ἐρεῖ, δώσ⟨ε⟩ι Β | ὅταν τις ὑμῶν βινῆ ἀλλοτ⟨ρ⟩ίαν γυνή, δώσ⟨ε⟩ι (δραχμὰς) A 'if anyone of you defames, he shall give 2,000 dr.; when one of you violates somebody else's wife, he shall give 1,000 dr.'; *BGU* XIV 2371, l. 4 (Heracleopolites, first century BC), *P. Lond.* VII 2193, ll. 15–19 (69–58 BC), *P.Mich.* V 243, ll. 3 and 6–8 (Tebtynis, AD 14–37). San Nicolò 1927: 276 interprets the punishment for adultery with the wife of a co-member as an expression of ethico-religious norms; however, in an associative context, adultery signifies the breakdown of trust among members and therefore undermines solidarity among them and could lead to insults, blows and injuries. Adultery has thus the potential to unravel the cornerstones of associative life, trust and solidarity: see Monson 2006: 229–32 and 2007: 772. It is particularly pertinent the interpretation of Kloppenborg 2013: 204 to the clauses enforcing attendance in associations. He regards, perhaps excessively, deliberate absence from assemblies and meetings as 'snubs of the honoree and are thus aggressive acts that subvert the fabric of the association'. One may object that not all meetings dealt with award of honours. On the regulation of obligatory participation, see Eckhardt in Chapter 3. For the rhetoric of ideals and their mild transgression during banquets, see Harland 2013b.

[25] Most recently in Kloppenborg and Ascough 2011: no 49 and Ascough, Harland and Kloppenborg 2012: no 8. For the expression πέρα κρίσεως see San Nicolò 1927: 295 according to whom the exaction of the fine does not require any further legal proceedings but it is immediately enforceable. A comparison between the laws of Greco-Roman religious associations and the Christian *Didache* is provided by Öhler 2005.

[26] From the list of violations mentioned by San Nicolò 1927: 262–3 only breach of members' obligations against the association (i.e. payment of contributions, disobedience, abstention from assemblies and festivities) and against other members of the group (insulting, fighting, injuring, etc.) are attested in Athens. In contrast to Egyptian material (both in Demotic and Greek), there is no reference to a duty to observe specific moral rules, like avoidance of adulterous relations (if indeed one interprets these clauses as imposing morals and not, what I think more likely, as

officials are attested in Hellenistic honorary decrees. In the normative clauses scattered in these texts, associations regulate and penalise the non-performance of duties by their magistrates (in particular, crowning and the public proclamation of the crown) and later the non-acceptance of magisterial duties.[27] In the Hellenistic normative texts, the non-payment of fees and the violation of any corporate decision, especially of the entrenchment clause, are regarded as offences. In Roman times, a distinct category of offences appears, aiming at the deviant behaviour of members against their fellows.[28]

Organs Imposing Sanctions

Usually there are two organs involved in imposing and enforcing penalties: the assembly of the members and the individual magistrates. A distinctive

---

undermining corporate trust and solidarity, see above n. 24) and rules pertaining to professional activities, San Nicolò 1927: 270-3 and 276.

[27] Non-performance of duties: *IG* II² 1328, 11–16: [ἐὰ]ν [δ]ὲ παρὰ ταῦ|τα ποιεῖ, κύριοι ἔ[σ]τωσαν οἱ ὀργεῶνες ζημιοῦντε[ς τὴ]ν [π]α[ρ]αβαίνουσά[ν] | τι τῶν γεγραμμένων μέχρι δραχμῶν π[εν]τήκον[τα κα]ὶ εἰσπραττ[όν]|των τρόπωι ὅτωι ἂν [δύνωνται· μ]ὴ ἐξεῖναι δὲ μηθενὶ μηδ' ἐπιψηφίσαι | τὸν εἰθισμένον ἔπαινον αὐταῖς 'and if someone acts against these provisions, the *orgeones* will have the power to impose a fine on the defaulter of the written provisions up to 50 drachmas and to exact it in whatever way they can; it is not allowed to anyone to put to vote the customary praise for them'; *IG* II² 1328, ll. 18–20: δ[ι]ς δὲ τὴν αὐτὴν [μὴ ἐξεῖ]|ναι καταστῆσαι ἕως ἂν ἅπασαι διέλθωσιν, εἰ δ[ὲ μή], ἔν[οχ]ος ἔ[στω] | ἡ ἱέρεια τοῖς αὐτοῖς ἐπιτιμίοις 'it is not allowed that she (*sc.* the priestess) is appointed twice till all of them fill the office, otherwise the priestess will be liable to the same punishment'. In contrast, magistrates are honoured when they comply and perform their duties properly, *IG* II² 1284, ll. 23–4: διώ[ικηκεν τὰ πρ]οστατταττόμεν' αὐτῶι ὑ[πὸ τ]ῶν νόμων ὀρθῶς καὶ δικαίως 'he administered what is ordained by the laws correctly and fairly' and similarly *IG* II² 1291, ll. 3–6; *SEG* 2:9, ll. 4–6; *SEG* 44:60, ll. 3–5. See Kloppenborg 2013: 213 who claims that these prescriptions target cases of withholding the honour due to magistrates and inducing other members to do so. No proclamation: *IG* II² 1263, ll. 43–5: ἐὰν δὲ μὴ ἀναγο|ρεύσωσι, ἀποτινέτωσαν τῶι κοινῶι | (50) δραχμάς 'if they do not proclaim the honours, they shall pay to the associations 50 drachmas' and similarly *IG* II² 1273, ll. 21–6; 1292, ll. 15–17; 1297, ll. 17–18. Refusal of appointment: *SEG* 31:122, ll. 23–7 with San Nicolò 1927: 270.

[28] Non-payment of fees: *IG* II² 1339, ll. 12–15: ἐὰν δὲ μὴ διδ[ῶσι | τὴν φοράν, ἔ]δοξεν μὴ μετέχειν αὐτο[ὺς | τοῦ ἐράν]ου ἐὰν μή τινι συμβῆι διὰ πέ[ν|θος ἢ διὰ ἀ]σθένειαν ἀπολειφθῆναι 'and if they do not pay the fee, it has been decided that they should not participate in the *eranos* (?), unless mourning or illness hinders anyone' and *IG* II² 1361, ll. 19–20. Non-compliance with decisions: *IG* II² 1275, ll. 12–17: ἐπειδὰν δὲ κυρώσωσι τὸν νόμ|ον οἱ θιασῶται, μηθὲν εἶναι τοῦ νόμου κυριώτερ|ον· ἐὰν δέ τις παρὰ τὸν νόμον ἢ εἴπει ἢ πράξει, κα|τηγορίαν αὐτοῦ εἶναι τῶι βουλομένωι τῶν θιασωτῶ|ν, καὶ ἂν ἕλει αὐτὸν τιμάτωσαν αὐτὸν καθότι ἂν δο|κεῖ τῶι κοινῶι 'when the *thiasotai* ratify the statute, nothing shall be more powerful than the statute; and if anyone says or acts contrary to the statute, anyone of the *thiasotai* who so wishes can prosecute him and if he is convicted, he shall be punished with a penalty, whatever seems proper to the association'. Punishment of deviant behaviour: *IG* II² 1368, ll. 72–95; 1369, ll. 40–4; *SEG* 31:122, ll. 5–9; *IG* IX.1².3 670, ll. 7–13. Kloppenborg 2013: 211 claims that most of the offences concern status challenges and they reflect a structural problem of the associations.

red line between the jurisdiction of the assembly and of magistrates depends on the perceived gravity of the offence for the well-being of the association. In Hellenistic times, the assembled members have the discretionary power to impose any penalty they wish on the member who violates the entrenchment clause (*IG* II² 1275, ll. 14–17) or on the priestess who does not comply with the rules introduced in *IG* II² 1328, lines 11–14. In Roman Athens, in the association of *Herakliastai en Limnais* it is the assembly's duty to decide how they are going to exact an imposed fine (*SEG* 31:122, ll. 8–9), while in the *Bakcheion* of *IG* II² 1368, the assembly convened by the priest decided cases of injury (ll. 84–94). The assembly usually exercises some, at least, discretionary power, although the extent of this authority may be delineated by an earlier decision of the group.

San Nicolò 1927 regards the judicial function of the assembly and of certain magistrates as similar to arbitration and therefore as an adequate basis for a right of appeal against verdicts of arbitrators to a polis court. However, this approach is deeply problematic since it presumes arbitration in cases that are far from what we know about the mechanics of arbitration in the Athenian jurisdiction (statement about the dispute, selection of arbitrators, decision and binding character). One could have argued that by joining an association, member(s) implicitly adhered to the rules of dispute resolution operative in this structure. Nevertheless, by joining an association, members were not stripped of their legal rights; they retained the right to use the polis legal machinery, be it for cases of insult, injury, defamation, property relations and so on. San Nicolò advocated, rather unconvincingly, a division between summary and ordinary procedure without defining their salient features; by implication, he considered as summary any procedure involving the assembly of members.[29] Rubinstein 2012 explores the role and the characteristic features of collective liabilities on boards of officials outside Athens in the late classical and Hellenistic periods. However, this concept is rarely employed by cult associations in late classical and Hellenistic Athens; in particular, I could find only one case, *IG* II² 1292 (215/4 BC), in which the association of *Sarapiastai* imposes a fine on *hieropoioi*. Nevertheless, we do not know their number, whether they were acting as a board when failing to proclaim the names of the honoured individuals after the sacrifice (crime of omission). There are,

---

[29] San Nicolò 1927: 289–90.

however, two cases (*IG* II² 1263 and 1297) in which the wording suggests a board but in fact it is a pseudo-collective since it refers to officials of consecutive years.

We usually assume that individual magistrates were responsible for imposing and collecting fines on recalcitrant members, especially those prescribed and fixed in a group's regulations. However, I found only weak indications in the Athenian 'corporate' epigraphy; in *IG* II² 1368, the priest is to decide whether a member has paid his contributions or not and therefore may participate in the celebrations (ll. 67–72), or in another case the treasurer may prohibit the entry to the association's premises to a member who has not paid a fine (ll. 99–102). San Nicolò 1927: 260 claims that the head of the group (*Vereinsvorstand*) had disciplinary authority policing the meetings and the festivals. This is not confirmed by Athenian evidence; only the *archeranistes* of *SEG* 31:122 seems to yield unfettered authority, but even he has to refer important questions to the assembly.[30] Equally difficult to answer is the question whether associations' magistrates had the authority to proceed to exacting the penalties. The parallel provided by other Greek poleis, thoroughly investigated by Lene Rubinstein, cannot shed any light, since only in *IG* II² 1273 and 1328 is there a hint about a similar grant of authority, with the substantial difference that no officials are authorised but only the association as a whole. The expression in *IG* II² 1273, lines 24–5 – ἡ δ'εἴσπραξις ἔστω τοῖς θιασώταις καθάπερ καὶ τἄλλα ὀφειλήματα 'the *thiasotai* shall exact (*sc.* the fines) as they do with other debts' – suggest that the fine imposed on a magistrate would have been dealt with exactly in the same way as debts for other reasons.[31] But this neat, modern picture of associations suing members over non-payment of subscriptions and fines defies realities. Recourse to the official channel of adjudication was only one option, perhaps the costliest; associations could have used other means to enforce their decisions, such as temporary expulsion from communal activities, social pressure (e.g. inscribing the name of debtors on a stele, *Agora* 16 161),

---

[30] More fruitful would have been to compare the imposition of fines by polis authorities (*proedroi* of the assembly, *strategoi* in *AthPol* 61.2 with Rhodes 1981: 684) (ἐπιβολαί) see *IG* I³ 82 (421/0 BC) and Harrison 1971: 4–5. See Ziebarth 1896: 174; the term *Vereinspolizei*, 'association's police', misrepresents the role of the officials. See also *P. Lond.* VII 2193, l. 17: μη|δὲ ἐπ[ικα]λήσειν καὶ μὲ κατηιγορή[σ]ειν [[α]] τοῦ ἑτέρου 'not to indict or to accuse another . . .', with Roberts, Skeat and Nock 1936: 53–4. Refusal or abstention from participating in an assembly to pass a verdict resulted in a fine, *IG* II² 1368, ll. 96–9 with San Nicolò 1927: 260–1 and *CID* I, 9 C, ll. 6–10 (Delphi, beg. of fourth century BC).

[31] Foucart 1873: 41 (recourse to polis tribunals), Ziebarth 1896: 175.

marginalisation of the individual, withdrawal of support by other members and so on. San Nicolò 1927: 291–2 and Boak 1937b: 214 underline the power of the head of an association in Hellenistic and Roman Egypt (attested in Greek and Demotic documents) to compel the payment of arrears or dues by seizing pledges at the expense of a recalcitrant member (in one case even the member himself), an authority not attested in Hellenistic or Roman Athens.[32]

Penalties

In principle, associations could impose one or a combination of the following three different legal sanctions on the members in enforcing their rules:[33]

    i.   a monetary fine, most often, of 50 dr., sometimes consecrated to the worshipped deity and some other time payable to the treasury of the association.[34] Penalties were fixed either by a statute or, less often, were left at the discretion of the assembly of the members;[35]

---

[32] Rubinstein 2010: 199–209 identifies four criteria that point to the conclusion that polis agents are vested with powers to actively proceed to exaction of imposed penalties: (i) combination of a *praxis* clause with a penalty clause directed against the officials responsible for the exaction; (ii) clause granting immunity to the agent of exaction from prosecution; (iii) cross reference to existing legislation or legal procedures that extend the authority of magistrates and/or define the method to be applied; and (iv) clause granting permission to officials to resort to any available means to exact the penalty.

[33] There is no question of the association imposing sanctions on non-members, despite San Nicolò 1927: 265–6. San Nicolò seeks parallels to penalties imposed by sanctuaries on their visitors; this is rather misleading since the sanctuary authorities were considered as sovereign in this enclosure but associations' authority extended only to their membership. Equally deceptive are the two examples in San Nicolò 1927: 266 n. 45 on the power of *demos* authorities exercising judicial function, since they operate in the context of a contract, in which the *demos* is one of the contracting parties.

[34] Fines consecrated: *IG* II² 1361, ll. 13–14 and 20 (ca. 330–324/3 BC); 1273, ll. 21–4 (265–3 BC); 1297, ll. 17–18 (236/5 BC); *MDAI (A)* 66 (1941): 228 no. 4, l. 19 (138/7 BC). For Poland 1909: 450 fines originally were designated to be paid to a deity and only later the association is designated as the recipient; but evidence from Athenian associations does not support this conclusion. San Nicolò 1927: 282 considers the reference to the exact amount of money to be paid as a protection against arbitrariness. His argument, however, is weakened by, at least, one case in which the penalty is left to the discretion of the assembly, *IG* II² 1275, ll. 14–17 (see above n. 26). For Egypt, see Boak 1937b: 218–19. San Nicolò 1927: 258–60 claims that the term παραχρῆμα, 'immediately', signifies the imposition of the penalty on the spot; see *IG* II² 1273 and 1323. However, in *SEG* 31:122, 17–18 παραχρῆμα is qualified as a period of a year. Fines payable to the association: *IG* II² 1263 (300/299 BC) and 1368 (AD 164/5). For the fines provided in Demotic documents in Egypt, see San Nicolò 1927: 273–5 and de Cenival 1972.

[35] Fixed by decree: *IG* II² 1263, ll. 43-6. Discretion of the assembly: *IG* II² 1275, ll. 14–17. See Ziebarth 1896: 173.

ii. expulsion or ejection from the activities of the group or the premises of the association;[36] and

iii. striking out a member from the ranks of the group.[37]

Two particularities require attention.

a. Striking out is very rarely invoked (and I suppose even more rarely was imposed); in *SEG* 31:122, lines 42–5 it is provided by the statute,[38] while in *IG* II² 1368 there is no provision imposing a similar penalty; in *IG* II² 1369 it is not clear whether the verb *ekballestho* (ἐκβαλλέσθω) signifies the removal or the expulsion, as it is accompanied by a fine.[39] *SEG* 31:122, lines 5–9, stipulates the following: ἐάν τις ἐν τῇ συνόδῳ | μάχην ποιήσῃ, τῇ ἐχομένῃ ἡμέρᾳ ἀποτινέτω προστείμ|ου ὁ μὲν ἀρξάμενος δραχμὰς δέκα ὁ δὲ ἐξακολουθή|σας δραχμὰς πέντε καὶ ἐξάνανκα πραττέσθω τῶν σ|[υ]νερανιστῶν ψῆφον λαβόντων ἐκβιβάσαι 'If someone in the assembly should cause a fight, on the following day let him pay a fine. The one who initiated the fight should pay ten drachmas and whoever joined in should pay five

---

[36] *IG* II² 1368, ll. 67–72; 82-3; 99–107 and 136–44. Foucart 1873: 40–2; Ziebarth 1896: 170–9; Poland 1909: 446–52; San Nicolò 1927: 279–81. San Nicolò 1927: 281 n. 177 is clearly wrong in criticising Poland 1909 who claimed that temporary expulsion could concur with a fine, see *IG* II² 1368, ll. 88-90: καὶ προστειμάσθω πρὸς χρόνον μὴ εἰσελθεῖν ὅσον ἂν δόξῃ καὶ ἀργυρίου μέχρι (δηναρίων) κε 'and he shall be barred from attending as long as the association decides and pay a fine up to 25 denarii'. For the term *stibas*, see now Jaccottet 2011 who argues that the term should be understood as the chief celebration/festival of the *Iobacchoi*. For the officials responsible to remove the recalcitrant member (*hippoi*), see Turcan 2003: 71.

[37] For the attitudes towards striking out a member in associations of the western part of the Roman empire, see Tran 2007.

[38] *SEG* 31:122, ll. 42–5: τὰς δὲ φορὰς | καταφέριν τῷ ταμίᾳ ἐπάναγκες ἰς τὰς ἐγδόσις· ὁ δὲ μὴ κατενένκας | ἀποτινέτω τὸ διπλοῦν ὁ δὲ μὴ δοὺς τὸ κάθολον ἐξέρανος | ἔστω 'The dues must be brought to the treasurer so that loans can be made. Whoever does not pay shall be fined a double amount. Whoever does not pay at all shall be expelled from the association' (tr. Ascough, Harland and Kloppenborg 2012: 19).

[39] For a parallel, see *IG* VII 2725, ll. 12–33 (Akraipheia-Boeotia, second century AD?): εἰ δέ τις | τὴν ἐπιγραφὴν ἐκκόψ|ῃ ἐκ τῆς παραστά[δο]]ς ἢ αὐτὴν ἄρῃ ἢ κακο[ποι]|ήσῃ, δώσι ὡς ὁμοίως | τῇ συνόδῳ τῶν ἡρω|ιαστῶν τῶν τέκν⟨ων⟩ μου | δηνάρια δισχίλια ὁμοίω|ς καὶ τῇ πόλι Ἀκρηφιῶν δ|ηνάρια δισχίλια πεντα|κόσια. καὶ τοὺς | ὑβρίσαντας τοὺς ἥρω|ας τῶν τέκνων ἡμῶν κα|ὶ ἐμὲ καὶ τὸν ἄνδρα μου Πυ|θίωνα καὶ ἐπιμένοντας | τῇ αὐθαδίᾳ οὐ βούλομαι μ|ετέχιν τῆς συνόδου τῶ|ν ἡρωιαστῶν τῶν τέκν|ων ἡμῶν Ἐπαμινώνδου | καὶ Θεοκρίν⟨η⟩ς μήτε ζώντω|ν ἡμῶν μήτε τελευτησ|άντων 'and if anyone damages the inscription from the pilaster or removes or damages the pilaster, he shall pay equally to the association of Worshippers of Our Children as Heroes two thousand denarii and equally to the city of Akraipheia two thousand five hundred denarii. And those who have abused the Worshippers of Our Children as Heroes and myself and my husband Python and insist on being insolent, I do not wish them to participate in the association of Worshippers of Our Children as Heroes, Epaminondas and Theokrine, neither while we are alive nor when we have passed away'. The crucial question in this case is whether *hybris* included the mutilation of the inscription alone or together with defaulting on the payment of the fine.

drachmas. After his fellow *eranistai* have taken a vote to expel him . . .'
(tr Ascough, Harland and Kloppenborg 2012: 18). Although this has
been rendered by the first editor of the document as imposing the
expulsion of the unruly member, the meaning of the term *ekbibasai*
(ἐκβιβάσαι) is not that unambiguous. In particular, the rationale of
imposing a monetary fine does not fit well with the compulsory
decision to expel a member. *Ekbibasai* could also mean 'to satisfy a
person's claim' (*P. Tebt.* II 398, l. 18, AD 142). Therefore, the passage
could be interpreted as 'his fellow-members shall compulsorily, after a
vote, force him to satisfy (the claim of paying the fine)'. In *IG* II²
1339, lines 12–15: ἐὰν δὲ μὴ διδ[ῶσι | τὴν φοράν, ἔ]δοξεν μὴ μετέχειν
αὐτο[ὺς | τοῦ ἐράν]ου ἐὰν μή τινι συμβῆι διὰ πέ[ν|θος ἢ διὰ
ἀ]σθένειαν ἀπολειφθῆναι 'and if they do not pay the fee, it has been
decided that they should not participate in the *eranos* (?), unless
mourning or illness hindered anyone', the restoration *eranos* instead
of *koinon* is adventurous. In the former case, it is conceivable that the
defaulting member may be exempted from the benefits of an *eranos*-
fund and not excluded from an *eranos*-association, as it would have
been the case when restoring *koinon*. Foucart 1873: 41–2 has already
doubted whether the phrase μὴ μετέστω αὐτῶι τῶν κοινῶν 'he will
not have a share in the common activites' in *IG* II² 1361, line 14 could
mean a definite exclusion, 'une exclusion définitive'; however, the
expression is preceded by a monetary fine, something that would
not make sense if the heavier penalty of exclusion was provided.

b.   There is no indication of corporal punishment provided for, with the
     exception of *IG* II² 1369.[40]

The associations' judicial competence is delimited, rather exclusively, by
the place in which the infringement took place (that is to say, premises of
the association) and on the identity of the involved parties; I do not know
any case of a non-member prosecuting or being prosecuted in front of
'corporate' judicial organs. To illustrate the above point, consider the
following case: Two members of a cult association had a commercial
dispute, and one punched the other in the *agora*. Which judicial organ

---

[40]   See the lack of references to officials like *rhabdophoroi vel similia* from the administrative board of
Athenian associations. Compare with *IG* IX.2 1109, ll. 23–30 (second century BC, oracle of Apollo
Koropaios near Demetrias) ῥαβδοῦχος . . . κωλύειν τὸν ἀκοσμοῦντα 'club-bearer . . . stops the
person who behaves improperly', *I.Ilion* 52 (Ilion?, second century BC?) ἔχειν ἐξουσίαν τοὺς
ἀκοσμοῦντας τῆι ῥάβδωι κολάζειν 'he has the power to punish with a club those behaving
improperly' and *IG* V.1 1390, ll. 41–5 (Andania, 91 BC?).

would have been competent to hear the case? Assuming that the ban on approaching public judicial agents provided in *IG* II² 1368, lines 90–4, was a persistent feature of Athenian associations, then prima facie there was concurring jurisdiction of both association and polis and therefore the victim of the attack could choose the course of action. However, it is more likely that the dispute would have been resolved by the polis' judiciary and not by the association's, since the provisions of *SEG* 31:122, lines 5–6, *IG* II² 1368, lines 72–4 and 94–5, clearly specify the location of the infringement as ἐν τῇ συνόδῳ 'on the premises of the association' or similar expressions.

Ideals Behind the Rules

Corporate rulings aim to ensure first and above all the preservation and the prosperity of the group along with solidarity and concord among its members. Officials are singled out and honoured when they contribute substantial amounts from their own purse to major refurbishment or reconstruction of dilapidating buildings, provide cash in cases of emergency or perform their duties irreproachably.[41] Solidarity among fellow-members is promoted and enhanced with prescriptions such as participation in processions (*IG* II² 1283) or other festivities, in the mourning for a deceased member and in his funeral or mutual help in cases of legal disputes (*IG* II² 1275 and 1258). This sense of community is elaborated, extended and further strengthened in Roman times when *Iobacchoi* are threatened with a monetary fine in case they circumvent the association and appeal to the polis' mechanism or the Roman authorities for justice.[42] The honorary vocabulary of Athenian cult associations includes values and predominantly civic qualities such as ἀρετή 'virtue', εὔνοια 'benevolence', εὐσέβεια 'piety towards the gods', δικαιοσύνη 'righteousness' and

---

[41] *IG* II² 1263, ll. 9–13: καὶ τοὺς λογισμοὺς ἀπέδωκεν ὀρθ|[ῶ]ς καὶ δικαίως καὶ εὐθύνας ἔδωκεν | ὧν τε αὐτὸς ἐκυρίευσεν καὶ [[τ]] ἃ πρὸς | τοὺς ἄλλους ἐξελογίσατο ὅσοι τι τ|ῶν κοινῶν διεχείρισαν 'and he provided their accounts correctly and justly and underwent a scrutiny of whatever he administered and he received accounts of those who administered anything of the common funds' and similarly *IG* II² 1271, ll. 6–8. On ἀνέγκλητος, see *IG* II² 1235 (ca. 274/3 BC), 1292 and 1328; see also the use of such expressions as λόγον καὶ εὐθύνας δεδώκασιν in *IG* II² 1199 (ca. 325/4 BC) and εὐθύνας διδόναι in *IG* II² 1174 (368/7 BC).

[42] *IG* II² 1368, ll. 90–4: ἔστω δὲ | τὰ αὐτὰ ἐπιτείμια καὶ τῷ δαρέντι καὶ | μὴ ἐπεξελθόντι παρὰ τῷ ἱερεῖ ἢ τῷ | ἀρχιβάκχῳ, ἀλλὰ δημοσίᾳ ἐνκαλέσαν|τι 'and the same penalties shall be applied to the person beaten and did not complain to the priest or to the *archibakchos*, but he proceeded to an accusation in the polis'. Compare Philostratus, *Vitas Sophistarum* (Polemon) 532.

φιλοτιμία 'love of honour, zeal'.[43] These five qualities appear in every possible combination, with only two standard parameters; piety appears in cases the honoured person had a sacral or cultic activity, righteousness in cases of successfully administering the affairs of the group. The remaining three usually designate a substantial financial contribution to the group. Only in the imperial era will *eukosmia* (clauses barring ill-talk, hubristic behaviour, fights and wounding) penetrate into the normative world of associations.[44] In this respect, associations do not innovate, do not cut through their own path; they follow the lead of the Athenian polis when it granted certain privileges (*proxenia, politeia*, etc.). What changes is the beneficiary; instead of the Athenian polis, it is the associations themselves who capitalise and channel the outcome of their members' activities.[45] As a consequence, associations appear to have been very well integrated into the social fabric of the Athenian polis.

Rules Reflecting Realities or Realities Shaping Rules?

It is a commonplace that in Athens, to a large extent, associations' rules reflect long-established strategies, inspired by what happens at the polis level, especially, and as far as controlling the powers of magistrates and channelling the competitive edge of members to the service of the association were concerned.[46] In organisational affairs, they follow the language of the polis, for example, the designation of the main assembly as *agora kyria* (in almost all the honorary decrees), *ekklesia kai syllogon poiein* (in *IG* II² 1361),[47] accountability procedures followed for magistrates leaving

---

[43] See the single instance of *andragathia*, 'bravery, manly virtue', in *IG* II² 1261 with Arnaoutoglou 2003: 117.

[44] Baslez 2004: 106–7 associates these occurrences with *eukosmia* in the world of gymnasia. The concern about *eukosmia* appears in the context of a gymnasium (*IG* XII.6 11, Samos, after 243/2 BC, Lazaridou 2015: 5 ll. 36–51, 24/23 BC), a sanctuary (*Agora* 16 123, 302/1 BC), oracle (*IG* IX.2 1109, Thessaly, second century BC), theatre (*Agora* 15 34, 343/2 BC), celebration (*SEG* 12:511, Cilicia, Magarsos-Antiochia, ca. 140 BC), of young women (εὐκοσμία τῶν παρθένων, *MDAI* (A) 37 (1912): 277 no 1; 35 (1910): 436 no 20, Pergamum; *I.Pergamon* 463, before AD 37?), a special archon ἐπὶ τῆς εὐκοσμίας (*IGR* IV 556, l. 69; *IGR* IV 582; *MAMA* IX no 38). Liu 2013: 136 rather hastily considers these rules as 'mechanism for exposing and punishing the non-conformist, whose reputation would consequently suffer'.

[45] See Arnaoutoglou 2003: 115–18.

[46] *IG* II² 1283, ll. 9–11: ὅπως ἂν οὖν φα|[ίν]ωνται καὶ οἱ ὀργεῶνες τῶι τε τῆς πόλεως νόμωι πειθαρ|χοῦντες 'so that the *orgeones* of the polis will appear to comply to the laws of the polis' and ll. 25–6: κατά τε τὰ πάτρια τῶν Θραικῶν καὶ τοὺς τῆς πόλ[εως νόμου]|ς 'according to the ancestral customs of the Thracians and to the laws of the polis'.

[47] Compare the use of the expression ἐπεμελήθησαν δὲ καὶ τῆς συλλογῆς τῆς τε βουλῆς κτλ in *Agora* 15 (passim).

office (*SEG* 2:9 and *I.Rhamnous* 167, ll. 25–7) and perhaps in *IG* II²
1275 initiating what looks like a trial with no fixed penalty (*atimetos agon*).
They use, though rarely, entrenchment clauses similar to that of the polis
decrees,[48] but not in the documents of the Roman era, in which the only
similar reference (or rather exhortation) occurs in *IG* II² 1368, lines 30–1:
εὐτονήσουσι γὰρ οἱ προεστῶτες τοῦ μηδὲν αὐτῶν λυθῆναι 'for the
presiding officers shall be empowered to prevent any of those decrees from
being violated' (tr. Ascough, Harland and Kloppenborg 2012: 13). In the
numerous honorary decrees, associations usually penalise the non-
performance of the ritual announcement of honours (*anagoreusis*), as in
IG II² 1263, lines 43–5 (*thiasotai*, 300/299 BC); 1273, lines 21–6 (*thiasotai*, 265-263 BC); 1297, lines 17–18 (*thiasotai*, 236/5 BC); 1292, lines
15–17 (*Sarapiastai*, 215/4 BC).[49]

Cult associations do not seem to have had any impact outside their
immediate surroundings; instead, they are influenced, at least in
Hellenistic times, by the reigning civic and legal culture, as they adopt
and use the mechanisms of dispute resolution, civic values and organisational details provided by the polis.[50] In a sense, associations orbit around
the organisational model of planet Polis. The situation does not significantly change once the centre of the 'political' universe shifts to Rome.
Associations are sticking to the old ways of doing things, therefore their
relation to the polis is not altered; however, they still have to respond to
the challenges posed by the new administration, they have to acknowledge,
even tacitly, the possibility of intervention by the Roman authority. This is
the reason they proceed to an unprecedented introduction of rules concerning the punishment of their members for fighting one another. In
order to stay clear of the Romans, the group of *Iobacchoi* went a step
further and decided not to allow recourse to dispute resolution mechanisms other than those provided by the group itself.

Hellenistic cult associations in Athens do not seem to be concerned
with providing a model of a well-ordered association. Despite the pre-
dominance of *eukosmia* in the world of Hellenistic gymnasia, Hellenistic
associations seem very little concerned (if at all!) with the stability and

---

[48] Compare the entrenchment clauses in *IG* II² 1275 and 1361 with the respective clauses in *IG* I³ 29
(ca. 450 BC); *IG* I³ 1453C (?ca. 449 BC); *IG* I³ 52 (434/3 BC); *IG* II² 43, ll. 51–61 (378/7 BC),
Agora 19 L4a, ll. 95–6. See San Nicolò 1927: 267.

[49] Fines on *demarchoi*, *IG* II² 1183 and 1194. Proclamation of crown (*anagoreusis stephanou*) occurs
also in *IG* II² 1235. Proclamation (*aneipein*) widely practiced at polis level, *IG* II³ 378; 870; 877; *IG*
II² 1178; 1186–7; 1193; 1202. Penalty (*epibole*, ἐπιβολή) imposed by a *demarchos*, *IG* II² 1177.

[50] See Koerner 1987 for the sanctions against magistrates in the archaic and classical polis.

orderly behaviour of their membership. This concern will emerge and predominate in Roman times. *IG* II² 1368 preserves two key terms, εὐστάθεια and εὐκοσμία, which roughly correspond to the modern notion of a 'well-ordered society'. My guess is that the drive to pursue similar aims was initiated by the heavy shadow of the Roman administration. Roman magistrates were inculcated with the fear that associations were the hotbed of unrest. There are numerous testimonies to that; in the first-century Ephesus (Paul, *Acts*, 19.23–41), Philo's description of the tense atmosphere in Alexandria (Philo, *Against Flaccus*, 135–8), the decision of a pro-consul (*I.Ephesos* 215) in second-century Ephesus about the bakers, the correspondence of Pliny with Trajan (Plin. *Ep.* 10.33–4 and 92–3).[51] At the bottom of this phobia lies the perception that deliberation and other forms of public consultation involving a certain amount of noise, murmuring (approving or disapproving), shouting, heckling and reaction to the speaker may quickly develop into challenges to the orderly life of a polis and to the Roman interests.[52] However, people's participation in deliberation and consultation, even in this form, was probably an everyday practice in the Greek cities; *thorybos* was present in the council, the assembly, the lawcourts and other venues. Therefore, a certain amount of it was acceptable, even normal. One may observe that *thorybos* appears also in *IG* II² 1368, in the acclamation of the members in support of the inscription of the rules. But this acclamation has nothing spontaneous; it sounds like a well-rehearsed performance – at least that is how the text presents it. It is this fundamental perception of people's participation in the process of deliberation and consultation as inherently destabilising that led to the adoption of disciplinary rules against each association's members, despite the Athenian long tradition of peaceful co-existence.

Therefore, one can observe a gradual modification in the deployment of legal sanctions and regulations between the Hellenistic era and Roman times in Athenian associations, a qualitative shift to purely disciplinary measures. This shift of focus may be due to the differing qualities of the epigraphic habit; many more associations' honorary decrees survive from

---

[51] For the abuse of beer and wine drinking in Egyptian religious associations, see Clarysse 2001. For instances of breakdown of law and order in Bithynia, see Talbot 2004.

[52] *Thorybos* in associations' gatherings: Philo, *In Flaccum*, 138, Ael. Arist. 18 (*Monodia epi Smyrne*) 8. *Thorybos* in deliberations of political organs outside Athens: *OGIS* 48 (Ptolemaïs Hermiou, Egypt, 278/7 BC) and in imperial Nicomedia (Bithynia), *TAM* IV 3, 7.

Hellenistic than from Roman Athens. It does not mean, however, that legal sanctions against 'corporate' officials disappear.[53] They are taken as granted, as part of the wider trend towards stability.

Nevertheless, even a well-intentioned reader would not fail to point out that, this being the case, we should have had more evidence from the western part of the empire. And, I am afraid, this evidence is not forthcoming ... What to make of the lack of disciplinary measures in Roman *collegia*, with the sole exception of the Lanuvian *cultores Salutaris Dianae et Antinoi* (*CIL* XIV 2112, II ll. 26–8)? Is it due to a tighter administrative control on the municipal life? Or were the disciplinary rules an invention of the associates in the Roman East to shed suspicion and prejudice? Finally, is what attested in the *Iobacchoi* inscription (*IG* II² 1368) but an isolated instance in which the figure of Claudius Herodes Atticus, priest of the *Sebastoi*,[54] played a pivotal role thanks to his social rank and status?

What remains to be answered is how Hellenistic and perhaps classical Athenian associations dealt with questions of animosity, instability, strife and fight in their ranks. To be more precise, how were members of associations restrained and made to abstain from insulting, fighting and injuring? It would have been naïve to assume that there were not any such worries; sporadic references to *homonoia* allude to such a concern. Since we do not hear anything in their numerous decrees and regulations, this suggests that associations did not aim to provide a sanitised context of common activities. There are several factors that, when combined, provide an explanation; first, associations in Hellenistic Athens were mainly cult groups, so there was little room for disagreements. Second, by tolerating *thorybos* and integrating it into the assembly business, they had at their disposal a mechanism to let off steam and avoid escalation. Third, there were informal channels of dealing with rowdy and recalcitrant members, such as peer pressure, competition for prestige and honour, withdrawal of support and/or contacts, marginalisation of the offending party and the 'name and shame' strategy mentioned in *IG* II² 1361 and *Agora* 16 161.

[53] See fine on *eukosmos* in *IG* II² 1368, ll. 144–6. For the office, see Turcan 2003: 66.
[54] Cl. Herodes is attested as priest of the imperial cult (ἀρχιερεὺς τῶν Σεβαστῶν) in AD 126/7 (*IG* II² 3603; 3607; 3608), as priest (ἱερεύς) in AD 132 (*IG* II² 3296) and involved in subsidising a new outfit of ephebes during their march to Eleusis in AD 165/6 (*IG* II² 2090). See Ameling 1983 (for Herodes' *cursus*) and Tobin 1997: 35.

Thus, the toleration of *thorybos* and the integration of *thorybountes* into the 'corporate' business may have provided an alternative method of dealing with competition, dissension and strife. If, however, things got out of control, associates could always rely on the judicial system of the polis.[55]

---

[55] After the completion of this chapter, an article exploring the different treatment of violence in democratic and oligarchic regimes appeared by Simonton 2017. His conclusion that democratic regimes tended not to regulate *in extenso* citizens' behaviour and thus defused any threats to their stability. Pending further detailed discussion, this seems to be very similar to my findings about the lack of extensive regulation of everyday activity in Athenian private associations.

CHAPTER 7

Private Affairs in a Public Domain
Regulating Behavioural Code towards Benefactresses and Planning a Strategy of Social Impact in Mantinean Associations

Sophia Zoumbaki

Despite the considerable number of private associations attested in the Peloponnese, epigraphic sources from this region only rarely allow us an insight into norms of the associations' internal organisation. Beyond a regulation for the use of an *hestiatorion*, 'banquet-hall', and a *chalkion* (in this context the term probably refers to 'bronze cooking utensils' or the place where they were stored) on a metal tablet from Sicyon (sixth/fifth century BC), which is followed by a list of seventy-three male names,[1] and an extremely fragmentary inscription from Mantinea,[2] which refers to a *nomos* and to imposition of fines, texts of this type are not preserved. Some indirect light on private associations' rules and regulations is further shed by a small number of honorific decrees originating in Peloponnesian towns. This chapter will focus on this category of texts from Mantinea.

Four honorific decrees have been singled out as an interesting homogeneous group of documents that are dated within a limited period of time and that display similarities in their content. All Mantinean inscriptions under discussion are dated from the second quarter of the first century BC to the first half of the first century AD: the *synodos* of the *Koragoi* (ἡ σύνοδος τῶν Κοραγῶν: 61/60 BC), the *synodos*, also referred to as *koinon*, of the priestesses of Demeter (ἁ σύνοδος/τὸ κοινὸν τᾶν ἱερειᾶν τᾶς Δάματρος: 43/42 BC), the *synodos* of the priests of Asclepius (ἡ σύνοδος τῶν Ἀσκληπιοῦ ἱερέων: first half of the first century AD) and the *synodos* of the priests of Zeus Epidotes (σύνοδος τῶν ἱερέων τοῦ Διὸς τοῦ Ἐπιδώτου: first half of the first century AD). A further common element of all these associations is that they were active within the broader scope of religious life, concentrated around popular cults of the town, and their decrees in

---

[1] Orlandos 1937/8: 5–12 no 1; Peek 1941: 200–7; Lejeune 1943 (*SEG* 11:244); Jeffery 1990: 143; Koerner 1993: 23 and 69–72 no 23; Van Effenterre and Ruzé 1994: 290–1 no 75; Lolos 2010.

[2] *IG* V.2 264; *IPArk* 10 (late second/early first century BC).

question passed in honour of prominent women for whom religion was the only field of activity in public life.

A religious dimension is to be found in every association, as it has been convincingly argued.[3] Our examination will not, however, concentrate on the religious activity of the Mantinean collectivities. Rituals will be regarded here merely as prescribed events in their schedule, which offer snapshots of their collegial life.[4] Our attempt will be first to gain an insight into the regulations that governed the associations and second to search for tangible traces of their interaction with local societies, since the degree of openness to public life and interplay with the external world could affect an association's organisation. The original set of rules at the moment of the establishment of the associations has been preserved in none of the cases under examination. Their honorific decrees allow us, however, to draw some indirect information about pre-existing rules and their internal organisation, as these texts refer on the one hand to predefined procedures that had to be followed, to codified sets of regulations and even to archives where important documents concerning their communal life were deposited; on the other hand, they contain new pieces of regulations that had to be henceforth respected by their members. These clauses further include punishment in cases of infringement and measures to secure the advertisement of the associations' decisions and regulations. These honorific decrees contain specific pieces of regulations that give us an idea of the groups' legislative corpora, which have not been preserved to us: in them, the image of an ordered environment emerges clearly. It is actually noteworthy that, despite the differences, remarkable similarities can be observed in the wording and the scheme of privileges granted to the benefactors in all honorific decrees under examination. Moreover, a similar set of ethical values that determined their practices and decisions is to be traced. All texts reveal the associations' aspiration to connect with members of the local elites and their effort to claim a role in the public life of the town.

The Association of the *Koragoi*

The name of *Koragoi* implies a connection with the celebration of the festival of Koragia in honour of Kore, a very popular goddess in Arcadia.[5]

---

[3] Scheid 2003: 61–74. On the role of religious devotion of private associations, cf. also Gabrielsen 2016b: 100–1.

[4] On regulations by associations concerning religious matters properly, see Carbon in Chapter 4.

[5] *IG* V.2 265; *IPArk* 11 (61/0 BC); cf. Jost 1985:297–355.

The *Koragoi* define themselves as a *synodos* at various points of their decree in honour of Nikippa, a prominent and wealthy woman whose statue was seen by Pausanias (8.6.9) in Mantinea almost two centuries later. From the record of Nikippa's numerous benefactions towards the *synodos* (*IG* V.2 265, ll. 1–26), we gain some details regarding the organisation of the *Koragia*, which should be regarded as the main event of the association's activity. Nikippa apparently undertook the costs (l. 13: τὰν λειτουργίαν lit. 'the service', with related expenses) of the festival that took place in the eighth month (l. 10) and included several ceremonies. Performance of the secret mysteries of the goddess (ll. 11–12; 20–1) should have been of central importance. A procession (ll. 15–16), sacrifices (ll. 11 and 17) and examination of the omens on behalf of the association (l. 17) are further mentioned. The new *peplos* that Nikippa offered to the cult statue of the goddess (l. 20) was apparently part of the ritual and not an expression of her personal generosity. The celebration also included a ritual carrying of the (cult statue of) the goddess to the priest's house,[6] perhaps as part of the procession (ll. 21–3); in this case, it was Nikippa who welcomed the statue of the goddess at home (we will return to this issue). Finally, she performed the conventional procedure (τὰ νομιζόμενα 'what is customary') connected to the opening of the temple on the 30th day (ll. 23–5). Since a temple was devoted to the cult of Kore and Nikippa took care of its additional building needs (ll. 25–6: προενοήθη δὲ καὶ ἃς προσεδεῖτο ὁ ναὸς [ο]ἰκοδομᾶς 'she also provided for the building work of which the temple was in need'), the question arises as to what the phrase ἐστέγασεν καὶ εὐσχημόνισεν τὰ περὶ τὰν θεὸν ἄρρητα μυστήρια means (ll. 20–1, literally, 'she gave a roof to the sacred mysteries and decorated them').[7] Furthermore, she gave 80 drachmas for an urgent, unspecified need (ll. 18–19).

The *Koragoi* served therefore a popular cult, displayed a long-lasting devotion to Kore, contributed to the needs of the cult and repeatedly accepted the benevolence of various benefactors. On the basis of the decree

---

[6] Jost 2003: 155 characterises this transportation of the cult statue as the 'essential moment' of the festival, a specifically Mantinean ritual either relating to the cycle of vegetation or celebrating the anniversary of the introduction of the cult or commemorating a divine visit. Bölte 1930: 1338–9 placed the origins of the cult of Kore to the old *demos* of Nestane and connected the place-name Nestane with Nostia interpreting it thus as an echo of the ritual of taking the statue of the goddess back to the temple, as it is described in the decree in honour of Nikippa.

[7] According to Jost 2003: 148 it means that she had the building repaired that was used at the same time for the Mysteries of Demeter and Kore (*IG* V.2 266) and for those of Kore only (*IG* V.2 265); Cronkite 1997: II 433 interprets the phrase in the sense that '… a temporary hut or shelter was erected so that rites could be performed in secret'.

in honour of Nikippa, we can draw indirect information about pre-existing rules of the association, such as those prescribing the annual schedule of the rites and the exact procedure that should be followed. Furthermore, common banquets are to be recognised as important events of their internal activity. It arises that certain individuals organised and hosted banquets on specific days, where they were supposed to invite the benefactors. Invitation of the benefactors to the banquets and sharing ritual food with them was a central element in the honours granted to all benefactors of the *synodos* (ll. 30–2): οἱ ἀεὶ ὑποδεχόμενοι,[8] 'those who each time host a meal' (or offer a sacrifice), were supposed to invite Nikippa ἐπὶ τὰ γέρα, 'to (offer her) perquisite', on specific days along with other individuals who had been honoured by the association. Further, αἶσα, 'her share' (of common meals or sacrifices where she apparently could not partake for ritual or personal reasons) was to be sent to her.[9] Sacrifices followed by a banquet and the sharing of sacrificial meat were therefore of crucial importance to the *synodos* of *Koragoi* (cf. ll. 29–34).

The honorific distinctions for Nikippa voted by the association were henceforth permanently in effect and their abolition entailed intervention of an official titled *epignoma*, who was expected to force the offender to fulfil the obligations towards the benefactor; if he still refused to do so, a penalty of 50 drachmas was to be imposed on him, as he would be considered guilty of having ignored the honours awarded by the *synodos*, which were in fact integrated into the set of 'regulations' that should be fostered by its members. The decisions of the *synodos*, as they are presented in the decree, aimed thus at permanent validity.

The decree further arranges the publication of the honours voted for Nikippa. The priests appointed eight men charged with the task to commission a stele bearing the decree (ll. 41–2: καταστασάτωσαν δὲ οἱ ἱερεῖς ... 'the priests shall set up ...'). The place for the erection of the stele is specified as 'the most prominent spot of the sanctuary'.[10] A copy of this decree was also to be deposited εἰς τὰν κοινὰν πινακίδα, 'in the common tablet', probably an archive of the association. The sanctuary mentioned in the decree, apparently the *Koragion*, which should have been the main setting of the *Koragoi*'s activity, was not a private clubhouse, but a public

---

[8] On ὑποδεχόμενοι see Poland 1909: 260.   [9] On *aisa* see Poland 1909: 259 and 436.
[10] On the regulation of space by associations, see Skaltsa in Chapter 5.

sanctuary, as it arises from the decree of the priestesses of Demeter, which will be discussed below.[11]

Rules regarding the internal structure, membership, various administrative issues or further events of the *Koragoi* remain unknown. What clearly arises from the decree is that functionaries and members were expected to respect a certain code of behaviour, which echoes basic values of the *synodos*. Compliance with the code of conduct towards the benefactors was so important that transgression meant the activation of a predetermined procedure: exhortation of the transgressor to comply with the regulations was the first step, and if not taken into account, a prescribed economic penalty was to be imposed on him. The emphasis given to the compliance with the conduct code within the association, the description of the steps from exhortation to punishment and the publication of the honorific decree at a prominent spot in parallel to the preservation of a copy in the association's archive show that decisions of the *synodos* should be indisputably obeyed and ethical values should be respected by its members. A set of these ethical values is reflected on the 'institutionalisation' of appropriate behaviour towards benefactors.[12] The ethical qualification of the honorand is underlined in stressing her *areta*, 'goodness', *dikaiosyne*, 'righteousness', *philanthropia*, 'benevolence' (towards people), *eusebeia*, 'piety' (towards gods), *eunoia*, 'favour' (towards the *synodos*) (ll. 2–6, 28–9). The moral code that was embraced by the association formalised reciprocity to the benefactor's generosity – namely, the tangible expression of the ethical qualification mentioned above – as a principle that should be obeyed; otherwise, a member whose behaviour would not be in compliance with that principle was regarded as [κατ]αλύων τὰ δεδόμενα ... [ὑπὸ τᾶς συνόδου] τίμια 'someone who abolishes the honours given by the *synodos*' (ll. 37–8), namely, as an offender of the reciprocity measures that had been voted by the *synodos* and hence been in power as rules that should be followed. Moreover, insistence on appropriate behaviour towards benefactors may reflect the strong need of the association to inspire further beneficial activity of the honorand or of others, since it is clearly stated in the decree that they maintained hopes for future benefactions (ll. 40–1). In this case, reciprocity would not be merely expected in a context of moral principles

---

[11] For the *Koragion* in combination with the *megaron* mentioned by the decree of the priestesses of Demeter, see n. 19 below.

[12] On the importance of the ethical code as a qualification of private associations, see Gabrielsen 2016b: 96–103.

of civility and politeness, but it would also form a necessary condition to continue attracting euergetism.

The Association of the Priestesses of Demeter

From the decree of the priestesses of Demeter in honour of Phaena, it is clear that she had already assumed the priesthood of the goddess.[13] During her term, she fulfilled in the most generous way her duties in respect both to the cult and to the priestesses of Demeter, as she spent profusely for any need of the cult or the priestesses (ll. 6–9). Μετὰ τὸ ἱεριτεῦσαι 'after serving as priestess', that is to say, when her term as priestess was over,[14] Phaena continued to hold splendid banquets and to spend for the cult of Demeter and the *synodos*. Moreover, she ordered her daughter and granddaughter to undertake the costs of the annual needs of the *synodos* in the case that she was unable to execute her duties. She donated 120 drachmas for the repair of the *megaron*, 'hall', or for the cover of any other need at the discretion of the priestesses, an action pointing out to the fact that the association possessed some sort of treasury and accepted funds.

For the ritual side of the association's activity, we have very limited information. From the phrase ἐν ταῖς γινομέναις ἀντ' ἐνιαυτοῦ θυσίαις τε καὶ σιταρχίαις 'both in the sacrifices and in the banquets (*sitarchiai*) which take place during the year' (ll. 35–6), we conclude that sacrifices and *sitarchiai* took place. In particular, ἀντ' ἐνιαυτοῦ is to be understood either as annual or as taking place throughout the year.[15] *Sitarchiai* are probably to be interpreted as ritual banquets of the association. The individual who was responsible for these banquets is called *sitarcho* (σιταρχώ).[16] Judging from the responsibilities of *sitarchos* mentioned by Harmodios of Lepreon in the context of the cults of Phigaleia (*FrGrH* 319), the *sitarcho* of the Mantinean association seems to be responsible for supplying food for the ritual banquet. The formulation of the text (ll. 36–7: ἀνακαλούσας τὰς ἀεὶ ἀντιτυγχανούσας ἱερείας τε καὶ σιταρχοῦς 'while anyone who may happen to serve both as priestess and as *sitarcho* will issue the invitation') may

---

[13] *IG* V.2 266; *IPArk* 12, l. 6 (ἱεριτευχε; 43/2 BC).

[14] Steinmüller 2008: 33 and 36 regards Phaena as an actual priestess and interprets the phrase μετὰ τὸ ἱεριτεῦσαι as 'beyond her function as a priestess'. That Phaena was still the current priestess of the association seems, however, incompatible with the perfect forms ἱερίτευχε (l. 6; cf. Schwyzer 1937: 41) and διαλέλοιπε (l. 14).

[15] Cf. Hesychius, *s.v.* mentions: ἀνθ' ἡμέρας· δι' ὅλης τῆς ἡμέρας.

[16] For the term, cf. Jost 1985: 346.

imply that both capacities, priesthood and *sitarchia*, could be combined in the same individual.

As it did to its benefactors in general (ll. 39–40), the association granted lifelong honours to Phaena and invited her to the *gera*, 'perquisites', at the banquets (*sitarchiai*) of the whole year (ll. 39–40). The quotation of the oral announcement of the invitation perhaps implies that it was announced loudly before the public (cf. ll. 36–40). Lifelong offering of γέρα τὰ εἰθισμένα 'customary perquisites' shows that they were standard for all benefactors. Failure to award these honours meant that the culprit was to be indicted, to be liable to prosecution and to the payment of a fine of 100 drachmas to the honorand and her off-spring. The judges are not named, but the phrase ὑπόδικος ἔστω καὶ ἐνδεικτός 'he/she shall be liable to trial and indictment' implies, according to K. Harter-Uibopuu, that the judges may have been civic appointees or the whole community that was aware of the honours, since they were publicly announced.[17] It is, however, not clear whether the judges were civic appointees and not functionaries of the association, as well as whether ἔνδειξις, 'indictment', refers to the whole community and not to its members.

As for the publication of the honours for Phaena, a stele bearing the decree was to be set up in the *Koragion*. The place of the erection of the stele was determined by the archons and the *synedroi* (ll. 40–2), namely, civic officers, a fact that leads us to guess that the *Koragion* was not a private place belonging to the association, but a sacred place belonging to the whole community. Although cults of Demeter and Kore[18] were interconnected, the placement of a stele erected by the priestesses of Demeter in the *Koragion* poses questions about the relationship of the *synodos* of the priestesses of Demeter with the *Koragoi* as well as about the topographical identification of the *Koragion* and the *megaron* whose repair was financially supported by Phaena.[19]

---

[17] Harter-Uibopuu 2013: 249–50 examines the judicial details of the whole procedure and stresses that the fine is much larger than the value of her share in common meals and sacrifices, but intends to reward her for a possible insult. Harter-Uibopuu further argues that if the judges are civic appointees or the whole community, the community seems to be regarded as a plaintiff, since a popular indictment (ἔνδειξις) is to be understood in the term ἐνδεικτός (l. 44).

[18] For the cult of Demeter and Kore in Arcadia, the rites and the *epikleseis* see Jost 2003: 144–6. She also stresses that 'in Arcadia proper, Artemis is associated with Despoina in the cult and probably the Mysteries of the *megaron* at Lykosoura'.

[19] A combination of the decrees of the *Koragoi* and the priestesses of Demeter with certain references in Pausanias's text poses further questions, since the chronological distance as well as the different points of view of the two sources cause several difficulties in understanding the topographical problems and various details of the cults. The inscriptions do not offer any details about the topographical identification of the *Koragion* and *megaron*. Pausanias (8.8, 1 and 4) refers to a

As in the decree of the *Koragoi*, special attention is paid to the proper behaviour towards the benefactress, who, moreover, gave instructions to her daughter and granddaughter to continue to support the *synodos* in case of her disability. That means that reciprocity between the benefactor and the association was important, perhaps – as we mentioned in the case of *Koragoi* – not only on a symbolic level of ethical values, but also on the practical level of the need for essentials, for whose cover the association could rely on benefactors.

Two Associations of Priests: The Priests of Asclepius and the Priests of Zeus Epidotes

Two *synodoi* of priests, those of Asclepius and of Zeus Epidotes,[20] honour the same outstanding woman, Iulia Eudia, for her donation of some plots of land to each group, a very important donation, if we take into account that landed property was an excellent source of income. The decree of the priests of Zeus Epidotes is very fragmentary, but it had apparently a similar content to that of the priests of Asclepius, which will be analysed here.

---

sanctuary of Demeter, defined as ἅγιον, which was located at Nestane at the slope of mount Alesion, at a considerable distance from the town of Mantinea (cf. Bölte 1930: 1338–9 who places the origins of the cult of Kore to the old *demos* of Nestane). He further records the sanctuary of Demeter and Kore under the sanctuaries of the town of Mantinea (8.9.2). The fact that Pausanias records one sanctuary devoted to both Demeter and Kore reflects, according to Stiglitz 1967: 75–6, the situation of Pausanias's age, when the cult of Demeter was already added to that of Kore in her urban sanctuary. The *Koragion* must be regarded as a different place, to which the association of *Koragoi* is apparently related, and its use by the priestesses of Demeter is interpreted by Stiglitz as a practical solution, because the sanctuary of Demeter at Nestane was far from the town, whereas the *Koragion* was in the town of Mantinea and thus more appropriate for advertising someone's honours. Stiglitz 1967: 75 takes further for granted that the *megaron* for whose repair Phaena donated 120 drachmas is to be placed in the sanctuary of Nestane and identified with the ἱερὸν ἅγιον of Demeter. Jost 1985: 127 separates the *megaron* from the *Koragion* and identifies the former with the sanctuary mentioned by Pausanias (8.9.2), where 'they keep a fire, taking anxious care not to let it go out' and where she places the mysteries recorded in *IG* V.2 265. Jost identifies further the temple mentioned in *IG* V.2 265 with the *Koragion* and wonders whether it could also be a hall for the meetings of the association of *Koragoi*. Jost 2003: 148, cf. 144–51 (discussion of further *megara* attested in Arcadia) suggests more clearly that the *megaron* was used both for mysteries of Demeter and Kore (*IG* V.2 266) and of Kore alone (*IG* V.2 265). According to Volanaki-Kontoleontos 1992–8: 473–90 (*SEG* 48:2185), a *megaron* is not to be necessarily identified with a subterranean chamber, but also with a building or an enclosure wall. For the identification of the cult places, see also Felten 2007: 241–2.

20 ἡ σύνοδος τῶν Ἀσκληπιοῦ ἱερέων (*IG* V.2 269; *IPArk* 13), σύνοδος τῶν ἱερέων τοῦ Διὸς τοῦ Ἐπιδώτου (*IG* V.2 270); both are to be dated to the first half of the first century AD. Pausanias mentions the cults of Asclepius and Zeus Epidotes (8.9, 1–2) in Mantinea. That the cult of Asclepius was very prominent in the Roman period is shown by the depiction of the deity on Mantinean coins of the Roman period bearing Plautilla's portrait on the obverse and Asclepius on the reverse, cf. *BMC* 27 (AD 202–5).

The priests of Asclepius decided for the advertisement of Eudia's benefactions through (public) praise, as well as for certain further acts, which would be permanent in effect. A painted portrait of the honorand in an *imago clipeata* was to be dedicated in the temple of Asclepius. Further, a new event was introduced to the association's annual schedule, namely, the celebration of Eudia's birthday in the fifth month, which included sacrifices to Asclepius and Hygeia for her and her husband's safety. The *synodos* was expected to invite Eudia and her husband *epi ta gera*, 'to the perquisites', at every banquet of the priests. A portion (*aisa*) was to be sent to her on the occasion of the banquets referred to as *Isiaka kai pyrophorika deipna*[21] – in which priests of Asclepius apparently partook, but they did not organise them. Failure to invite the honorand resulted in a trial and a financial penalty of 50 drachmas was to be paid by the offender to Eudia, her descendants and the priests. It gives the impression that abolishment of these honours was to be taken as an insult not only to the benefactress, but also to the *synodos* that voted for them. The whole procedure was supervised by the *epignoma*.

The new event that was introduced into the association's annual programme, the celebration of Eudia's birthday, was not integrated into an existing set of events, but it created a new one that enriched its schedule. It shows that the internal organisation of the association's life was not a fossilised set of rules, but a flexible and ongoing process.[22] The high honours voted for the benefactress and the punishment that was foreseen for any transgressors reflect the moral rules that formed the basis of the members' behaviour. Moreover, the association not only voted for various honours for the benefactress, but also wished to advertise them, so that everybody be informed that it did express its gratitude in a tangible way, as it is formulated (ll. 34–7). As it was the case with the aforementioned Mantinean associations, reciprocity was apparently not only a matter of civility, but also a policy aiming at the attraction of further benefactions.

Remarks to the Associations of Mantinea

In the cases analysed above, all Mantinean associations in question were attached to popular traditional cults of the town, as further epigraphic,

---

[21] Jost 1985: 505–6 suggests that *pyrphorika deipna* were organised by the *pyrphoroi* and the *Isiaka deipna* by the functionaries of the cult of Isis. Felten 2007: 242 does not exclude the possibility that these banquets were organised in the shrine of Asclepius, given the connection between Isis and Asclepius, which is to be observed at several places.

[22] Cf. Gabrielsen 2016b: 87–111, esp. 102.

literary and archaeological evidence confirm. Devotion of private associations to the most important state cults is to be observed at several places, including other Peloponnesian towns, and obviously served strategies of both state and associations.[23] Beyond the service of traditional civic cults, further common elements are to be observed in regard to their regulations concerning honours and privileges of their benefactresses.

Regulations concerning the Grant of Honours: A Common Scheme Dictated by Moral Values and Historical Circumstances

The expression of gratitude of the *synodoi* resulted in granting a common scheme of privileges to the benefactors, such as invitation to common banquets, sharing of sacrificial meat and sending of *aisa*, erection of honorific monuments or publication of the honours at prominent spots of a sanctuary. The priests of Asclepius decided further for the addition of a new event to their annual schedule in honour of their benefactress; this is the only element that deviates from the common pattern of honours.

Inviting benefactors to the banquets and offering them a share from the sacrifices appears in all cases as an extremely important element. As a perquisite from sacrifices was a privilege of the priests, this honour assumes a special significance for benefactors who either had held the office of a priest (e.g. Phaena) or had undertaken priestly duties without having officially assumed the function of a priest (e.g. Nikippa).[24] Showing a long-lasting respect to the benefactresses as well as maintenance of their privileges appear as the main concern and pursuit of the associations' decrees. Moreover, voting and publishing honours for them meant that a common unwritten ethical code of values assumed the form of concrete written regulations. According to these regulations, the abolition of honours to benefactors led in all cases to appeal to the judgement of arbiters and to the punishment of the offenders.

In order to perceive the insistence of the associations on a strict code of behaviour, we should place the activity of the three Mantinean benefactresses and the associations connected with them into their historical context. For this purpose, it is perhaps significant to take into account the conditions prevailing in Mantinea in the first century BC and the first

[23] Suys 2005: esp. 214. For the Peloponnese in particular cf. *ha synodos ha ton Asklapiastan ton en Panakeia* in Epidauros (*IG* IV² 1 679), a *synodos* devoted to the cult of Asclepius, the most popular deity of the region, whose sanctuary was of outstanding fame.
[24] Pirenne-Delforge 2005: 25; 2010: 122–3.

decades of the Imperial period. Generally, for Peloponnesian towns, it is a phase of reconstruction and overcoming of economic difficulties caused by the long preceding period of hardship. Wars, changes of alliances and the exhaustion of human and economic resources during the Hellenistic period (cf. Plb. 36.17.5–6), followed by the annihilation of Corinth by Mummius in 146 BC, put severe strain on the towns and led to their gradual decline. The second half of the second century BC was marked by shrinkage of various aspects of public activity in the Peloponnese, which is obvious in the sharp drop in production of public texts and in the limited activity or even cessation of local mints. The dissolution of the important economic network earlier centred at Corinth, which certainly included numerous Peloponnesian towns, resulted in the region's stagnation, introversion and poverty, which favoured the flourishing of Delos (Str. 10.5.4 (486)). This situation combined with piracy, which took full action, especially at the southern shores of the Peloponnese and impeded commercial activity, had a huge impact on local economies. The towns could not really recover throughout the second half of the second century BC and continued to experience further drainage of economic reserves and human capital during the Mithridatic wars and the Roman social wars, due to enormous Roman demands for recruitments and supplies of various kinds, as literary and epigraphic sources show.[25]

In order to cope with this situation during the first century BC, the towns energised all existing mechanisms, above all euergetism. Inscriptions from various Peloponnesian towns of the first century BC imprint the scale of private initiatives of benefactors on various levels of public life in an attempt to return to normality. Cultic activities had been also neglected in several cases in the Peloponnese, and sanctuaries were left to collapse due to economic difficulties. Inscriptions of the first century BC attest to private individuals who undertook the restoration of sanctuaries or took up priesthoods of neglected cults.[26]

It is thus understandable that euergetic activity of prominent women in Mantinea was very important during a period of reconstruction on all levels. It is further understandable that activity of private associations could offer a significant contribution to keeping various cultic procedures and celebrations upright and was for this reason apparently welcomed by civic authorities and communities. The social placement of private associations is obvious in an inscription from the Augustan age from Mantinea (IG V.2 268) recording honours awarded by the polis and the Roman *negotiatores*

[25] Zoumbaki 2019: 33–5.   [26] Giannakopoulos 2017.

to an outstanding individual, Euphrosynos, son of Titus, and his wife Epigone. Under their benefactions, it is mentioned that ταμεῖα συνόδοις ἐχαρίσαντο 'they donated (private) chambers to the *synodoi*' (l. 37), which implies that the position of the *synodoi* in the town's life was prominent enough to attract support of members of the elite. Euergetism towards associations was thus of high importance for the survival of these organisms and their capability to keep on their activity, which, in turn, ensured the continuity of performance of popular cults of the town. Under these circumstances, it becomes understandable why concrete regulations in the honorific decrees insisted on ensuring that privileges awarded to benefactors would not be abolished. Obviously, this reflects not merely a set of moral principles, but also awareness of the associations' vital need for material support.

Internal Regulations or External Interventions? The Elusive Limits between Private and Public

In this context, the relationship of the associations with public authorities and the possibility of transfer of responsibilities from the public sphere to the level of a private association should be expected. In the Mantinean decrees in question, limits between public and private in several cases fluctuate. Elusive limits between public and private are to be observed at several places,[27] where private associations appear as an integral part of religious life and they seem not to contradict with public religious authorities, but to contribute to the organisation of the rites and to support financially any need of the ritual or material aspect of the cults.

Although the question of what belongs to the public sphere and what falls into an association's private level is not the focus of this chapter, this aspect is not irrelevant to our discussion, as it is important to clarify what concerns the associations' internal organisation and what belongs to the wider religious landscape of the polis, especially in crucial aspects of the associations' activity, such as the field of justice. It is interesting to examine whether certain of the associations' rules exclusively stipulated in-house settlement of their issues or allowed or invited external authorities to intervene and regulate internal affairs, such as punishment of delinquent behaviour. So, we can wonder whether the *epignoma*, who was supposed to force members of the *Koragoi* and the association of the priests of Asclepius to fulfil their obligations towards the benefactors, is to be regarded as a

---

[27] Rüpke 2013: 268–9; Suys 2005: 205–7, 211–18.

public authority, since he is attested as such in several cases in the Peloponnese and beyond.[28] Because private associations often imitate public organisation and functions, it is very well possible that the *epignoma* was a magistrate of the association.

In some cases, it is obvious that Mantinean associations collaborated with public authorities. So, for example, the exact place of the publication of the honorific decree for Phaena issued by the *synodos* of the priestesses of Demeter was to be determined by the archons and the *synedroi* (ll. 40–2), namely, civic officers of the highest rank. As already mentioned, the fact that these officers decided to erect the stele in the *Koragion* indicates that it was a public sacred place, since public authorities could not decide on the exact place of publication of a private decree at a private space. The *Koragion* was apparently connected with the activity of the *Koragoi* as well. A public sanctuary could be used with the consent of civic authorities by two private associations attached to the interconnected cults of Demeter and Kore, obviously because these private associations played such an important role in covering the needs of the cults and the sanctuary that they could in fact perform their activity seamlessly there – although civic authorities maintained supervision of the public sanctuary. Since the associations in question were attached to civic cults and performed cere-monies partially or exclusively in a public sanctuary[29] – even if they also possessed private clubhouses – their processions and celebrations were apparently, at least to some degree, publicly visible. Therefore, we are not dealing with marginal associations totally focused on their internal and private affairs only, but with organisms open to the public, enjoying wide respect, collaborating in some cases with public authorities and even undertaking to some degree the town's role in the finance of popular cults.

---

[28] The *epignoma/epignomas/epignomon* is attested in several Peloponnesian towns. His responsibilities included the supervision of the sanctuary's smooth functioning and perhaps oversight of some financial aspects. He is mentioned on fragmentary Archaic period inscriptions on slabs covering Mycenaean underground passages – originally used for water supply – at the NW side of the acropolis of Tiryns; see Verdelis, Jameson, Papachristodoulou 1975 (*SEG* 30:380); Lupu 2005: 191–204, no 6. A board of officials, ἁ ἐπιγνόμα, consisting of eight *synepignomonas*, is attested in the records of the bronze tablets of the treasury of Pallas (where the sacred funds of Hera were also kept) in Argos: here two *epignomones* from each Argive tribe and a *grammateus* make up a board, which is in charge of a sum of money called *epignomonikon* (Kritzas 2013: 283–4). In a manumission of a later date from Mantinea, an official, called *epignomoneuon*, is listed after the priest of Poseidon (*IG* V.2 275).The *episophos* on Thera (*IG* XII.3 330, l. 199), who is attested in the context of a private association, may have had identical or similar functions. The term *epignomon* is attested in later literary texts always in the sense of 'inspector', e.g. in the Epistles of Maximus Confessor (*Patrologia Graeca* 91).

[29] Mylonopoulos 2006 generally on sanctuaries as places of communication through rituals.

Their honorific decrees imitate the style of civic equivalents, borrowing clauses from civic honorific texts, and their pompous wording resembles that of civic documents. Although we know very little about their internal organisation, it is possible that they also imitated the civic structure or adopted civic titles for their functionaries.

A further confusion arises as to whether priests and priestesses mentioned in the decrees are to be understood as functionaries of the associations or as civic priests. A civic priest was expected to perform official sacrifices on behalf of the whole community – often followed by sacrificial meals for the community. For example, the fact that the priests of Asclepius decided to celebrate Eudia's birthday with sacrifices reinforces the assumption that the association does not act as a college of priests in an official polis capacity, since the beneficiary of the sacrifice was not the citizens' community but rather private individuals. The priests of the decrees under examination acted as private groups, which organised private events and accepted the benevolence of certain individuals whom they honoured privately. Common banquets organised by the associations, where the benefactors were invited, were not sacrificial meals for the whole community, but belonged to a private sphere and the priests were totally legitimised to single out certain individuals as guests.[30] It appears clearly in the case of the priests of Asclepius, who invited Iulia Eudia and her husband to their banquets but not to the *Isiaka kai pyrophorika deipna*, which were obviously not organised by them. Certainly priests were also expected to perform private sacrifices on behalf of isolated supplicants of the sanctuaries[31] or to perform rites outside the official scope of the city, yet these rites did fall within the framework of tradition.[32] Therefore, a priest could be activated both on a public and on a semi-private level, namely, public and private capacity could be combined in one and the same individual, but both capacities remained clearly separate and each could be used depending on circumstances. As Carbon and Pirenne-Delforge state,[33] '"private" worship was an integral part of the wider "public" context, of the so-called "*polis*-religion" framework', and this seems to be true for Mantinean associations.

Given the important social and economic role of these associations in the religious life of their towns, their openness to the public, their collaboration with public authorities as well as imitation of various elements of

---

[30] Cf. an analogous situation from a completely different cultural environment, see Raja 2015.
[31] Pirenne-Delforge 2010: 123.   [32] Carbon and Pirenne-Delforge 2013: 65–6.
[33] Carbon and Pirenne-Delforge 2013: 66.

civic structure, titles, wording, it becomes clear why limits between public and private appear – at least for the modern researcher – fluid. In the internal affairs of Mantinean associations, the public aspect is omnipresent.

Conclusions

The associations discussed above were activated in the wider spectrum of religion in Mantinea, being integral parts of social life. Despite the differences, remarkable common elements are obvious in their honorific decrees, which formed the basis of our investigation. In all cases, honorific decrees not only included the description of a common pattern of honours and privileges granted to benefactresses, but also regulated the members' conduct and enforced respect to the benefactresses in a similar manner. This code of behaviour goes beyond politeness and gratitude and assumes the form of written internal regulations with long-lasting effect.

Thus, all associations were open to external benefactors and did not hesitate to share part of their communal activities, such as ritual food, with them. Participation in communal activities was apparently of such importance for these collectivities that the clause καλεῖν ἐπὶ τὰ γέρα 'invite to the perquisites' appears as a central privilege of the benefactors, whose abolishment led to punishment. Generally, privileges and honours were not to be abolished and severe measures of punishment were always foreseen for cases of infringement. Not only common moral values but also the importance of euergetism for the survival of the associations and careful strategy for attraction of prominent protectors and sponsors are traceable in the regulations in all cases under discussion.

This considerable openness to the external world, observed in all cases, and the abundant support of outstanding individuals allowed the associations to organise events of a decent, if not luxurious, standard. The sums of 80 and 120 drachmas donated to the *synodoi* of *Koragoi* and the priestesses of Demeter by Nikippa and Phaena, respectively, are important donations and show the high economic status of both women as well as the impact of the associations on local society. If we take into consideration the general economic situation of the Peloponnesian towns during the second half of the second century and the first century BC, it is understandable why important state cults sought support of outstanding associations that prolonged public organisation of certain rites and added magnificence and splendour by paying for building needs or performance of ceremonies. The role of euergetism becomes clear under these circumstances and the reciprocity to the benefactors appears as a central element of the internal behavioural code of the associations. The affiliation of outstanding individuals and highlighting their goodwill towards the associations were obviously the groups' strategic choices in order to secure their financial support and, further, to gain prestige in the local communities. Conversely, displaying an euergetic activity towards associations that enjoyed public respect was for members of the elite an excellent opportunity to enhance their reputation. Placed in societies that depended much on euergetism, both associations and prominent individuals could profit from cooperation.

Openness to the public sphere, common to all associations examined here, certainly affected their internal organisation and the strategy of their activity. Their activity was highly visible to the public; they erected their monuments or documents in public places, obviously because they wanted them to be accessible to the public. The fact that special attention was paid to the place of publication of the honorific decrees may have been aimed at representing the *synodoi* as powerful, influential and visible organisms at the most conspicuous religious spaces. Moreover, they obviously aspired to present themselves as well-organised, strictly structured micro-societies that were governed by concrete rules, whose internal life obeyed ethical principles. Thus, associations represented themselves as respectful bodies within the town.

CHAPTER 8

A World Full of Associations
Rules and Community Values in Early Roman Egypt[*]

Micaela Langellotti

Introduction

This chapter investigates the nature of the relations between the rules of professional associations and the shaping of community values in early Roman Egypt.

The ancient world was full of associations. From West to East, in urban as well as rural centres, individuals gathered in more or less formalised groups, each displaying specific purposes and connotations, and over time the associative model, or *fenomeno associativo*, was widespread across all of the Mediterranean countries – and beyond.[1] Being part of a group reflected a primary human desire, thus providing individuals with a sense of belonging and contributing to the shaping of one's social identity. Multiple reasons, social and cultural as well as political and economic, lie behind the development of this phenomenon.[2] The religious element, in particular, was common to all types of ancient associations.[3] Some groups had a very distinctive religious character, as their main purpose revolved around the worship of a particular deity; in modern scholarship, these are generally referred to as 'religious associations'.[4] Economy, broadly speaking, also played a role in the formation and evolution of associations; indeed, individuals sharing the same occupation are attested to have

---

[*] I am grateful to the editors for the invitation to give a first version of this chapter at a stimulating conference in Athens in 2014 and for offering helpful feedback to the version submitted here. I also thank the anonymous readers for careful comments and criticisms and for pointing out to me new bibliography, which has helped clarify several issues. All remaining errors are my own.

[1] On the associative model, see Cracco Ruggini 1971: 59–64 and 1976. On the origins of associations there is a vast bibliography; see, for example, Poland 1909 and Waltzing 1895–1900. See also De Salvo 1992: 373–4 for associations in Italy (*collegia*) and van Nijf 1997 for a tradition of associations in the East. For Egypt, see Boak 1937b, San Nicolò 1972 and Muhs 2001. For associations as global Eurasian phenomenon, see Evers in Chapter 10.

[2] See Gibbs 2008 and 2011; Hawkins 2016: 66–129; Paganini 2020c; Venticinque 2010 and 2016.

[3] See also Carbon in Chapter 4.

[4] On religious associations in Egypt, see in general de Cenival 1972.

formed what today we usually call professional or trade associations.[5] The separation between religious and professional associations, however, was not definite and the boundaries between the two groups were rather blurred.[6] Religious elements were to be found in associations that had a prominent economic character and vice versa, as we shall see later in this chapter.

Associations with a more pronounced professional (or economic) focus grew in number during the early Roman period.[7] The evidence shows that such groups normally had a well-defined internal structure and sets of regulations, *nomoi*, which governed individual behaviour as well as communal activities. From Roman Egypt three sets of regulations have survived, all coming from the same village, Tebtynis, in the Fayum (ancient Arsinoite district), and dated to the mid-first century AD: of a non-identified association; of the *apolysimoi* of the imperial estate of Claudius, that is, imperial farmers who were exempt from certain liturgies; and of the salt merchants (*halopolai*).[8] The three *nomoi* were formally recorded at the local record office (*grapheion*), which reflected a common practice among associations; indeed, the contemporary register of contract titles attests the registration of several *nomoi* for the year AD 45/6 (see discussion below).[9]

Thanks to the availability of a significant number of contemporary documents from the same site, we are also well informed about the social, economic and administrative environment in which these associations operated and their rules functioned.[10] This gives us a unique opportunity

---

[5] For a definition of professional associations, see Cracco Ruggini 1971: 64–5: 'Collectivity of men who gather together with a common and permanent objective (or at least felt as such in the conscience of the members), which represents the ideological link at the base of the continuity of this system. This objective establishes another characteristic feature (of the associations), that is, their stable organisation, independent from any change which members might experience' (the translation is mine). See also Cracco Ruggini 1973: 272–3. Some scholars use the definition of 'trade associations'; see, for example, Gibbs 2008, 2011 and 2015.

[6] For a discussion of terminology, see Gabrielsen 2016a: 131–2.

[7] The general consensus holds that the Romans did not create professional associations, but took advantage of the associative model for their own administrative purposes. See, for example, van Minnen 1987: 53. Van Nijf 1997: 8 also notes that 'the associations of the Greek East did not spring into existence ex nihilo, although Waltzing suggests that professional associations were a conscious innovation, imported by the Romans together with their own political institutions'.

[8] *P.Mich.* V 243 (AD 14–37), 244 (AD 43) and 245 (AD 47).   [9] *P.Mich.* II 123 *recto*.

[10] A large number of documents of various types and several archival groups survive from Tebtynis in the first two centuries AD, including the archive of the record office (*grapheion*), the archive of Kronion son of Cheos (see Foraboschi 1971) and the archive of the descendants of Patron (see Bagnall 1973 and Kehoe 1992: 74–92). It is the first-century record office archive that provides the best evidence regarding the community in which the rules of associations were established. See Husselman 1970 and Langellotti 2016a.

to explore the issues that are put forward in this volume: the place of association rules in the local community and their role in producing and shaping social values.

The aim of this chapter is twofold: first, to identify the values embedded in the regulations of the professional associations of early Roman Egypt and establish how far these values reflected those of the local community; second, to determine whether these rules aimed to create a well-ordered society (and whether they succeeded in doing so).

Regulations of Associations in Roman Egypt

In Egypt, associations had a long-standing tradition, which can be traced back to the Saite period.[11] As mentioned in the introduction, in the Roman period there was a proliferation of associations with a more professional characterisation, and it is remarkable to note that in Egypt many of these groups operated in rural communities. In the first century AD in the village of Tebtynis only there were at least eighteen associations that displayed a professional character; they exhibited a high level of specialisation and professionalism, mainly to do with textile production (weavers, dyers, fullers, cloak-makers, cloak-beaters and wool merchants) and metal work (coppersmiths and goldsmiths).[12] The role and importance of these groups have not gone unnoticed. Recent studies have focussed in particular on their economic dimension, suggesting that membership in a formalised group provided protection and clear financial advantages.[13] In this period, associations were private and voluntary enterprises, which means that there was no formal imposition on individuals to band together.[14] Nevertheless, a large proportion of the population participated in associations, and this was not a phenomenon limited to Egypt. Usually these groups were headed by a president, who was elected by the majority of the members and was in charge of enforcing the rules.[15]

---

[11] See Gibbs 2015: 242, with previous bibliography in n. 2. The most common Greek term for association is *synodos*, but *koinon* and *plethos* are also well attested. For an analysis of the terminology employed by associations in the Ptolemaic period, see now Paganini 2018.

[12] For a list of associations in early Roman Tebtynis, see Langellotti 2016b: 113–15. For a list of professional associations in the Roman East, see Arnaoutoglou 2002: 29–30; also Arnaoutoglou 2005: 213–16, who collects the evidence related to associations in the late first century BC and first century AD. For a general overview and discussion of different types of associations in Roman Egypt, with a focus on the first two centuries AD, see now Paganini 2020c. On professions and craft specialisation in the Eastern Mediterranean under the Romans, see Ruffing 2008.

[13] See, for example, Gibbs 2011 and Verboven 2011.   [14] Wilson 1996: 9–10.

[15] In the papyri, the president is usually referred to as *hegoumenos*. Other terms, such as *epimeletes*, *kephalaiotes* and *prostates*, are also used.

However, some particularly large associations, like the public farmers (*demosioi georgoi*) and the fishermen (*halieis*), had a board of officials called elders (*presbyteroi*), as the management of their activities would have been more demanding and in this way duties could be shared.[16] In the daily administration they were assisted by a secretary (*grammateus*).[17]

In the Roman period Egyptian associations had sets of rules which were agreed upon by the majority of the members and formally registered at the record office, as confirmed by the case of mid-first-century Tebtynis.[18] As notarial agreements (*demosioi chrematismoi*), these documents were legally binding. This means that members of an association committed to the compliance of the rules from a private as well as legal perspective; in other words, violation of rules could result in formal legal action, should the association deem it necessary, even though internal resolution of disputes seems to have been the preferred method for members (see below).[19]

Boak was the first to note that the procedure by which associations' rules were validated voluntarily by their members was to be found in the Athenian private associations before Alexander the Great and suggested that their 'contractual basis was introduced into Egypt under Greek influence'.[20] The traditional view holds that the *nomoi* had a one-year validity.[21] While this seems to have been the norm in the Ptolemaic period, this was definitely not the case under the Romans.[22] As I suggested elsewhere, the president was in charge for one year, whereas the rules had a variable validity, which could be longer than one year.[23] The role of the president, with his power to enforce the association rules and collect fees and fines, was not necessarily or exclusively one of social prestige, but could also be a burden. Normally, presidents had other occupations to keep them busy; an example is given by Petheus son of Petheus, president and secretary of the weavers of Kerkesoucha Orous.[24] His daily schedule must have been quite hectic: as a weaver, he was

---

[16] See, for example, *P.Mich.* V 313 and *PSI* VIII 901. Kruse 2020 suggests that under special circumstances the elders and the president could have co-existed.

[17] The same structure is to be found in associations of royal farmers of the Ptolemaic period. See also Gibbs 2015: 251, who also notes the existence of an overlapping terminology between state officials and officials of trade associations.

[18] *P.Mich.* V 243, ll. 13–14; V 244, ll. 45–6; V 247, ll. 17–18; V 248, ll. 8–9. See Boak 1937b, Gibbs 2011 and Venticinque 2016: 77–85.

[19] See, for example, Venticinque 2016: 58–60.   [20] Boak 1937b: 220.   [21] Boak 1937b: 213.

[22] Monson 2007: 770–1. For the Ptolemaic period, there is, however, at least one exception – the association of the weavers of Coptos who engraved their regulations in Demotic to be valid 'forever and eternally': *Short Texts* I 158 (22 Tybi = 19 January 30 BC).

[23] Langellotti 2016b: 117–18. See also Gabrielsen 2016b: 93–4.

[24] *P. Mich.* II 121 *verso*, III l. 13 = *recto* IV vi. See also Langellotti 2016a: 1731–2.

engaged in textile production; as a president and secretary of an association, he had to perform regular administrative and other social tasks.
Although in the ancient world occupational patterns were normally rather
fluid, the involvement in different roles and activities of varying degrees of
responsibility must have been demanding; therefore, the temporary nature
of an association president's mandate would have made this role more
attractive. It is likely that the annual turnover of presidents also contributed to ensuring that a certain level of fairness was kept in the internal set-
up of the group and in the management of the various activities. In this
way, no one would have been given the chance to establish and foster long-
term power relations.

The rules, on the other hand, did not need to be modified every year;
the president was in charge of their enforcement, and in the case of
violation he had the authority to arrest the defaulter (*enechyrazein*) and
'hand him over' (*paradidonai*), most likely to the local authorities.[25] The
main purpose of these regulations was to create a social and administrative
order within whose boundaries individuals could operate and interact with
each other; this also created what we might call a 'sub-legal' system within
the established judicial system.[26] Although associations, in the role of their
president, had the right to enforce their rules, there is no evidence
suggesting that they had their own judicial system. Instead, it appears that
members tended to favour, when possible, internal resolution of disputes,
as recently noted by Cameron Hawkins and Philip Venticinque.[27] The
fact that *nomoi* were registered at the record office means that the central
government was informed of the associations' affairs, but also, and most
importantly, that the associations were making a conscious effort to align
themselves and their rules with the state's practice of registration.[28]

---

[25] Right to arrest: *P.Mich.* V 244, ll. 19–20 and 245, ll. 37–42; right to exact pledges: *P.Mich.* V 243,
l. 3. Arnaoutoglou 2002: 43 notes that these provisions regarding the president's power were also to
be found in Greece in the second century, concluding that they might have been a Roman
introduction. However, a similar role (i.e. chasing of defaulters and collection of fees and fines) is
attested for the 'representatives of the house' as outlined in the Ptolemaic Demotic regulations,
which may speak against the idea of a Roman introduction (at least for Egypt).

[26] Gibbs 2015: 258–60 examined the relationship between state laws and regulations of trade
associations in the Ptolemaic period. He points out that 'the notion of internal jurisdiction was
very important. Disputing members would presumably seek redress through the *nomoi* that all
members had agreed upon, before going to the state to resolve the issues.'

[27] Hawkins 2016: 118–19; Venticinque 2016: 58–60. For Roman Egypt, see in particular the clause
included in the unnamed association, *P.Mich.* V 243, ll. 6–7: 'If anyone prosecutes another or
defames him, let him be fined eight drachmas' (transl. Boak).

[28] Recent scholarship has argued that the Roman legislation which issued bans and restrictions on
associations was not implemented in Egypt. For an overview of state restrictions on associations, see
Cotter 1996 and Arnaoutoglou 2002: 30–6; for a discussion of the application of Roman legislation

In general, this attitude of conforming to the values of the central power was typical of associations in the Roman East.[29]

For the Ptolemaic period, we have several rules of religious associations in Demotic from Tebtynis.[30] Using the network model theorised by Charles Tilly, Andrew Monson interpreted the ethical rules of these groups as a vehicle to create an institutionalised trust network that would facilitate cooperation between members.[31] In his view, economic reasons were secondary to social relations when joining an association. Was this still true in the Roman period? Did rules of associations and their underlying values change over time, adapting to new socio-economic and political circumstances? And finally, can the network model still be applied to the so-called professional associations of the Roman period? The following sections will attempt to answer these questions.

The Evidence

The village of Tebtynis provides us with particularly valuable evidence about rules of associations: three full sets of regulations and a notarial register dated to AD 45/6 in which at least six other associations recorded their rules. Of these, the title of only two is given: of the shepherds (*poimenes*) and of the builders (*oikodomoi*).[32] The surviving three sets of rules regulated three separate types of associations, each reflecting a specific dimension of the local community; some of the rules are in common, some

---

in Egypt in the first century AD, see Arnaoutoglou 2005, who argues that in this province the government, in the person of the prefect Flaccus, took temporary measures only towards the Alexandrian associations. See also Arnaoutoglou 2002.

[29] Arnaoutoglou 2002: 29. The inclusion in the *Gnomon of the Idios Logos* of a regulation mentioning a fine of 500 drachmas for members of associations has been used to argue in favour of a hostile attitude of the state towards such groups. However, given the existence of a large number of associations in the Roman world, recent scholarship has proposed that fines against associations were limited to specific contingencies and are not to be regarded as a means to discourage the formation of new formalised groups; see now Venticinque 2016: 176–8. The *Gnomon* was a collection of rules concerning legal status, inheritance, marriage etc. compiled first under Augustus; see *BGU* V 1210 and *P.Oxy.* XLII 3014.

[30] For a list of Demotic rules of associations in the Ptolemaic period, see Arlt and Monson 2011: 211. Cf. Table 1.1 in Chapter 1. See also Monson 2006, 2007 and Muhs 2001. For a study of trade associations in the Ptolemaic period see now Gibbs 2015.

[31] Monson 2006. See also Venticinque 2010, esp. 277, for the use of the network model to suggest that ethical rules aimed at reinforcing familial bonds between members.

[32] Shepherds: *P.Mich.* II 123 *recto*, XVI l. 12 (23 May 46); builders: *P.Mich.* II 123 *recto*, XVII l. 39 (17 June 46). One set of regulations is submitted by a certain Psosneus who is said to be an oil-producer, which suggests that he was a member of the relevant association and acting on its behalf (*P.Mich.* II 123 *recto*, VI l. 18, 28 October 45). For the other regulations, see *P.Mich.* II 123 *recto*, IX l. 45 (2 January 46), X l. 6 (4 January 46) and XI l. 36 (30 January 46).

others are unique to each group. All three ordinances include a provision regarding the election of an annual president who was given the power to enforce the laws of the association, a provision on the attendance of monthly banquets and a number of provisions on the prosecution of lawbreakers, which varied from one group to another (Table 8.1).[33] They also include a number of ethical rules, which regulated the social relations between the members and set the correct line of conduct. These constituted a well-ingrained tradition in Egyptian associations, and their presence in the ordinances of the Roman period attests to a line of continuity in the life of these groups.[34] The rules of an ethical nature are prominent in the ordinance of the non-identified association. The *nomos* of this group exhibits an essentially convivial character. Their explicit purpose was to hold monthly banquets to which all members had to contribute through the payment of dues. According to Boak, the reference to the purchase of a flock of sheep as an event to be celebrated might suggest the possibility that we are dealing here with the association of the cattle graziers (*probatoktenotrophoi*). However, this is not a convincing argument. In this document it is clear that the purchase of a flock has the same value as the purchase of a property (*to eggaion*), and in the same provision other events are envisaged as occasions for celebration. It is possible that members of this group engaged in some type of collective activity (economic or administrative) and that their rules, though not directly regulating this particular aspect of communal life, facilitated these non-convivial operations.

That conviviality was the main feature of this association is also suggested by the number of provisions on social gatherings and ethical behaviour, mutual support and respect, which are not to be found in the

---

[33] Boak 1937b provided a clear analysis of the three Greek *nomoi* from Tebtynis and compared the rules of Greek and Demotic texts. For a critique of the dichotomy Greek–Egyptian in Ptolemaic associations, see Paganini 2017. See also Muhs 2001, esp. 4–5, who supports the generally accepted view that there was an independent Egyptian tradition of religious associations, which can be seen in the very early evidence for associations in Egypt. This tradition would have been later adopted by Greek-speakers in the formation of the so-called professional associations. Rules about social behaviour are to be found also in associations outside Egypt; see, for example, the case of the *Iobacchoi* of Athens (e.g. Moretti 1986). Gibbs 2015: 248–9 points out that the early professional associations in the Hellenistic Mediterranean had a distinctive organisational structure 'that was preferred among all others', and that this structure is partly reflected in the *nomoi*. He suggests that there might have been a common institution that was derived from Greek precedents, and this Greek model 'could be grafted onto existing traditional indigenous institutions'.

[34] Venticinque 2010: 286 suggests that behind these regulations there is the association's concern to protect 'the reputation for reliability and trustworthiness of the guild'. See also Arnaoutoglou 2002: 43, who thinks that the purpose of rules on ethical behaviour was to keep social turmoil under control 'without any immediate cost to the Roman administration'.

Table 8.1. *Common features in the regulations of the first-century Tebtynis associations*

PROVISIONS	Non-identified association	*Apolysimoi* of the imperial estate of Claudius	Salt merchants
Election of a president	Yes	Yes	Yes
Main payment of members	Monthly contribution (set at 12 dr.)	Poll-tax and expenses	Trade taxes
Main purpose of the association	Monthly banquets	Payment of poll-tax and expenses	Payment of trade taxes and division of areas for sale of salt and gypsum
Monthly banquets	Yes (12th)	Yes (8th)	Yes (25th)
Prosecution of misbehaving members	Yes	Yes	Yes
Attendance of meetings	Non-attendance punished by fines	Non-attendance punished by fines	Non-attendance punished by fines
Arrangement of seating plan at banquets	Yes (Fine: 3 ob.)	No	No
Prosecution or defamation of members	Yes (Fine: 8 dr.)	No	No
Intrigue and corruption of a member's home	Yes (Fine: 60 dr.)	No	No
Payment for birth, marriage, purchase of property, of sheep and of cattle	Yes	No	No
Mutual support	Failure punished by fines (8 dr.)	No	No
Mutual assistance for debt	Yes	Yes	No
Attendance at a member's funeral	Yes (Fines: 4 dr. for not shaving; 4 dr. for not attending)	Yes (Fine: 4 dr. for not attending)	No

other two extant *nomoi*. Members were required to follow a good conduct and to make a financial contribution when another member married, had a child and bought a property, cattle or a flock of sheep; members were also expected to help a fellow member in trouble and to be considerate when taking seats at a banquet, and were forbidden to prosecute and to corrupt a fellow member. Finally, a provision was included regulating behaviour in the event of a member's death, whereby members had to shave, feast for one day and contribute with 1 drachma and two loaves of bread each. The importance of these ethical rules is reflected in their respective fines, which ranged from a minimum of 3 obols for shoving other members at the banquets, to 8 drachmas for denying help to a fellow member, for prosecuting him or slandering him, to a maximum of 60 drachmas for intriguing against a member or corrupting his home. It emerges clearly that fines were directly proportional to the seriousness of the violation, thus revealing the values that the group perceived as of the utmost importance and that therefore should not be infringed. For this association, it was the act of scheming against another member (*hyponomeuein*) or corrupting his home (*oikophthoreuein*) that was viewed as the most appalling offence of all, with a fine of 60 drachmas. By ensuring good conduct and mutual respect, ethical rules encouraged the creation and maintenance of strong relations of trust and solidarity. The inclusion in the *nomos* of such rules (and associated fines) combined with a monthly fee of 12 drachmas per member and occasional additional contributions made membership of this group rather costly. As Philip Venticinque has noted, an annual membership of 144 drachmas would have been sufficient to support a family of four for a year, thus suggesting that members were relatively well off.[35] The enforcement of fines that added to the members' financial burden no doubt would have been a good way to ensure proper behaviour.

In the *nomos* of the *apolysimoi* and in that of the salt merchants, rules on social behaviour are limited to provisions on mutual support in case of debt and attendance of funerals for the former and to participation of meetings only for the latter. An early provision states the main purpose for the *apolysimoi*, that is, to pay their share of the poll-tax (*laographia*) and other expenses (*dapanai*) to their president.[36] This rule is of particular

---

[35] Venticinque 2016: 14–15.

[36] *P.Mich.* V 244, ll. 2–7: 'Having met together, the undersigned men of Tebtynis, *apolysimoi* of an estate of Tiberius Claudius Caesar Augustus Germanicus Imperator, voted unanimously to elect one of their number, an excellent man, Kronion, son of Herodes, to be superintendent for one year from the month Sebastos of the coming fourth year of Tiberius Claudius Caesar Augustus Germanicus Imperator, the same Kronion to collect the public revenues of the poll-tax of the

significance, for two reasons: first, because it highlights the administrative and practical aspect of their gathering into a formalised group; second, because it reveals that members of this group were not exempt from the main capitation tax, but from liturgies.[37] Paying taxes as a collective was not without advantages, mainly because it avoided that members must deal directly with tax collectors.[38] Another noteworthy aspect of their regulations is the formalised link with the emperor Claudius; a provision required that members hold a party on the eighth day of each month, in honour of the emperor's birthday, with the president providing drinks for the celebrations and toasts. No provision is to be found that regulated other collective activities of the group, but some entries listed in the contemporary register of contract titles suggest that the *apolysimoi* occasionally made contracts as a collective. One contract, for example, mentions the 'group of *apolysimoi*' (*plethos apolysimon*).[39] A group of *apolysimoi* is also attested, jointly with the cattle graziers, in two affidavits (*cheirographiai*) registered at the record office in AD 45/6.[40] It is unclear whether these *apolysimoi* are to be identified with the *apolysimoi* of the estate of Claudius or with the farmers of another estate, but it is interesting to note that the two associations had shared interests (perhaps leasing of pasture land) and engaged in collective actions (one of the affidavits mentions the maintenance of some canals). The association of the *apolysimoi* with an imperial estate and their potential collaboration with groups of professional cattle breeders suggest that their activities included farming and livestock grazing. It is not surprising that these activities were not officially regulated by a *nomos*, as they were in fact 'state' activities, whose main terms were dictated by the Roman government and therefore there was no need, or freedom, for enforcing specific rules. However, the fact that the imperial farmers made contracts as a collective guaranteed some degree of flexibility in their economic enterprises. The rules of their associations did not give instructions as to how make bid applications or any other type of contracts, but facilitated these transactions by introducing a provision on debt, whereby members were given security for a set period of time (thirty or

---

same *apolysimoi* and all the expenses of the said association' (transl. Boak). It is worth noting that paying taxes collectively was a novelty in Egypt and seems to have been connected with formalised associations; see van Minnen 1987: 48–56. It was not, however, a Roman introduction; see, for example, the payment of the *eisphora*, a direct tax paid in periods of particular needs, like war, in Classical Athens: Christ 2007b.

[37] Boak, Introduction to *P.Mich*. V 244. See also *P.Gen*. II 91.   [38] Hanson 1984.

[39] *P.Mich*. II 123 *recto*, XX l. 44.

[40] *P.Mich*. II 123 *recto*, III l. 40 and VIII l. 26. See Parassoglou 1978: 61 and n. 67; also Langellotti 2016b: 122–4.

sixty days) in case they incurred in a private debt of up to 100 drachmas. Membership itself served as a protective measure in financial dealings.

A provision on debt is missing in the *nomos* of the salt merchants, but nine out of twelve regulations deal with the arrangement for the distribution of salt and gypsum among the members in the Fayum region. The reason behind the lack of a clause on debt probably lies in the fact that the salt merchants already enjoyed rights and privileges that other traders did not have, which was reflected in the careful subdivision of areas among the members. The sale of salt, at least in the Fayum, constituted a government concession, and salt merchants were required to submit bidding applications (*anaphoria*) to the state in order to acquire this right, as is attested by the local record office evidence dated to AD 45/6.[41] Membership in an association aimed at strengthening the position of the salt merchants in the various activities connected with their trade, from the application process to the sale of the finished product.[42] For the association to work efficiently, precise rules were needed as how to divide the market among the members.[43] This was all the more important due to the presence in the area of

---

[41] Written bids by salt merchants are attested in *P.Mich.* II 123 *recto*, VII l. 27 (15 November 45), *P.Mich.* II 123 *recto*, XXI l. 40 (14 August 46) and *P.Mich.* II 123 *recto*, XXII l. 27 (23 August 46). For an up-to-date discussion of *anaphoria* as written bids, see now Langellotti 2016b: 129–34. On the sale of salt in the Greek world, see Carusi 2008, esp. 207–14 on Graeco-Roman Egypt. She notes that it is still unclear to what extent the production of salt was under state control during the Roman period and how its exploitation was managed. See also Wallace 1938: 183–4 and Adams 2013: 273.

[42] Gabrielsen 2016b: 92–5 argues against the consensus that holds that the salt merchants were a professional association, suggesting instead that they formed a sort of partnership. Whether or not the salt merchants constituted what we call a regular association, it is impossible to ascertain; it is conceivable, however, that other associations also functioned like the salt merchants, meaning that this was not a unique case, but rather the manifestation of a wider phenomenon (i.e. formation of associations with a more economic character).

[43] The list of current members appended to the *nomos* of salt merchants is damaged and shows only the ages and distinctive marks of five signatories, which might mean that the association had only five members, including the president. These regulations are stated in *P.Mich.* V 245, ll. 9–34: 'And (they have decided) that all alike shall sell salt in the aforesaid village of Tebtynis, and that Orseus alone has obtained by lot the sole right to sell gypsum in the aforesaid village of Tebtynis and in the adjacent villages, for which he shall pay, apart from the share of the public taxes which falls to him, an additional sixty-six dr. in silver; and that the said Orseus has likewise obtained by lot from Kerkesis, alone to sell salt therein, for which he shall likewise pay an additional eight dr. in silver. And that Harmiusis also called Belles, son of Harmiusis, has obtained by lot the sole right to sell salt and gypsum in the village of Tristomos also called Boukolos, for which he shall contribute, apart from the share of the public taxes which falls to him, five additional dr. in silver. Upon condition that they shall sell the good salt at the rate of two and one-half obols, the light salt at two obols, and the lighter salt at one and one-half obol, by our measure or that of the warehouse. And if anyone shall sell at a lower price than these, let him be fined eight dr. in silver for the common fund and the same for the public treasury. And if any of them shall be found to have sold more than a stater's worth of salt to a merchant, let him be fined eight dr. in silver for the common fund and the same for the public treasury. But if the merchant shall intend to buy more than four drachmas' worth, all must

other groups of the same type, namely, the salt merchants of Talei and
Theogonis and those of Ibion Eikosipentarouron [44] The inclusion of
legally binding rules on the subdivision of localities for the sale of salt
must be seen as a way to regulate the competition and to set defined and
clear parameters by which each member was required to abide. Needless to
say, failure to do so resulted in the payment of fees, which was probably a
good deterrent for misbehaving members.

While the expectation in all three sets of rules that members attended
monthly meetings is a good indication of the strong social character of
these groups, some associations felt the need to add rules that regulated
more closely the ethical behaviour of their members. The exact nature of
each of these associations is difficult to ascertain. If we go by the content of
their *nomoi* and their titles, we may conclude that the non-identified
association was a convivial club, while the *apolysimoi* and the salt merchants constituted more professional groups. This distinction, however, is
not a fair reflection of the realities behind these groups. As Vincent
Gabrielsen pointed out, associations that did not display in their title an
occupational connotation did not necessarily lack an economic role in the
community and, therefore, should not be excluded from our economic
analysis. [45]

The regulations of the exempt farmers of the imperial estate of Claudius
and those of the salt merchants reveal two fundamental dimensions of
communal life in the early Roman period: first, the desire to fit into the
new Roman administrative system, which is clearly shown by the formalised commitment of the *apolysimoi* to pay taxes collectively; second, the
social values of conviviality and sociability, which are the reflection of a
society where personal relations were central, and trust among individuals
was continuously fostered.

A significant aspect of communal life that emerges from the three sets of
regulations is geographical mobility. Members of associations regularly
travelled from their village of residence to other villages of the region
and to the district capital, Ptolemais Euergetis, in order to attend monthly
meetings in the context of which social networks were established and
maintained. Reasons to travel outside Tebtynis were either business or
participation in religious festivals and other social events; the salt

sell to him jointly. And if anyone shall bring in gypsum and shall intend to sell it outside, it must be
left on the premises of Orseus, son of Harmiusis, until he takes it outside and sells it' (transl. Boak).
[44] Talei and Theogonis: *P.Mich.* II 123 *recto*, XXI l. 40; Ibion Eikosipentarouron: *P.Mich.* II 123 *recto*,
XXII l. 27.
[45] Gabrielsen 2016b: 89.

merchants, for example, who held the concession for the sale of salt and gypsum in Tebtynis and nearby villages, were expected to travel around the district and have business relations with merchants and other buyers living outside Tebtynis. Provisions on meetings in the *nomoi* clearly attest this type of mobility. Members of the three associations were required to attend all the meetings called by the president, which could take place in the village, in a place outside the village or in the district capital. Although the nature of these meetings is not specified, variation in fines for failing to attend them suggests that their importance depended on their location, and those happening in the district capital were of particular significance: between 1 and 2 drachmas if the meeting was in the village, 4 drachmas if it was outside the village, 4 and 8 drachmas if it was in the district capital.[46] It appears that the non-identified association was less mobile; its members did not have meetings in other villages and the fine for missing a meeting in Ptolemais Euergetis was lower (4 instead of 8 drachmas). We do not know how far members of other associations established social or economic relations with individuals in other villages and in the district capital, but the very fact that some of their meetings took place outside Tebtynis, where the association was based, unveils the existence of a net of connections between Tebtynis, its neighbouring villages and Ptolemais Euergetis. It is most likely that one of the purposes of their meetings and banquets was that of providing the members with the possibility of networking, which would have facilitated potential economic dealings by creating trust networks.

An important fact to be noted is the inclusion of ethical rules in the ordinance of the non-identified association, which are missing in the other two ordinances (the exempt farmers of the imperial estate of Claudius do have provisions for mutual assistance and funerals, but none on ethical behaviour). Does this mean that these values were less important for the purpose of being a member of a professional association? Did the salt merchants not value the contribution of ethical rules? As membership in an association was not mutually exclusive, it is possible that those who were part of a more professional association also joined a social club, like that of the non-identified association, in order to enjoy the privileges of mutual support. Certain rules were agreed upon by the members on the basis of their particular needs, which clearly differed from one group to another. The relations between members of a professional association seem to have relied on rules that were dictated by conscious economic decisions

---

[46] On regulation of compulsory participation in associations, see Eckhardt in Chapter 3.

more than on social rules, suggesting that the members were aware that this group was in fact an economic enterprise.

Table 8.1 includes a list of provisions to be found in the three surviving sets of regulations (of the non-identified association, of the *apolysimoi* and of the salt merchants), thus revealing which terms were common to all, which were common to two associations only and, finally, which terms were unique to one association only. It emerges clearly that, although associations were free to devise their personalised sets of rules according to their own needs, they all shared three core provisions – election of a president, obligation to attend monthly banquets and prosecution of lawbreakers – which can be regarded as the distinctive markers of an officially recognised association, at least in the Roman period.

The World of Professional Associations: A Well-Ordered Society?

The regulations of associations that survived from early Roman Egypt reveals the existence of a set of social values that underpinned the behaviour and activities of these groups and the relations between their members. These values were of two types: ethical (solidarity, trust and sociability) and practical (mobility and desire to integrate into the Roman administrative and economic framework). The fact that a large number of people joined one or more of these associations confirms that these values were not unique to specific groups but reflected those of the entire community. Although the percentage of individuals who were members of specific formalised groups cannot be calculated, the evidence from Tebtynis gives us a pretty good idea of the magnitude of this phenomenon. Assuming that each association had an average of twenty to thirty members, I calculated elsewhere that 10 to 15 per cent of the male population in the village might have belonged to an association.[47]

Trust and solidarity were not simply theoretical notions, but core values at the base of the contractual economy of Roman Egypt. Mobility too was not a prerogative of members of associations, but a phenomenon widely attested among all strata of the population. Traders and craftsmen, for example, were not the only social groups who travelled around their own region and beyond. Shepherds too, who, incidentally, might have formed an association, occasionally had to relocate their flocks to different areas (sometimes outside their own district) to find pastures; state officials, slaves and freedmen who worked in administrative roles regularly travelled on

---

[47] Langellotti 2016b: 119.

business, and many individuals of Hellenic descent resided half-time in the district capital, half-time in the village, therefore making frequent journeys between their two residences.[48]

The increase of professional associations under the Romans was not a product of chance, but a phenomenon strictly connected with the proliferation of state concessions, which in many cases replaced the old Ptolemaic monopolies.[49] This new situation led to the development of ad hoc rules that reflected the new needs of these groups' members. The case of the salt merchants in this respect is illustrative, as it shows the necessity to regulate a specific economic activity – the distribution of salt and gypsum – within a wide region and was not a unique case. As the evidence from first-century Tebtynis shows, many economic enterprises were now organised as state concessions and revolved around a relevant association: the fishermen, the builders, the weavers, the dyers, the cattle graziers and so on.[50]

The *nomoi* of these groups have not come down to us, but the example of the salt merchants suggests that some of their rules also covered their economic dimension. Such associations most likely had regulations that covered the financial aspects of their business; the weavers, for example, paid their trade tax (*cheironaxion*) collectively, a condition that was probably included in their *nomos*.

The values introduced by the new rules reflected primarily the need of the individuals to acquire enhanced support and protection in the bidding procedure.[51] The old social and ethical rules, conversely, were not abandoned, as they were strongly embedded in institutionalised social networks.

In this respect, the *nomoi* of the Roman period associations reflect a community that was different from the one in place in the Ptolemaic period. This society had new needs and concerns; the livelihood of families and individuals depended now on an economic set-up mainly based on an organised system of licence fees that required initiative and resourcefulness on the part of the bidders. State concessions enhanced competition and gave individuals the possibility to be involved actively and voluntarily in a number of activities. It was a chance for more profit, but it also meant

---

[48] Bagnall 1973.   [49] Wallace 1938: 181–3.

[50] Gibbs 2015: 261–2 suggests that the trade associations of the Ptolemaic period would have been involved in the system of state monopolies, whereby contractors, through an auction, would agree to produce a fixed amount of product at a fixed price. In the Roman period, state concessions replaced the Ptolemaic monopolies, allowing for more flexibility in an open market.

[51] See Arnaoutoglou in Chapter 6 for the impact of the Romans on Athenian associations.

financial risk. The associative model, based on those ethical values that had
characterised the Egyptian society for a long time, proved to be a useful
way to deal with this new scenario.

The economic situation in Egypt rapidly changed from the first to the
second century AD.[52] Associations were put under stricter control and
soon were required to perform administrative duties on behalf of the
state.[53] The change in the administrative and economic set-up would have
led inevitably to a change in community values – in many cases, fear was
probably more prominent than desire for profit, and ethical and protectionist norms might have had a privileged place in associations' *nomoi*. The
character of associations and their rules adapted to the increasingly and
ever-changing society, demonstrating not only that they were a fundamental social institution, but also that they were flexible and easily adjustable to
different situations. Some rules, however, did not disappear, for example,
the ones related to burial of members and members' relatives.[54] While
various political and economic contingencies gradually modified the
ancient Egyptian society, community values that mirrored the new needs
of the individuals (to conform to the Roman administration) emerged.
This was an attempt on the part of associations to align their values (and
those of their own community) with the values of the central authority.
Things, of course, did not always run smoothly. Conflicts and disagreements can be seen in petitions in which members of associations filed
complaints in matters of taxation, an inevitable result considering that by
the second century AD associations became fully involved in the administrative state machinery.[55]

The creation of ad hoc rules that would conform to new circumstances
confirms the willingness of associations to survive and maintain a certain
order in which they could exist. From this point of view, it could be argued
that rules were established to create a well-ordered society; whether members of associations were influenced or inspired by the Greek idea of 'good

[52] For Roman Asia, Harland 2003: esp. 89–112 argues that associations participated fully in 'civic
vitality' and were not to be seen as 'compensatory phenomena in a period of civic decline'. Cf.
Cracco Ruggini 1976. See also Gillihan 2012, whose analysis of the Dead Sea scrolls reaches
similar conclusions.

[53] See, for example, *Stud.Pal.* IV pp. 70–1 (Ptolemais Euergetis, AD 73) and *P.Tebt.* II 287 (Tebtynis,
AD 161–9)

[54] Craft guilds in late Medieval England, for example, provided their members with two types of
religious activities: Sunday gatherings at church and postmortem services (funerals and burials).
These were well-structured organisations with rules that regulated both ethical conduct and
administrative and economic activities of their members. See also Richardson 2005: esp. 149 and
156–63.

[55] Venticinque 2015: 357.

order', is, however, difficult to prove. Though deeply ingrained in the native Egyptian strata of the population, associations had a long tradition that combined both Egyptian and Greek models; 'good order' might have been embedded in the Greek model, but there is no clear evidence. More likely, the reason why associations, with their rules, strove to achieve a social order lies in their need for preservation. The associative model provided a useful social (and, to an extent, economic) framework that their members did not want to give up. They created rules that allowed their associations to function the best way possible under different political, administrative and economic scenarios.

It is very tempting to suggest that the values that were at the core of professional associations in the early Roman period and beyond, that is, trust, solidarity and mutual support, had a universal character. These were to be found in Egypt well before Christianity and continued to be an integral part of the identity and rules of associations in later periods and in different regions outside Egypt.[56] In her analysis of medieval craft guilds and market order in the sixteenth century, Mougeot points out that 'although they conveyed the values required to set up an economy of exchange, these craft guilds remained influenced by the values of mutual assistance which was a feature of primitive society'.[57] Their rules of conduct, which regulated ethical behaviour to ensure good business, were approved by the legal authorities. Admittedly, late antique and medieval associations were different from earlier institutionalised groups. However, members still found a way to preserve the ethical values that were at the core of their own establishment.[58]

---

[56] See also Evers in Chapter 10. Carrié 2002: 311 pointed out that professional associations in late antiquity were characterised not only by the fiscal obligations to which they were subjected, but also by 'sociability, conviviality, and cultural practice'. Hughes 1974: 61–2 suggested erroneously that medieval guilds, 'many of which had as their most notable feature the sharing of a common meal', were based on familial feelings, which found their roots in the Bible. In fact, feelings of familiarity are to be found in ancient associations well before the advent of Christianity.

[57] Mougeot 2003: 170; also Richardson 2005: 140 notes that 'the rational-choice approach to the analysis of organization behavior suggests the performance of an organization (such as a guild) depends upon the rules by which it operates and how effectively those rules are enforced. Rules encourage individuals to contribute toward collective goals and discourage them from taking advantage of their colleagues.' For a comparison between ancient associations and medieval guilds, see van Nijf 1997: 11–18, in which the similarities between the two institutions are stressed. See also Carrié 2002: 328–31.

[58] See Rosser 2015: 37–87.

CHAPTER 9

Ordo corporatorum

The Rules of Roman Associations and the collegia at Ostia in the Second and Third Centuries AD

Nicolas Tran

The abundance of private and voluntary associations was a key character-istic of the Roman world, in the West and in the East, during the late Republic and the High Empire.[1] Most of the time, those communities were called *collegia*, *corpora* or *sodalicia* and their social recruitment was rooted in the urban *plebs*, the plebeians.[2] From a certain point of view, they were very diverse. Indeed, their specific names suggested that their members decided to unite for different reasons: because they had the same occupation, the same geographical origin or the same devotion to a specific god, for instance. Nevertheless, they were usually engaged in very similar activities. All of them were religious associations.[3] Feasts gave opportuni-ties to have convivial banquets amongst friends, often in a common meeting-place. This collective life followed precise rules that, in some cases, were written down in a single document: a proper regulation.[4] In a very few cases, associations had such a text engraved and displayed as their *lex collegii*, 'law of the *collegium*'. This expression appears on three long inscriptions and corresponds to a set of rules that members gave to themselves, of their own accord or at the request of a benefactor. The jurist Gaius defined such association rules as a *pactio*, 'agreement, contract', that members were free to draw up, as long as they did not break public laws.[5]

---

[1] For the global Eurasian character of the associational phenomenon, see Evers in Chapter 10.

[2] Modern historiography of Roman *collegia* started with Mommsen 1843, Cohn 1873 and Waltzing 1895–1900, followed by de Robertis 1955. Ausbüttel 1982 and Flambard (especially 1981 and 1987) explored the same field, before van Nijf 1997, Tran 2006, Verboven 2007 and Liu 2009. Perry 2006 offered a historiographical overview.

[3] The importance of religion within associations is underlined in several chapters of this volume: see also Chapter 4 by Carbon, Chapter 5 by Skaltsa, Chapter 7 by Zoumbaki and Chapter 8 by Langellotti.

[4] We ignore how frequent these documents – written on perishable material – were. Yet a comparison with Egyptian papyri suggests that they would not have been so rare. On the Egyptian evidence, see also Langellotti in Chapter 8.

[5] *Dig.* 47.22.4 (Gaius, *Ad leg. XII tab.* 4): *Sodales sunt, qui eiusdem collegii sunt, quam Graeci ἑταιρίαν uocant. His autem potestatem facit lex pactionem quam uelint sibi ferre, dum ne quid ex publica lege*

In fact, associations' regulations included calendars of meetings and ceremonies, as well as various clauses of internal regulation. Nonetheless, they do not provide a global and rational vision of the whole organisation. For example, they do not describe any decision-making procedure, although preserved decrees demonstrate that such a procedure was very codified. Yet this incompleteness is not surprising. Inscriptions of city charters, in particular from *Hispania*, are a useful parallel in this respect: although they are much longer than associations' regulations, they still do not offer a global description of city governance either. The *leges collegiorum*, 'laws of the *collegia*', form a very narrow category of Roman documents, in general, and of inscriptions engraved by associations, in particular. However, we cannot ignore them, and the first part of this chapter intends to briefly present the evidence. However, these *leges* cannot answer all of our questions by themselves only: they are no doubt fascinating inscriptions, but they become even more interesting when we compare them with the whole epigraphic production of Roman associations and complete their content with information given by other kinds of inscriptions. In fact, lists of members, decrees, honorific inscriptions, religious dedications or association titles inscribed on epitaphs reflect inner regulations too. This epigraphic production reveals a scrupulous attention paid by associations to formal procedures and internal hierarchies.

In this respect, the city of Ostia in the second and third centuries AD provides a great viewpoint on this phenomenon.[6] A good number of *collegia* and *corpora* have left many inscriptions of all kinds, especially lists of members. Ostian epigraphy, like the evidence from other great harbours of the western Mediterranean, preserves the existence of several associations. Many of them were professional associations that gathered individuals who had the same occupation. Some of their crafts and trades were harbour occupations, strictly speaking. For instance, associations of *lenuncularii*, 'tugboatmen', are quite well known:[7] they were local boatmen who tugged maritime ships or unloaded cargoes at sea. Some of them were called *lenuncularii auxiliarii*, 'auxiliary tugboatmen', because their workboats helped seagoing crafts. Other *lenuncularii* and/or *scapharii* were related to a specific *traiectus*, 'ferry service', especially the *traiectus Luculli* and the *traiectus Rusticeli*, which were probably linked to specific docks. All

---

corrumpant, 'Companions are those who belong to the same association, what the Greeks call *hetairia*. The law gives them the power to enter in any agreement they like, so long as they do not contravene the public law.'

[6] About *collegia* at Ostia, see Rohde 2012: 79–274.   [7] Tran 2012a and 2014.

of the *lenuncularii* were divided into five *corpora lenunculariorum Ostiensium*, 'corporations of Ostian tugboatmen', from the first decades of the third century at the latest.[8] Furthermore, some professional associations unrelated to sea trade also played a great part in Ostia's urban life. For instance, at the end of the second century AD, the *collegium fabrum tignuariorum Ostiensium*, 'association of Ostian carpenters (working with beams)', had more than 300 members:[9] although strictly speaking they were carpenters, they also ran building enterprises. In Ostia as much as elsewhere, the cult of a specific god or the celebration of a specific rite was also the *raison d'être* of many associations. For example, the *dendrophori* (literally 'tree-bearers') every 22 March performed a procession in honour of the goddess Cybele, parading a pine-tree symbolising Attis.[10] Professional and other associations from Ostia, in particular those mentioned above, give practical information about functioning rules: the second part of this chapter will emphasise this point. Finally, some inscriptions present few Ostian *corpora* as orders (*ordines*). The third part of this study investigates the meaning and interpretation of this concept: this is in fact crucial to the understanding of Roman *collegia* as 'well-ordered' groups.

The Preserved *Leges Collegiorum*

During the High Empire, a few Italian associations engraved their own regulations: these are the object of review in this section.

The *lex familiae Siluani*, 'law of the family (that is to say, association) of the god Silvanus', from Trebula Mutuesca and three other blocks of travertine were part of the same epigraphic monument.[11] One of them mentions the consuls in charge during the summer and the autumn of AD 60; it also indicates the precise date of 15 July. The regulation was added to an *album*, 'membership list', of seventy-eight *cultores*, 'worshippers, members', maybe shortly after the making of that list. Its clauses were essentially financial: they aim at regulating the use of common funds and at inflicting fines on members who were disrespectful towards the regulations. Rules punished fights and disorder but the *familia* was essentially concerned with worship, funerals and banquets: it was strictly forbidden to

---

[8] *CIL* XIV 170, 352, 4144.   [9] *CIL* XIV 4569. On these builders, see DeLaine 2003; Tran 2017.
[10] On the religious (and not professional) nature of the *collegia dendrophorum*, I agree with Liu 2009:
       52–4.
[11] *AE* 2002 no 397; Buonocore and Diliberto 2003; Friggeri and Magnani Cianetti 2014: 110–15
       (no 28).

invite to ceremonies people who were not officially members of the *collegium* and thus registered on the *album*.[12] The monument was erected at the expenses of the donor M. Valerius Dexter;[13] however, M. Valerius Firmus,[14] probably Dexter's son, seems to have paid for engraving the law.

The second and very famous *lex collegii* is the regulation inscribed by the *cultores*, 'worshippers', of Diana and Antinous from Lanuvium.[15] L. Caesennius Rufus, patron of the city and benefactor of the *cultores*, asked them to engrave the inscription during a general meeting held in June AD 136.[16] But the *collegium* did exist from AD 133. The marble table had the practical utility of recalling common rules. Yet the *cultores* had not felt the need for it for three years, before their benefactor wished to emphasise his generosity: he had in fact instituted a perpetual foundation of 16,000 sesterces in order to finance annual ceremonies in honour of the *collegium*'s deities. Moreover, the table of Lanuvium not only was an internal regulation but also alluded to a *senatus consultum*, a decree of the Roman Senate, whereby the *collegium* had received the *ius coeundi*, 'right of association'. It reminded the common goal: to contribute in order to celebrate the funerals of deceased members. Various clauses then formed the *lex collegii* itself: it dealt with an entry fee, with the payment of a *funeraticium*, 'funerary indemnity', to the relatives of the deceased – which would cover costs of funerals – and with the organisation of banquets. The *collegium* did not provide any *funeraticium* if the deceased had not properly paid his contributions to the association. Some specific cases were also considered, such as death far from Lanuvium, intestate (that is to say, in absence of a will), without burial because of masters' cruelty or by suicide. About drinks and banquets, dispositions dealt with the calendar of the ceremonies, with privileges and duties of the dignitaries and with correct behaviour.

---

[12] *Cum ad | sacrum uentum erit, ne quis litiget | neue rixam faciat neue extrane|um inuitet ea die: si ita fecerit, d(are) d(ebeat) (sestertios) XX*, 'When one comes to the sacred ceremony, he shall not quarrel, fight or invite a stranger on this day: if he behaves like that, then he shall pay 20 sesterces' (ll. 6–9).

[13] *Siluano consacrauit et familiae M(arcus) [Va]lerius M(arci) f(ilius) Dexter, impensa su[a] | donum dedit*, 'Marcus Valerius Dexter, son of Marcus, devoted (this monument) to Silvanus and gave it to the association (*familia*) at his expense' (*AE* 2002 no 397b).

[14] *M(arcus) Valerius Firmus titulum adiecit ap* (!) *se d(ecreto) f(amiliae)*, 'Marcus Valerius Firmus added the inscription by himself, by virtue of a decree of the association (*familia*)' (*AE* 2002 no 397d).

[15] *CIL* XIV 2112. Its discovery dates back to 1816 and inspired the young Th. Mommsen to write a fundamental study on *collegia* (Mommsen 1843). Bendlin 2011 (with an English translation partly quoted below) published an important reappraisal of this document.

[16] *Praecepit legem ab ipsis constitutam sub tetra[stylo A]ntinoi parte interiori perscribi*, 'he enjoined the law (*lex*) established by them to be written out in full at the bottom of the *tetrastylon* of Antinous on the inner side' (*CIL* XIV 2112, I ll. 6–7).

The regulation of the Roman *negotiantes eborarii et citrarii*, 'ivory and citrus-wood workers', also dates back to the Principate of Hadrian.[17] The inscription comes from the Trastevere district, where the *eborarii et citrarii* had their meeting-place (*schola*). Its text is fragmentary and focuses on banquets and money distributions, which celebrated birthdays of a donor, of his son and of the emperor. Only one general clause, about inclusion of new members, is preserved: it established the dismissal of officials, if they had admitted in the *collegium* individuals who were not actual *eborarii* or *citrarii*. In that case, the *collegium* had to remove the name of those unscrupulous *curatores*, 'officials', from its *album*.

The *lex collegii Aesculapi et Hygiae*, 'law of the association of Asclepius and Hygieia', seems so specific that some historians have considered it a simple decree, much more than a real law.[18] Yet the words '*lex collegii*' do appear on this stone, engraved in AD 153. It describes a foundation instituted by Salvia Marcellina and her brother-in-law, the imperial freed-man P. Aelius Zeno: they were the *collegium*'s mother and father. Above all, the so-called law precisely set a festive calendar. It also reveals funerary activities, as in Lanuvium and Trebula Mutuesca. The inscription also refers to a fine inflicted on officials (*quinquennales* or *curatores*) who would not enforce the rules – however, given its deterrent amount of 20,000 sesterces, it is likely that the *collegium* never imposed such a penalty.[19]

In addition to regulations proper, a very few inscriptions contain reference to *leges collegiorum*. In Pozzuoli, the *corpus Heliopolitanorum*, 'association of Heliopolitans', gathered the *cultores Iouis Heliopolitani Berytenses qui Puteoli consistent*, 'Berytian worshippers of Heliopolitan Jupiter, who are settled in Pozzuoli'.[20] This religious association of Levantine migrants possessed a field, with a *cisterna*, 'cistern', and *tabernae*, 'stalls': its property consisted in a *ius possessorum* (literally a 'right of holders') that the *cultores* could keep, if they did nothing against the association law.[21] Finally, we may leave Italy just for a moment and mention a wax-tablet discovered in Alburnus Maior in Dacia with the act of dissolution of a *collegium Iouis Cerneni*, 'association of Jupiter

---

[17] *CIL* VI 33885.

[18] *CIL* VI 10234. The *collegium* voted its law on 11 March AD 153. See Flambard 1987: 234.

[19] *Si aduersus ea quid fecerint q(uin)q(uennalis) et curatores s(upra) s(cripti) uti poenae nomine arkae n(ostrae) inferant HS XX m(ilia) n(ummum)*, 'if they do something else, then the above-mentioned president and supervisors will pay as a penalty into our treasury the sum of 20,000 sesterces' (ll. 21–22).

[20] *CIL* X 1579.

[21] ... *nihil aduersus lecem et conuentionem eius corporis*, 'nothing against the law and the covenant of this *corpus*'.

Cernenus[22] Its *curatores* had in fact rendered their accounts for good: the number of contributors had become too low to ensure the proper functioning of the association and the *cultores* of Jupiter *Cernenus* had not met on the days prescribed by their law for a long time.[23]

This small group of documents recording regulations by *collegia* has recently grown, thanks to three new documents from Ostia published by N. Laubry and F. Zevi.[24] Amongst these three fragments, one belongs to an already-known document; the two others are independent. They are related to three unknown communities, which organised funerary services for their members. The first of them might have been related to the cult of Cybele, given its discovery in the *Campus Magnae Matris*, the area in the southern part of Ostia where a temple complex of Cybele was built in the Hadrianic period.[25] The second fragment is an opisthograph:[26] the vestige of an *album* appears on one side, whereas the text inscribed on the other side is identical to the first fragment. This makes hypothetical restorations easier, even though only a very small part of the original inscription can be determined. At any rate, we are able to recover its general meaning. The text recalls an important decision of the Roman Senate, taken at the request of the emperor in AD 121. In fact, during the Principate of Hadrian, the right of association, settled by Augustus around 7 BC, went through a significant shift: this change might have consisted in the recognition of funerary activities as a criterion of public usefulness, whereby associations could be formally authorised.[27] Apparently, the inscriptions from Ostia aimed at celebrating a public decision: by engraving such a document, the main goal of the *collegia* had probably nothing to do with the regulation of their common life, from an internal point of view – even though rules about funerary activities may have of course followed the quotation of the *senatus consultum*. The third fragment certainly belonged to a *lex collegii*:[28] it dealt with money distribution during members' funerals (*exequiarium*) and with the *curatores* in charge of these ceremonies; it further mentions the contribution of one amphora of wine, in uncertain

---

[22] *CIL* III 924; *ILS* 7215; *IDR* I 31.
[23] ... neq(ue) | quisquam ta[m magno tempore diebus qui]bus legi | continetur conuenire uoluerint aut confer|re funeraticia siue munerar..., 'that no one had been willing, since such a long time, to attend meetings on the days required by the law or to contribute funeral services or fees ...'
[24] Laubry and Zevi 2010 and 2012.   [25] *AE* 2010 no 242.   [26] *AE* 2010 no 243.
[27] On the link between *ius coeundi*, 'right of association', and *utilitas publica*, 'public usefulness': see *Dig.* 50.6.6.12; Laubry and Zevi 2012: 321 and passim.
[28] *AE* 2012 no 312.

circumstances, as well as a procedure of accountability that had to be followed; fines were also inflicted in case of dispute or fight.

To sum up, the fragments from Ostia, the *lex familiae Siluani* and the *lex collegii Dianae et Antinoi* obviously belong to the same typology of documents and attest a common practice, with interesting similarities and dissimilarities between them. The recent publication of new evidence gives us hope for progress in the field; however, we should probably not raise our expectations too high. New discoveries will scarcely change the picture, because Roman associations did not usually engrave their regulations. It was a much less common practice than the drawing-up of an *album*: it suffices to compare, for instance, the three possible fragments of *leges collegiorum* with the much higher number of fragmentary membership lists preserved from Ostia.[29] Most of the time, regulations were not inscribed for their own sake but only to celebrate a benefaction: a financial gift or a favourable public decision. As a result, we have to consider the whole epigraphic production of Roman associations to better appreciate their internal rules.

The Rules at Work in the Epigraphic Habit of Associations

The epigraphic production of Ostian associations, in general, reveals information concerning internal rules. First, few inscriptions point to the fact that associations kept their own archives. In Ostia, two secretaries of a professional association of carpenters, the *collegium fabrum tignuariorum*, are attested on an *album* engraved in AD 198 and on the epitaph of C. Similius Philocyrius.[30] This man ran the association as president (*magister quinquennalis*) between AD 235 and 239. When he was a secretary, he probably wrote official acts, to ensure that the association had carried out formal procedures in compliance with its rules.[31] Those archives constitute a 'lost memory', to which few Ostian inscriptions give an indirect access.

---

[29] See e.g. *CIL* XIV 246–52, 256–8, 4569, 4572–3, 5356–7, 5361, 5374 ... and dozens of smaller fragments.

[30] *CIL* XIV 418, 4569. The *lex collegii* from Lanuvium mentions also *scribae*, 'secretaries', who received a half time greater share at distributions (*CIL* XIV 2112, II ll. 19–20).

[31] Associations needed archives in case of litigation, which could happen quite a long time after a collective decision. The *cultores* from Lanuvium thought of possible controversies against members' heirs: *ne ... ne postmodum queraris aut heredi tuo | controuer[si]am relinquas*, 'in such a manner that later you may not make a complaint or leave a dispute to your heir' (*CIL* XIV 2112, I ll. 18–19).

Some of the texts refer to admission and exclusion procedures. Admission in a *collegium* was called *adlectio* and required the payment of an entry fee. Cn. Sentius Felix's epitaph reflects this procedure.[32] Many Ostian associations picked him out as a patron and, in his later years, that is to say in the first decades of the second century AD, he became a public magistrate of Ostia. Before that, he had made his fortune in maritime trade, as shown by his membership in associations of ship-owners and of wine merchants. On his funerary altar, his adoptive son, Cn. Sentius Lucilius Gamala Clodianus, called him a *gratis adlectus inter nauicularios maris Hadriatici et ad quadrigam fori uinarii*, 'member admitted for free to the ship-owners of the Adriatic sea and to the association of the wine market'. In order to pay homage to him, both associations exempted him from an admission fee. Cn. Sentius Felix's exemption seems very honorific, because the *lex collegii* from Lanuvium insists on *cultores* paying their fee.[33] In fact, the word *adlectio* appears in three laws, engraved by the *negotiantes eborarii et citrarii*, 'ivory and citrus-wood workers', the *cultores Dianae et Antinoi*, 'worshippers of Diana and Antinous' and the *cultores Aesculapi et Hygiae*, 'worshippers of Asclepius and Hygieia'. Therefore, Cn. Sentius Felix's epitaph implies the existence of rules mentioned sporadically by *leges collegiorum*. Those are fundamental rules, insofar as they reveal the voluntary nature of Roman associations: as a matter of fact, admissions required an application, which could be approved or rejected.[34]

Moreover, associations could expel members who refused to follow common rules.[35] Laws give almost no information about this exclusion procedure. Only the regulation of the ivory and citrus-wood workers threatens dishonest *curatores* with dismissal.[36] Yet, many associations would have pronounced exclusions when the other sanctions – fines especially – had been inefficient. The epigraphic habit seems to shed light on such procedures through erasures on membership lists. Those hammered-out obliterations tend to reveal expulsions, not only simple

---

[32] *CIL* XIV 409. See Tran 2006: esp. 68–70; 2012a: 331.

[33] The *lex collegii* addressed *Tu qui nouos in hoc collegio | intrare uole[s]* 'You who want to enter this *collegium* as a new member' and its very first clause is: *[Placu]it uniuersis, ut quisquis in hoc collegium intrare uoluerit, dabit kapitulari nomine HS C n(ummos) et u[ini] boni amphoram*, 'It was agreed by all that whoever wants to enter this *collegium* shall give as a fee of 100 sesterces each and an amphora of good wine' (*CIL* XIV 2112, I ll. 17–18 and 20–1).

[34] For the same practice in the Greek world, see Giannakopoulos in Chapter 2.

[35] Tran 2007: 125–7 (in particular).

[36] A dismissed president of the *collegium fabrum tignuariorum* at Rome appears in *AE* 1971 no 71, ll. 59–60: a new *magister quinquennalis* was appointed between AD 74 and 78 *in loc(o) Fla[ui - - -], summo(ti)*, 'in place of Flavius ... who had been removed'.

updates. In fact, the Greek letter *theta*, engraved next to a name, could indicate a member's death,[37] while expulsion from associations may have led to a form of *damnatio memoriae*.[38] Although the *album* of the *corpus corporatorum qui pecuniam ad ampliandum templum contulerunt*, 'association of the members who collected funds for the enlargement of the temple', has unfortunately been lost for centuries,[39] several early modern copies exist and are reliable for the restitution of the text. The *corporati*, 'members', who contributed to enlarge their temple were in fact members of the *corpus scaphariorum et lenunculariorum traiectus Luculli*, 'association of ship-men and tugboatmen of the ferry service of Lucullus', one of the five associations of boatmen working in the harbour system of Ostia and Portus.[40] They had their list completed from AD 140 to 172 and erased the names of three *corporati*. It is tempting to link their probable exclusion with the contributions imposed. Another erasure appears on a later list of *nomina corporatorum*, 'members' names', inscribed in AD 262.[41] It mentions patrons and members of a *plebs*, amongst whom were many *Titi Tinucii*. Their community was considered as unknown until now, but the comparison between this document, a fragmentary honorific text and a piece of an *album* allows a possible hypothesis for identification:[42] the Ostian *corpus*, in which the *Titi Tinucii* are so numerous during the second third of the third century AD, might be the *corpus traiectus Rusticeli*, 'association of the ferry service of Rusticelus', another of the five *corpora* of the boatmen of Ostia. A third and last small fragment is characterised by an erasure, but the *corporati* who had the list inscribed remain unknown.[43]

Epigraphy provides evidence about decision making and elections too. The structure of Ostian membership lists implies procedures that aimed at assigning titles to patrons and dignitaries. Patrons did not belong to

---

[37] E.g. on *CIL* XIV 256 (*album* of the *corpus fabrum naualium*, 'association of the boat builders', from Portus).

[38] In any case, a few *corpora* chose to leave erasures visible. Conversely, the *familia Siluani* from Trebula Mutuesca erased seven names from its *album* and replaced them with others (*AE* 2002 no 397): therefore, the intention to highlight the estrangement of some members from the *familia* is much less clear.

[39] *CIL* XIV 246, III l. 3, IV l. 28, V l. 4.   [40] Tran 2012a: 327–30.   [41] *CIL* XIV 5357, I l. 18.

[42] *CIL* XIV 431; Cicerchia and Marinucci 1992: 223–4 (C112, fig. 152). The first inscription is a tribute to a dignitary of the *corpus traiectus Rusticeli*, paid by Veturia Q. f. Rufina and Q. Veturius Q. f. Felix Socrates, who were probably his children. The son's name can be restored on the fragmentary *album*, amongst the *patroni corporis*, 'association's patrons'. This list might also allude to C. Veturius Testius Amandus, known as *patronus et defensor quinque corporum lenunculariorum Ostiensium*, 'patron and protector of the five associations of Ostian tugboatmen', during the first decades of the third century AD (see Tran 2014, about *CIL* XIV 4144).

[43] *CIL* XIV 5372, l. 10.

associations themselves:[44] as protectors, they were in fact not amongst the group, but above it; therefore, they were listed at the top. Senators and then Roman knights are sometimes named with precedence.[45] A codified procedure granted the rank of patron but neither the *leges collegiorum* nor the inscriptions from Ostia give information about it; conversely, this is known from few *tabulae patronatus*, 'patronage's records', from other Italian cities. For instance, a bronze slab, given in AD 256 by an association of craftsmen (*collegium fabrum*) from Pisaurum to its new patrons, describes a procedure modelled on senatorial and decurional decrees.[46] The speech of the magistrates in front of all the members (*'uniuersi collegae conuenerunt'*) preceded a formal vote (*'censuer(unt)'*). A deputation had to announce the decision to the patrons, to whom the *tabula* was offered.

Likewise, the mention of officials implies specific rules about elections and title assignment.[47] In Ostia, the most frequent title for a president was *quinquennalis* or *magister quinquennalis*.[48] Furthermore, many inscriptions refer to the *lustrum*, the five-year term of office, of each *magister quinquennalis* of the *fabri tignuarii*.[49] For example, C. Similius Philocyrius served during the thirty-sixth *lustrum* of the *collegium*. As a matter of fact, the term of office was precisely defined in every Ostian association. In the best-known communities, the number of *quinquennales* in charge also reflects a high level of stability: the *fabri tignuarii* always had three *quinquennales*, certainly in accordance with a formal rule, observed for two centuries. Furthermore, in a few Ostian associations, there was a hierarchy between *quinquennales* (incumbent officials) and former *quinquennales*. Those who had received the title of honorary president were styled *quinquennales perpetui*; before this formal recognition, they were only called *quinquennalicii*. For a long time, the *corpus lenunculariorum traiectus Luculli* was the only association known for this organisation. But a small fragment of an *album* suggests that it did exist amongst the *lenuncularii tabularii auxiliarii*, 'auxiliary tugboatmen', too.[50] The distinction between

---

[44] Clemente 1972.   [45] E.g. *CIL* XIV 251.   [46] *CIL* XI 6335.

[47] Only one inscription (*CIL* XIV 2630), the epitaph of T. Flavius Hilario, a former *magister quinquennalis* of the *collegium fabrum tignuariorum* at Rome between AD 74 and 78, sheds some light on elections in *collegia*. During his career in the association, Hilario assisted in the voting procedure as *nungentus ad subfragia*, 'official to the elections', and then, after his presidency, he assumed the office of *censor bis ad magistros creandos*, 'censor for the election of presidents'.

[48] Royden 1988.

[49] The era of the Ostian builders started in AD 60. The earliest president attested is L. Aquillius Modestus, *magister quinquennalis collegii fabrum tignuariorum Ostiensium lustri II* (*CIL* XIV 299).

[50] *AE* 2001 no 622. See Zevi 2001, completed by Tran 2014: 134–6.

quinquennalicii and *quinquennales perpetui* underlined a strong attachment to codified procedures.

The decision-making process, which led associations to adopt decrees, involves precise functioning rules too. They probably dealt not only with meetings and voting procedures but also with enforcement of common decisions. The expression *cura agentibus*, 'through the care of', followed by the names of officials, is quite frequent in Ostian inscriptions: it is mainly inscribed on statue bases,[51] but we can also read it on a temple architrave, one that the *collegium fabrum tignuariorum* dedicated to the deified emperor Pertinax.[52] In that case, the words *cura(m) agentibus* suggest an acceptance of work that may have legal implications. The tribute paid to the Roman knight Q. Calpurnius Modestus by the association of the Ostian grain merchants during the mid-second century AD is interesting too.[53] It describes an action of this *corpus* through the application of a common decree by two *quinquennales* and two *quaestores*, 'treasurers'. The reference to these financial magistrates recalls the accountability briefly mentioned in a few regulations.[54] Hence, the use of common funds required formal rules that *quaestores* had to follow.

Finally, epigraphy does not simply reflect rules: epigraphic habit was sometimes a means for ensuring the respect for rules. We have seen that several regulations have been inscribed on stone in the context of foundations: benefactors wanted to be sure that associations would not forget or neglect their will. Display of inscriptions in common headquarters results from this concern. Conversely, the Ostian *dendrophori* honoured their benefactors and displayed the self-awareness of their duties towards them with another kind of inscription: a marble slab placed in their *schola*, 'clubhouse', listed all the benefactors' birthdays that the worshippers of Cybele and Attis had to celebrate.[55] One of the benefactors was the patron and *quinquennalis perpetuus* C. Iulius Cocilius Hermes, who apparently cared a lot about the permanency of his foundation: he gave 6,000 sesterces to the *dendrophori*, in addition to a silver statue, and required them to celebrate his birthday, using the interest accruing from his gift for the payment of the related expenses – otherwise, the money would be given to the *fabri tignuarii Ostienses*.[56] Another example is A. Egrilius Faustus, *quinquennalis* of the *lenuncularii traiectus Luculli*, who

---

[51] *CIL* XIV 128, 160, 4142, 5336, 5344, 5345; *AE* 1974 no 123 (inscribed by the *collegium fabrum tignuariorum Ostiensium*). *CIL* XIV 106, 168 (honours paid by the *nauicularii codicarii*, 'skippers', and the *fabri nauales*, 'boat builders').
[52] *AE* 1971 no 64 = *CIL* XIV 4365+4362.   [53] *CIL* XIV 161.
[54] Laubry and Zevi 2012: 330–1.   [55] *CIL* XIV 326.   [56] *AE* 1987 no 198.

had instituted a testamentary foundation for the benefit of his *corpus*: it was written on its *album*, which gave great publicity to Faustus' generosity and effort.[57] Membership lists could also indicate and ensure exemptions from contributions granted to members: amongst the plebeians of his *corpus*, Sergius Bictor, a shipbuilder from Portus, is described as an *immunis*, 'exempt';[58] another one was a *sesquiplicarius*, 'official entitled to an extra share and a half', who – like the officials amongst the *cultores Dianae et Antinoi* – received one and a half more during distributions. Therefore, an *album* could be a reference document, recording formal decisions.

Furthermore, like the *cultores* from Lanuvium did above their *lex collegii*, Ostian associations indicated that they had received a formal authorisation from the Roman Senate. On their *album* or on other inscriptions, they called themselves associations of *corporati quibus ex Senatus consulto coire licet*, 'association's members to whom right of association has been granted by decree of the Senate'.[59] The practice was quite frequent, although not systematic: this mention was therefore not at all compulsory. It stemmed from a desire to appear as well-established and thus respectable communities. The fact that some associations presented themselves as an *ordo*, 'order', was part of the same behaviour.

Collegia or Ordines?

Even if available documents give a very partial view of the situation, Roman associations followed precise internal rules. Therein, they intended to constitute well-ordered societies, even though they did not always achieve this objective. Beyond their regulations, the way associations called themselves on inscriptions further shows that they wished to appear as 'well-ordered societies'. Probably exactly for this purpose, they used the expression *ordo corporatorum*, 'order of association's members', at the beginning of several Ostian membership lists. A still-unpublished fragment illustrates this point: it belonged to the *album* engraved in AD 192 by the *corpus lenunculariorum pleromariorum auxiliariorum*, 'association of auxiliary boatmen on lighters [used to unload larger freighters]'.[60] Until now, these boatmen have been known only by another list, from AD 200.[61]

---

[57] *CIL* XIV 246.   [58] *CIL* XIV 256.
[59] *CIL* XIV 10, 168–9, 256, 4573; *AE* 1955 nos 175 and 177; Marinucci 2012: 108–9 (no 129).
[60] Site of Ostia Antica, inventory number 6335 a–b (F. Zevi and I intend to publish it soon).
[61] *CIL* XIV 252. See also *CIL* XIV 253.

Both inscriptions employed the words *ordo corporatorum*, as it was the appropriate formulation in such a context. As a matter of fact, the unpublished fragment completes a small series of well-known inscriptions. Two of them are membership lists established by the *corpus lenuncular-iorum traiectus Luculli*, also known as the *ordo corporatorum qui pecuniam ad ampliandum templum contulerunt*, 'association of the members who collected funds for the enlargement of the temple'.[62] Likewise, on their membership lists, the *lenuncularii tabularii auxiliarii* seem to have always defined their group as an *ordo corporatorum*. Three different lists from AD 152, 192 and 213 tend to prove this.[63] The true significance of the practice of calling themselves '*ordines*' is difficult to understand, because the notion of *ordo* is complex. The word itself is polysemous: we must try to determine its exact meaning on inscriptions engraved by *collegia*.

On the one hand, this term was partly used in a concrete sense; on the other hand, its use resulted from a practice of imitation. But neither explanation is completely sufficient. The word *ordo* could mean very concretely a line of things or men placed next to each other: a row. Therefore, one can wonder if Ostian *ordines corporatorum* were nothing but ordered lists of association members. The expression *nomina corpor-atorum*, 'members' names', was sometimes engraved instead of *ordo corpor-atorum*, which designated the *album* as a register.[64] Yet, on other inscriptions, *ordo* indisputably meant more than 'register' and did not only define a group listed in a hierarchical fashion. Associations' regulations contribute to prove it.

In the *lex collegii Aesculapi et Hygiae*, for instance, *ordo* designated the *collegium* itself, as an active entity. At the end, the document is in fact presented as a decree passed by 'our order' during a general meeting: *hoc decretum ordini n(ostro) placuit in conuentu pleno*, 'our *ordo* issued this decree in a general assembly'. Just before this, the inscription alluded to decisions *quos ordo collegi n(ostri) decreuit*, 'which the *ordo* of our associa-tion decreed'.[65] A statue base from Lavinium, in Latium, helps to under-stand what *ordo* could mean in such a context.[66] It was inscribed first in

[62] *CIL* XIV 246, 5356.   [63] *CIL* XIV 250, 251; Bloch 1953: no 42.
[64] *CIL* XIV 5357. In Lanuvium, the *collegium Dianae et Antinoi* used the word *ordo* in a very concrete sense: presidents of the dinners (*magistri cenarum*) are designated according to the *album*'s order (*ex ordine albi*).
[65] *CIL* VI 10234, ll. 23 and 20.
[66] Nonnis 1995–6; Liu 2015 (*AE* 1998 no 282). Text IV (ll. 3–5): *In Caesareum quod est in foro cum ordo collegi dendropho|rum L(aurentium) L(auinatium) conuenisset, ibi Cornelius Trophimus et Varenius | Legitimus, quinquennales, uerba fecerunt*, 'When the *ordo* of the *collegium dendrophorum* of Lavinium had convened in the *Caesareum* which is in the forum, Cornelius Trophimus and

September AD 227, in honour of C. Servilius Diodorus, a Roman knight who had just become a *Laurens Lauinas* priest. A stone copy of several documents appears on three faces: the dossier deals with a perpetual foundation, which benefitted the local *collegium dendrophorum*. In return, C. Servilius Diodorus received the title of patron in AD 228 and sent a letter of thanks. Then, a formal decree was added to the epigraphic dossier on another side of the base. At the beginning of this fourth text, the group gathered to vote the decree is called the *ordo collegii dendrophorum*: in this document, too, the word *ordo* seems to designate the group itself, without being a simple synonym of *collegium*, if we admit that the expression *ordo collegii* is not totally redundant. Its use may aim at highlighting which kind of community the *collegium* was, especially when its members met in a general assembly.[67] In this solemn occasion, the group was 'ordered', insofar as the members had gathered officially, hierarchically and sitting next to each other – in rows – to make a legitimate decision. In fact, this point makes the regulation of the *negotiantes eborarii et citrarii* clearer: members of the *collegium* convened in a formal assembly, that is to say, as an *ordo*, and were entitled to erase from the *album* the names of dignitaries guilty of fraudulent admission, that is to say, to vote their revocation.[68]

However, Roman associations were not *ordines* in the same way as the senatorial order or the equestrian order. They were neither *ordines* in the same way as the orders of *apparitores*, 'attendants', assisting the Roman magistrates, nor as the *ordines* of city councillors or even of *Augustales*.[69] Indeed, Roman *collegia* were private and voluntary associations. They gathered *priuati*, 'private persons', and were free to recruit, or not,

---

Varenius Legitimus, the presidents, made proposals …'. See also, ll. 11–13: *idque ordi|ni n(ostro) maxime placere tam bono uiro bene merenti gratias age|re*, 'and that it greatly pleases our *ordo* to give thanks to such a worthy good man'.

[67] Likewise, in AD 206, the fishermen and divers of the Tiber decided to honour a dignitary through a formal procedure (*CIL* VI 1872). They insisted on the solemnity of their decision making, through these words: *ex decreto | ordinis corporis piscatorum | et urinatorum totius alu(ei) Tiber(is) | quibus ex s(enatus) c(onsulto) coire licet*, 'by a decision made by the *ordo* of the fishermen and divers' association of the whole Tiber bed, who are allowed to gather by senatorial decree'. See also *CIL* V 56: decree voted by the *collegium dendrophorum* from Pola in AD 227, on which the words *[decretum ordi]nis n(ostri)* are restored.

[68] *CIL* VI 33885, ll. 4–6: *ut si alius quam negotiator eborarius aut citriarius [p]er | [fr]audem curatorum in hoc collegium adlectus esset, uti curatores eius | [cau]sa ex albo raderentur ab ordine*, 'if someone else than an ivory or citrus-wood worker is admitted in this *collegium* through a deceit of the supervisors, then for this reason the *ordo* will erase the supervisors from the *album*'.

[69] On *ordines* of *apparitores*, see Cohen 1984. About *ordines Augustalium* (or *seuirorum Augustalium*) and the debate on their nature, see Abramenko 1993: 13–37; Mouritsen 2011: 249–61.

individuals who wanted to join them. On the contrary, membership in the
'real' *ordines* resulted from a public decision made by a civic authority and
not from a co-optation.[70] The legal status of Roman *collegia* was very
different. The choice of calling themselves *ordines* was part of a more
general behaviour, which underlines the strong integration of *collegia* to a
broader socio-cultural environment: Roman associations imitated public
structures meticulously to gain respectability. For instance, the presidents
of the *collegium fabrum tignuariorum Ostiensium* bore the title of *magister
quinquennalis*; however, they obviously had almost nothing to do with the
'real' magistrates from a legal and public point of view. They remained
private individuals. Is the expression *ordo corporatorum* part of the same
behaviour? The *collegium dendrophorum* from Lavinium was defined as an
ordo when they voted a decree, which looked exactly like a *decretum
decurionum*, 'decree of city councillors'. O. M. van Nijf has defined an
'*ordo*-making' process to qualify this mimetic attitude:[71] it consisted in 'a
form of collective self representation as a respected status group in society,
that adopted the form of self representation of the Roman elites'. Hence,
Roman associations imitated groups and structures socially and legally very
different from them. These higher *ordines* fascinated the wealthiest members of *collegia*, who were also the most keen for social climbing: many
association dignitaries expected to join an *ordo Augustalium* or an *ordo* of
apparitores;[72] they would have entered an *ordo decurionum*, 'decurional
order', with enthusiasm, but their social condition or – in the case of the
numerous freedmen amongst them – their legal status usually prevented
them from doing so.[73] Hence, they placed this ambition on their sons,
who sometimes became *decuriones* or even members of the equestrian
order. To some extent and due to the social motivations of their members,
associations would have pretended to be *ordines*, but were not 'real' *ordines*.
Yet, although this explanation is partly right, it is not completely
convincing either.

The expression *ordo corporatorum* reflects the will to appear as 'well
ordered' communities; however, the notion of *ordo* is very polymorphic.[74]
Few social groups, different from orders formally defined by public
authorities, were also called *ordines* – and not in a concrete sense. Private
associations were no exception. According to Cl. Nicolet, these uses of *ordo*

[70] Flambard 1981: 154: 'l'association n'est jamais une donnée externe qui préexiste à la volonté de ses
constituants' ('the association is never an external fact prior to the will of its constituents').
[71] Van Nijf 1997: 245–7.   [72] Tran 2006: 211–32.   [73] Tran 2006: passim.
[74] Cohen 1975; Tran 2006: 335–46.

were metaphorical and hence 'inappropriate'.[75] Nonetheless, it is very difficult to distinguish metaphorical usage from realities resulting from imitation. Terminology, behaviours and concrete organisation of Roman associations were closely connected. Of course, the *corporati* knew that their associations and the senatorial order, for instance, had not much in common. But in their minds, their *corpus* was a 'real' *ordo*, because it was:

- a formally circumscribed group, whose list of members could be precisely established;
- a group, whose membership depended on an individual procedure, which provided each member with a hierarchical position (higher or lower);
- a group, whose dignitaries exercised an authority on ordinary members, in particular a coercive power in case of fraud or disorder (as shown by fines and exclusions mentioned above);
- a group able to make collective decisions (*decreta*) through formal procedures of deliberation, vote and archiving.

Therefore, the strong connection between the designation as an '*ordo corporatorum*' and the existence of formal rules for common life must be stressed. Roman associations wanted to appear as well and strongly structured as possible.

A further example of a similar behaviour may be mentioned here. As far as we know, the *collegium fabrum tignuariorum Ostiensium* never claimed to be an *ordo*, but its members were supposed to form a *numerus caligatorum*, 'group/unit of booted men (*sc.* soldiers)'.[76] This expression clearly belonged to military vocabulary and presented the *collegium* as something it was not: a military unit. Unlike the members of many *collegia fabrum* in the Roman West, the *fabri tignuarii Ostienses* did not serve as firefighters, because 'real' soldiers detached from the cohorts of the *uigiles*, 'watchmen, police force', from Rome assumed this task.[77] Therefore, Ostian builders seem to have had no reason to call themselves as an infantry unit, other

---

[75] Nicolet 1984: 9 'mais si j'ose dire, tous les *ordines* ne sont pas vraiment des *ordines*: il est des emplois trompeurs, ou abusifs, de ce mot' ('if I may say so, all the *ordines* are not really *ordines*: it is a deceptive or improper usage of this word') and 13.

[76] *CIL* XIV 128, 160, 374, 4569. See Zevi 2008: 493–4. *Caligae* were boots worn by Roman soldiers: a *caligatus* was a common soldier. The reference to the army is even more explicit in the first inscription, which quotes (in AD 285) *honorati et decurion(es) et numerus militum caligatorum*, 'notables and officials and the group of booted soldiers'.

[77] Sablayrolles 1996: 45–55 and 289–314.

than their desire to appear as 'ordered' as possible, that is to say, as organised and hierarchical as possible. In this respect, we must keep in mind that the word *ordo* could also mean 'a line of soldiers standing side by side'. After all, the way in which the *collegium fabrum tignuariorum Ostiensium* is called does not seem so odd, even though it is definitely ambiguous.[78]

Conclusion

One should not misunderstand what inscriptions display: in fact, it is an ideal and idealised view. This construction does not simply reflect ancient realities. Roman associations were not always a world of 'well-ordered societies'. In fact, rules and means to enforce them responded to potential disorders or faults in organisation and discipline – things that could be fatal for an association, as the wax tablet with the act of dissolution of the *collegium Iouis Cerneni* in Alburnus Maior illustrates. This also points to the important aspect that association rules were not simply ideological: although they certainly reflected the civic values of association members, they also served very practical purposes. In a certain way, the rules and the internal organisation, which they sketched, were more than vital, as they lay at the core of what defined an association proper and distinguished it from another group. An association proper was closed, permanent and organised. Without admission and functioning rules, those characteristics are by default missing: an association did not exist without rules, because rules gave birth to it. Etymologically, a *collegium* might have united individuals under the same *lex*, under the same rules.[79] This is what epigraphic evidence and epigraphic habit of Roman associations also emphasise – regardless of etymology. The well-ordered organisation of Roman *collegia* demonstrates that their members had completely interiorised values and habits, created and embodied with the greatest intensity by other social categories: the elites. Associations' regulations and their other inscriptions reveal norms of behaviour, festive practices and procedures shaped on those of the city. This reproduction at the scale of *collegia* was

---

[78] Likewise, in Tran 2012b I tried to demonstrate how ambiguous the adjective *publicus* was, when Roman *collegia* used it in inscriptions.

[79] Ernout and Meillet 1932: 515, *s.v.* '*lex*'.

not at all gratuitous and disinterested: this process was a matter of participation, a matter of civic and social integration. *Corporati* aimed to gain positions in social hierarchies in the most favourable manner. For dignitaries, in particular, a *collegium*'s respectability, attained through the image of a strictly ordered community, was often a springboard in a quest for prestige beyond associations.

CHAPTER 10

Rules and Regulations of Associations
The Eurasian comparandum*

Kasper G. Evers

Historical Overview

In order to learn more about the origins of and motivations behind charters of rules and regulations laid down by ancient groups to define themselves as associations proper, that is, with codified laws,[1] scholars have traditionally opted for units of study comprising distinct cultural and political entities, such as 'Classical Greek,' 'Hellenistic,' or 'Roman' associations. Occasionally, though, Greek and Roman traditions for associating have been treated as an implicit case of Mediterranean institutional unity, constituting one overarching *fenomeno associativo*, 'associational phenomenon'.[2] Thus, particularly the older historiography of the subject reflects this basic premise of wider Greco-Roman institutional connectedness and compatibility, in that even though the two subjects are most often dealt with separately, they are assumed to add up to a mutually coherent framework for interpreting one or the other or both.[3] However, even if we employ an augmented Greco-Roman perspective, this

---

* Special abbreviations employed:

> *Arthash.:*   Kangle (1965-72).
>
> *Periplus:*   Casson (1989)

Moreover, the documents from Dunhuang are conventionally identified as follows:

> O.:   Ōtani Documents, Library of Ryūkoku University, Kyoto.
>
> P.:   Pelliot Dunhuang Collection, Bibliothèque Nationale, Paris.
>
> S.:   Stein Dunhuang Collection, British Library, London.

[1] As defined by Gabrielsen and Paganini in Chapter 1.
[2] Phrase chosen from the title of de Robertis 1955.
[3] Poland 1909 includes associations of Roman citizens in the East in later Hellenistic times and associations of Greeks in *Italia*. Likewise, Waltzing 1895–1900 readily includes a number of Greek associations of the Roman East in his monumental account. San Nicolò 1972 encompasses both the Ptolemaic and Roman periods in his study of associations in Egypt.

'Mediterrano-centric' view of events might cause us to miss out on (or conveniently ignore)[4] the greater picture, namely, of a much wider institutional development and associational phenomenon encompassing the width and breath of Eurasia.

Accordingly, this chapter will endeavour to briefly survey and compare the institutional set-up, as constituted by charters of rules and regulations, of Greco-Roman associations of the Mediterranean from the Principate onwards with similar and roughly contemporary organisations of South and East Asia, the time span ranging from the first to tenth centuries AD. By way of a brief general overview, there is evidence for a comparable but much older associational habit amongst the peoples of the Near East. Although this was an indigenous development, it interacted with Greek forms of association from at least the third century BC onwards and merged with them in Roman times, causing distinctive local hybridisation.[5] Likewise, first the Hellenistic states, particularly those of the Seleucids and the Ptolemies, and afterwards seagoing Roman traders of the Red Sea and Indian Ocean, came into contact with Indian craftsmen and merchants traditionally organised in their own organisations, the most conspicuous types being the *shreni* and the *nigama*, respectively.[6] Finally, Buddhist networks of scholastic transmission from northern India came increasingly into contact with autochthonous Chinese religious institutions during the third to fourth centuries AD, effecting the creation of *she* associations native to China from no later than the early seventh century AD.[7]

Picking out the Indian and Chinese associations for comparison with their Greco-Roman counterparts, it becomes possible to trace the historical trajectories of this particular kind of institution across the largest possible spatial framework, namely, Eurasia. Thus, three different 'association phenomena' can be studied in isolation and interaction, which explains the need for the largest possible area of study, and comparison of roughly synchronic Roman and Indian associations with their later Chinese ditto. Although it would have been highly interesting to conduct a strictly synchronic comparison of medieval European, Indian and Chinese associations, too,[8] such a monumental study is, sadly, beyond the scope of this chapter.

---

[4] As argued about the Western invention of an exceptional 'Antiquity' generally by Goody 2012: 26–67.
[5] McLaughlin 2001; Maciá 2007; specific case studies of hybridisation in Ameling 1990, Stern 2007 and Brock 2009 (the latter kindly brought to my attention by Dr Ilias Arnaoutoglou).
[6] Majumdar 1920; Thaplyal 1996.   [7] Yamamoto et al. 1988–89; Ning and Hao 1997.
[8] E.g. Ogilvie 2011 (Western Europe); Maniatis 2009 (Byzantium); Abraham 1988 (South India).

More specifically, the focus here will be restricted to the rules and regulations of associations with memberships explicitly, but by no means exclusively, defined by profession, with the partial exception of the medieval Chinese associations, rather acting as a general East Asian *comparandum*. This is a necessary methodological requirement to ensure that the units to be compared have a certain minimum of meaningful characteristics in common. While comparisons with associations whose memberships were not defined by inter alia profession can be very useful, if their limitations are duly recognised, they easily become misleading when used too extensively instead of non-extant *leges*, 'laws', of professional *collegia*.[9]

In the following analysis of rules and regulations of Roman, Indian and later medieval Chinese associations, three interconnected issues will be explored – namely, which values or behavioural norms the associations sought to promote through their sets of rules, how the private ordering of associations worked in relation to states and what *raison d'être* associations appear to have had in their host societies.

Rules and Regulations of Roman Associations

Starting out at Rome, the earliest development of associations in the Mediterranean really goes back to the ancient Greek city states,[10] subsequently diffused in Hellenistic times to other parts of the Mediterranean world, from Magna Graecia to the Levant.[11] While later Roman historians ascribed the establishment of occupational *collegia* to the legendary king Numa, whose reign tradition dated to the later eighth to early seventh century BC,[12] the first inscriptions by *collegia* and *corpora* crop up in the epigraphic record from the early second century BC and they are

---

[9] An example of the former is Broekaert 2011: 227, 234; while an example of the latter is Hawkins 2012: 190–3. In other words, associations with all or most members sharing a joint profession were also always 'religious' in practicing elements of a communal cult, whereas the devotees of a specific deity united in a common cult by membership of a specific association will not have had shared professional or economic interests as a group, most likely exercising differing vocations as private individuals.

[10] Poland 1909; Jones 1999; Arnaoutoglou 2003.

[11] Gabrielsen 2016a shows that the birth of the association phenomenon cannot be narrowed down to early Hellenistic times. Rather, the development leading up to this 'take-off' is attested epigraphically from no later than the beginning of the fourth century BC. Gabrielsen 2007 elaborates on the far-reaching 'industrious revolution' that the Greek association phenomenon constituted.

[12] Plin. *HN* 34.1, 35.46; Plu. *Num.* 17.2. Gabba 1984 debunks the tradition's historical credibility.

mentioned in the literary sources from the sixties BC.[13] The earliest preserved charters of association rules, however, only date from the mid-first to mid-second centuries AD,[14] and only one of these pertains to a *collegium* defined by profession, to be treated in the following.

This association is attested by an inscription found in Trastevere, across the Tiber from Rome, dating from the reign of Hadrian, AD 117–38. The membership of the *collegium* consisted of *negotiatores eborarii et citriarii*, that is, 'ivory and citrus-wood traders', but, sadly, only half of the charter, on admission rules, annual banquets, handouts, rotation of offices and the management of communal funds, survives.[15] The historical context for the combination of such different lines of trade in one organisation was the particular circumstance that luxurious composite furniture made from polished citrus wood supported by or adorned with carved ivory was very much in vogue during the mid-first to later second centuries AD.[16]

Significantly, the *lex*, 'law', states at the top of its preserved second column that 'if anyone but an ivory or citrus-wood trader is admitted into this association (*collegium*) by deceit of the officials (*curatores*), the officials should for this [rea]son be struck from the membership list (*album*) by the members' assembly (*ordo*)'. Moreover, prospective members also had to be approved of by one or more presidents, *quinquennalis/-es*.[17] This rule is

---

[13] For the earliest origins, see Waltzing 1895–1900, I: 61–90; III: 1–2; Ausbüttel 1982: 106–7, Tran 2006: 1–21; Diosono 2007: 24–33.

[14] On a firm basis, the earliest Roman specimen is the *Lex familiae Silvani*, ca. AD 60 (*AE* 1929 no 161; Buonocore and Diliberto 2003), while the *Lex collegii aquae* (*CIL* VI 10298) dates back to late Republican times, but it is contested whether this group constituted an occupational *collegium*, so Moschetta 2005, or a board of municipal magistrates, so Berger 1951: 108–15. The other charters are those of the *collegium salutare* of Diana and Antinous (*CIL* XIV 2112, AD 136; Bendlin 2011) and *collegium* of Asclepius and Hygieia (*CIL* VI 10234, AD 153; Ascough, Harland and Kloppenborg 2012: 207–10), which can be cautiously compared with the preserved *nomos* of the Athenian *Iobacchoi* (*IG* II² 1368, AD 164/5; Kloppenborg and Ascough 2011: 241–56): see also Arnaoutoglou in Chapter 6. In addition, a fragment has survived of an inscription granting permission by the Senate in AD 121 to an otherwise unknown Ostian association to convene as a *collegium*, the extant quoted clauses being verbatim to corresponding passages in the *lex* of the *collegium* of Diana and Antinous (above) concerning funerary practices (*CIL* XIV 4548; Laubry and Zevi 2010): see also Tran in Chapter 9. The *collegium* of *negotiatores eborarii et citriarii* is treated in detail below.

[15] *CIL* VI 33885 = *ILS* 7214. Cf. Borsari 1887; Waltzing 1895–1900: III 316 no 1347; Tran 2007: 122–3; specifically, only half of the four-line preamble and the second half of the main text have been preserved.

[16] On citrus wood and its uses, see Meiggs 1982: 286–91. For a brief summary of ancient references to citrus-wood tables with ivory legs and the latter's possible importation as single carved pieces from India, see Karttunen 1997, and on the role of this particular *collegium* in such a proposed trade between Rome and India, Evers 2017: 13–47.

[17] *CIL* VI 33885, ll. 4–7: *si alius quam negotiator eborarius aut citriarius* [p]*er* | [fr]*audem curatorum in hoc collegium adlectus esset uti curatores eius* | [cau]*sa ex albo raderentur ab ordine debebunt utique*

somewhat surprising, seeing as it is the only known example of its kind,[18] making for a homogeneous membership base restricted to two select and highly specialised commercial occupations. Thus, this membership clause underlines the exclusive and close-knit nature of the organisation for those eligible and willing to participate.

In addition, unlike other contemporary *collegia* with surviving *leges*, the association of citrus-wood and ivory traders took active steps to be a highly egalitarian organisation.[19] All members received equal portions of money back from the club coffers at the end of the association's fiscal year and at the stipulated celebrations on New Year's Day, the day of Hadrian's accession, as well as on the emperor's, patron's and patron's son's birthdays, all received the same cash handouts and were to be treated to the same food and drink.[20] In consequence, neither the boards of officials, being the *curatores* and *quinquennalis/-es*, nor more well-to-do traders or well-connected members, received any more back of any kind than ordinary members.[21] In fact, this egalitarian feature seems to be further emphasised by the fact that all members were eventually appointed as *curatores* according to rotation based on the order of the membership list, *album*.[22] Consistent with an ideal of equality amongst members, a procedure like this highlights that no one had privileged access to the blessings and burdens of the association's basic communal office – unfortunately, we do not know how they elected their *quinquennalis/-es*.

Furthermore, we learn that this association must have regularly constituted itself as a formal assembly of its own, an *ordo* or 'status group unto itself', authorised to make internal communal decisions and enforce them, amongst other things, regarding the admission of new members and the potential expulsion of *curatores* who had failed in their duties.[23] Whatever other authority the *ordo* of the *collegium* might have had over the members might well have been stated explicitly in the lost first half of the regulations, but the one surviving clause we have about the power of the *ordo*

---

curatores de eo | [*que*]*m adlecturi fuerint ante ad quinq*(*uennales*) *re*[*fe*]*rre*. Note that the length of office of the Roman 'five-year presidents' could be less than five years, cf. Royden 1989.

[18] Tran 2007: 122; Ausbüttel 1982: 37–8. That is, although no other charters of occupational *collegia* are preserved from the Roman West, numerous membership lists, *alba* and honorific dedications reveal that patrons and benefactors, in particular, were freely admitted no matter their vocation; e.g. *CIL* XI 2702; XIII 5154; XIV 409. Obviously, though, other (non-occupational) *collegia* also strove to exclude freewheeling non-members from their banquets, etc.; e.g. Tran 2007: 123.

[19] Contrary to: *CIL* VI 10234, ll. 10–12; XIV 2112, II ll. 17–22; *IG* II² 1368, ll. 117–24.

[20] *CIL* VI 33885, ll. 8–19, 22.   [21] Bäumler 2014: 72–3, 75.   [22] *CIL* VI 33885, ll. 19–20.

[23] *CIL* VI 33885, l. 6. On Roman *ordines* of the West in general: Tran 2006: 335–46; on this *ordo* specifically, Tran 2007: 124.

over internal matters indicates a strong mechanism for private ordering amongst these two combined groups of traders.

Accordingly, in order for people of quite different trades to merge into a more or less coherent group able to make joint decisions, the establishment through codification of a principle of equal worth amongst the members seems an eminent idea. In practice, this egalitarian principle was enacted at the half dozen annual celebrations following a strictly defined format (set handouts and banquets), serving to create trustworthy and functional relations between individual members, at one level, and the two trades more generally. Thus, the group constituted itself as a formal body through the very procedure regulating stipulated communal activities.[24]

Summing up on this particular occupational *collegium*, it was an organisation created intentionally in response to a strong demand for composite citrus-wood and ivory furniture. As such, it is a prime example of vocational dependency facilitated by associational bonding, made possible by embedding transactional relationships of profession in social relations of fellow-members enshrined in associations' regulations.

Significantly, a recently discovered inscription from Miletus in Roman Asia Minor sheds a sidelight on the intentional creation and deliberate organisation of occupational associations.[25] The text is a reply from emperor Hadrian, dated AD 131, granting permission for the establishment of an *oikos naukleron*, 'house of the shippers', and at the same time ratifying the *nomos* in accordance with which it was to be organised.[26] Accordingly, the Milesian *naukleroi* must have previously drafted a set of rules setting out the arrangements of their prospective 'house of shippers' and attached them to a petition seeking imperial approval for the formal foundation of such an organisation.[27] In fact, the *collegium* of *negotiatores eborarii et citriarii* is likely to have established itself through the very same process, seeing as imperial approval for the creation of associations was not

---

[24] Bäumler 2014: 77–9, drawing on Luhmann 1969.

[25] On professional associations in the Greek-speaking East of the Roman Empire, see generally Dittmann-Schöne 2001 and Zimmermann 2002.

[26] Ehrhardt and Günther 2013: 200, ll. 10–13.

[27] Whereas *oikos* was used in Hellenistic times to refer to an association's property, being its meeting place (or clubhouse), e.g. *I.Délos* I 520 (ll. 3, 10) and 774, the word came to denote in the Roman East an association itself, most (perhaps even all) of *naukleroi*, whereas their physical 'house' could now be called an *oikos nauklerikos*, cf. *TAM* IV.1 22 (with IV.1 33). Other known *oikoi naukleron* are: *IScM* 60, 132 and 153; *BCH* 25 (1901): 36 no 184; *SEG* 51:2016. On which, see Poland 1909: 114; Vélissaropoulos 1980: 104–6; and Dittmann-Schöne 2001: 42. The great value of the new inscription from Miletus is that it informs us that these groups not only shared joint profession, owned property, elected officials and made communal dedications, but also abided by formally established sets of rules.

only required by law,[28] but that this particular group actively advertised appreciation for the emperor by celebrating his birthday and accession to the purple, marked by greater handouts and, as regards the latter day, a proper dinner instead of the regular banquets.[29] Imperial favour of occupational *collegia* (and *oikoi*) was thus not only a formal requirement, but also seems to have been proudly advertised as a group value in the guise of collective reverence for the emperor.

Indeed, the fundamental importance of charters of rules for the foundation of associations whose members were primarily involved in economic activities is further borne out by two inscriptions from Puteoli, the great maritime hub of Rome. One, from AD 116, tells us that the port hosted Berytian worshippers of Jupiter Heliopolitanus, while another in all likelihood refers to the same group as a *corpus Heliopolitanorum*, possessing land, a cistern and *tabernae*, as well as a set of rules and shared norms, *lex et conventio*, which anyone entering the area had to abide by.[30] Thus, although the members of this group shared both geographical origins (Berytus), religious confession (Jupiter Heliopolitanus) and presumably profession (merchants and shippers operating out of Puteoli, as the Tyrians to be treated shortly), they still felt the need to express their formal nature as a corporate association by reference to their common rules (the *lex*) and principles (*conventio*), which members and non-members alike had to abide by in their little part of town. Previously, a second-century BC association of Berytian merchants, shippers and forwarding agents,[31] being worshippers of Poseidon, had been equally well organised as a group with common property, funds, rules, magistrates and court proceedings, on Hellenistic Delos, revealing a long-term Berytian penchant for setting up associations governed by meticulous regulations.[32]

A similar situation is revealed by an inscription put up by a dwindling community of Tyrians resident in Puteoli in AD 174, being those who

---

[28] E.g. *Dig.* 3.4.1 (Gaius, second century AD), mentioning, in particular, permissions granted by the Senate or emperor for *corpora naviculariorum* in the provinces; 47.22.3.1 (Marcianus, early third century AD). Pliny the Younger also mentions in passing that Trajan was consulted about the establishment of *collegia* (*Pan.* 54.4)

[29] *CIL* VI 33885, ll. 10–11, 17–18; cf. Bäumler 2014: 75, 78–9.

[30] *CIL* X 1634 and 1579, respectively = Tran Tam Tinh 1972: S. 12–13; Terpstra 2013: 84–5.

[31] *I.Délos* I 520. 'Forwarding agents' is a translation of the ambiguous Greek term *egdocheis*, following Fraser 1972b: 185f and 319f with n. 428; whereas Rostovtzeff 1941: II 1268, interpreted the group as 'warehouse owners'. One might also settle for calling them 'warehousemen'. However, Fraser's translation better brings out an active role, comparable to that of *emporoi* and *naukleroi*, rather than implying passive (or even absentee) owners of storage space or the people working in such buildings. Compare *P.Cair.Zen.* 59021, ll. 9–11 (258 BC).

[32] See Tod 1934: 140–59.

originally settled in town to service their fellow merchants and shippers sailing out of Tyre.[33] From the details of the inscription, we learn that the Tyrians jointly possessed a *statio* in town, being an actual building of some size and considerable embellishment, where worship of their ancestral gods was conducted and around which the Tyrian community's participation in and payment for public festivals was organised – if all of this was not governed by an explicit *lex*, then, at least, they too adhered to a common *conventio* grounded in shared ethnicity and common worship of ancestral gods.[34] Significantly, moreover, the Tyrian settlers at Puteoli seem to have been in possession of some kind of authoritative document, perhaps a founding *lex* of sorts, which ensured their eventual success in securing from the city council of Tyre support for the status and independence of their community vis-à-vis a similar establishment of their countrymen in Rome.[35] And, just as with their Berytian contemporaries in Puteoli, Tyrian merchants and shippers had been established and formally organised as an association of worshippers of Heracles, on second-century BC Delos, proving an equally long-standing tradition for well-ordered societies of Tyrian economic agents.[36]

Having by now studied the principles behind the *lex* of the *collegium* of *negotiatores eborarii et citriarii*, the role of *leges* for the foundation and organisation of associations consisting of traders and craftsmen more widely and the importance of official ratification of an association's regulations by the central authorities, we shall now briefly consider the potential of charters for facilitating corporate economic activity by professional associations. From the theoretical perspective of Roman law, persons formally permitted to constitute a *corpus* in the manner of a *collegium* or *societas* or other organisation were allowed to possess common property and funds (as we have already seen, all of the associations treated in the above did to various extents) and to authorise a person to act as agent (*actor*) or representative (*syndicus*) of the entire group, anything this person transacted or did being on behalf of all.[37] However, this article merely defines that associations were considered corporate bodies in the eyes of the law and, therefore, leaves us none the wiser about actual corporate economic activity by ancient associations.

---

[33] *CIG* V 853. Terpstra 2013: 70–9

[34] All of this being embedded in a strong Tyrian religious community, apparently created by the official transhipment from their motherland to Puteoli of a native god in AD 79. *IGR* I 420 = Tran Tam Tinh 1972: 137, S. 18; and Torrey 1948–49.

[35] As argued by Sosin 1999.   [36] *I.Délos* I 519.   [37] *Dig.* 3.4.1.1 (Gaius, second century AD).

In support of a guild- or firm-like corporate potential of *collegia, corpora, oikoi*, etc., evidence of associations from Ptolemaic and Roman Egypt is often employed.[38] One specific document stands out:[39] a papyrus from Tebtynis in the Fayyum of Roman Egypt, dated AD 47, which was lodged in the village record office by local salt merchants, *halopolai*, and contained a detailed account of how their mutual business was to be organised for the following year, in the area for which they had jointly acquired the public concession to sell salt.[40] A supervisor and collector of their trades' public taxes was elected, rights of salt and gypsum sale for different localities were distributed amongst them, fixed prices for salt and gypsum were agreed upon as well as upper limits for individual transactions with third parties, different fines were stipulated for transgression of the rules, the date for a monthly meeting (involving the consumption of beer) was set, and, finally, the right to arrest any member who came to owe the group money was vested in the person of the supervisor. Significantly, perhaps, in light of the above analysis, no party to the agreement seems to be accorded undue privileges based on considerations of status external to their businesslike compact.

While this might at first glance appear to be monopolistic behaviour by a sort of *koinon halopolon* acting much in the same manner as an archetypical merchants' guild of medieval Europe,[41] the special context constituted by the economy of Roman (and Hellenistic, for that matter) Egypt should, in fact, cause us to think otherwise.[42] Rather, local Egyptian *koina* of craftsmen and traders, like that of the salt merchants of Tebtynis, were to a considerable extent united for contractual reasons to do with their subleases of greater public or private monopolies in their trades,[43] and for reasons of public utility, such as the collection of trade taxes. Several cases of occupational groups being held liable for their profession's trade taxes by government collectors are known from throughout the Roman period.[44] In other words, we should probably consider such Egyptian *koina* of craftsmen and traders more in the sense of annually renewable professional partnerships[45] operating within the special framework of an indigenous

---

[38] On professional associations in Egypt generally, see, in particular, San Nicolò 1972; Gibbs 2011, 2015; Venticinque 2016; and Langellotti in Chapter 8.

[39] E.g. van Nijf 1997: 13–14; Broekaert 2011: 246–7.   [40] *P.Mich.* V 245. Boak 1937a, 1937b.

[41] As defined by Ogilvie 2011: 19–40.   [42] Liu 2009: 15; Gibbs 2011: 296.

[43] Gibbs 2011: 298–9, especially n. 30; for Ptolemaic times, Gibbs 2015: 261.

[44] E.g. *Stud.Pal.* IV pp. 58–78, ll. 378–431 (potters, AD 73); also *P.Tebt.* II 287 (fullers and dyers, AD 161/9); cf. Johnson 1936: 394–7, nos 248–9. On associations paying taxes collectively, see van Minnen 1987: 48–9. See also Langellotti 2016b and in Chapter 8.

[45] Gabrielsen 2016b: 92–5.

Egyptian tradition for both associations[46] and the collective leasing of monopoly concessions.[47] Accordingly, this particular set of circumstances sets the 'charter' of the Tebtynian salt merchants apart from the *leges* and *nomoi* of formal and permanent associations of craftsmen and traders in the rest of the Empire, with which it cannot therefore be properly compared.

However, there is one tantalising example of a professional association organising the work of its members in such a way as to resemble corporate business, if we turn to a Late Antique inscription, dating to AD 459, from Lydian Sardis in Asia Minor. This inscription constitutes a formal agreement between a builders' association and the local magistrate, the aim of which was to force builders to comply with the contracts they entered into.[48] Thus, this agreement made the association itself responsible for the conduct of its members, so that if any defaulted on their contracts, the organisation was liable to pay fines and reimburse the losses of employers, pledging 'under a lien both general and individual, all our property present and future of every kind and sort'.[49] However, this was only one side of the deal, the other being that the association secured a range of formal rights for its members, thus making the deal mutually beneficent, both parties obtaining desired guarantees. Such legally binding agreements were only possible if the association in question had a set of rules, a *lex*, to organise work, both at the level of communal contracting and as regards the work of individual members, and if they had regulations in place to ensure, through monitoring and enforcement, that agreements with third parties were honoured. Whether this very late example can meaningfully be employed to shed light on the *leges* of professional *collegia* of the first to second centuries AD must remain an open question, though.[50]

---

[46] Cf. *P.Cair.* II 30606 (Dem.) = de Cenival 1972: 45–51 (mid-second century BC) and *P.Lond.* VII 2193 (early first century BC), which charters are both stated to be authoritative for one year only, presumably to be reaffirmed and archived annually, as well as the contemporary charter of fellow inhabitants of Tebtynis preserved in *P.Mich.* V 243 (Tiberian, apparently pastoralists). But cf. also Langellotti in Chapter 8.

[47] A parallel example to the Tebtynian salt merchants is that of *myropolai* contracting for and dividing up the concession for the perfume monopoly in the Arsinoite nome in both Ptolemaic (*SB* X 10296; cf. Skeat 1966) and Roman times (*P.Fay.* 93; cf. Johnson 1936: no 238); a *koinon* of such *myropolai* declaring the market prices of their wares is known from the early fourth century AD Oxyrhynchus: *P.Oxy.* LIV 3731, 3733 and 3766, V l. 80.

[48] *Sardis* VII.1 18. Garnsey 1998: 77–87.

[49] *Sardis* VII.1 18, ll. 53–6; translation pulled from Buckler and Robinson 1932: 43, clause 7.

[50] Earlier comparable organisations, conspicuously employed by state authorities as transport contractors for grain, exist, though: the *hippodromitai naukleroi* of first-century BC Memphis in Egypt (*BGU* VIII 1741), cf. Gibbs 2015: 260; the *naukleroi tou poreutikou Alexandreinou stolou*, later second century AD (*IG* XIV 917–18), cf. Rohde 2012: 116 n. 223; and the *navicularii marinii Arelatensii quinque corporum*, third century AD (*CIL* III 14165), cf. Broekaert 2011: 248.

Rounding off, for now, on the primary characteristics of Roman professional associations, the fragmentarily preserved – but only surviving –
specimen of an actual *lex collegii* highlights strong principles of member
equality. Moreover, there is compelling evidence to suggest that the
would-be members of new associations perceived the role of formal rules
as vital for the foundation and management of enduring organisations.
The importance of explicit ratification of charters by the emperor or of
codified conduct appealing for imperial favour generally serves only to
emphasise this point further. Finally, it appears that although members of
Roman associations were allowed to hold funds and property in common,
that is, as belonging to the coffers of the organisation independent of the
fortunes of its individual members, and conduct business collectively on
behalf of the membership, this only rarely led to anything resembling
guild- or firm-like economic activities. In the following section, moreover,
a number of additional points will be made about the formal rules
governing Roman associations as compared with their Indian counterparts.

Rules and Regulations of Indian Associations

Next, we turn to early historical Indian associations. From the subconti-
nent, a large number of sources are available, epigraphical as well as
literary, being spread out over a wide geographical area and with a
chronology spanning more than a millennium. However, whereas nearly
all Indian epigraphs concerning or set up by associations pertain to
endowments, the Indian literary sources, conversely, mainly concern
themselves with formalistic matters, in particular the relationship between
state and associations, as well as the internal rules and regulations of the
latter. Accordingly, the epigraphic and literary evidence yields different
but, fortunately, supplementary information on ancient Indian
associations.[51]

Although the earliest literary sources shedding some light on the internal
ordering of Indian organisations allegedly date back as far as the early fifth
century BC (or even earlier),[52] these were orally transmitted and not put
down in writing until the third century BC at the very earliest and in all
likelihood not even for a few centuries after that. Potentially later dates for

---

Furthermore, the historiographical tradition of distinguishing sharply between early and late
collegia, on the basis of their assumed relation with the Roman government, has been refuted by
Sirks 1993.
[51] Thaplyal 1996: 2–6.   [52] Majumdar 1920: 9–13; Thaplyal 1996: 20–6.

the earliest literary sources on the subject also fit better with the epigraphical record, which attests the existence of an Indian association phenomenon from the second century BC.[53] Nonetheless, even if we recognise that the Indian literary evidence cannot be securely dated beyond the beginning of the Common Era, we must also acknowledge that texts may contain elements of greater antiquity, such as represented by parts of Buddhist texts preserved on Ashokan rock inscriptions of the mid-third century BC.[54]

A case in point is the work *Arthashastra*, being a theoretical treatise on statesmanship traditionally attributed to around 300 BC.[55] Detailed stylistic analysis has revealed that different parts seem to have been composed at different times, while the extant written version of the work was compiled as late as the mid-third century AD.[56] Controversy, therefore, flourishes about which chapters, if any, date back to the Mauryan period and which parts are later constructs, adaptions or interpolations, with the best fit for an actual ancient Mauryan content being chapter two of the treatise.[57]

Notwithstanding whether it actually dates back to the third century BC, chapter two of the *Arthashastra* contains interesting information about associations, variously named, often as *sangha*, traditionally translated as 'corporations,'[58] or *shreni*, translated as 'guilds',[59] advocating a state policy aimed at regulating the economic activities of associations by appointing different markets in villages and neighbourhoods for different groups, a practice also concretely attested in a royal charter to a market town in western India, from the later sixth century AD.[60] Even more significantly, for present purposes, is the bureaucratic directive that in each city the public superintendent of accounts should enter the 'laws, transactions, customs and fixed rules' (in the context of supervising the economic life of

---

[53] Epigraphical evidence from the (later) second century BC: Mahadevan 2003: nos 3, 6 (Mangulam, S. Deccan); Lüders 1912: no 1335 (Bhattiprolu, E. Deccan); Deshpande 1959: 77 (Pitalkhora, W. Deccan). From Central India there is evidence dated to 50–25 BC: Bühler 1894: 378, no 200 = Lüders 1912: no 345 (Sanchi).

[54] Thapar 1995: 81–2, 85.   [55] Shamasastry 1915; Kangle 1965–72.

[56] Trautmann 1971. For a critique of the work of the former, see now Mital 2004, who raises some highly interesting objections to Trautmann's methods.

[57] Thapar 2004: 184–5.

[58] E.g. *Arthash.* 2.7(2), 3.14(12). Attempt at terminological clarification in Thaplyal 1996: 164.

[59] E.g. *Arthash.* 2.4(16), 4.1(2). Cf. Thaplyal 1996: 7–8.

[60] *Arthash.* 2.1(32), 2.4(16). Significantly, we find this practice reflected in the much later municipal charter of Vishnusena, issued to the merchant community, *vanijgama*, of Lohata in Kathiawar, Gujarat, dated to AD 592; Sircar 1953–54: 171, no 12.

the city) of inter alia corporations in state registers.[61] Remarkably, this passage fits well with other early Indian literary sources exhorting professional groups to lay down their customary rules in accordance with religious precepts and subsequently to make the king acquainted with these rules, which he should in turn ratify and respect.[62] Such laws of an association were codified in a document that officers and ordinary members alike had to abide by and that applicants could sign to become new members. Violations of it were to be prosecuted.[63]

Accordingly, Indian associations had charters containing rules and regulations and the state wanted to both ratify and file these, as did the authorities in the Roman Empire, as set out above. Indeed, a similar practice is echoed as far east as Late Sassanian Mesopotamia by a detailed charter of Christian craftsmen.[64] Elsewhere in the Roman Mediterranean, new members of an association also had to swear to abide by its established regulations, the latter often being inscribed on stone and agreed on by vote.[65]

As regards the legal validity of such internal rules of an association, the *Arthashastra* informs us in another book that agreements made or transactions conducted between parties to a 'secret' or 'private union', that is, any form of non-public mutual association, were legally binding.[66] In the following sections of the same chapter, moreover, it is spelled out that such transactions could, for instance, concern partition of inheritance, which was to be made in accordance with 'whatever be the customary law' of the corporation,[67] or the collective responsibility of workmen belonging to a corporation contracting for jobs.[68] In consequence, agreements, such as formal rules, between members of associations were considered binding.

These stipulations contained in the *Arthashastra* compare very well with Roman legal sources. First, let us compare the *Arthashastra*'s statement about the authority of agreements entered into by members of Indian associations with the well-known, so-called Solonic Law on associations

[61] *Arthash.* 2.7(2); Thaplyal 1996: 73.
[62] Thaplyal 1996: 25 (*Gautama Dharmasutra*), 34 n. 117 (*Manusmriti*).
[63] Thaplyal 1996: 37–9, 74 (drawing on the *Brihaspatismriti* and *Katyanasmriti*).
[64] Brock 2009: 62, no 32.
[65] *CIL* VI 10234, ll. 23–4; XIV 2112, I ll. 6, 17–19; *IG* II² 1368, ll. 10–32. Or the signed papyrus charter of Roman Tebtynis, *P.Mich.* V 243, ll. 12–31.
[66] *Arthash.* 3.1(11). The key term is *mithaḥsamavāya*, a compound of *mithas-*, meaning 'in secret or private, secretly, privately', and *-samavāyḥ*, meaning 'union, multitude, close connection, cohesion', cf. Apte 1957–59, s. v.
[67] *Arthash.* 3.7(40); cf. Kangle's note, the *Manusmriti* (8.41) states that all matters regarding corporations, not just inheritance, were to be handled in accordance with their customary laws.
[68] *Arthash.* 3.14(12–18).

allegedly of the sixth century BC, but reproduced in the second-century AD commentary of Gaius, the jurist, to be found in the sixth-century AD *Digest* of Justinian: 'whatever they [that is, members of various groups and kinds of associations] agree between themselves will be valid unless forbidden by public statutes'.[69] This fits quite well with the wording and intent of the clause in the *Arthashastra* and even better if we add to this the additional admonitions in Indian literary sources about laying down rules, mentioned above, stating that such laws of associations should be sanctioned by the king.

Indeed, according to the literary sources, laws of Indian associations on the one hand regulated relations between members, as well as between members and their elected officials, assemblies having the power to contest the decisions of their chief or officers, in which case the dispute was to be decided by a royal court.[70] On the other hand, they could even act as public courts, following procedures similar to those of the royal courts, the laws of an association having the force of state laws,[71] which, in fact, appears to be borne out to some degree by at least three inscriptions attesting the authority of presidents of Indian associations over civic matters. The first instance concerns a royal endowment consisting of two principal sums entrusted at interest with different craftsmen's associations (*shrenis*) of weavers at Govardhana, near Nashik in the Western Deccan, which was to be registered with and therefore presumably subsequently monitored by the 'assembly of the merchant's association' (*nigama sahhā*) in that town.[72] The second is a similar example from the Eastern Deccan, in which an endowment entrusted at interest with four different associations (*shrenis*) of craftsmen was to be supervised by the local merchants' association (*nigama*), which was explicitly charged with enforcing the stipulated use of the annually occurring interests.[73] Finally, administrative copper plate documents from a town in north India reveal how the local leaders of associations (apparently the three heads of the town's traders, travelling merchants and artisans, respectively) served on the municipal board administering district matters together with the appointed state representative.[74]

---

[69] *Dig.* 47.22.4; translation by Arnaoutoglou 1998a.   [70] Thaplyal 1996: 53–4 (*Brihaspatismriti*).
[71] Thaplyal 1996: 96–106.
[72] Senart 1905–6: no 12, l. 4, with amendment in Thaplyal 1996: 11, 90 (Nashik, later first century AD). On the nature of and differences between *shreni* and *nigama*, see Thaplyal 1996: 6–12; 1972: 227–9; and Ray 1986: 111–12.
[73] Sircar 1963–64: 7, l. 7 (Nagarjunakonda, AD 333); cf. Thaplyal 1996: 11.
[74] Basak 1919–20: 129–32, plate 1 (Damodarpur, AD 443–44), being the *nagara shreshthin*, *sārthavāha* and *kulika*. Such boards of joint officials are also known from some 270 sealings attesting their role in judiciary and administrative processes, e.g. Thaplyal 1996: 170, 174 C.

In a somewhat similar manner, Greco-Roman associations could function as courts for internal purposes, mimicking the procedures of their host polity and thereby in theory vesting association assemblies with democratic power of majority vote over presidents, club officials and defaulters – just as the *ordo* of the *collegium* of *negotiatores eborarii et citriarii* could strike members from the membership list, *album*, treated above.[75] The laws of Greco-Roman associations could also have consequences for members in their daily lives 'outside' the organisation, as several charters stipulate that disputes between members or debts to the organisation were to be handled by internal adjudication and settlement.[76] In light of the fragmentary nature of our source material for associations generally, it is clear that documents attesting actual internal proceedings of associations must be few and far between. However, a few examples of internal or external enforcement of the rules of an association spring to mind, shedding a sidelight on the legal authority of charters over their signatories, that is, the members.

Early evidence is preserved in a late third-century BC Ptolemaic papyrus from Egypt, in which the relative of a deceased member of an association complained to state officials that the association (*thiasos*) did neither furnish a funeral for the deceased, nor recompense the relative for arranging one, which was in open breach of the group's rules, the *thiasitikos nomos*. Significantly, the regional Ptolemaic official ordered his local representative to reconcile the parties in accordance with the regulations of the association.[77] A second case is known from a wax tablet unearthed in the Roman mining town of Alburnus Maior in the province of Dacia, where a *collegium* took the unusual step of formally disbanding itself in AD 167, because too many members (thirty-seven out of fifty-four) had ceased to pay their subscriptions in outright transgression of their charter. Accordingly, the remaining seventeen members officially denounced the rights of the thirty-seven defaulters to a funeral paid for by the common coffers, thus, using the rules to terminate their joint organisation, perhaps in order to establish afresh a new association of more conscientious members.[78] Finally, there is the well-attested practice of so-called erasures known from the inscribed membership lists, *alba*, of Roman associations.[79] Although we cannot tell exactly how or why these individuals

[75] Other *collegia* seem to have exercised similar exclusions of officials, cf. Tran 2007: 124f.

[76] E.g. *CIL* XIV 2112. ll. 23–8; *P.Mich.* V 243, ll. 2–3; *IG* II² 1368, ll. 84–95; even the Sassanian craftsmen's association, cf. Brock 2009: 59 no 11.

[77] *P.Enteux.* 20 (221 BC). A similar procedure seems to have been followed in the corresponding case of *P.Enteux.* 21 (218 BC), cf. l. 11.

[78] *CIL* III 924. See Biró 1969.   [79] Tran 2007: 125–30.

had their membership status terminated and were therefore physically erased from the names on the list, it is clear that the specific associations in question had decided to formally exclude them in accordance with their rules, such as documented in the *lex* of the *collegium* of *negotiatores eborarii et citriarii* or the announcement by the *collegium* at Alburnus Maior.

Furthermore, the *Arthashastra* details how corporations of workmen could be held collectively responsible for non-performance of agreements entered into as a group and that the members could divide earnings equally or by mutual agreement, fines or eventual expulsion being employed against defaulting members,[80] which is corroborated by later Indian law-makers of the fifth to sixth centuries AD, according to whom an association's assembly could, by majority vote, authorise any member to enter into a contract on behalf of the entire group.[81] By way of general comparison, this fits quite well with both the case of the corporate responsibility of the builders' association of Lydian Sardis and the article from the *Digest* (3.4.1.1) on the corporate nature of associations.

Finally, a unique inscription goes beyond the theoretical literature of the ancient Indian lawmakers by shedding a remarkable light on the internal life and workings of an ancient Indian association (*shreni*) of craftsmen, namely, silk weavers, dating from the fifth century AD.[82] Evidently attempting to lay claim to intellectual sophistication and civic recognition, this group paid a somewhat second-rate local Brahman poet to compose a Sanskrit poem about their recent history and accomplishments. Thus, we learn that 'men famed throughout the world for their craft came from the region of Lata', lying immediately east of the important ancient port of Barygaza[83] in what is today southern Gujarat, 'to Dashapura, bringing their children and kinsfolk', being the central city in a small tributary kingdom some 250 km further north.[84] In their new home, they retained their social identity as a group, but some, it seems, drifted into alternative professions, while others remained 'excellent in their craft', everyone nonetheless exhibiting a trustworthy and helpful conduct, their *shreni* being altogether the most glorious and pious of all[85] – such profuse praise of one's group's moral and religious integrity being customary in inscriptions of associations in the Greek[86] and Roman[87] worlds, too.

---

[80] *Arthash.* 3.14(12–18).   [81] Thaplyal 1996: 41–2 (*Brihaspatismriti*).
[82] Fleet 1888: III 84–8 no 18; later editions in Basham 1983 and Thaplyal 1996: 180–94.
[83] *Periplus* 41-9, 64 (mid-first century AD).   [84] Basham 1983: 95, stanzas 4–5.
[85] Basham 1983: 97–8, stanzas 15–17.   [86] Gabrielsen 2007: 195; 2016b: 100–3.
[87] Verboven 2007.

The main purpose of this particular epigraph, though, was, on the one hand, the commemoration of a specific event in the group's recent history in Dashapura: 'the silk weavers, who had formed a guild (*shreni*), skilled in their craft, with hoarded wealth had this incomparably noble temple made for the god with burning rays (*sc.* the Sun)' in the year AD 436.[88] On the other hand, it was to mark the restoration of this temple of the Sun, having fallen into disrepair during a period of apparent instability, in the year AD 473, the stone being set up on this occasion.[89] Accordingly, we learn that *shreni*s were very tight-knit organisations, being not merely defined by vocation but also overarching ties of kinship, religion and cooperation – profession nonetheless remaining the key identifying group characteristic, as with the Greco-Roman organisations treated above. Moreover, they could finance substantial collective endeavours, such as a temple, and possessed the longevity to move from place to place and maintain communal possessions for decades.

In summary, the historical and institutional developments of Roman and Indian associations of traders and craftsmen mirror each other to a surprising degree. From a formal perspective, an analysis of the associations' rules and regulations reveal that these were surprisingly similar. The same can be said, moreover, about their relations to host polities, and, remarkably, their combination of economic, social and religious activities within one communal framework. While diffusion of a sort of 'associational archetype' or 'institutional blueprint' from one part of the world to the other is out of the question, in light of the separate and synchronous developments of the two phenomena outlined here, the underlying explanation is rather to be found in the 'independent invention' of parallel institutional answers to similar circumstances.[90]

Rules and Regulations of Early Medieval Chinese Associations

Indeed, this interpretation is further borne out by correlating the Greco-Roman and Indian association phenomena with their Chinese counterpart, in this chapter constituting a slightly later *comparandum* acting as 'control group' for the principal characteristics of ancient and medieval associations more widely, not just those of traders and craftsmen.[91]

---

[88] Basham 1983: 101, stanza 29; dating: 103, stanzas 34–5.
[89] Basham 1983: 103–4, stanzas 36–9.   [90] Steward 1929.
[91] Significantly, though, Chinese *she* associations could also be based on shared profession, e.g. soldiers, watchmen, carriers, irrigation channel managers, Buddhist clergy, etc., cf. Yamamoto et al. 1988–89: 18–20; Rong 2013: 299.

The earliest Chinese type of association proper, the *yi*, traditionally translated as 'religious association,' crops up in the epigraphic record from the later fifth century AD, being local organisations brought into being to facilitate communal Buddhist offerings through collection of voluntary donations from the membership, which could number from little more than a dozen to as many as 200 to 300.[92] In the later sixth to seventh centuries AD, the *yi* became supplanted by a different type of Buddhist association, the *she* (in the older literature often translated as 'club'),[93] an institution developed from Chinese peasant communities worshipping ancestral gods of the land and its harvest, in particular the Sun, now appropriated by local Buddhist monks and lay followers as their chosen unit of organisation.[94] Accordingly, by the time of the late Tang and early Song dynasties, ninth to eleventh centuries AD, when we have documents produced by *she* associations preserved from Dunhuang – being the westernmost city of ancient China and road junction of all routes leading to Central Asia – ancient Chinese traditions had merged with imported Buddhist practices[95] to create an entirely new kind of organisation native to China.[96]

The documents in question have been preserved in the so-called library cave of Dunhuang, not because they contained information pertaining to associations, but because monks from a local monastery in around 1002 AD stowed a huge amount of re-used paper-rolls containing religious scripture, which they had been collecting for an archive, in a small side chapel that they walled up due to an invasion of Turkic-speaking Uighurs.[97] As it happens, some 300 texts produced by *she* associations resident in Dunhuang from around the mid-ninth century AD up to the year of the sealing of the cave have been preserved, because they constitute the recto or verso of documents stored for the religious content on the other side of the sheet. Moreover, by a singular stroke of luck, three *she* documents produced elsewhere in the Tarim Basin have survived in the dry sands of the Taklimakan Desert, indicating that the copious production of paperwork by *she* associations was not a phenomenon restricted to Dunhuang alone.[98]

---

[92] E.g. Chavannes 1914: 13–29, nos III–IV (sixth century AD).

[93] *She* (or *shê*) is the conventional English transliteration, whereas it is rendered *chö* in French.

[94] Gernet 1956: 252–5.

[95] E.g. the association-like Buddhist *sangha* of third–fourth century AD Niya on the southern edge of the Tarim Basin: Burrow 1940: no 489; elucidated in Hansen 2012: 51; van Schaik 2014: 272–3.

[96] Cf. also Yamamoto et al. 1988–89: 6; Rong 2013: 296.

[97] Hansen 2012: 177–9; based on Rong 1999–2000.

[98] Yamamoto et al. 1988–89: 30-1, nos 304 (O. 2355), 305 (O. 1529), 306 (O. 1535); from Turfan and Kucha along the northern edge of the Tarim Basin, eighth century AD.

Although the majority of the Dunhuang corpus is made up of circulars, that is, summons to *she* members to assemble,[99] there are also nineteen written sets of regulations preserved that are equivalent to the charters of Greco-Roman associations and the corpus of rules laid down by lawmakers concerning Indian associations. Accordingly, this collection of regulations provides us with quite a coherent picture of the rules of Chinese *she* associations from the mid-ninth to later tenth centuries AD, and, in particular, the way in which these compare well with the earlier precedents from the Mediterranean and South Asia.

First of all, the perceived importance of formal charters for the creation of durable groups is reflected by the prominence attached to rules and regulations by the members of the organisations thus called into being and given institutional existence. One *she* association consisting of fifteen women, most or all of them nuns, reaffirmed their charter of regulations on the third day of the new year AD 959, stating that 'the rules are designed to be as suitable for members as water is for fish; they are to swear by the hills and streams, with the sun and moon as witnesses; and that as a precaution against bad faith these rules have been written down to serve as a memorandum for those who come after'.[100] In fact, it was so self-evident for potential would-be fellow members in Dunhuang that sets of formal rules were the vital constitutive nuclei for establishing viable associations that generic charters, acting as style sheets for drawing up the regulations of an actual association, circulated throughout town.[101] One tenth century AD style sheet suggests the following communal declaration on the authority of the corpus of rules agreed upon: 'According to the will of those present, we draw up this document in order to form an association. ... The above clauses represent the basic rules of the association, which are arrived at one by one by those present and drawn up into clauses that shall not be altered. In order to avoid preposterous libels in the future, we set them down in writing, so they may serve as proof for eternity.'[102]

Moreover, both actual charters as well as the style sheets on which they were based often followed a conventional layout: first, a preamble setting out in somewhat verbose language the purpose of the association; second, the main text setting out rules regarding all obligations between members

---

[99] Yamamoto et al. 1988–89: 17–25, nos 36–153.   [100] S. 527. Paraphrase from Giles 1943: 156.

[101] From Late Sassanian Mesopotamia we have a charter of Christian craftsmen that the local bishop evidently intended to be used as a model for similar associations, thus, providing a parallel to the Chinese style sheets from Dunhuang; cf. Brock 2009: 52.

[102] S. 6537. Translation in Rong 2013: 297.

and formal administrative processes (including detailed and specific punishments for violation of any of the regulations); and, last, a signed membership list confirming the regulations and binding members to abide by them.[103] A dozen of such charters survive, having been produced by actual *she* associations, duly signed by their members, sealed and stored away for use in case of disputes.[104] Remarkably, this practice is surprisingly similar to the activities of Greco-Roman and Indian associations in laying down their rules, affirming them by democratic majority and documenting them for internal purposes as well as for approval by the relevant central authorities.[105]

Other institutional parallels contained in the regulations and documents of Chinese *she* associations, in addition to member equality in decision making (as represented in the two quoted examples above), include the right to fine defaulting members or physically punish them, or both,[106] strict admittance and exit rules,[107] set mandatory banquets and offerings on specific days of the year,[108] the validity of agreements between members,[109] exhortations to provide mutual assistance in times of distress[110]

---

[103] Yamamoto et al. 1988–89: 7, 12–13; nos 5, 7, 8, 15, 16, 18 and 19, are considered style sheets.
[104] Yamamoto et al. 1988–89: 10; nos 1–4, 6, 9–14, 17.   [105] Compare nn. 61–5.
[106] S. 527: 'If in the club there is anyone who disregards precedence in small things and great, in unruly fashion creates disturbance at a feast, and will not obey the verbal instructions of her superior, then all the members shall repair to the gateway and fine her of enough alcohol for a whole feast, to be partaken of by the rest of the company' (translation from Hansen 2000: 254), see also the next note on cane blows; P. 3989 (paraphrased in Gernet 1956: 266). Compare nn. 70–9.
[107] S. 527: 'Any person wishing to leave the Club shall be sentenced to three strokes with the bamboo' and be fined (translation in Giles 1943: 156). See also application for admittance: P. 3216 (translation in Gernet 1956: 260); and exit: S. 5698 (translation in Rong 2013: 298) – generally, Yamamoto et al. 1988–89: 14–15, nos 20–8. Compare n. 17 and *CIL* VI 10234, ll. 5–7; XIV 2112, I ll. 20–3; *IG* II² 1368, ll. 33–41; Brock 2009: no 28; as well as the papyrus *P.Mich.* IX 575 (AD 184).
[108] S. 527: 'On feast days, the members of this mutual benefit society are each to contribute 1 *ko* (i.e. 1/10 pint) of oil, 1 pound of white flour, and 1 gallon (*tou*) of wine; and on the day in the first moon set apart for "the establishment of merit", 1 *tou* of wine and 1 bowl of lamp-oil' (paraphrase by Giles 1943: 156); P. 3544 (annual feasts and contributions detailed in Yamamoto et al. 1988–89: 10 no 1). Compare n. 20 and *CIL* VI 10234, ll. 9–17; XIV 2112 ll. 11–13; *IG* II² 1368, ll. 42–4; Brock 2009: no 2 (and 14).
[109] S. 527: 'In dealing with friends, a single word may serve as a bond of faith' (translation in Giles 1943: 156); P. 3989 (paraphrased in Gernet 1956: 266). Compare nn. 66–9. On the importance of friendship for the workings of Hellenistic associations, see Gabrielsen 2016b: 96–100.
[110] S. 527: 'Our parents give us life, but friends enhance its value: they sustain us in time of danger, rescue us from calamity' (translation in Giles 1943: 156). Yamamoto et al. 1988–89: 7–8; Hansen 2012: 193; Rong 2013: 299. Yang 1950 even argues that the *she* acted as an early example of the 'rotating credit association' attested in China in pre-modern times, but while this is plausible, it appears to be nowhere explicitly stipulated in the surviving *she* documents – mutual *assistance* is not the same as mutual *financing*. Compare *P.Mich.* V 243, ll. 9–10; V 244, ll. 9–10 (both require members to bail an arrested fellow out of jail); and Brock 2009: 61, nos 20 (standing surety for jailed fellows) and 25 (general support).

and help in providing fitting funerals for family members.[111] Indeed, this
list could be expanded further if one wanted to compare not only rules and
regulations as such, but also organisational hierarchies or the administration of communal cult and banquets. Conversely, Chinese founding
charters also include apparently unique motivations, such as those that
were established primarily to maintain or repair specific Buddhist temples
or hermitages.[112]

In brief summary, then, before passing on to the conclusion proper, this
superficial comparison of the rules and regulations of Chinese *she* associations of the ninth to tenth centuries AD with their earlier Greco-Roman
and Indian counterparts provides serious food for thought. Specifically, it
appears that across some ten centuries and ten thousand kilometres,
ancient and medieval associations of the Mediterranean, South Asia and
China not only attached the same prominence to formal written regulations as the basis for creating and perpetuating community, but also,
remarkably enough, developed parallel traditions for the creation of private
associations, exhibiting highly similar institutional characteristics.

Conclusion

As regards the underlying principles contained in the rules and regulations
surveyed, a number of values appear to have been held in common by
Greco-Roman and Indian associations of craftsmen and traders specifically,
as well as by Chinese associations generally: the authority of written rules
affirmed and signed by all; member equality and the authority of the
membership assembly; the right to enforce the rules of the association
amongst the members (private ordering); the embedding of professional,
religious and social ties within fellow member relations that were considered binding in the case of agreements and transactions; and group
boundary creation controlling entrance and exit – to name but some of
the more conspicuous principles shared to some extent by all three
association phenomena.

When it comes to relations with states, rules of Greco-Roman and
Indian professional associations had to be in accordance with the legal
corpora of host societies, which latter insisted on the right to monitor and

---

[111] P. 3489, 3989 (both paraphrased in Gernet 1956: 266) and S. 5698 (translation in Rong 2013: 298), more generally Gernet 1956: 258–9; Yamamoto et al. 1988–89: 25–7, nos 221–50. In comparison, funerary aid looms large in *CIL* III 924; XIV 2112; *P.Mich.* V 243, ll. 9–12; and Brock 2009: nos 7–10, 21, 27.
[112] S. 3540 and 5828.

validate the regulations of any potentially subversive groups defining themselves as distinct sub-units of society. Charters would often contain rules codifying a more pious and moral conduct between members, as well as between the group as a whole and wider society. Furthermore, arbitration between members and punishment of defaulters was, common to all three traditions, considered the prerogative of an association's assembly, consequently supplanting public courts.

Finally, the role of associations in their host societies appears to have been the creation of sufficient group cohesion through communal social, religious and economic activities to enable private ordering, mutual assistance and professional collaboration – that is, making a formalised unit with solidified ties (an association) out of a matrix of ephemeral social, religious and economic interactions between individuals (the would-be members), who acknowledged membership with the benefits and burdens that this entailed. Thus, members attained a measure of order to interaction between one another and states obtained corporate entities to deal with and hold responsible, as circumstances dictated. As concerns the Greco-Roman and Indian associations of craftsmen and traders, organisation sometimes developed, first, some degree of economic corporeality and, later, possibly a propensity for communal contracting as a group.[113]

In conclusion, all three association phenomena developed comparable rules and regulations with minor differences in the way that they were implemented. All three considered the production of thorough rules put down in writing of the utmost importance. All three traditions were based on at least semi-democratic member assemblies, although neither early historical India nor early medieval China had known either Greek democracy or Roman republicanism. And just as the rules and regulations of Greek and Roman associations were shaped by both the civic and religious institutions of their host societies, we see how this also applies to Indian and Chinese associations, the more conspicuous because Buddhism played an important role for both of the latter. All this being said, it is of course also possible to point to differences, but these are in effect more akin to variations caused by specific historical circumstances. On the whole, we might in conclusion venture to state that from a perspective of comparative institutional analysis, these three association

---

[113] A detailed analysis of the economic functions of associations in Roman and Indian society, vis-à-vis each other, is available in Evers 2017.

phenomena appear to have developed along remarkably similar lines. Hence, *il fenomeno associativo* was most emphatically not unique to Mediterranean Antiquity, but, rather, as a superficial analysis of the rules and regulations of Indian and Chinese associations reveals, a Eurasian phenomenon in its own right.

CHAPTER II

Conclusion
Associations in Their World

Vincent Gabrielsen and Mario C. D. Paganini

A World of Associations

Following the overarching theme of associations' regulations, the chapters of this book have provided the reader with different insights into a large variety of ancient associations that were embedded in as many local realities, in an attempt on the one hand to highlight similar patterns but on the other hand also to stress the vivacity and diversity of the *fenomeno associativo*, 'associational phenomenon': although common traits certainly emerge, one should in no way expect uniformity. The world of associations was in fact a complex one: this book has mainly explored associations active in the Greek-speaking world, but even in this 'common cultural sphere' one sees a great variety of different options at play, which mirror the character of their various societies. The ways in which associations operated were a result of the strategies adopted by them on the basis of the different challenges they encountered and the way in which they appear to us is also linked to the contingent production and preservation of the sources, which varied depending on location and time. It is therefore not surprising that the picture we have gained from late Hellenistic and early Roman Athens is a different one from that of contemporary Mantinea, for instance: in Athens, as we have seen in the discussion by Arnaoutoglou in Chapter 6, associations made full use of the polis' general directions, trends and mechanisms in the regulation of members' behaviour so as to enhance their profile and foster their autonomy, room of action or survival, by providing an image that matched the expectations of the public adminis- tration. Chapter 7 by Zoumbaki, on the other hand, has shown how in Mantinea associations found specific scope of action during the recovery from a period of socio-economic difficulties in somewhat replacing the involvement of public institutions and by recruiting forces – and resources – from the ranks of local female notables for the purpose, in particular to guarantee the survival of (public) cult practices that were being neglected by public authorities.

Egypt is another case in point: associations operated in a socio-cultural, political and administrative landscape, which is often rather unfamiliar to the reader who is accustomed to the Greek world. However, this is not because Egypt was different in absolute terms – no more than Athens was different from Corinth, Halicarnassus from Pergamum, Rhodes from Lesbos or Macedonia from Boeotia, for instance. Recent scholarship has in fact refuted the notion of 'exceptional position' – *Sonderstellung* – that Egypt would have allegedly occupied and which made it incompatible with historical comparison with the other parts of the Hellenistic and, especially, Roman world.[1] Rather, Egypt displays typicalities with which scholars of the Greek world simply need to become more familiar: polis status was not the standard and more common political-administrative feature of the majority of the country and complex cultural identities were at play in the society with the coexistence of different traditions, while legal systems and practices cohabitated side by side. Furthermore, papyri give us an insight into a range of dealings, which mostly remain unattested for the other parts of the Hellenistic and Roman worlds. As the discussion by Langellotti in Chapter 8 has shown, for the associations of Egypt we have a good number of accounts, lists, dispositions, requests, receipts, regulations and contracts that allow more thorough investigations of an economic and administrative nature. The associations in the other provinces of the Roman Empire may well have behaved exactly in the same way but we simply do not have evidence to that regard, because of the different nature of our sources.

The snapshots gained in Chapter 9 of the associations of Ostia by Tran and in Chapter 10 of the Far East by Evers provide comparative material with associations outside the Greek-speaking Mediterranean and also beyond antiquity: the evidence presented opens up larger perspectives and nicely illustrates the spectrum of strategies that associations adopted in varying circumstances. In Ostia, for instance, associations embodied behaviours, values and procedures typical of the elites of the city, including their political overtones. This, however, was not much different from what one sees in action in some poleis of the Greek world. In fact, similar patterns of behaviour can also be identified in Indian and Chinese

---

[1] Egypt's *Sonderstellung* was rendered canonical by Wilcken 1912: I.I xv; for its removal (or at all events, review), see Lewis 1970 and 1984; Bowman 1976: 160–1; Keenan 1982–83: 30–1; Geraci 1989; Heinen 1989; Rathbone 1989; Bowman and Rathbone 1992; Bagnall 2005; Rathbone 2013.

associations, in particular regarding the creation of regulations endorsing specific behaviour and concerning the image they wanted to project to their political hosting communities. What we have before us was indeed a world of associations: although each association was unique and embedded in its local society (against which it needs to be accessed) and developed ways of furthering its agenda depending on circumstance and place, the chapters of this book have showed that common traits existed, because they emerged from similar concerns. This demonstrates the global character of the *fenomeno associativo*. With this comparative approach it is hoped the authors have offered an insight into the multifaceted world of associations for the benefit of a larger readership, not only for historians of the Greco-Roman world.

In all the examples investigated in the book, we see associations actively involved in the assertion of specific common values for their own purposes. The spectrum covered is large and stretches from values of mutual support, equality amongst members, fairness, reciprocal generosity, economic help to ideals of respect, obedience of the laws and the superiors, piety, sense of belonging and duty. A finding to be especially noted is that these values could encompass those shared by the larger community but could also include others that are not typically recognisable or largely diffused in their contemporary societies – these may be ideas of equality in political systems without an active tradition of democratic values, such as most of Egypt, India or China, for instance. Associations established strategies with the aim to achieve specific goals and to attain a particular profile in their communities, which allowed them to play a specific role and to promote their agenda. The various aspects embraced by the regulations and investigated in this volume cover the large interests that ancient associations had at heart: from financial and economic aspects, to moral and ethical features, behaviour, religion and regulation of space.

As appears clearly in their regulations, associations considered of great importance that these aspects were somehow codified and that the members were given directives. The image that they were giving of themselves to the outside world – as much as to the members themselves – mattered enormously. Through the implementation of several – sometimes punctilious – rules, associations were doing something vital for claiming their place in society by shaping themselves as 'well-ordered' groups. The following pages are devoted to some concluding remarks drawn from the previous chapters with a focus on the impact that associations exercised on their local communities, precisely thanks to the profile attained through the implementation of their regulations. The discussion is organised around four main axes, which embody associations' spheres of action: their relation with the state, their role as social phenomena, their position within the local economy and their input to cultural life. These 'spheres' are not to be thought as separate from one another. They are coterminous, overlapping and interlinked; they are here addressed separately for convenience of argumentation only.

Associations and the State

It is often said that associations imitated the state: this is true, at least to a large extent, as this volume demonstrates. The view that associations were the result of the decline of civic life and copied the democratic polis as the only way of perpetuating dying traditions in Hellenistic times has been now dismissed as false: besides the shortcomings of assumptions of civic decline, associations existed before Philip's and Alexander's new regimes.[2] The polis is generally regarded as the model of Greek private associations.[3] However, the parallels from (pharaonic) Egypt, India and China, as the discussion by Evers in Chapter 10 has shown, suggest that the development of associations based on an idea of equality and shared participation was not necessarily linked with democratic (political) ideals. It is therefore not always true that it was the democratic polis that was being imitated – one may wonder whether an ('aristocratic'?) concept of 'a group of few equals' was ultimately behind associations' ethics.[4] For the Greek world, we are faced with a further intricate question of whether associations may have predated the emergence and formation of the polis: if so, imitation might have occurred the other way round. Future studies may be able to uncover any substance in this.

At all events, as repeatedly pointed out in the chapters of this volume, associations shared with state institutions much of the terminology used. The designation of officials often recalls those of the state (and of the temples, in the case of titles in Demotic texts of Egypt, for instance), the formulae adopted in associations' inscriptions and official decisions nicely reproduce those by civic institutions and the regulation by associations of sacred space and of religious practices recalls directives by states and sanctuaries. Associations employed procedures that could also be adopted

---

[2] See Harland 2003: 90–7, with critique of previous scholarship. On pre-Hellenistic associations, see Gabrielsen 2016a.

[3] See Gabrielsen 2007, for instance.

[4] Voting practices attested in Demotic regulations from Egypt, for instance, cast doubts on the purported 'Greek (democratic) model': see Paganini 2016, *contra* Boak 1937b and Muhs 2001.

by the state machinery: voting practices, rotation of offices and mechanisms for scrutiny and accountability, for instance. It is clear that associations adopted specific formal aspects that could link them to entities – state or religious institutions – which were obviously considered of some authority, worth and prestige. From these, associations could further boost their profile. The chapters of this volume have shown how values and ideals – whether taken from state ideology, democratic principles or from elsewhere – did not remain purely ideological. They were adapted to suit associations' needs for very practical purposes.

As the discussion by Giannakopoulos in Chapter 2 has argued, for instance, the *orgeones* of Bendis in fourth-century Piraeus (*CAPInv.* 230) adopted an examination of newcomers on the model of civic institutions, although slightly adapted to the association's needs for sake of convenience and time. Besides responding to practical needs for a controlled entrance into the group, by choosing to reproduce state procedures the association elevated the prestige and respectability of the group as a whole and of the single individual members, who could boast to have undergone strict scrutiny on a par with Athenian citizens and magistrates. Similarly, the third-century AD *gerousia* of Asclepius of Hyettus in Boeotia (*CAPInv.* 984), by adopting a name that recalled public bodies and distinguished groups of elders affiliated with mythical figures, was strategically hinting at a link with those prestigious counterparts. On their part, the Roman *collegia*, with their specific choice of terminology and self-definition as *ordines*, 'social orders, classes', were also mirroring public structures in order to gain respectability, as well as reproducing norms of behaviour and practices shaped on those of the city in order to elevate their profile to that of civic officialdom. This is one of the insights of Chapter 9 by Tran. It has been further noted by Evers in Chapter 10 how religious institutions offered a model of paramount importance, next to state institutions, for Indian and Chinese associations, as Buddhism played an important role in both. This attitude is noticeable for most of the ancient world: state and religion were not separable; often they were not even two distinct things. The official administrative apparatus of the political communities in which associations were active also represented a source of inspiration for the more practical aspects of associations' governance. As pointed out in Chapter 3 by Eckhardt and in Chapter 8 by Langellotti, some of the competences of presidents of associations in Hellenistic and Roman Egypt, for instance, recalled those of local officials, who could seize non-complying individuals and bring them to justice.

In order to avoid being unlawful, associations obviously had to obey local legislation on matters that may be relevant to them. This is what is ratified in the allegedly Solonic legislation – as echoed in the Digest via Gaius centuries later – and what is specifically mentioned in the regulations of Indian associations.[5] This general attitude of obedience to the laws of the state is not surprising, as everyone is expected to comply with them. However, associations went a step further by specifically portraying themselves as respectful members of society, as honourable individuals, good citizens and loyal subjects. They wanted to display themselves as very well integrated into the public sphere and they operated in a way that showed their attachment to their local communities.[6] For instance, Arnaoutoglou in Chapter 6 has stressed how the Thracian *orgeones* of Bendis in third-century BC Piraeus (*CAPInv.* 232) made a point to mention clearly in one of their decrees that they were complying with the laws of Athens that prescribed the performance of the procession from the city centre to the harbour. The associations of Hellenistic Egypt, on the other hand, stressed with particular force, both in the (Demotic) regulations and in other texts, their devotion to the Royal House and their active involvement in cults in favour of the rulers.[7] A similar attitude has been underlined by Skaltsa in Chapter 5 for the second-century BC *Asklepiastai* (*CAPInv.* 857): this association probably gathered members of the local garrison and was created by the commander of a fortress in the Pergamene hinterland, who was making quite a statement of loyalty by founding a new sanctuary in honour of Asclepius and by manifestly promoting the cult of one of the major deities endorsed by the Attalid Kings.

Another insight of our study is that, in order to assert their social profile, it was of paramount importance for associations to cooperate and comply with the practices codified by the state. The purity rules of associations, for instance, paralleled those of their immediate regional context and hosting communities, as underlined by Carbon in Chapter 4. Thanks to Langellotti's analysis in Chapter 8, we have seen that associations in the village of Tebtynis in Roman Egypt were making a conscious effort to follow state directives concerning the registration of official documents. Their regulations were registered in the local record office, thus being officially recognised as valid by the state. Although reaping a few

---

[5] *Dig.* 47.22.4, also with Evers in Chapter 10. The value of the alleged Roman ban on associations has been challenged: Arnaoutoglou 2002 and 2005. See also Harland 2003: 162–73.

[6] For associations' attachment to the polis and participation in civic life in the Roman East, see also Harland 2003: 101–12.

[7] See now Paganini 2020a.

advantages from the practice (collection of registration fees and tally of associations – and their affairs – in a given place), the state did not officially require associations to register their regulations; associations decided to do so. The reasons are probably linked to some form of prestige or respectability, which the registration brought with it. The fact that registered regulations (as contractual agreements) could be officially used in courts seems to have been of secondary importance for associations, given that the practice was explicitly despised and avoided almost at all costs. Furthermore, associations in Roman Egypt developed the tendency to cooperate with the state machinery, in particular in matters of tax collection. In addition to practical advantages for members and for the state, the practice linked them with the public sphere even more tightly. A similar picture of close cooperation between state and associations emerges from the discussion by Evers in Chapter 10 about the associations in India too: their regulations were ratified and filed by the state and associations' assemblies could even act as public courts, following procedures similar to them, as the laws of an association had the force of state laws.

In the development of their procedures, associations also followed general trends typical of the socio-political climate in which they lived, sometimes to the detriment of some of the associations' leading principles. This can be noted, for instance, in the practice of euergetism and the ensuing awarding of honours to benefactors by associations: both followed well established patterns of the elites in Hellenistic and Imperial times. However, Giannakopoulos in Chapter 2 has argued that this custom promoted hierarchies between members of associations – beyond officials – against usual practice, and in the case of exemption from membership fees for benefactors, this constituted a deviation from the general associative principle of equal liability for regular contributions.[8] It has also been noted that dispositions concerning reduced entrance-fees for descendants of members were clearly codified only in the Imperial period: this reflected a general socio-political tendency of the time, also in public and semi-public bodies, by which a regularisation of the continuous presence of certain families over several generations was economically facilitated. A similar attitude is identified by Tran in Chapter 9 for the Roman *collegia*: they showed that they had internalised habits of the elites in the well-ordered organisation of their structure according to codified procedures.

[8] See also Arnaoutoglou 2003: 147–53.

However, compliance with state models was not the only option associations could decide to follow. In some cases, they deviated from state procedures and practices, creating something for themselves. If by demanding regular contributions from the members, associations were acting like a state exacting revenue, they, however, adopted a different approach. Associations employed a system of equal taxation, as the regular fees for membership (usually monthly) were exacted in the same amount from all members; on the other hand, state taxes were normally levied on the basis of wealth or income. In the case of honours for benefactors, the poleis did not normally grant exemption from taxation or levies, but associations frequently offered immunity from entrance-fees, membership fees and other levies as honours. In the case of democratic regimes, the Greek cities neither demanded compulsory participation in civic institutions or cults (with the exclusion of specific age categories) nor had norms to that effect. Associations, on the other hand, expected it and punished – more or less severely – those who did not show up: participation was in fact not only vital for the economic survival of associations but also essential for the promotion of an image of active, united, vibrant and important communities. These are some of the points made by Giannakopoulos in Chapter 2 and by Eckhardt in Chapter 3.

In very few cases it also happened that associations' regulations were somewhat in tension or diverged from those of the political hosting community: in this case, associations were suggesting a parallel system in competition with state channels. This can be observed in the case of regulations concerning dispute resolution mechanisms between members: by forbidding or hindering their members from bringing charges before the public organs of justice, associations were trying to substitute state courts and state officials with procedures of internal justice administered by the association's assembly or by (some of) its officials. This was presented not as an alternative but implemented 'by force' as the sole option for dispute resolution imposed on association's members – whether successfully or not is another matter. Dispositions concerning this occupy an important position in the Demotic regulations of the associations of Egypt in Hellenistic times and the practice was also favoured in Roman times, as Chapter 8 by Langellotti stresses.[9] In Athens, on the other hand, this procedure is absent in Hellenistic times but surfaces during the Roman period, namely, in the second-century AD regulations of the *Iobacchoi* (*CAPInv.* 339), which punished anyone who brought their

[9] See also Paganini in press b.

complaints before polis lawcourts or Roman authorities. This has been interpreted by Arnaoutoglou in Chapter 6 as a desire by the association to stay clear of Roman intervention in their affairs. Arbitration between members and punishment of defaulters were dealt with internally, as one of the major prerogatives of an association's assembly in lieu of public courts, also in the associations of India from the third century BC onwards, as emerges from Evers' analysis in Chapter 10. In addition to offering a more inexpensive and theoretically more favourable place for dispute resolution than the official courts – one may also wonder whether associations believed it to be better than state tribunals – by asking their members to abstain from the usual channels for justice and to deal with their disputes internally, associations were requiring their members to have a deeper trust in the group than in the state courts. More than that: associations were ultimately expecting their members to display a deep sense of loyalty towards the group, by putting the association's reputation and well-being before their own. In fact, besides shunning a possible unnecessary state meddling in their affairs, associations wanted to avoid washing their dirty linen in public, so to speak: they strove to maintain an image of trustworthy, honest, respectful, correct and peaceful people to the outside world.

Associations as Social Agents

Associations played a role of fundamental importance as features able to influence, shape and enrich the society of their communities, through a parallel process of social conservatism and of innovation.

The value of tradition, as noted by Carbon in Chapter 4, played a particularly important role for the codification of purity rules by associations, which often relied on existing regulations, recorded or not by the city and the community. In Hellenistic Athens, associations made a point to follow the paths offered by the polis, adopting its procedures and mechanisms, without a noticeable desire to innovate, at least in the formal aspects, in order to be fully integrated into the social fabric of the polis. When in Roman times associations started to put particular emphasis on concepts such as 'proper behaviour' or 'stability' – previously tacitly acknowledged – this has been seen by Arnaoutoglou in Chapter 6 as a response to please the conservative attitudes of the Roman administration. More manifestly, the conservatism by associations could also include the preservation of procedures that had been long abandoned in the general running of state affairs. In his analysis in Chapter 2, Giannakopoulos has drawn the attention to the case of some second-century AD Athenian associations such as the *eranistai* from Paiania (*CAPInv.* 308) or the *Iobacchoi* (*CAPInv.* 339), for instance, where we see that they still preserved procedures, such as sortition, which had been associated with classical democracy but had long been abandoned in public proceedings by Athens. At the same time, they also stressed conservative values of family tradition, which were, however, very fashionable in the contemporary civic discourse. The Roman *collegia*, on their part, followed the standards established by the local elite in their eagerness for propriety and regulation, thus presenting themselves as *ordines* in a conservative attempt to foster respectability, as Tran has argued in Chapter 9. Reverence towards rulers is another feature of the conservative attitudes adopted by associations for the assertion of their profile within society.[10]

The idea of equality of members that associations fostered in their regulations could also be seen as a conservative position in the perpetuation of old traditions, which did not match – any longer – the model upon which their contemporary societies operated. However, such an idea may in fact recall an elitist concept of 'equality of the few chosen'. As a matter of fact, the concept of 'well-ordered groups' promoted by associations and their general conservatism often embodied – or at any rate mirrored – the ideology of the higher end of contemporary society, with connotations of propriety, privilege and exclusivity. Rather than purportedly recalling old democratic ideas in a way that could have been perceived as somewhat subversive, they were more likely adopting the mainstream rhetoric of the local elites. Associations did not want to be regarded as dissidents, revolutionaries or modernisers; they strove to blend in with conventionality as much as possible.

At the same time as presenting themselves as more royalist than the King, associations nonetheless silently managed to act as innovators by easing new features or unconventional practices into society. Associations provided social and, in some cases, even legal scope of action for sections of the population that were otherwise barred from or limited in their official activity. This has been seen in many of the examples offered in the chapters of this volume. In the Greek poleis, for instance, foreigners contributed to the local society in a more formalised way thanks to their involvement in

---

[10] On associations upholding Imperial cults and loyalty in the Roman East, see also Harland 2003: 115–36.

associations, in particular in cities where foreign presence was particularly lively for commercial reasons. They could own land and have the right to tombs for their afterlife through membership in association: all these things were otherwise impossible for them. Furthermore, mixed associations of citizens and foreigners provided specific occasions for social integration, which the law either tended to discourage or at any rate did not envisage. This is the case of the Thracian *orgeones* of Bendis in third-century BC Piraeus (*CAPInv.* 232), who played an active part in the religious life of the city and managed to lobby the Athenian assembly to grant them the right to own land, or of the Hellenistic *koinon* of the Sidonians in Piraeus (*CAPInv.* 331), who owned a temple and were involved in its cults as one gathers from a bilingual Phoenician–Greek decree set up by the group. The association of the *Haliadai kai Haliastai* on second-century BC Rhodes (*CAPInv.* 10) welcomed into their ranks high-profile foreigners, to whom they also granted honours and tombs, and an association of *Temenitai* in first-century BC Miletus (*CAPInv.* 1001) gathered citizens and foreigners together and were in all likelihood providing tombs as one of the perks of membership. An association of *thiasotai* in third-century BC Athens (*CAPInv.* 284) was also formed by Athenian citizens and foreigners alike, both women and men, whereas the *Sabaziastai* in second-century BC Piraeus (*CAPInv.* 353) had only men, but both Athenian citizens and foreigners together – and even a slave. The *Heroistai Samothrakiastai* of Rhodian Peraea in the early Imperial times also welcomed foreigners into their midst, as did an association of purple-dyers in second-century AD Thessalonica (*CAPInv.* 786), whereas the *Geremellenses* of third-century AD Puteoli (*CAPInv.* 1080) probably gathered foreigners of Semitic origin and owned a temple in the city. The possibilities for active agency offered to foreigners by membership in associations were particularly exploited by those for whom travel or residency abroad was a fundamental part of their profession – associations provided logistic advantages to their business enterprises. Thanks to their mercantile character and strategic geographical position for commerce as maritime hubs, Delos and Puteoli became the ideal seat of associations that advertised their identity as foreign merchants and contributed in a fundamental way to the cities' vibrant economic, social and cultural life, while also leaving substantial traces in the topography. Examples of these are, on the one hand, the second/first-century BC Berytian *Poseidoniastai* (*CAPInv.* 9), with their impressive clubhouse, and the second-century BC Tyrian *Herakleistai* (CAPInv. 12) on Delos; and are, on the other hand, the second-century AD Berytian worshippers of

Jupiter Heliopolitanus (*CAPInv.* 1082) and the Tyrian *stationarioi* (*CAPInv.* 1079) in Puteoli.[11]

Associations operated as means for the social integration not only of foreigners but also of freedmen; they could furthermore provide opportunities for social climbing to others, whose social conditions did not allow them to enter the higher ranks of local society. This is what happened, for instance, in the Roman *collegia*, as pointed out by Tran in Chapter 9: their wealthiest members often used membership in a *collegium* and the undertaking of the collegial offices – with the possibilities of publicity and prestige this bestowed – as means to climb the social hierarchies beyond the associations for themselves or for their sons. Slaves were also sometimes included in associations with freeborn members or with freedmen: examples are a *synodos* of Heracles in second-century BC Athens (*CAPInv.* 36; in addition to slaves, this group included Athenian citizens and foreigners too), an association of *threskeutai* of Zeus *Hypsistos* in third-century AD Pydna in Macedonia (*CAPInv.* 41) and possibly some *mystai* of Dionysus in first/second-century AD Byzantium (*CAPInv.* 315).

Women, who largely did not enjoy civil rights, found in associations a way to create impact and a channel to express themselves as a group in a society that constitutionally silenced them, in particular in the Greek world. Examples of women-only associations are, for instance, a *thiasos* of women in third-century BC Miletus (CAPInv. 1238), the *koinon* of the priestesses of Demeter in first-century Mantinea (*CAPInv.* 430), a *thiasos* of women in the Egyptian village of Kerkethoeris in the third century BC (*CAPInv.* 766) and a *thiasus* of Maenads in first/second-century AD Philippi in Macedonia (*CAPInv.* 708). It is not surprising that the evidence of women-only associations tends to point towards a religious component, as religion was the main area of possible action for women in antiquity: that said, although providing some ground for social innovation, associations still remained generally conservative. Furthermore, the existence of associations (beyond familial associations) with mixed membership, that is to say, gathering both men and women, represented one of the very few opportunities in the ancient world to temporarily bridge the gap between the sexes and bring together in a formalised fashion two worlds that were normally kept separate in public life. Religious ceremonies, in particular civic cults, were the other occasion in which men and women at the same time could both have an active role in the proceedings, although the two

[11] See also the discussion by Evers in Chapter 10.

groups did normally not interact with each other.[12] Men and women appear, for instance, in associations of *thiasotai* in fourth- and third-century BC Athens (*CAPInv.* 268, *CAPInv.* 269, *CAPInv.* 276, *CAPInv.* 284), in the *dekadistai kai dekadistriai* on third/second-century Delos (*CAPInv.* 218), in an association of *Temenitai* in second-century BC Miletus (*CAPInv.* 998), in the *Athenaistai* of early Imperial Tanagra in Boeotia (*CAPInv.* 935), in an association of *eranistai* in first-century AD Athens (*CAPInv.* 321), in the Dionysiac *thiasos* of Amandos in second-century AD Locris (*CAPInv.* 437), in the *thiasus Placidianus* of second/third-century AD Puteoli (*CAPInv.* 1088) and in an association of *threskeutai* of Zeus *Hypsistos* in third-century AD Pydna in Macedonia (*CAPInv.* 41). The exact level and nature of the interaction between men and women in these associations remain, however, mostly unclear, due to the lack of further details in the sources.

In the case of the role of associations as social agents vis-à-vis women specifically, the example from Mantinea offered by Zoumbaki's analysis in Chapter 7 represents a unique case. Four associations only (*CAPInv.* 428, *CAPInv.* 430, *CAPInv.* 432, *CAPInv.* 433), dating to the first centuries BC and AD, are attested with certainty in the polis and women were involved in all of them (either as members, benefactresses or both), whereas in the evidence from the whole of the Greek-speaking world, the presence of women in the context of associations is around 6 per cent only. Much of the picture derived for Mantinea certainly depends on the poor epigraphic evidence for the region; however, the fact that all attestations of associations date to this specific period of time and that all of them involve women is noteworthy. In fact, it shows how associations seized the opportunity for agency during a period of economic recovery and focussed their efforts in a field left unattended by public institutions, namely, some public cults, using the strategy of attracting euergetism – exactly as their contemporary civic bodies were doing. Mantinean associations, both of priests and priestesses, for their own purposes and for the benefit of the entire community mobilised social entities, such as (wealthy) women, which traditionally had not had much scope in public life in the past.[13] However, also in this case conservatism and the general trends of contemporary society dictated the rules: women's intervention was mainly centred

---

[12] For the interesting and uncommon case of mixed priesthoods, contemporarily held by men and women, see Ackermann 2013.

[13] On a re-evaluation of the social standing of priests and priestesses in the Greek cities in the Hellenistic and Roman periods, see Mylonopoulos 2013.

on acts of benefaction and focussed around religion. From the late Hellenistic period onwards, in fact, the involvement of women as bene-factresses at the public level increased, as the undertaking of civic offices became more a simple matter of wealth: for this they received various honours – above all, statues – by the civic communities.[14] The women's role in the case of Mantinean associations is certainly less remarkable than that of the Acmonian women in Phrygia. These set up a public monument in AD 6/7 and acted as a public body in their own right.[15] The rich women of Mantinea did not do anything comparable. However, they were 'hunted' by local associations – did men prefer to be rather involved in benefactions that brought more civic visibility? – and they were given a potential stage for the assertion of some 'involvement', although codified in the traditional pattern of euergetism in the religious sphere and at the time when civic institutions were doing the same. In the case of men-only associations, women could really venture into unchartered territory and dip their toes – even physically, if they decided to show up to the banquets to which they were invited as honours for their generosity – into an environment that was otherwise off limits for them.

In order to appreciate further the example of women's agency in associations at Mantinea expounded by Zoumbaki in Chapter 7, it may be useful to provide a brief parallel from Hellenistic Rhodes. Unlike in other Hellenistic cities, women are largely absent from priesthoods and from civic honorific habit on Rhodes: their scope of action was limited to the private sphere, and when they appear in public inscriptions, they mainly do so with an 'aristocratic' focus on familial networks.[16] According to the traditional attitudes of Rhodian society, women seem to have had few opportunities for visibility and agency in the private settings of local associations, which were usually happy to capitalise on 'underestimated' sections of society. Women were involved in some way in only about 3 per cent of the many Rhodian associations recorded in the sources and they pretty much only appear as honorands together with their husbands. In one case only, a woman is honoured by a Rhodian associa-tion in her own right: Stratonika was granted by the second-century BC association of the *Haliadai kai Haliastai* (*CAPInv.* 10) a statue, an olive wreath, the title of benefactress and honours after her death for her generosity towards the association – it is probable that she was a member

[14] See generally Kron 1996; van Bremen 1996; Ma 2013. For the Roman West, see Meyers 2019.
[15] *MAMA* XI 99: Thonemann 2010.   [16] Zachhuber 2018, with further bibliography.

herself. However, she was not Rhodian but came from Halicarnassus. Perhaps the lack of Rhodian family lineage, so important for a woman on the island (and of a Rhodian husband, who would take care of her public image?) prompted Stratonika in her direct involvement with an association, which was well disposed towards (generous) foreigners – another member honoured by the *Haliadai kai Haliastai* was an Alexandrian, who was also a benefactor and probably member of three other local associations.

Although representing an almost unique setting for fostering integration and agency of social categories that were normally limited in their opportunities for impact, associations (at least those that had a public profile and left traces in the written sources) still remained to a large extent a business for men – as did most of the other aspects of the ancient world.

The impact on local society by associations can be also analysed in terms of exclusivity and inclusivity, not only on the social fabric but also on the physical space. In many cases, associations functioned as markers of distinction by excluding others from their activities and premises (which could, however, become local landmarks): this is exemplified by the Hellenistic familial foundations of Diomedon of Cos (*CAPInv.* 1919), Poseidonios of Halicarnassus (*CAPInv.* 830) and Epikteta of Thera (*CAPInv.* 1645). These associations regulated both membership and attachment to a specific place in terms of strict exclusivity, as Skaltsa's analysis in Chapter 5 has shown. Membership could also be strictly based on a specific profession or social status: the rules of the second-century BC association of Amon-Opet in Thebes of Egypt (*CAPInv.* 1480), for instance, established exclusive membership for the choachytes, 'water pourers', a branch of religious personnel in charge of funerary rituals. The choachytes largely belonged to interconnected families, so that membership in the association of Amon-Opet was also ultimately dictated by family membership. Other associations were open to a broader base: even so, it was important to present membership as an exclusive feature and a mark of prestige. This boosted the association's profile, made membership appealing for outsiders and attracted euergetism. In some cases, associations adopted a more inclusive approach: as noted by Skaltsa in Chapter 5, for instance, the third-century BC *Amphieraistai* of Rhamnous (*CAPInv.* 356) and the second-century BC *Asklepiastai* of Yaylakale in the Pergamene hinterland (*CAPInv.* 857) restored or built their own sanctuaries, which were, however, thereafter open to the local community.

Associations as Economic Agents

As already mentioned in Chapter 1, several studies have shown the important role and impact of associations on the ancient economy.[17] There is no need to repeat their content here, beyond reminding once again that associations – especially, but not only, those referred to as 'professional associations' by traditional scholarship – could facilitate economic transactions in a number of ways, including provision of social capital, increase and diffusion of know-how and price information, decrease of transaction costs, risk management, organisation of labour, building of networks, implementation of trust and human capital, supply of capital, coordination of resources, optimisation of transport, organisation of local production and distribution and management of distant trade. Besides access to capital, the main reason why associations could operate as successful economic agents was their profile: thanks to the implementation of values and regulations that presented them as 'well-ordered groups', associations could successfully build economic networks that relied on trust, reputation, mutual respect and reliability. Individually, members of an association could count on the financial support of the group in the form of loans, as well as on the other advantages that membership in a successful and respected organisation brought with it in economic terms.

In the case of Egypt, as already noted, the nature of the evidence allows us a closer direct insight into various economic aspects in the life of associations, which we generally lack for the other parts of the ancient world: it is therefore not surprising that the material lends itself to investigations with a more economic focus. The analysis by Langellotti in Chapter 8 has argued that, while fostering traditional values of sociability, conviviality and personal relations, many associations developed specific economic strategies, such as collective action or a protectionist outlook, in order to increase their chances of economic success and limit risk, as a response to the economic set-up of Roman Egypt, which was increasingly organised according to a system of licence fees. In addition to associations' regulations, papyri have preserved to us a variety of texts that testify the financial vivacity of (some) associations and allow us a close look into their economic dealings: accounts, lists, transactions, contracts and

---

[17] See, for instance, van Minnen 1987; van Nijf 1997; Gabrielsen 2001; Monson 2006; Gabrielsen 2007; Liu 2009; Broekaert 2011; Gibbs 2011; Tran 2011; Verboven 2011; Venticinque 2013; Gibbs 2015; Venticinque 2015; Gabrielsen 2016b; Langellotti 2016b; Venticinque 2016: esp. 35–66; Evers 2017; Gabrielsen in press.

agreements. From these we also note that associations became increasingly more involved in financial transactions at the state level, from tax collection and compulsory services to the performance of administrative duties on behalf of the state.[18] Roman associations and Indian associations, in particular those gathering craftsmen and traders, displayed similar features and trends: as remarked by Evers in Chapter 10, they had some degree of economic corporeality and showed a progressive propensity for communal contracting as a group. This is something on which the evidence from other areas of the ancient world is largely silent.

However, one may still gather some information on the economic position of associations within local society even from sources that are less explicit on financial matters, and not just for those associations that we may think as primarily interested in business. The role of any association in attracting euergetism, for instance, was of significance to stimulate capital flow; in periods of stagnation or recession, this was even more important for boosting the local economy, as Zoumbaki has stressed in Chapter 7 in the case of Mantinea.

Associations' main source of income derived from members' fees and contributions, which went to cover the cost of running the group's activities. Realty could also form part of an association's assets and could be (partly) let out to third parties, thus constituting an additional source of revenue. When associations had at their disposal extra liquidity, they usually invested it (mostly through moneylending) and employed the accruing interest for financing their activities, evidence of their entrepreneurial mindset. The money that associations accumulated was mostly reinvested in the local market: this made them partly responsible for the economic vivacity of a place. Associations were consumers of marketed goods and services, as we can indirectly derive from their inscriptions and from direct evidence in the papyrus accounts: they spent money on a variety of items and services, from the more extravagant portraits, immovables (either rented or bought) and crowns of precious metals to the more mundane oil for lamps, foodstuff, drinks and sacrificial animals. Depending on the association's size and dealings, they also provided employment to various staff, from stone carvers, scribes, artisans of various kind, artists and musicians to cooks, architects, guards, cleaners and other servants.

This brings us to a further issue concerning the economic makeup of associations: were they rich? As is often the case, the answer is: it depends.

---

[18] See van Minnen 1987: 48–56 and Venticinque 2015.

Some associations sat at the higher end of the spectrum of economic wealth, others at the bottom end. However, those that left traces in our evidence were certainly positioned towards the upper end of the scale and were rich enough to afford carving inscriptions, bestowing honours, commemorating events, setting their regulations on stone or papyrus and making their existence tangibly noticeable in the public domain. Others had more limited means and did not leave traces behind: of them we know nothing. This bias of the ancient sources, which reflect a biased image of ancient society, is common and every historian has to come to terms with it.

What about the members? Some were very rich and could afford to make outstanding donations, others managed just about to pay the membership fees. Although quantifying the level of wealth is often difficult, it is safe to say that members had at their disposal means and time that they could spend in the framework of associations: this suggests that on average they were not in financial distress. In fact, fees of associations were often not inconsiderable sums of money and membership could be relatively expensive. An unnamed association of first-century AD Tebtynis in the Arsinoites of Egypt (*CAPInv.* 1408), for instance, required its members to pay a monthly membership fee of 12 drachmas, for a total of 144 drachmas a year: it has been suggested that this sum could be sufficient to support a family of four for a year; one would therefore surmise that the members of this association were relatively well off.[19] The same has been noted for the associations of the Arsinoites in Hellenistic times: Demotic regulations and accounts suggest that the members of these associations (men and women) belonged to relatively wealthy families that had somewhat high standards of living.[20] The evidence from the Greek world for the most part does not allow quantifications of this type. However, the fact that some associations, such as the third/second-century BC *eranistai ton Adoniazonton* in the Rhodian Peraea (*CAPInv.* 1124) or the second-century BC *Haliadai kai Haliastai* of Rhodes (*CAPInv.* 10), granted *ateleia*, exemption from membership fees, as one of the honours for their benefactors suggests that the disbursement of money for membership was not insignificant – otherwise, the value of the honour would have been trivial. Therefore, it seems that the members of most associations that left traces in our sources were to some degree well off – even though with a large range of gradation. However, their financial abilities could vary due to some contingent circumstances, and some may have found themselves unable to afford

[19] Venticinque 2016: 14–15.   [20] Monson 2006: 224–8.

membership any longer. This is exactly what happened to a certain Epiodoros, who on 25 July AD 184 wrote to the president and fellow members (*synoditai*) of an unnamed association of Karanis in the Arsinoites of Egypt (*CAPInv.* 1380): 'Since I am doing poorly (financially) and I am unable to remain in the association, I ask you to accept my resignation.'[21]

Associations as Cultural Agents

Thanks to their activities and the profile they attained in local society, associations could leave their mark also on the larger cultural sphere. We shall briefly focus here on two major cultural aspects: religion and material culture, in particular architecture and visual space.

The involvement of associations in the religious sphere is attested in almost every single piece of evidence concerning them. Virtually every association performed religious activities of some kind, as they were a very important part of communal life, in the building of the group's specific profile: religion solemnised proceedings, embodied the group's piety and devotion and was a means to deepen the feeling of belonging to the group and to seal practices that strengthened bonds of trust between members. However, associations were not simple passive performers; they often occupied a position of active prominence in the development of the local religious landscape.

As stressed in the analysis by Skaltsa in Chapter 5, some associations were responsible for the 'invention' of completely new cults: the family foundation of Epikteta on Hellenistic Thera (*CAPInv.* 1645), for instance, established the cult of the diseased members as heroes; this involved the creation of priestly offices (first held by Epikteta's grandson) and the regulation of specific rituals to be performed regularly. In other cases, associations introduced or facilitated the spread of 'foreign' cults, either unadulterated or with some form of *interpretatio*, 'adaptation': this is the case of the *xenoi Apolloniatai* of Hermopolis Magna in Egypt (*CAPInv.* 194), who in 79/8 BC dedicated a temple to Apollo, Zeus and the companion gods and introduced their own – in all likelihood, Idumaean – rituals that they continued to perform 'in foreign tongue' even three centuries later.[22] Finally, associations often set up or restored sanctuaries and temples (which often belonged to them) of traditional deities, thus rejuvenating local religious practices: Chapter 5 by Skaltsa has drawn our attention to the third-century BC *Amphieraistai* of Rhamnous

---

[21] *P.Mich.* IX 575, ll. 4–8.   [22] See Paganini 2020b: 204–6.

(*CAPInv.* 356), who restored a temple of Amphiaraus for the advantage of all the faithful, and to the second-century BC *Asklepiastai* in the Pergamene hinterland (*CAPInv.* 857), who founded a new sanctuary in honour of Asclepius and opened it to the larger community by encouraging practices such as incubation, thus enriching the religious life of those living in the vicinity.

The involvement of some associations for the preservation of specific (civic) cults has been particularly stressed in case of Mantinea by Zoumbaki in Chapter 7. One can observe that associations took on the responsibility of the organisation, upkeep and financial survival of ritual and material aspects of the cults. They ensured the continuity of the performance of popular cults of the city, thus playing a fundamental role as integral constituents of local religious life well beyond the confines of the association. The same was the case of the Thracian *orgeones* of Bendis in third-century BC Piraeus (*CAPInv.* 232), who were in charge of performing a procession from the city to the harbour, or the Tyrian *stationarioi* (*CAPInv.* 1079) in second-century AD Puteoli, as Chapter 10 by Evers has recalled: they took part in the larger religious life of the city, by participating in the public festivals, for the organisation of which they also partly paid – in addition to worshipping their own ancestral gods. The involvement of associations in larger religious ceremonies can also be envisaged in many other cases, for which evidence is, however, mostly lacking.[23]

Associations could even foster new trends in traditional religious practices or a new interpretation of traditional beliefs. By embedding cults for the rulers – as well as other cults – within their activities, the associations of Hellenistic Egypt, for instance, may have acted as the diffusers of more intimate and personalised forms of group cult, in addition to the largely distant state religion and temple celebrations: the Royal House and the other gods were made part of the communal life of private individuals, still in a codified and somewhat institutionalised way but beyond the high walls of the temples and their priestly personnel.[24] Another interesting case is the one of the precepts dictated by Dionysios for his *oikos* in Philadelphia (*CAPInv.* 348): as the analysis by Carbon in Chapter 4 has noted, they have a strong ethical dimension, rather than focussing on a series of cases of impurity with the correlated behaviour to neutralise them, as the norms of purity usually do. The possible followers of Dionysios were required to abide by a series of detailed moral principles: rather than following norms

---

[23] See also van Nijf 1997: 191–206.   [24] Paganini 2020a.

for the purity of the sanctuary, they were asked to shape their character according to the moral principles established by the founder. Associations could therefore contribute to shaping the larger cultural values of reference of their local societies; this has been argued also by Arnaoutoglou in Chapter 6 and by Langellotti in Chapter 8 in the case of Roman Athens and Roman Egypt, respectively, where associations adapted or stressed specific community values in order to meet new needs, arisen to conform to the Roman administration.

On a more tangible level, associations exercised a not inconsiderable impact on material culture, in particular on the visual space of their communities. By setting up inscriptions in various parts of the public and private space, associations were leaving a recognisable mark on the topography of the places where they were active. In the village of Tebtynis in Roman times, for instance, the associations' presence was particularly felt along the processional avenue of the temple, which was dotted with banqueting halls and inscriptions signalling the meeting-place of associations; the same practice is also well attested in the Hellenistic period.[25]

With their clubhouses or with the erection of sanctuaries or shrines primarily for their use, associations were establishing a physical place for themselves in the local urban fabric. Archaeological remains are often difficult to link with certainty to associations; in the few cases when this has been possible, such as on Delos, at Athens or Ostia, complexes of considerable dimensions and structure testify even nowadays to the impact that these buildings had on the local topography.[26] With their specific choices of architecture and ornaments, associations were further setting visual trends, often vesting space with special symbolism: as stressed in Chapter 5 by Skaltsa, the monumentalisation of the founding act and the testamentary dispositions of Epikteta on Thera (*CAPInv.* 1645) on a large pedestal, for instance, with further display of statues of the heroised dead, enclosed in a larger memorial, created an important new element in the local topography and became a prominent reminder of the role of the association in the local societal and physical landscape.

Associations could also shape the local necropolis: this is particularly recognisable on Cos and on Rhodes in Hellenistic times, where associations set up tombs and monuments that often functioned as landmarks in

---

[25] Paganini 2020b.
[26] Trümper 2011; Skaltsa 2016; Zevi 2008. See also www.ostia-antica.org/dict.htm for floorplans and pictures of Ostian clubhouses.

the necropolis' landscape. In the case of Rhodes, associations built even larger funerary complexes in which members regularly gathered in order to perform communal activities of remembrance and honour for deceased members. In this way, associations were affecting not only the cities of the living but also the world of the dead.[27]

[27] Cos: Maillot 2013. Rhodes: Fraser 1977; Gabrielsen 1994.

Bibliography

Abraham, M. 1988. *Two Medieval Merchant Guilds of South India.* New Delhi. Manohar Publications.

Abramenko, A. 1993. *Die munizipale Mittelschicht im kaiserzeitlichen Italien: zu einem neuen Verständnis von Sevirat und Augustalität.* Frankfurt. Lang.

Ackermann, D. 2013. 'Les prêtrises mixtes: genre, religion et société', in J. Rüpke, M. Horster and A. Klöckner (eds.), *Cities and Priests: Cult Personnel in Asia Minor and the Aegean Islands from the Hellenistic to the Imperial Period.* Berlin and Boston. De Gruyter: 7–39.

Adams, C. P. E. 2013. 'Natural resources in Roman Egypt. Extraction, transport, and administration', *BASP* 50: 265–81.

Aleshire, S. B. 1989. *The Athenian Asklepieion: The People, Their Dedications, and the Inventories.* Amsterdam. Gieben.

Ameling, W. 1983. *Herodes Atticus II. Inschriftenkatalog.* Hildesheim. Olms.

    1985. 'Der Archon Epaphrodeitos', *ZPE* 61: 133–47.

    1990. 'Κοινὸν τῶν Σιδωνίων', *ZPE* 81: 189–99.

Amis, W. D., and Stern, S. E. 1974. 'A critical examination of theory and functions of voluntary associations', *Nonprofit and Voluntary Sector Quarterly* 3: 91–9.

Aneziri, S. 2003. *Die Vereine der dionysischen Techniten im Kontext der hellenistischen Gesellschaft. Untersuchungen zur Geschichte, Organisation und Wirkung der hellenistischen Technitenvereine.* Stuttgart. Franz Steiner Verlag.

    2020. 'Associations and endowments *sub mondo* in the Hellenistic and Roman period: a multifaceted relationship', in A. Dimopoulou, A. Helmis and D. Karambelas (eds.), *Ιουλίαν Βελισσαροπούλου ἐπαινέσαι. Studies in Ancient Greek and Roman Law.* Athens. Greek Epigraphic Society: 1–34.

Apte, V. S. 1957–59. *Revised and enlarged edition of Prin. V. S. Apte's The Practical Sanskrit-English Dictionary.* 3 vols. Poona. Prasad Prakashan.

Arlt, C., and Monson, A. 2010. 'Rules of an Egyptian religious association from the early second century BCE', in H. Knuf, C. Leitz and D. von Recklinghausen (eds.), *Honi soit qui mal y pense. Studien zum pharaonischen, griechisch-römischen und spätantiken Ägypten zu Ehren von Heinz-Josef Thissen.* Leuven. Peeters: 113–22.

    2013. 'Rules of an Egyptian religious association from the early second century BCE', in R. Ast, H. Couvigny, T. M. Hickey and J. Lougovaya (eds.),

Papyrological Texts in Honor of Roger S. Bagnall (P. Bagnall). Durham, NC. American Society of Papyrologists: 209–13.

Arnaoutoglou, I. N. 1994. Ἀρχερανιστής and its meaning in inscriptions', *ZPE* 104: 107–10.

1998a. *Ancient Greek Laws: A Sourcebook*. London and New York. Routledge.

1998b. 'Between *koinon* and *idion*: legal and social dimensions of religious associations in ancient Athens', in P. Cartledge, P. Millet and S. von Reden (eds.), *KOSMOS: Essays in Order, Conflict and Community in Classical Athens*. Cambridge University Press: 68–83.

2002. 'Roman law and *collegia* in Asia Minor', *RIDA* 49: 27–44.

2003. *Thusias heneka kai sunousias. Private Religious Associations in Hellenistic Athens*. Athens. Academy of Athens.

2005. '*Collegia* in the province of Egypt in the first century AD', *AncSoc* 35: 197–216.

2011a. 'Craftsmen associations in Roman Lydia: a tale of two cities?', *AncSoc* 41: 257–90.

2011b. '"Ils étaient dans la ville, mais tout à fait en dehors de la cité." Status and identity in private religious associations in Hellenistic Athens', in O. M. van Nijf and R. Alston (eds.), *Political Culture in the Greek City after the Classical Age*. Leuven. Peeters: 27–48.

2015. 'Cult associations and politics: worshipping Bendis in Classical and Hellenistic Athens', in V. Gabrielsen and Ch. A. Thomsen (eds.), *Private Associations and the Public Sphere. Proceedings of a Symposium held at the Royal Danish Academy of Sciences and Letters, 9–11 September 2010*. Copenhagen. Royal Danish Academy: 25–56.

2016a. 'The Greek text of D. 47.22.4. (*Gai 4 ad legem duodecim tabularum*) reconsidered', *Legal Roots* 5: 87–119.

2016b. 'Θόρυβος, εὐστάθεια καὶ τὸ κανονιστικό πλαίσιο τῶν ἀθηναϊκῶν λατρευτικῶν σωματείων', *EHHD* 46: 23–78.

Ascough, R. S., Harland, Ph. A. and Kloppenborg, J. S. (eds.) 2012. *Associations in the Greco-Roman world. A sourcebook*. Waco, TX. Baylor University Press.

Assmann, J. 2011. *Cultural Memory and Early Civilization: Writing, Remembrance, and Political Imagination*. Cambridge University Press.

Ausbüttel, F. M. 1982. *Untersuchungen zu den Vereinen im Westen des römischen Reiches*. Kallmünz. Laßleben.

Bagnall, R. S. 2005. 'Evidence and models for the economy of Roman Egypt', in J. G. Manning and I. Morris (eds.), *The Ancient Economy: Evidence and Models*. Stanford University Press: 187–204.

Bagnall, W. S. 1973. 'The Archive of Laches: prosperous farmers of the Fayum in the second century'. Unpublished PhD thesis, Duke University.

Barton, S. C., and Horsley, G. H. R. 1981. 'A Hellenistic cult group and the New Testament Churches', *Jahrbuch für Antike und Christentum* 24: 7–41.

Basak, R. 1919–20. 'No. 7. The five Damodarpur copper-plate inscriptions of the Gupta period', *Epigraphia Indica* 15: 113–45.

Basham, A. L. 1983. 'The Mandasor inscription of the silk-weavers', in B. Smith (ed.), *Essays on Gupta Culture*. New Delhi. Motilal Banarsidass: 93–105.

Baslez, M.-F. 2004. 'Les notables entre eux. Recherches sur les associations d'Athènes à l'époque romaine', in S. Follet (ed.), *L'Hellénisme d'époque romaine: Nouveaux documents, nouvelles approches (Ier s. a.C.–IIIe s. p.C.). Actes du colloque international à la mémoire de Louis Robert, Paris, 7–8 juillet 2000*. Paris. De Boccard: 105–20.

2006. 'Entraide et mutualisme dans les associations des cités grecques à l'époque hellénistique', in M. Molin (ed.), *Les régulations sociales dans l'antiquité*. Rennes University Press: 157–68.

Bäumler, A. 2014. 'Prestigekohärenz bei römischen Festen? Vergemeinschaftung und Distinktion bei Festen von römischen Vereinen am Beispiel der *lex collegia eborariorum et citriariorum* (*CIL* 6, 33885),' in B. Backes and C. von Nicolai (eds.), *Kulturelle Kohärenz durch Prestige*. Munich. Utz: 59–82.

Bekker-Nielsen, T. 2008. *Urban Life and Roman Politics in Roman Bithynia: The Small World of Dio Chrysostom*. Aarhus University Press.

Bendlin, A. 2011. 'Associations, funerals, sociality, and Roman law: The *collegium* of Diana and Antinous in Lanuvium (*CIL* 14.2112) reconsidered,' in M. Öhler (ed.), *Aposteldekret und antikes Vereinswesen: Gemeinschaft und ihre Ordnung*. Tübingen. Mohr Siebeck: 207–96.

Berger, A. 1951. 'Some remarks on D. 1.2.1 and *CIL* 6.10298,' *IURA* 2: 102–15.

Bers, V. 1985. 'Dikastic *thorubos*', in P. A. Cartledge and F. D. Harvey (eds.), *Crux. Essays in Greek History Presented to G. E. M. de Ste Croix on His 75th Birthday*. London. Duckworth: 1–15.

Biró, J. 1969. 'Das *Collegium funeraticium* in Alburno maiore,' in M. N. Andreev (ed.), *Gesellschaft und Recht im griechisch-römischen Altertum. Eine Aufsatzsammlung*, vol. 2. Berlin. Akademie-Verlag: 1–19.

Bloch, H. 1953. 'Iscrizioni rinvenute tra il 1930 e il 1939', *Notizie degli Scavi di Antichità* 78: 239–306.

Boak, A. E. R. 1937a. 'An ordinance of the salt merchants', *AJPh* 58(2): 210–19.

1937b. 'The organization of gilds in Greco-Roman Egypt', *TAPhA* 68: 212–20.

Bogaert, R. 1968. *Banques et banquiers dans les cités grecques*. Leiden. Sijthoff.

Bollmann, B. 1998. *Römische Vereinshäuser. Untersuchungen zu den Scholae der römischen Berufs-, Kult- und Augustalen-Kollegien in Italien*. Mainz. Von Zabern.

Bölte, F. 1930. 'Mantinea', in *RE* XIV.2: 1290–344.

Borsari, L. 1887. 'Di un importante frammento epigrafico rinvenuto nel Trastevere,' *BCAR* 15: 3–7.

Bouchon, R., and Decourt, J.-C. 2017. 'Le règlement religieux de Marmarini (Thessalie): nouvelles lectures, nouvelles interprétations', *Kernos* 30: 159–86.

Bowden, H. 2009. 'Cults of Demeter Eleusinia and the transmission of religious ideas', in Malkin, Constantakopoulou and Panagopoulou (eds.): 70–82.

Bowman, A. K. 1976. 'Papyri and Roman Imperial history, 1960–75', *JRS* 66: 153–73.

Bowman, A. K., and Rathbone, D. 1992. 'Cities and administration in Roman Egypt', *JRS* 82: 108–27.

Bramoullé, Y., Galeotti, A. and Rogers, B. (eds.) 2016. *The Oxford Handbook of the Economics of Networks.* Oxford University Press.

Brennan, G., and Pettit, P. 2004. *The Economy of Esteem.* Oxford University Press.

Bresciani, E. 1994. 'Nuovi statuti demotici di "Confraternite" dalla necropoli dei Coccodrilli a Tebtynis (P.Vogl. demot. Inv. 77 e Inv. 78)', *Egitto e Vicino Oriente* 17: 49–67.

Brock, S. 2009. 'Regulations for an association of artisans from the late Sasanian or early Arab period', in P. Rousseau and M. Papoutsakis (eds.), *Transformations of Late Antiquity. Essays for Peter Brown.* Farnham, UK, and Burlington, USA. Ashgate: 51–61.

Broekaert, W. 2011. 'Partners in business: Roman merchants and the potential advantages of being a *collegiatus*', *AncSoc* 41: 221–56.

Buckler, W. H., and Robinson, D. M. (eds.) 1932. *Greek and Latin Inscriptions. Part I, Sardis.* Leiden. American Society for the Excavation of Sardis.

Bühler, G. 1894. 'Further votive inscriptions from the Stûpas at Sañchi (II),' *Epigraphia Indica* 2: 366–407.

Buonocore, M., and Diliberto, O. 2003. 'L'*album* e la *lex* della *Familia Silvani* di Trebula Mutuesca. Nuove considerazioni,' *RPAA* 75: 327–93.

Burrow, T. 1940. *A Translation of the Kharosthi Documents from Chinese Turkestan.* London. Royal Asiatic Society.

Burt, R. 2005. *Brokerage and Closure: An Introduction to Social Capital.* Oxford University Press.

Campanelli, S. 2016. 'Family cult foundations in the Hellenistic age. Family and sacred space in a private religious context', in M. Hilgert (ed.), *Understanding Material Text Cultures. A Multidisciplinary View.* Berlin and Boston. De Gruyter: 131–202.

Carbon, J.-M. 2013. 'Appendix: The stele of Poseidonios', in Carbon and Pirenne-Delforge: 99–114.

2016. 'The Festival of the *Aloulaia* and the association of the *Alouliastai*: notes concerning the new inscription from Larisa/Marmarini', *Kernos* 29: 185–208.

Carbon, J.-M., and Peels, S. (eds.) 2018. *Purity and Purification in the Ancient Greek World: Texts, Rituals, and Norms (Kernos Supplement 32).* Liège University Press.

Carbon, J.-M., and Pirenne-Delforge, V. 2012. 'Beyond Greek sacred laws', *Kernos* 25: 163–82.

2013. 'Priests and cult personnel in three Hellenistic families', in M. Horster and A. Klöckner (eds.), *Cities and Priests: Cult Personnel in Asia Minor and the Aegean Islands from the Hellenistic to the Imperial Period.* Berlin and Boston. De Gruyter: 65–119.

Carrié, J.-M. 2002. 'Les associations professionnelles à l'époque tardive: entre *munus* et convivialité', in J.-M. Carrié and R. Lizzi Testa (eds.), *Humana sapit: Mélanges en l'honneur de Lellia Cracco Ruggini.* Turnhout. Brepols: 309–32.

Carusi, C. 2008. *Il sale nel mondo greco, VI a.C.–III d.C.: luoghi di produzione, circolazione commerciale, regimi di sfruttamento nel contesto del Mediterraneo antico.* Bari. Edipuglia.

Caruso, A. 2016. *Mouseia. Tipologie, contesti, significati culturali di un'istituzione sacra (VII–I sec. a.C.) (Studia Archaeologica 209).* Rome. L'Erma di Bretschneider.

Chaniotis, A. 2002. 'Foreign soldiers – native girls? Constructing and crossing boundaries in Hellenistic cities with foreign garrisons', in A. Chaniotis and P. Ducrey (eds.), *Army and Power in the Ancient World.* Stuttgart. Steiner: 99–113.

2013. 'Mnemopoetik: die epigraphische Konstruktion von Erinnerung in den griechischen Poleis', in O. Dally, T. Hölscher, S. Muth and R. M. Schneider (eds.), *Medien der Geschichte. Antikes Griechenland und Rom.* Berlin and Boston. De Gruyter: 132–69.

Chankowski, V. 2007. 'Les catégories du vocabulaire de la fiscalité dans les cités grecques', in J. Andreau and V. Chankowski (eds.), *Vocabulaire et expression de l'économie dans le monde antique.* Pessac. Ausonius: 299–329.

Chavannes, E. 1914. *Six Monuments de la Sculpture Chinoise.* Brussels and Paris. Hachette.

Christ, M. R. 2007a. *The Bad Citizen in Classical Athens.* Cambridge University Press.

2007b. 'The evolution of the *eisphora* in Classical Athens', *CQ* 57: 53–69.

Cicerchia, P., and Marinucci, A. 1992. *Scavi di Ostia XI: Le Terme del Foro o di Gavio Massimo.* Rome. Istituto Poligrafico e Zecca dello Stato.

Clarysse, W. 2001. 'Use and abuse of beer and wine in Graeco-Roman Egypt', in K. Geus and K. Zimmermann (eds.), *Punica-Libyca-Ptolemaica. Festschrift für Werner Heuß zum 65. Geburtstag dargebracht von Schülern, Freunden und Kollegen.* Leuven. Peeters: 159–66.

Clemente, G. 1972. 'Il patronato nei *collegia* dell'impero romano', *Studi Classici e Orientali* 21: 142–229.

Cohen, B. 1975. 'La notion d'"ordo" dans la Rome antique', *Bulletin de l'Association Guillaume Budé* 2: 259–82.

1984. 'Some neglected *ordines*; the apparitorial status-group', in Nicolet (ed.): 23–60

Cohn, M. 1873. *Zum römischen Vereinsrecht. Abhandlungen aus der Rechtsgeschichte.* Berlin. Nabu.

Coleman, J. S. 1988. 'Social capital in the creation of human capital', *American Journal of Sociology* 94. Supplement: S95–S120.

Constantakopoulou, C. 2015. 'Beyond the polis', in Taylor and Vlassopoulos 2015a: 213–36.

Cotter, W. 1996. 'The *collegia* and Roman law: State restrictions on voluntary associations, 64 BCE – 200 CE', in Kloppenborg and Wilson (eds.): 74–89.

Coulton, J. J. 1976. *The Architectural Development of the Greek Stoa.* Oxford. Clarendon Press.

Cracco Ruggini, L. 1971. 'Le associazioni professionali nel mondo romano-bizantino', in *Artigianato e tecnica nella società dell'alto Medioevo occidentale, Settimane di Studio del Centro Italiano di Studi dell'Alto Medioevo 18, 2–8 aprile 1970*. Spoleto. Centro Italiano di Studi sull'Alto Medioevo: 59–277.

   1973. 'Stato e associazioni professionali nell'età imperiale romana', in *Akten des VI. Internationalen Kongresses für Griechische und Lateinische Epigraphik, München 1972*. Munich. Beck: 271–311.

   1976. 'La vita associativa nelle città dell'Oriente greco: tradizioni locali e influenze romane', in D. M. Pippidi (ed.), *Assimilation et résistance à la culture gréco-romaine dans le monde ancien: travaux du VIe Congrès international d'Études classiques (Madrid, Septembre 1974)*. Paris. Les Belles Lettres: 463–92.

Cresswell, T. 2015. *Place: An Introduction*. Chichester/Oxford. Wiley-Blackwell.

Cronkite, S.-M. 1997. 'The sanctuary of Demeter at Mytilene: a diachronic and contextual study'. Unpublished PhD thesis, University of London.

Davies, J. K. 2009. 'Pythios and Pythion: the spread of a cult title', in Malkin, Constantakopoulou and Panagopoulou (eds.): 57–69.

   2015. 'Retrospect and prospect', in Taylor and Vlassopoulos 2015a: 241–56.

De Angelis, F. 2010. '*Ius* and space: an introduction', in F. De Angelis (ed.), *Spaces of Justice in the Roman World*. Leiden. Brill: 1–25.

de Cenival, F. 1967/8. 'Les associations dans les temples égyptiens d'après les documents démotiques', *École pratique des hautes études. 4e section, Sciences historiques et philologiques. Annuaire* 1967–8: 591–7.

   1972. *Les associations religieuses en Égypte d'après les documents démotiques*. Cairo. Institut français d'archéologie orientale du Caire.

   1986. 'Comptes d'une association religieuse thébaine datant des années 29 à 33 du roi Amasis (P.Démot. Louvre E 7840 bis)', *REgypt* 37: 13–28.

   1988. 'Papyrus Seymour de Ricci: le plus ancien des règlements d'association religieuse (4ème siècle av. J.-C.) (Pap. Bibl. Nationale E 241)', *REgypt* 39: 37–46.

de Hoz, M. P. 2017. 'The regulations of Dionysios in the so-called *Lex Sacra* from Philadelphia in Lydia: elevated strict moral code or current civil behavioural norms?', *EA* 50: 93–108.

de Robertis, F. M. 1955. *Il fenomeno associativo nel mondo romano, dai collegi della Repubblica alle corporazioni del Basso Impero*. Rome. L'Erma di Bretschneider.

De Salvo, L. 1992. *Economia privata e pubblici servizi nell'impero romano: i corpora naviculariorum*. Messina. Samperi.

Decourt, J.-C., and Tziafalias, A. 2012. 'Un nouveau règlement religieux de la région de Larissa', in A. Mazarakis-Ainian (ed.), *Proceedings of the Third Archaeological Work of Thessaly and Central Greece, Volos 12.3–15.3.2009*. Volos. University of Thessaly Press: 463–73.

   2015. 'Un règlement religieux de la région de Larissa: cultes grecs et "orientaux"', *Kernos* 28: 13–51.

Degen, R. 1977. 'Review of H. Kaufhold, *Die Rechtssammlung des Gabriel von Basra und ihr Verhältnis zu den anderen Sammelwerken der Nestorianer*, Berlin 1976', *Oriens Christianus* 61: 145–50.

DeLaine, J. 2003. 'The builders of Roman Ostia: organisation, status and society', in S. Huerta (ed.), *Proceedings of the First International Congress on Construction History. Madrid, 20th–24th January 2003*. Vol. 3. Madrid. Instituto Juan de Herrera: 723–32.

Delli Pizzi, A. 2011. 'Impiety in epigraphic evidence', *Kernos* 24: 59–76.

Demont, P. 2003. 'Le κληρωτήριον ("machine à tirer au sort") et la démocratie athénienne', *Bulletin de l'Association Guillaume Budé* 1: 26–52.

Deshours, N. 2006. *Les mystères d'Andania: étude d'épigraphie et d'histoire religieuse*. Paris. Ausonius.

Deshpande, M. N. 1959. 'The rock-cut caves of Pitalkhora in the Deccan', *Ancient India* 15: 63–93.

Dignas, B. 2002. *The Economy of the Sacred in Hellenistic and Roman Asia Minor*. Oxford University Press.

Diosono, F. 2007. *Collegia. Le associazioni professionali nel mondo romano*. Rome. Quasar.

Dittmann-Schöne, I. 2001. *Die Berufsvereine in den Städten des kaiserzeitlichen Kleinasiens*. Regensburg. Roderer.

Dobias-Lalou, C. 2000. *Le dialecte des inscriptions grecques de Cyrène* (*Karthago* 25). Paris. Centre d'études archéologiques de la Méditerranée.

Dreyer, B. 2004. 'Die *Neoi* im hellenistischen Gymnasion', in D. Kah and P. Scholz (eds.), *Das hellenistische Gymnasion*. Berlin. Akademie: 211–36.

Durrbach, F., and Radet, G. A. 1886. 'Inscriptions de la Pérée rhodienne', *BCH* 10: 245–69.

Dyck, A. R. 1985. 'The function and persuasive power of Demosthenes' portrait of Aeschines in the speech On the Crown', *G&R* 32: 42–8.

Ebel, E. 2004. *Die Attraktivität früher christlicher Gemeinden. Die Gemeinde von Korinth im Spiegel griechisch-römischer Vereine*. Tübingen. Mohr Siebeck.

Ecker, A., and Eckhardt, B. 2018. 'The *Koinon* of Kosadar in Maresha: A Hellenistic private association in the Levant', *Israel Exploration Journal* 68: 192–207.

Eckhardt, B. 2016. 'Romanization and isomorphic change in Phrygia: the case of private associations', *JRS* 106: 147–71.

 2017a. 'Heritage societies? Private associations in Roman Greece', in T. M. Dijkstra, T. M. Kuin, N. I. Inger, M. Moser and D. Weidgenannt (eds.), *Strategies of Remembering in Greece under Rome (100 BC–100 AD)*. Leiden. Sidestone: 71–81.

 2017b. 'Temple ideology and Hellenistic private associations', *Dead Sea Discoveries* 24: 407–23.

Ehrhardt, N., and Günther, W. 2013. 'Hadrian, Milet und die Korporation der milesischen Schiffseigner. Zu einem neu gefundenen kaiserlichen Schreiben', *Chiron* 43: 199–220.

Eidinow, E. 2011. 'Networks and narratives: a model for ancient Greek religion', *Kernos* 24: 9–38.

Engelmann, H. 1976. *Die Inschriften von Kyme*. Bonn. Habelt.

Ernout, A., and Meillet, A. 1932. *Dictionnaire étymologique de la langue latine. Histoire des mots*. Paris. Les Belles Lettres.

Evers, K. G. 2017. *Worlds Apart Trading Together. The Organisation of Long-Distance Trade between Rome and India in Antiquity*. Oxford. Archaeopress.

Faraguna, M. (ed.) 2013. *Archives and Archival Documents in Ancient Societies* (*Legal Documents in Ancient Societies* IV). University of Trieste Publications.

Felten, I. M. 2007. 'Raum und Religion im kaiserzeitlichen Griechenland – Die sakralen Landschaften der Argolis, Achaias und Arkadiens'. Unpublished PhD thesis, University of Würzburg.

Fenn, N., and Römer-Strehl, C. (eds.) 2013. *Networks in the Hellenistic World. According to the Pottery in the Eastern Mediterranean and Beyond*. Oxford. British Archaeological Reports.

Ferguson, W. 1944. 'The Attic *orgeones*', *HThR* 37: 61–140.

  1949. 'Orgeonika', in *Commemorative Studies in Honor of Theodore Leslie Shear, Hesperia Supplements* 8: 130–63.

Fernoux, H.-L. 2004. *Notables et élites des cités de Bithynie aux époques hellénistique et romaine (IIIe siècle av. J.-C.–IIIe siècle ap. J.-C.). Essai d'histoire sociale.* Lyon. Maison de l'Orient méditerranéen.

  2007. 'L'exemplarité sociale chez les notables des cités d'Asie Mineure à l'époque impériale', in H.-L. Fernoux and Ch. Stein (eds.), *Aristocratie antique. Modèles et exemplarité sociale.* Dijon University Publications: 175–200.

  2011. *Le Demos et la Cité. Communautés et assemblées populaires en Asie Mineure à l'époque impériale*. Rennes University Publications.

Feyel, Ch. 2009. *ΔΟΚΙΜΑΣΙΑ. La place et le rôle de l'examen préliminaire dans les institutions des cités grecques*. Nancy. A.D.R.A.

Flambard, J.-M. 1981. '*Collegia compitalicia*: phénomène associatif, cadres territoriaux et cadres civiques dans le monde romain à l'époque républicaine', *Ktema* 6: 143–66.

  1987. 'Éléments pour une approche financière de la mort dans les classes populaires du Haut-Empire. Analyse du budget de quelques collèges funéraires de Rome et d'Italie', in F. Hinard (ed.), *La mort, les morts et l'au-delà dans le monde romain*. Caen University Press: 209–44.

Fleet, J. F. 1888. *Corpus Inscriptionum Indicarum: Inscriptions of the Early Guptas*. Vol. 3. Calcutta. Archaeological Survey of India.

Foraboschi, D. 1971. *L'archivio di Kronion*. Milan. Cisalpino-La Goliardica.

Foucart, P. 1873. *Des associations religieuses chez les Grecs, thiases, éranes, orgéons*. Paris. Klincksieck.

Fraser, P. M. 1972a. 'Notes on two Rhodian Institutions', *ABSA* 67: 113–24.

  1972b. *Ptolemaic Alexandria*. 3 vols. Oxford. Clarendon Press.

  1977. *Rhodian Funerary Monuments*. Oxford. Clarendon Press.

Freu, C. 2012. 'L'identité sociale des membres des collèges professionnels égyptiens (Ier–VIe s. p.C.)', in M. Dondin-Payre and N. Tran (eds.), *Collegia. Le phénomène associative dans l'Occident romain*. Bordeaux. Ausonius: 229–47.

Friggeri, R., and Magnani Cianetti, M. 2014. *Terme di Diocleziano: il chiostro piccolo della certosa di Santa Maria degli Angeli*. Milan. Mondadori Electa.

Fröhlich, P. 2004. *Les cités grecques et le contrôle des magistrates (IVe–Ier siècle avant J.C.)*. Geneva. Droz.

Fröhlich, P., and Hamon, P. (eds.) 2013a, *Groupes et associations dans les cités grecques (IIIe siècle av. J.-C.–IIe siècle apr. J.-C.) Actes de la table ronde de Paris, INHA, 19–20 juin 2009*. Geneva. Droz.

Fröhlich, P., and Hamon, P. 2013b. 'Histoire sociale et phénomène associatif dans les cités grecques d'époque hellénistique et impériale', in Fröhlich and Hamon 2013a: 1–27.

Gabba, E. 1984. 'The *collegia* of Numa: problems of method and political ideas', *JRS* 74: 81–6.

Gabrielsen, V. 1987. 'The *antidosis* procedure in Classical Athens', *C&M* 38: 7–38.

  1994. 'The Rhodian associations honouring Dionysodoros from Alexandria', *C&M* 45: 137–60.

  1997. *The Naval Aristocracy of Hellenistic Rhodes*. Aarhus University Press.

  2001. 'The Rhodian associations and economic activity', in Z. H. Archibald, J. Davies, V. Gabrielsen and G. J. Oliver (eds.), *Hellenistic Economies*. London and New York. Routledge: 215–44.

  2007. 'Brotherhoods of faith and provident planning: the non-public associations of the Greek World', *Mediterranean Historical Review* 22(2): 183–210 = in Malkin, Constantakopoulou and Panagopoulou 2009: 176–203.

  2013. 'Finance and taxes', in H. Beck (ed.), *A Companion to Ancient Greek Government*. Malden, MA, and Oxford. Wiley-Blackwell: 332–46.

  2015. 'Naval and grain networks and associations in fourth-century Athens', in Taylor and Vlassopoulos 2015a: 177–212.

  2016a. 'Associations, modernization and the return of the private network in Athens', in C. Tiersch (ed.), *Die Athenische Demokratie im 4. Jahrhundert. Zwischen Modernisierung und Tradition*. Stuttgart. Steiner: 121–62.

  2016b. 'Be faithful and prosper: associations, trust and the economy of security', in K. Droß-Krüpe, S. Föllinger and K. Ruffing (eds.), *Antike Wirtschaft und ihre kulturelle Prägung – The Cultural Shaping of the Ancient Economy*. Wiesbaden. Harrassowitz: 87–111.

  2017. 'A new inscription attesting to associations from the necropolis of Rhodes (with an appendix by N. Christodoulides)', *Tyche* 32: 15–40.

Gabrielsen, V. in press. 'Social networks and trade', in S. von Reden (ed.), *Cambridge Companion to the Greek Economy*. Cambridge University Press.

Gabrielsen, V., and Thomsen, Ch. A. 2015. 'Introduction: Private Groups, Public Functions?', in V. Gabrielsen and Ch. A. Thomsen (eds.), *Private Associations and the Public Sphere. Proceedings of a Symposium held at the Royal*

Danish Academy of Sciences and Letters, 9–11 September 2010. Copenhagen. Royal Danish Academy: 7–24.

Gans, H. J. 2002. 'The sociology of space: a use-centered view', *City & Community* 1(4): 329–39.

Garland, R. 1992. *Introducing new Gods. The Politics of Athenian Religion*. Ithaca and New York. Cornell University Press.

Garnsey, P. 1998. *Cities, Peasants, and Food in Classical Antiquity. Essays in Social and Economic History*. Cambridge University Press.

Gauthier, Ph., 1980. 'Études sur des inscriptions d'Amorgos', *BCH* 104: 197–220.

1985. *Les cités grecques et leurs bienfaiteurs*. Paris. French School at Athens.

1990. 'L'inscription d'Iasos relative à l'*ekklesiastikon* (I. Iasos 20)', *BCH* 114: 417–43.

Gauthier, Ph., and Hatzopoulos, M. B. 1993. *La loi gymnasiarchique de Beroia* (*Meletemata* 16). Athens/Paris. Research Centre for Greek and Roman Antiquity, National Hellenic Research Foundation.

Gawlinski, L. 2012. *The Sacred Law of Andania: A New Text with Commentary*. Berlin and Boston. De Gruyter.

Geagan, D. J. 1967. *The Athenian Constitution after Sulla*. Princeton. American School of Classical Studies at Athens.

1992. 'A family of Marathon and social mobility in Athens of the first century B.C.', *Phoenix* 46: 29–44.

Geraci, G. 1989. 'L'Egitto romano nella storiografia moderna', in L. Criscuolo and G. Geraci (eds.), *Egitto e storia antica dall'ellenismo all'età araba: bilancio di un confronto*. Bologna. CLUEB: 55–88

Gernet, J. 1956. *Les aspects économiques de Bouddhisme dans la Société chinoise du Ve au Xe siècle*. Saigon. French School of the Far East.

Gherchanoc, F. 2012. *L'Oïkos en fête. Célébrations familiales et sociabilité en Grèce ancienne*. Paris. Sorbonne University Publications.

Giannakopoulos, N. 2008. *Ο Θεσμός της Γερουσίας των ελληνικών πόλεων κατά τους ρωμαϊκούς χρόνους*. Thessaloniki. Vanias.

2012. *Θεσμοί και λειτουργία των πόλεων της Εύβοιας κατά τους ελληνιστικούς και τους αυτοκρατορικούς χρόνους*. Thessaloniki. University Studio Press.

2013. 'The Gerousia of Akmonia', *Gephyra* 10: 13–31.

2017. 'Decrees awarding offices for life and by hereditary right as honours', in A. Heller and O. M. van Nijf (eds.), *The Politics of Honour in the Greek Cities of the Roman Empire*. Leiden. Brill: 220–42.

Gibbs, M. 2008. 'Professional and Trade Associations in Ptolemaic and Roman Egypt'. Unpublished DPhil dissertation, University of Oxford.

2011. 'Trade associations in Roman Egypt: their *raison d'être*', *AncSoc* 41: 291–315.

2015. 'The trade associations of Ptolemaic Egypt', in V. Gabrielsen and Ch. A. Thomsen (eds.), *Private Associations and the Public Sphere. Proceedings of a Symposium held at the Royal Danish Academy of Sciences and Letters, 9–11 September 2010*. Copenhagen. Royal Danish Academy: 241–69.

Gieryn, T. F. 2000. 'A space for place in sociology', *Annual Review of Sociology* 26: 463–96.

Giles, L. 1943. 'Dated Chinese manuscripts in the Stein Collection, VI, tenth century', *Bulletin of the School of Oriental and African Studies* 11(1): 148–73.

Gillihan, Y. M. 2012. *Civic Ideology, Organization, and Law in the Rule Scrolls. A Comparative Study of the Covenanters' Sect and Contemporary Voluntary Associations in Political Context*. Leiden and Boston. Brill.

Goody, J. 2012. *The Theft of History*. Cambridge University Press.

Granovetter, M. 1983. 'The strength of weak ties: a network theory revisited', *Sociological Theory* 1: 203–33.

Guarducci, M. 1974. *Epigrafia greca III. Epigrafi di carattere privato*. Rome. Istituto Poligrafico e Zecca dello Stato.

Haake, M. 2015. 'Philosophical schools in Athenian society from the fourth to the first century BC: an overview', in V. Gabrielsen and Ch. A. Thomsen (eds.), *Private Associations and the Public Sphere. Proceedings of a Symposium Held at the Royal Danish Academy of Sciences and Letters, 9–11 September 2010*. Copenhagen. Royal Danish Academy: 57–91.

Hansen, M. H. 1976. *Apagoge, Endeixis and Ephegesis against Kakourgoi, Atimoi and Pheugontes. A Study in the Athenian Administration of Justice in the Fourth Century B.C.* Odense University Press.

  1991. *The Athenian Democracy in the Age of Demosthenes: Structure, Principles, and Ideology*. Oxford. Blackwell.

Hansen, V. 2000. *The Open Empire. A History of China to 1600*. New York and London. Norton & Co.

  2012. *The Silk Road. A New History*. Oxford University Press.

Hanson, A. E. 1984. 'Caligulan month-names at Philadelphia and related matters', in *Atti del XVII Congresso internazionale di Papirologia: Napoli, 1983*. Naples. Centro internazionale per lo studio dei papiri ercolanesi: 1107–18.

Harland, Ph. A. 2003. *Associations, Synagogues, and Congregations: Claiming a Place in Ancient Mediterranean Society*. Minneapolis. Fortress Press.

  2005. 'Familial dimensions of group identity: "brothers" (ἀδελφοί) in associations of the Greek East', *Journal of Biblical Literature* 124 (3): 491–513.

  2009. *Dynamics of Identity in the World of the Early Christians. Associations, Judeans and Cultural Minorities*, New York and London. Clark.

  2013a. *Associations, Synagogues and Congregations. Claiming a Place in Ancient Mediterranean Society*, 2nd ed. Kitchener.

  2013b. 'Banqueting values in the associations: rhetoric and reality', in D. E. Smith and H. Taussig (eds.), *Meals in the early Christian world: Social formation, experimentation, and conflict at the table*. New York and Basingstoke. Palgrave Macmillan: 73–85.

  2014. *Greco-Roman Associations: Texts, Translations, and Commentary, II. North Coast of the Black Sea, Asia Minor*. Berlin and Boston. De Gruyter.

Harris, E. M. 2008. *Demosthenes, Speeches 20–22*. Austin. University of Texas Press.

  2015. 'Towards a typology of Greek regulations about religious matters: a legal approach', *Kernos* 28: 53–83.

2018. 'Pollution for homicide after 400 BCE: more evidence for the persistence of a belief', *Dike* 20: 143–9.

Harrison, A. R. W. 1971. *The Law of Athens*. vol. 2 Oxford University Press.

Harter-Uibopuu, K. 2010. 'Erwerb und Veräußerung von Grabstätten im grie-chisch-römischen Kleinasien am Beispiel der Grabinschriften aus Smyrna', in G. Thür (ed.), *Symposion 2009. Vorträge zur griechischen und hellenistischen Rechtsgeschichte*. Vienna. Austrian Academy of Sciences: 247–70.

2013. 'Auf dass Ehren ewig währen – Epigraphische Zeugnisse zum Schutz von Auszeichnungen', in R. Breitwieser, M. Frass and G. Nightingale (eds.), *Calamus. Festschrift für Herbert Graßl zum 65. Geburtstag*. Wiesbaden. Harrassowitz: 245–60.

Hawkins, C. 2012. 'Manufacturing', in W. Scheidel (ed.), *The Cambridge Companion to the Roman Economy*. Cambridge University Press: 175–94.

2016. *Roman Artisans and the Urban Economy*. Cambridge University Press.

Heinen, H. 1989. 'L'Égypte dans l'historiographie moderne du monde hellénistique', in L. Criscuolo and G. Geraci (eds.), *Egitto e storia antica dall'ellenismo all'età araba: bilancio di un confronto*. Bologna. CLUEB: 105–35.

Hellmann, M.-Ch. 1992. *Recherches sur le vocabulaire de l'architecture grecque d'après les inscriptions de Délos*. Athens. Libraries of the French School at Athens and Rome.

2006. *L'architecture grecque 2: Architecture religieuse et funéraire*. Paris. Picard.

Hepding, H. 1907. 'Die Arbeiten zu Pergamum 1904–1905. Die Inschriften', *MDAI(A)* 32: 241–377.

Herzog, R. 1928. *Heilige Gesetze von Kos*. Berlin. Prussian Academy of Sciences.

Hiller von Gaertringen, F. 1914. Ἐπιγραφαὶ Ῥόδου, Θήρας, Νάξου, Ἀρκαδίας', *AEph*: 130–35.

Hofmann, K. P., Bernbeck, R. and Sommer, U. (eds.) 2017. *Between Memory Sites and Memory Networks. New Archaeological and Historical Perspectives*. Berlin. Topoi.

Hornblower, S. 2009. 'Did the Delphic amphiktiony play a political role in the Classical period?', in Malkin, Constantakopoulou and Panagopoulou (eds.): 39–56.

Hughes, D. O. 1974. 'Toward historical ethnography: notarial records and family history in the Middle Ages', *Historical Methods Newsletter* 7(2): 61–71.

Hurtado, L. W. 2016. *Destroyer of the Gods: Early Christian Distinctiveness in the Roman World*. Waco. Baylor University Press.

Husselman, E. 1970. 'Procedures of the record office of Tebtunis in the first century A.D.', in D. Samuel (ed.), *Proceedings of the Twelfth International Congress of Papyrology*. Toronto. A. M. Hakkert Ltd.: 223–38.

Isager, S. 2014. 'New inscriptions in the Bodrum Museum: a Hellenistic foun-dation from the area of Mylasa', *Opuscula. Annual of the Swedish Institutes at Athens and Rome* 7: 185–92.

Ismard, P. 2010. *La cité des réseaux. Athènes et ses associations, VIe–Ier siècle av. J.-C.* Paris. Sorbonne University Publications.

Jaccottet, A.-F. 2003. *Choisir Dionysos: Les associations dionysiaques ou la face cachée du dionysisme*. 2 vols. Zürich. Akanthus.

2011. 'Integrierte Andersartigkeit. Die Rolle der dionysischen Vereine', in R. Schlesier (ed.), *A Different God? Dionysos and Ancient Polytheism*, Berlin and Boston. De Gruyter: 413–31.

Jeffery, L. H. 1990. *The Local Scripts of Archaic Greece. A Study of the Origin of the Greek Alphabet and Its Development from the Eighth to the Fifth Centuries B.C.* Rev. ed. Oxford. Clarendon Press.

Johnson, A. C. 1936. *Roman Egypt to the Reign of Diocletian* (*An Economic Survey of Ancient Rome*, vol. 2). Baltimore. The Johns Hopkins University Press.

Jones, C. P. 2008. 'A Hellenistic cult-association', *Chiron* 38: 195–204.

Jones, N. F. 1987. *Public Organization in Ancient Greece: A Documentary Study*. Philadelphia. American Philosophical Society.

1999. *The Associations of Classical Athens: The Response to Democracy*. Oxford University Press.

Jost, M. 1985. *Sanctuaires et cultes d'Arcadie*. Paris. Vrin.

2003. 'Mystery cults in Arcadia', in M. Cosmopoulos (ed.), *Greek Mysteries. The Archaeology and Ritual of Ancient Greek Secret Cults*. London and New York. Psychology Press: 143–68.

Juhel, P. O., and Nigdelis, P. M. 2015. Ἕνας Δανός στη Μακεδονία του τέλους του 19ου αιώνα. Ο Karl Frederik Kinch και οι επιγραφικές του σημειώσεις. Thessaloniki. Ionian University.

Just, R. 1989. *Women in Athenian Law and Life*. London. Routledge.

Kaizer, T. 2002. *The Religious Life of Palmyra. A Study of the Social Patterns of Worship in the Roman Period*. Stuttgart. Steiner.

Kamps, W. 1937. 'Les origines de la fondation cultuelle dans la Grèce ancienne', *Archives d'histoire du Droit Oriental* 1: 145–79.

Kangle, R. P. (ed.) 1965–72. *The Kautilya Arthashastra*. 3 vols. Bombay. Motilal Banarsidass.

Karttunen, K. 1997. 'Wooden tables with ivory legs,' in R. Allchin and B. Allchin (eds.), *South Asian Archaeology 1995: Proceedings of the Thirteenth International Conference of the European Association of South Asian Archaeologists, Cambridge, 5–9 July 1995*. Vol. 2. New Delhi and Calcutta. Ancient India and Iran Trust: 557–62.

Kaufhold, H. 1976. *Die Rechtssammlung des Gabriel von Basra und ihr Verhältnis zu den anderen juristischen Sammelwerken der Nestorianer*, Berlin and Boston. De Gruyter.

Keenan, J. G. 1982–83. 'Papyrology and Roman history: 1956–1980', *CW* 76: 23–31.

Kehoe, D. P. 1992. *Management and Investment on Estates in Roman Egypt during the Early Empire*. Bonn. Habelt.

Keil, J., and von Premerstein, A. 1911. *Bericht über eine zweite Reise in Lydien*. Vienna. Hölder.

1914. *Bericht über eine III. Reise in Lydien und den angrenzenden Gebieten Ioniens*. Vienna. Hölder.

Keil, K. 1855. *Schedae Epigraphicae*. Naumburg. Sieling.

Kloppenborg, J. S. 2013. 'Membership practices in Pauline Christ groups', *Early Christianity* 4: 183–215.

    2014. 'The moralizing of discourse in Greco-Roman associations', in C. J. Hodge, S. M. Olyan, D. Ullucci and E. Wasserman (eds.), *'The One Who Sows Bountifully': Essays in Honor of Stanley K. Stowers*. Providence. Society of Biblical Literature: 215–28.

Kloppenborg, J. S., and Ascough, R. S. 2011. *Greco-Roman Associations: Texts, Translation and Commentary I. Attica, Central Greece, Macedonia and Thrace*. Berlin and New York. De Gruyter.

Kloppenborg, J. S., and Wilson, S. G. (eds.) 1996. *Voluntary Associations in the Graeco-Roman World*. London and New York. Routledge.

Koerner, R. 1987. 'Beamtenvergehen und deren Bestrafung nach frühen griechischen Inschriften', *Klio* 69: 450–98.

    1993. *Inschriftliche Gesetzestexte der frühen griechischen Polis. Aus dem Nachlaß von Reinhard Koerner*. Edited by K. Hallof. Cologne and Vienna. Böhlau.

Kohl, M. 2002. 'Das Nikephorion von Pergamon', *RA*: 227–53.

Konstan, D. 1997. *Friendship in the Classical World*. Cambridge University Press.

Krauter, S. 2004. *Bürgerrecht und Kultteilnahme. Politische und kultische Rechte und Pflichten in griechischen Poleis, Rom und antikem Judentum*. Berlin and New York. De Gruyter.

Kritzas, Ch. 2013 'Οι νέοι χαλκοί ενεπίγραφοι πίνακες από το Άργος. ΙΙ. Πρόδρομη ανακοίνωση', in D. Mulliez (eds.), *Sur les pas de Wilhelm Vollgraff. Cent ans d'activités archéologiques à Argos, Actes du colloque international organisé par la IVe EPKA et l'École française d'Athènes, 25–28 septembre 2003*. Athens. French School at Athens: 275–301.

Kron, U. 1996. 'Priesthoods, dedications and euergetism; what part did religion play in the political and social status of Greek women?', in P. Hellström and B. Alroth (eds.), *Religion and Power in the Ancient Greek World: Proceedings of the Uppsala Symposium 1993*. Uppsala. Ubsaliensis S. Academiae: 139–82.

Kruse, Th. 2020. 'The organisation of the state farmers in village administration in Roman Egypt', in M. Langellotti and D. W. Rathbone (eds.), *Village Institutions in Egypt in the Roman to Early Arab Periods* (*Proceedings of the British Academy* 231), Oxford University Press: 82–93.

Kunnert, U. 2012. *Bürger unter sich. Phylen in den Städten des kaiserzeitlichen Ostens*. Basel. Schwabe.

Langellotti, M. 2016a. 'Contracts and people in early Roman Tebtunis: a complex affair', in T. Derda, A. Łajtar, and J. Urbanik (eds.), *Proceedings of the 27th International Congress of Papyrology, Warsaw 19 July–3 August 2013* (*JJP* Supplement). Warsaw: 1725–36.

    2016b. 'Professional associations and the State in Roman Egypt: the case of first-century Tebtunis', *CE* 91: 111–134.

Lanni, A. 1997. 'Spectator sports or serious politics? *Hoi periestekotes* and the Athenian lawcourts', *JHS* 117: 183–9.

    2012. 'Publicity and the courts of classical Athens', *Yale Journal of Law and the Humanities* 24: 119–35.

Laubry, N., and Zevi, F. 2010. 'Une inscription d'Ostie et la législation impériale sur les collèges,' in M. Silvestrini (ed.), *Le tribù romane. Atti della XVIe Rencontre sur l'épigraphie (Bari 8–10 ottobre 2009)*. Bari. Edipuglia: 457–67.

2012. 'Inscriptions d'Ostie et phénomène associatif dans l'Empire romain: nouveaux documents et nouvelles considérations', *Archeologia Classica* 63: 297–343.

Laum, B. 1914. *Stiftungen in der griechischen und römischen Antike. Ein Beitrag zur antiken Kulturgeschichte*. 2 vols. Leipzig and Berlin. Teubner.

Lazaridou, K. D. 2015. ῾Εφηβαρχικὸς νόμος ἀπὸ τὴν Ἀμφίπολη', *AEph* 154: 1–48.

Le Dinahet, M.-Th. 2014. 'Les nécropoles cycladiques du Ier au IIIe s. apr. J.-C.', *Topoi* 19(1): 335–99.

Le Guen, B. 2001. *Les associations de technites dionysiaques à l'époque hellénistique*. 2 vols. Paris. De Boccard.

Leão, D. F., and Rhodes, P. J. 2015. *The Laws of Solon*. London. Tauris.

Lejeune, M. 1943. 'En marge d'inscriptions grecques dialectales. I.', *REA* 45: 183–98.

Lewis, D. M. 1974. 'Entrenchment-clauses in Attic decrees', in D. W. Bradeen and M. F. McGregor (eds.), *Phoros. Tribute to B. D. Meritt*. New York. Augustin: 81–9.

Lewis, N. 1970. 'Greco-Roman Egypt: fact or fiction?', in D. H. Samuel (ed.), *Proceedings of the Twelfth International Congress of Papyrology: Ann Arbor, 1968*. Toronto. Hakkert: 3–14.

1984. 'The romanity of Roman Egypt: a growing consensus', in *Atti del XVII Congresso internazionale di Papirologia: Napoli, 1983*, Naples. Centro internazionale per lo studio dei papiri ercolanesi: 1077–84.

Liddel, P. 2007. *Civic Obligation and Individual Liberty in Ancient Athens*. Oxford University Press.

Lipsius, J. H. 1905. *Das attische Recht und Rechtsverfahren*. Vol. 1. Leipzig. Olms.

Liu, J. 2008. 'The economy of endowments: the case of Roman associations', in K. Verboven, K. Vandorpe and V. Chankowski (eds.), *Pistoi dia tèn technèn. Bankers, Loans and Archives in the Ancient World. Studies in Honour of Raymond Bogaert*. Leuven. Peeters: 231–56.

2009. *Collegia Centonariorum: The Guilds of Textile Dealers in the Roman West*. Leiden and Boston. Brill.

2013. 'Trade, traders and guilds (?) in textiles: the case of southern Gaul and northern Italy (1st–3rd centuries AD)', in M. Gleba and J. Pásztókai-Szeőke (eds.), *Making Textiles in Pre-Roman and Roman Times. People, Places, Identities*. Oxford. Oxbow Books: 126–41.

2015. 'AE 1998, 282: a case study of public benefaction and local politics', in J. Bodel and N. Dimitrova (eds.), *Ancient Documents and their Contexts. First North American Congress of Greek and Latin Epigraphy (2011)*. Leiden and Boston. Brill: 248–62.

Lolos, Y. 2010. 'A bronze inscribed tablet from the Sikyonian countryside. A reappraisal', in G. L. Reger, F. X. Ryan and T. F. Winters (eds.), *Studies in Greek Epigraphy and History in Honour of Stephen V. Tracy*. Bordeaux. Ausonius: 275–92.

Lüddeckens, E. 1968. 'Gottesdienstliche Gemeinschaften im Pharaonischen, Hellenistischen und Christlichen Ägypten', *ZRGG* 20: 193–211.

Lüders, H. 1912. *Appendix to Epigraphia Indica and Record of the Archaeological Survey of India Vol. X: A List of Brahmi Inscriptions from the Earliest Times to about A.D. 400 with the Exception of Those of Asoka.* Calcutta. Superintendent Government Printing, India.

Luhmann, N. 1969. *Legitimation durch Verfahren.* Frankfurt. Suhrkamp.

Lupu, E. 2005. *Greek Sacred Law. A Collection of New Documents (NGSL).* Leiden and Boston. Brill.

Ma, J. 1999. *Antiochos III and the Cities of Western Asia Minor.* Oxford University Press.

2005. *Antiochos III and the Cities of Western Asia Minor.* 2nd ed. Oxford University Press.

2013. *Statues and Cities: Honorific Portraits and Civic Identity in the Hellenistic World.* Oxford University Press.

Maciá, L. 2007. *Marzeah y thiasos. Una institución convival en el Oriente Próximo Antiguo y el Mediterráneo.* Madrid. Ediciones Complutense.

Madsen, J. M. 2009. *Eager to be Roman: Greek Response to Roman Rule in Pontus and Bithynia.* London. Bloomsbury.

Mahadevan, I. 2003. *Early Tamil Epigraphy: From the Earliest Times to the Sixth Century A.D.* Cambridge, MA, and London. Harvard University Press.

Maillot, S. 2013. 'Les associations à Cos', in Fröhlich and Hamon 2013a: 199–226.

Maiuri, A. 1925. *Nuova silloge epigrafica di Rodi e Cos.* Florence. Le Monnier.

Majumdar, R. C. 1920. *Corporate Life in Ancient India.* 2nd ed. Calcutta. Mukhopadhyay.

Malay, H., and Petzl, G. 2017. *New Religious Texts from Lydia.* Vienna. Austrian Academy of Sciences.

Malkin, I. 2011. *A Small Greek World: Networks in the Ancient Mediterranean.* Oxford University Press.

Malkin, I., Constantakopoulou, Ch., and Panagopoulou, K. (eds.) 2009. *Greek and Roman Networks in the Mediterranean.* Oxford and New York. Routledge.

Malkin, I., Constantakopoulou, Ch., and Panagopoulou, K. 2007. 'Preface: Networks in the ancient Mediterranean', *MHR* 22(1): 1–9.

Malkopoulou, A. 2015. *The History of Compulsory Voting in Europe: Democracy's Duty?* London. Routledge.

Maniatis, G. C. 2009. *Guilds, Price Formation and Market Structures in Byzantium.* Farnham. Routledge.

Marchand, F. 2015. 'The associations of Tanagra: epigraphic practice and regional context', *Chiron* 45: 239–66.

Marinucci, A. 2012. *Disiecta membra. Iscrizioni latine da Ostia e Porto 1981–2009.* Rome. Soprintendenza speciale per i Beni archeologici di Roma, sede di Ostia.

Matthaiou, A. P. 2000–3, 'Φρατερικὸς νόμος Πάρου', *Horos* 14–16: 307–10.

McInerney, J. 1997. 'Parnassus, Delphi, and the Thyades', *GRBS* 38(3): 263–83.

McLaughlin, J. 2001. *The marzēaḥ in the Prophetic Literature. References and Allusions in Light of the Extra-Biblical Evidence.* Leiden, Boston and Cologne. Brill.

Meiggs, R. 1982. *Trees and Timber in the Ancient Mediterranean World.* Oxford University Press.

Menard, H. 2014. '*Convicium et clamor*: la justice romaine face aux cris de la foule', in Fr. Chauvaud and P. Prétou (eds.), *Clameur publique et émotions judiciaires de l'antiquité à nos jours.* Rennes University Press: 211–20.

Meyers, R. 2019. 'On her own: practices of female benefaction in the western Roman Empire', *AncSoc* 49: 327–50.

Migeotte, L. 2010. 'Pratiques financières dans un dème attique à la période classique: l'inscription de Plôtheia IG I³, 258', in G. Thür (ed.), *Symposion 2009. Vorträge zur griechischen und hellenistischen Rechtsgeschichte.* Vienna. Austrian Academy of Sciences: 53–66.

Mikalson, J. 1998. *Religion in Hellenistic Athens.* Los Angeles. University of California Press.

Mital, S. 2004. *Kautiliya Arthashastra Revisited.* New Delhi. Centre for Studies in Civilizations.

Mommsen, Th. 1843. *De collegiis et sodaliciis Romanorum.* Kiel. Libraria Schwersiana.

    1850. 'Römische Urkunden. III: Die *lex* des *collegium aquae*', *Zeitschrift für geschichtliche Rechtswissenschaft* 15: 345–53.

Monson, A. 2005. 'Private associations in the Ptolemaic Fayyum: the evidence of Demotic accounts', *Papyrologia Lupiensia* 14 (M. Capasso and P. Davoli eds., *New Archaeological and Papyrological Researches on the Fayyum*): 179–96.

    2006. 'The ethics and economics of Ptolemaic religious associations', *AncSoc* 36: 221–38.

    2007.'Religious associations and temples in Ptolemaic Tebtunis', in J. Frosen, T. Prola and E. Salmenkivi (eds.), *Proceedings of the 24th International Congress of Papyrology. Helsinki, 1–7 August 2004.* Helsinki. Societas Scientiarum Fennica: 769–79.

Moretti, L. 1986. 'Il regolamento degli Iobacchi ateniesi', in *L'association dionysiaque dans les sociétés anciennes. Actes de la table ronde organisée par l'École Française de Rome (24–25 Mai 1984).* Rome. French School at Rome: 261–73.

Moschetta, G. 2005. '"Collegium Aquae". Un collegio tra pubblico e privato', *RDR* 5: 1–12.

Mougeot, C. 2003. 'From the tribal to the open society: the role of medieval craft guilds in the emergence of a market order', *The Review of Austrian Economy* 16(2/3): 169–81.

Mouritsen, H. 2011. *The Freedman in the Roman World.* Cambridge University Press.

Muhs, B. 2001. 'Membership in private associations in Ptolemaic Tebtynis', *Journal of the Economic and Social History of the Orient* 44: 1–21.

Müller, H. 2003. 'Pergamenische Parerga, III. Die Athenapriesterin Brimo und die pergamenischen Nikephorien', *Chiron* 33: 433–45.

2010. 'Ein Kultverein von Asklepiasten bei einem attalidischen Phrourion im Yüntdağ', *Chiron* 40: 427–57.

Müller, H., and Wörrle, M. 2002. 'Ein Verein im Hinterland Pergamons zur Zeit Eumenes' II.', *Chiron* 32: 191–235.

Muñiz Grijalvo, E. 2005. 'Elites and religious change in Roman Athens', *Numen* 52: 255–82.

Muszynski, M. 1977, 'Les associations religieuses en Égypte d'après les sources hiéroglyphiques, démotiques et grecques', *OLP* 8: 145–74.

Mylonopoulos, J. 2006. 'Greek sanctuaries as places of communication through rituals: an archaeological perspective', in E. Stavrianopoulou (ed.), *Ritual and Communication in the Graeco-Roman World* (*Kernos Supplément* 16). Liège University Press: 69–110.

2011. 'Das griechische Heiligtum als räumlicher Kontext antiker Feste und Agone', in *Thesaurus cultus et rituum antiquorum (ThesCRA) VII: Festivals and contests*. Los Angeles. Paul Getty Museum: 43–78.

2013. 'Commemorating pious service: images in honour of male and female priestly officers in Asia Minor and the eastern Aegean in Hellenistic and Roman times', in J. Rüpke, M. Horster and A. Klöckner (eds.), *Cities and Priests: Cult Personnel in Asia Minor and the Aegean Islands from the Hellenistic to the Imperial Period*. Berlin and Boston. De Gruyter: 121–53.

Nemeth, G. 1994. 'Μεδ' ὄνθον ἐγβαλῖν. Regulations concerning everyday life in a Greek *temenos*', in R. Hagg (ed.), *Ancient Greek Cult Practice from the Epigraphical Evidence. Proceedings of the second international seminar on ancient Greek cult, organized by the Swedish Institute at Athens, 22–24 November 1991*. Stockholm. Swedish Institute at Athens: 59–64.

Nicolet, C. (ed.) 1984. *Des ordres à Rome*. Paris. Sorbonne University Publications.

Nielsen, I. 2014. *Housing the Chosen. The Architectural Context of Mystery Groups and Religious Associations in the Ancient World*. Turnhout. Brepols.

Nigdelis, P. M. 2010. 'Voluntary associations in Roman Thessalonike: in search of identity and support in a cosmpolitan society', in L. Nasrallah, Ch. Bakirtzis and S. Friesen (eds.), *From Roman to Early Christian Thessalonike: Studies in Religion and Archaeology*. Cambridge, MA, and London. Harvard Divinity School: 13–47.

Ning, K., and Hao C. 1997. *Dunhuang sheyi wenshu jijiao*. Nanjing.

Nonnis, D. 1995–96. 'Un patrono dei dendrofori di Lavinium. Onori e munificenze in un dossier epigrafico di età severiana', *Rendiconti della Pontificia Accademia Romana di Archeologia* 58: 235–62.

Norsa, M. 1937. 'Elezione del κεφαλαιωτής di una corporazione', *ASNP* 6(1): 1–7.

Oetjen, R. 2014. *Athen im dritten Jahrhundert v. Chr. Politik und Gesellschaft in den Garnisonsdemen auf der Grundlage der inschriftlichen Überlieferung.* Duisburg. Wellem.

Ogilvie, S. 2004. 'The use and abuse of trust: social capital and its deployment by early modern guilds', *CESifo Working Paper* no 1302 = *Jahrbuch für Wirtschaftsgeschichte* 2005(1): 15–52 (available online: www.cesifo-group .de/w/krlsrcrj).

2011. *Institutions and European Trade. Merchant Guilds, 1000–1800.* Cambridge University Press.

Öhler, M. 2005. 'Die Didache und antike Vereinsordnungen – ein Vergleich', in M. Pratscher and M. Öhler (eds.), *Theologie in der Spätzeit des Neuen Testaments. Vorträge auf dem Symposion zum 65. Geburtstag von K. Niederwimmer.* Vienna. Evangelical-Theological Faculty: 35–65.

Oliver, J. H. 1941. *The Sacred Gerusia* (*Hesperia Supplement* 6). Baltimore. American School of Classical Studies at Athens.

1963. 'The main problem of the Augustus inscription from Cyme', *GRBS* 4: 115–22.

1970. *Marcus Aurelius. Aspects of Civic and Cultural Policy in the East.* Princeton. American School of Classical Studies at Athens.

Orlandos, A. K. 1937–38. Ἐπιγραφαὶ τῆς Σικυωνίας', *Hellenica* 10: 5–18.

Osborne, R. 2009. 'What travelled with Greek pottery?', in Malkin, Constantakopoulou and Panagopoulou (eds.): 83–93.

Paganini, M. C. D. 2016. 'Decisional practices of private associations in Ptolemaic and early Roman Egypt', in T. Derda, A. Łajtar, and J. Urbanik (eds.), *Proceedings of the 27th International Congress of Papyrology, Warsaw 19 July – 3 August 2013* (*JJP* Supplement). Warsaw: 1889–901.

2017. 'Greek and Egyptian associations in Egypt: fact or fiction?', in B. Chrubasik and D. King (eds.), *Hellenism and the Local Communities of the Eastern Mediterranean, 400 BCE–250 CE.* Oxford University Press: 131–54.

2018. 'A terminological analysis of private associations in Ptolemaic Egypt', in A. Di Natale and C. Basile (eds.), *Atti del XVI Convegno di Egittologia e Papirologia: Siracusa 29 settembre – 2 ottobre 2016* (*Quaderni del Museo del Papiro* 15). Siracusa. Museo del Papiro: 459–78.

2020a. 'Cults for the rulers in private settings: gymnasia and associations of Hellenistic Egypt', in S. Caneva (ed.), *Materiality of Hellenistic Ruler Cults* (*Kernos Supplément* 36). Liège University Press: 125–45.

2020b. 'Epigraphic habits of private associations in the Ptolemaic *chora*', in A. K. Bowman and C. Crowther (eds.), *The Epigraphy of Ptolemaic Egypt.* Oxford University Press: 179–207.

2020c. 'Private associations and village life in early Roman Egypt', M. Langellotti and D. W. Rathbone (eds.), *Village Institutions in Egypt in the Roman to Early Arab Periods* (*Proceedings of the British Academy* 231). Oxford University Press: 41–65.

Paganini, M. C. D. in pressa. 'Religion and leisure: a gentry association of Hellenistic Egypt', in A. Cazemier und S. Skaltsa (eds.), *Associations and Religion in Context: the Hellenistic and Roman Eastern Mediterranean* (*Kernos Supplément* 39). Liège University Press.

    in pressb. 'Keep it for yourself: private associations and internal dispute resolution in Ptolemaic Egypt', in S. Waebens and K. Vandorpe (eds.), *Two Sides of the Same Coin. Dispute Resolution in Greco-Roman and Late Antique Egypt* (*Studia Hellenistica*). Leuven. Peeters.

Paliou, E., Lieberwirth, U., and Polla, S. (eds.) 2014. *Spatial Analysis and Social Spaces. Interdisciplinary Approaches to the Interpretation of Prehistoric and Historic Built Environments.* Berlin and Boston. De Gruyter.

Papazarkadas, N. 2011. *Sacred and Public Land in Ancient Athens.* Oxford University Press.

Parassoglou, G. M. 1978. *Imperial Estates in Roman Egypt.* Amsterdam. Hakkert.

Parker, R. C. T. 1996a. *Athenian Religion. A History.* Oxford. Clarendon Press.

    1996b. *Miasma: Pollution and Purification in Early Greek Religion.* 2nd ed. Oxford. Clarendon Press.

    2010. 'A funerary foundation from Hellenistic Lycia', *Chiron* 40: 103–21.

    2018a. 'The new Purity Law from Thyateira', *ZPE* 205: 178–83.

    2018b. 'Miasma: old and new problems', in Carbon and Peels (eds.): 23–33.

Parker, R. C. T., and Scullion, S. 2016. 'The mysteries of the goddess of Marmarini', *Kernos* 29: 209–66.

Paul, S. 2013. *Cultes et sanctuaires de l'île de Cos* (*Kernos Supplément* 28). Liège University Press.

Peek, W. 1941. 'Heilige Gesetze', *MDAI (A)* 46: 171–217.

Peels, S. 2016. *Hosios: A Semantic Study of Greek Piety* (*Mnemosyne Supplement* 387). Leiden and Boston. Brill.

Perry, J. S. 2006. *The Roman Collegia. The Modern Evolution of an Ancient Concept.* Leiden and Boston. Brill.

Petrakos, V. 1999a. *Ο δήμος του Ραμνούντος. Σύνοψη των ανασκαφών και των ερευνών (1813–1998). I. Τοπογραφία.* Athens. Archaeological Society at Athens.

    1999b. *Ο δήμος του Ραμνούντος. Σύνοψη των ανασκαφών και των ερευνών (1813–1998). II. Οι Επιγραφές.* Athens. Archaeological Society at Athens.

Petrovic, A. 2017. 'Greek sacred laws', in J. Kindt, E. Eidinow and R. Osborne (eds.), *Oxford Handbook of Ancient Greek Religion.* 2nd ed. Oxford University Press: 339–52.

Petrovic, A., and Petrovic, I. 2016. *Inner Purity and Pollution in Greek Religion, Volume I: Early Greek Religion.* Oxford University Press.

    2018. 'Purity of body and soul in the cult of Athena Lindia: on the eastern background of Greek abstentions', in Carbon and Peels (eds.): 225–58.

Petzl, G. 1994. *Die Beichtinschriften Westkleinasiens.* Bonn. Habelt.

Pirenne-Delforge, V. 2005. 'Personnel de culte', in *Thesaurus cultus et rituum antiquorum (ThesCRA) V: Personnel of cult, Cult instruments.* Los Angeles. Paul Getty Museum: 1–31.

2010. 'Greek priests and "cult statues": in how far are they unnecessary?', in J. Mylonopoulos (ed.), *Divine Images and Human Imaginations in Ancient Greece and Rome.* Leiden and Boston. Brill: 121–44.

Pittakes, K. S. 1842. 'No. 861', *Ephemeris Archaiologike*: 520–1.

Pleket, H. W. 1958. *The Greek Inscriptions in the 'Rijksmuseum van oudheden' at Leyden.* Leiden. Brill.

1998. 'Political culture and political practice in the cities of Asia Minor in the Roman Empire', in W. Schuller (ed.), *Politische Theorie und Praxis im Altertum.* Darmstadt. Wissenschaftliche Buchgesellschaft: 204–16.

Podes, S. 1993. 'Pay and political participation in Classical Athens. An empirical application of Rational Choice Theory', *Journal of Institutional and Theoretical Economics* 149: 495–515.

Poland, F. 1909. *Geschichte des griechischen Vereinswesens.* Leipzig. Teubner.

Price, P. L. 2013. 'Place', in N. C. Johnson, R. H. Schein and J. Winders (eds.), *The Wiley-Blackwell Companion to Cultural Geography.* Chichester. Wiley-Blackwell: 118–29.

Price, S. R. F. 1984. *Rituals and Power. The Roman Imperial Cult in Asia Minor.* Cambridge University Press.

Pugliese Carratelli, G. 1939/40. 'Per la storia delle associazioni in Rodi antica', *ASAA* 22: 147–200.

Radt, W. 1999. *Pergamon, Geschichte und Bauten einer antiken Metropole.* Darmstadt. Primus.

Raja, R. 2015. 'Staging "private" religion in Roman "public" Palmyra. The role of the religious dining tickets (banqueting tesserae)', in Cl. Ando and J. Rüpke (eds.), *Public and Private in Ancient Mediterranean Law and Religion.* Berlin, Munich and Boston. De Gruyter: 165–86.

Ramsay, W. 1889. 'Inscriptions d'Asie Mineure', *REG* 2: 17–37.

Rathbone, D. W. 1989. 'The ancient economy and Graeco-Roman Egypt', in L. Criscuolo and G. Geraci (eds.), *Egitto e storia antica dall'ellenismo all'età araba: bilancio di un confronto.* Bologna. CLUEB: 159–76.

2013. 'The romanity of Roman Egypt: a faltering consensus?', *JJP* 43: 73–91.

Raubitschek, A. E. 1981. 'A new Attic club (ERANOS)', *The J. Paul Getty Museum Journal* 9: 93–8.

Ray, H. P. 1986. *Monastery and Guild. Commerce under the Satavahanas.* New Delhi and New York. Oxford University Press.

Renberg, G. 2017. *Where Dreams May Come: Incubation Sanctuaries in the Graeco-Roman World.* 2 vols. Leiden and Boston. Brill.

Rhodes, P. J. 1981. *A Commentary on the Aristotelian* Athenaion Politeia. Oxford. Clarendon Press.

1982. 'Problems in Athenian *eisphora* and liturgies', *AJAH* 7: 1–13.

Rhodes, P. J., with Lewis, D. 1997. *The Decrees of the Greek Cities.* Oxford. Clarendon Press.

Richardson, G. 2005. 'Craft guilds and Christianity in late-medieval England. A rational-choice analysis', *Rationality and Society* 17(2): 139–89.

Riethmüller, J. W. 2005. *Asklepios: Heiligtümer und Kulte*, 2 vols. Heidelberg. Archaeology and History Press.

Robert, L. 1945. *Le sanctuaire de Sinuri près de Mylasa*. Paris. De Boccard.

1979. 'Deux inscriptions de l'époque impériale en Attique', *AJPh* 100(1): 153–65.

Roberts, C., Skeat, Th. C., and Nock, A. D. 1936. 'The gild of Zeus Hypsistos', *HThR* 29: 39–88.

Roesch, P. 1982. *Etudes béotiennes*. Paris. De Boccard.

Rohde, D. 2012. *Zwischen Individuum und Stadtgemeinde. Die Integration von Collegia in Hafenstädten*. Mainz. Antike.

Roller, L. E. 1999, *In Search of God the Mother: The Cult of Anatolian Cybele*. Berkeley, Los Angeles and London. University of California Press.

Rong, X. 1999–2000. 'The nature of the Dunhuang Library Cave and the reasons for its sealing,' trans. V. Hansen, *Cahiers d'Extreme-Asie* 11: 247–75.

2013. *Eighteen Lectures on Dunhuang*. Translated by Imre Galambos. Boston and Leiden. Brill.

Ross, L. 1845. *Inscriptiones Graecae Ineditae*, vol. 3. Berlin. Prussian Academy.

Rosser, G. 2015. *The Art of Solidarity in the Middle Ages: Guilds in England 1250–1550*. Oxford University Press.

Rostovtzeff, M. 1941. *The Social and Economic History of the Hellenistic World*. 3 vols. Oxford. Clarendon Press.

Royden, H. L. 1988. *The Magistrates of the Roman Professional Collegia in Italy from the First to the Third Century A.D.* Pisa. Giardini.

1989. 'The tenure of office of the *quinquennales* in the Roman professional *collegia*,' *AJPh* 110(2): 302–15.

Rubinstein, L. 2010. '*Praxis*: the enforcement of penalties in the late classical and early Hellenistic periods', in G. Thür (ed.), *Symposion 2009. Vorträge zur griechischen und hellenistischen Rechtsgeschichte*. Vienna. Austrian Academy of Sciences: 193–216.

2012 'Individual and collective liabilities of boards of officials in the late classical and early Hellenistic period', in B. Legras and G. Thür (eds.), *Symposion 2011. Vorträge zur griechischen und hellenistischen Rechtsgeschichte. Paris, 7.–10. September 2011*. Vienna. Austrian Academy of Sciences: 329–55.

Rudorff, A. A. F. 1850. 'Die sogenannte *lex de Magistris Aquarum*, eine altrömische Brunnenordnung', *Zeitschrift für geschichtliche Rechtswissenschaft* 15: 203–73.

Ruffing, K. 2008. *Die berufliche Spezialisierung in Handel und Handwerk: Untersuchungen zu ihrer Entwicklung und zu ihren Bedingungen in der römischen Kaiserzeit im östlichen Mittelmeerraum auf der Grundlage griechischer Inschriften und Papyri*. Rahden. VML.

Rüpke, J. (ed.) 2007. *Gruppenreligionen im römischen Reich. Sozialformen, Grenzziehungen und Leistungen*. Tübinen. Mohr Siebeck.

Rüpke, J. 2013. 'Individuals and networks', in L. Bricault and C. Bonnet (eds.), *Panthée: Religious Transformations in the Graeco-Roman Empire*. Leiden and Boston. Brill: 261–77.

Rutherford, I. 2007. 'Network theory and theoric networks', *MHR* 22(1): 23–37.

2009. 'Network theory and theoric networks', in Malkin, Constantakopoulou and Panagopoulou (eds.): 24–38.

2013, *State Pilgrims and Sacred Observers in Ancient Greece: A Study of Theōriā and Theōroi*. Cambridge University Press.

Saba, S. 2012. *The Astynomoi Law of Pergamon. A New Commentary*. Mainz. Antike.

Sablayrolles, R. 1996. *Libertinus miles. Les cohortes de vigiles*. Rome. French School at Rome.

San Nicolò, M. 1927. 'Zur Vereinsgerichtsbarkeit im hellenistischen Ägypten', in *Epitymbion Heinrich Swoboda dargebracht*. Reichenberg. Stiepel: 255–300.

1972. *Ägyptisches Vereinswesen zur Zeit der Ptolemäer und Römer*. 2 vols. 2nd. rev. ed. Munich. Beck.

Santamaría Álvarez, M. A. 2010. 'Los misterios de Esquines y su madre según Demóstenes (*Sobre la Corona* 259–260)', in F. Cortés Gabaudan and J. V. Méndez Dosuna (eds.), *Dic mihi, Musa, virum. Homenaje al profesor Antonio López Eire*. Salamanca University Press: 613–20.

Sartre, M. 1991. *L'Orient romain: provinces et sociétés provinciales en Méditerranée orientale d'Auguste aux Sévères (31 avant J.C.–235 après J.C.)*. Paris. Seuil.

Schäfer, A. 2002. 'Raumnutzung und Raumwahrnehmung im Vereinslokal der Iobakchen von Athen', in U. Egelhaaf-Gaiser and A. Schäfer (eds.), *Religiöse Vereine in der römischen Antike. Untersuchungen zu Organisation, Ritual und Raumordnung*. Tübingen. Mohr Siebeck: 173–220.

Scheid, J. 2003. 'Communauté et communauté. Réflexions sur quelques ambiguïtés d'après l'exemple des thiases de l'Égypte romaine', in N. Belayche and S. C. Mimouni (eds.), *Les communautés religieuses dans le monde gréco-romain: Essais de définition*. Turnhout. Brepols: 61–74.

Schmidt, J. 1890. 'Statut einer Municipalcurie in Africa', *RhM* 45: 599–611.

Schnöckel, K. H. 2006. *Ägyptische Vereine in der frühen Prinzipatszeit. Eine Studie über sechs Vereinssatzungen (Papyri Michigan 243–248)*. Konstanz University Press.

Schuler, Ch. (ed.) 2007. *Griechische Epigraphik in Lykien. Eine Zwischenbilanz. Akten des internationalen Kolloquiums München, 24.–26. Februar 2005 (Denkschriften der philosophisch-historischen Klasse 354. Ergänzungsbände zu den Tituli Asiae Minoris 25)*. Vienna. Austrian Academy of Sciences.

Schwartzberg, M. 2004. 'Athenian democracy and legal change', *American Political Science Review* 98: 311–25.

2010. 'Shouts, murmurs and votes: acclamation and aggregations in ancient Greece', *The Journal of Political Philosophy* 18: 1–21.

Schwyzer, E. 1937. 'Zwei Perfektformen aus Arkadien', *Zeitschrift für vergleichende Sprachforschung* 64: 41.

Scott, M. 2013. *Space and Society in the Greek and Roman Worlds*. Cambridge University Press.

Seidl, E. 1962. *Ptolemäische Rechtsgeschichte*. 2nd ed. Glückstadt. Augustin.

Senart, E. 1905–6. 'The inscriptions in the caves at Nasik', *Epigraphia Indica* 8: 59–96.

Shamasastry, R. (ed.) 1915. *Kautilya. Arthashastra*. Bangalore. Government Press.

Sherwin-White, A. N. 1966. *The Letters of Pliny. A Historical and Social Commentary*. Oxford. Clarendon Press.

Simonton, M. 2017. 'Stability and violence in classical Greek democracies and oligarchies', *ClAnt* 36: 52–103.

Sircar, D. C. 1953–54. 'Charter of Vishnusena, Samvat 649', *Epigraphia Indica* 30: 163–81.

   1963–64. 'More inscriptions from Nagarjunakonda', *Epigraphia Indica* 35: 1–36.

Sirks, A. J. B. 1993. 'Did the late Roman government try to tie people to their profession or status?', *Tyche* 8: 159–75.

Skaltsa, S. 2016. '"Housing" private associations in Hellenistic Athens: three case-studies for a place to meet and worship the gods', in O. Rodríguez Gutiérrez, N. Tran and B. Soler Huertas (eds.), *Los espacios de reunión de las asociaciones romanas. Diálogos desde la arqueología y la historia, en homenaje a Bertrand Goffaux*. Sevilla University Press: 79–92.

Skeat, T. 1966. 'A fragment on the Ptolemaic perfume monopoly (P. Lond. inv. 2859A),' *JEA* 52: 179–80.

Sokolowski, F. 1954. 'Fees and taxes in the Greek cults', *HThR* 47(3): 153–64.

   1969. *Les Lois Sacrées des cités grecques*. Paris. De Boccard.

Sosin, J. D. 1999. 'Tyrian *stationarii* at Puteoli', *Tyche* 14: 275–84.

   2005. 'Unwelcome dedications: public law and private religion in Hellenistic Laodicea by the Sea', *CQ* 55(1): 130–9.

Spatharas, D. 2006. 'Persuasive *gelōs*: public speaking and the use of laughter', *Mnemosyne* 59: 374–87.

Spawforth, A. 2012. *Greece and the Augustan Cultural Revolution*. Cambridge University Press.

Stavrianopoulou, E. 2006. *'Gruppenbild mit Dame': Untersuchungen zur rechtlichen und sozialen Stellung der Frau auf den Kykladen im Hellenismus und in der römischen Kaiserzeit*. Stuttgart. Steiner.

Steinhauer, J. 2014. *Religious Associations in the Post-Classical Polis*. Stuttgart. Steiner.

Steinmüller, M. 2008. 'Gleichheit, Freiheit, Geschwisterlichkeit. Möglichkeiten geschlechtlicher Egalität in antiken Vereinen und frühchristlichen Gemeinden'. Unpublished PhD thesis, University of Vienna.

Stern, K. 2007. 'The *marzeah* of the East and the collegia of the West: inscriptions, associations and cultural exchange in Rome and its eastern provinces,' in M. Olivé, G. Baratta and A. Almagro (eds.), *Acta XII Congressus Internationalis Epigraphiae Graecae et Latinae*. Vol. 2. Barcelona. Institute of Catalan Studies: 1387–404.

Steward, J. H. 1929. 'Diffusion and independent invention: a critique of logic,' *American Anthropologist, New Series* 31(3): 491–5.

Stiglitz, R. 1967. *Die grossen Göttinnen Arkadiens. Der Kultname ΜΕΓΑΛΑΙ ΘΕΑΙ und seine Grundlagen.* Vienna. Austrian Archaeological Institute.

Stowers, S. K. 1998. 'A cult from Philadelphia: *oikos* religion or cultic association?', in A. J. Malherbe, F. W. Norris and J. W. Thompson (eds.), *The Early Church in Its Context: Essays in Honor of Everett Ferguson (Supplement to Novum Testament* 90). Leiden. Brill: 287–301.

Suys, V. 2005. 'Les associations cultuelles dans la cité aux époques hellénistique et impériale', in V. Dasen and M. Piérart (eds.), *Ἰδίᾳ καὶ δημοσίᾳ. Les cadres 'privés' et 'publics' de la religion grecque antique.* Liège University Press: 203–18.

Tacon, J. 2001. 'Ecclesiastic *thorubos*: interventions, interruptions, and popular involvement in the Athenian assembly', *G&R* 48: 173–92.

Talbot, F. 2004. 'Désordres civils et droit d'association dans les cités de Bithynie sous le règne de Trajan', *Cahiers des Études Anciennes* 41: 92–111.

Taylor, C. 2007. 'From the whole citizen body? The sociology of election and lot in Athenian democracy', *Hesperia* 26: 323–45.

Taylor, C., and Vlassopoulos, K. (eds.) 2015a. *Communities and Networks in the Ancient Greek World.* Oxford University Press.

Taylor, C., and Vlassopoulos, K. 2015b. 'Introduction: an agenda for the study of Greek history', in Taylor and Vlassopoulos 2015a: 1–31.

Teixidor, J. 1981. 'Le thiase de Bêlastor et de Beelshamên d'après une inscription récemment découverte à Palmyre', *CRAI*: 306–14.

Terpstra, T. 2013. *Trading Communities in the Roman World: A Micro-Economic and Institutional Perspective* (Columbia Studies in the Classical Tradition 37). Leiden and Boston. Brill.

Thapar, R. 1995. 'The first millennium BC in northern India (up to the end of the Mauryan period)', in R. Thapar (ed.), *Recent Perspectives of Early Indian History.* Bombay. Popular Prakashan: 80–141.

2004. *Early India. From the Origins to AD 1300.* Berkeley and Los Angeles. University of California Press.

Thaplyal, K. 1996. *Guilds in Ancient India. A Study of Guild Organization in Northern India and Western Deccan from circa 600 B.C. to circa 600 A.D.* New Delhi. New Age International.

Thonemann, P. 2010. 'The women of Akmoneia', *JRS* 100: 163–78.

Thür, G., and Taeuber, H. 1994. *Prozessrechtliche Inschriften der griechischen Poleis: Arkadien (IPArk).* Vienna. Austrian Academy of Sciences.

Tilly, C. 2005, *Trust and Rule.* Cambridge University Press.

Tobin, J. 1997. *Herodes Attikos and the city of Athens. Patronage and conflict under the Antonines.* Amsterdam. Brill.

Tod, M. N. 1932. *Sidelights on Greek history: Three Lectures on the Light Thrown by Greek Inscriptions on the Life and Thought of the Ancient World.* Oxford. Blackwell.

1934. 'Greek inscriptions at Cairness House', *JHS* 54(2): 140–62.

Torrey, C. 1948–49. 'The exiled god of Sarepta', *Berytus* 9: 45–9.

Tracy, S. V. 1995, *Athenian Democracy in Transition. Athenian Letter-Cutters of 340 to 290 B.C.* Berkeley. University of California Press.

Tran Tam Tinh, V. 1972. *Le culte des divinités orientales en Campanie en dehors de Pompéi, de Stabies et d'Herculanum.* Leiden. Brill.

Tran, N. 2006. *Les membres des associations romaines. Le rang social des collegiati en Italie et en Gaule sous le Haut-Empire.* Rome. French School at Rome.

  2007. 'Les procédures d'exclusion des collèges professionnelles et funéraires sous le Haut-Empire: pratiques épigraphiques, normes collectives et non-dits', in C. Wolff (ed.), *Les exclus dans l'antiquité. Actes du colloque organisé à Lyon les 23–24 septembre 2004.* Paris. De Boccard: 119–38.

  2011. 'Les collèges professionnels romains: "clubs" ou "corporations"? L'exemple de la vallée du Rhône et de CIL XII 1797 (Tournon-sur-Rhône, Ardèche)', *AncSoc* 41: 197–219.

  2012a. 'Un Picton à Ostie: M. Sedatius Severianus et les corps de lénunculaires sous le principat d'Antonin le Pieux', *Revue des Études Anciennes* 114(2): 323–44.

  2012b. 'Associations privées et espace public: les emplois de "publicus" dans l'épigraphie des collèges de l'Occident romain', in M. Dondin-Payre and N. Tran (eds.), *Collegia. Le phénomène associatif dans l'Occident romain.* Bordeaux. Ausonius: 63–80.

  2014. 'C. Veturius Testius Amandus, les cinq corps de lénunculaires d'Ostie et la batellerie tibérine au début du IIIe siècle', *Mélanges de l'École Française de Rome. Antiquité* 126(1): 131–45.

  2017. 'Entreprises de construction, vie associative et organisation du travail dans la Rome impériale et à Ostie', *L'Antiquité Classique* 86: 115–27.

Trautmann, T. 1971. *Kautilya and the Arthasastra: A Statistical Investigation of the Authorship and Evolution of the Text.* Leiden. Brill.

Travlos, J. 1986. Λεξικό αρχαίων αρχιτεκτονικών όρων. Athens. Archaeological Society at Athens.

Trümper, M. 2002. 'Das Sanktuarium des "Etablissement des Poseidoniastes de Bérytos" in Delos. Zur Baugeschichte eines griechischen Vereinsheiligtums', *BCH* 126: 265–330.

  2006. 'Negotiating religious and ethnic identity: the case of clubhouses in late Hellenistic Delos', in I. Nielsen (ed.), *Zwischen Kult und Gesellschaft: Kosmopolitische Zentren des antiken Mittelmeerraumes als Aktionsraum von Kultvereinen und Religionsgemeinschaften. Akten eines Symposiums des archäologischen Instituts der Universität Hamburg, 12–14 Oktober 2005 (Hephaistos* 24). Augsburg. Camelion: 113–40.

  2011. 'Where the non-Delians met in Delos. The meeting-places of foreign associations and ethnic communities in late Hellenistic Delos', in O. M. van Nijf and R. Alston (eds.), *Political Culture in the Greek City after the Classical Age.* Leuven. Peeters: 49–100.

Tsouli, Ch. 2013. Ταφικά και επιτάφια μνημεία της Κω. Συμβολή στη μελέτη της τυπολογίας και της εικονογραφίας των επιτάφιων μνημείων των ελληνιστικών και ρωμαϊκών χρόνων. Unpublished PhD thesis, University of Athens.

Turcan, R. 2003. *Liturgies de l'initiation bacchique à l'époque romaine (Liber). Documentation littéraire, inscrite et figurée.* Paris. De Boccard.

Unwin, T. 2000. 'A waste of space? Towards a critique of the social production of space', *Transactions of the Institute of British Geographers* 25(1): 11–29.

Ustinova, Y. 2005. '*Lege et consuetudine*: Voluntary cult associations in the Greek law', in V. Dasen and M. Piérart (eds.), Ἰδίᾳ καὶ δημοσίᾳ. *Les cadres 'privés' et 'publics' de la religion grecque antique.* Liège University Press: 177–90.

van Bremen, R. 1996. *The Limits of Participation: Women and Civic Life in the Greek East in the Hellenistic and Roman Periods.* Amsterdam. Gieben.

  2013. '*Neoi* in Hellenistic cities: age class, institution, association?', in Fröhlich and Hamon 2013a: 31–58.

Van Effenterre, H., and Ruzé, F. 1994. *Nomima. Recueil d'inscriptions politiques et juridiques de l'archaïsme grec.* Vol. 1. Rome. French School at Rome.

van Minnen, P. 1987. 'Urban craftsmen in Roman Egypt', *MBAH* 6(1): 31–88.

van Nijf, O. M. 1997. *The Civic World of Professional Associations in the Roman East.* Amsterdam. Brill.

van Nijf, O. M., and Alston, R. 2011. 'Political culture in the Greek city after the Classical Age: introduction and preview', in O. M. van Nijf and R. Alston (eds.), *Political Culture in the Greek City after the Classical Age.* Leuven. Peeters: 1–26.

Van Rossum, J. 1988. *De gerousia in de Griekse steden van het Romeinse Rijk.* Leiden University Press.

van Schaik, S. 2014. 'Married monks: Buddhist ideals and practice in Kroraina', *South Asian Studies* 30(2): 269–77.

Vélissaropoulos, J. 1980. *Les nauclères grecs: recherches sur les institutions maritimes en Grèce et dans l'Orient hellénisé.* Geneva. Droz.

Venticinque, Ph. F. 2010. 'Family affairs: guild regulations and family relationships in Roman Egypt', *GRBS* 50: 273–94.

  2013. 'Matters of trust: associations and social capital in Roman Egypt', *The Center for Hellenic Studies Research Bulletin* 1(2): online.

  2015, 'Counting the associations: co-operation, conflict and interaction in Roman Egypt', in V. Gabrielsen and Ch. A. Thomsen (eds.), *Private Associations and the Public Sphere. Proceedings of a Symposium held at the Royal Danish Academy of Sciences and Letters, 9–11 September 2010.* Copenhagen. Royal Danish Academy: 314–40.

  2016. *Honor among Thieves. Craftsmen, Merchants, and Associations in Roman and Late Roman Egypt.* Ann Arbor. University of Michigan Press.

Ventroux, O. 2017. *Pergame. Les élites d'une ancienne capitale royale à l'époque romaine.* Rennes University Press.

Verboven, K. 2007. 'The associative order. Status and ethos among Roman businessmen in late Republic and early Empire', *Athenaeum* 95(2): 861–93.

  2011 'Introduction – Professional collegia: guilds or social clubs?', *AncSoc* 41: 187–95.

Verdelis, N., Jameson, M., and Papachristodoulou, I. 1975. Ἀρχαϊκαὶ ἐπιγραφαὶ ἐκ Τίρυνθος', *AEph*: 150–203.

Bibliography

Villacèque, N. 2013. 'Thorubos tōn pollōn: le spectre du spectacle démocratique', in A. Macé (ed.), *Le savoir public. La vocation politique du savoir en Grèce ancienne.* Besançon. Franche-Comté University Press: 287–312.

Vittmann, G. 2011. 'Eine Urkunde mit den Satzungen eines Kulturvereins (P. dem. Mainz 10)', in F. Feder, L. D. Morenz and G. Vittmann (eds), *Von Theben nach Giza. Festmiszellen für Stefan Grunert zum 65. Geburtstag (Göttinger Miszellen Beihefte* 10). Göttingen: Department for Egyptology and Coptology: 169–79.

Vlassopoulos, K. 2007a. *Unthinking the Greek Polis.* Cambridge University Press.

2007b. 'Beyond and below the polis: networks, associations and the writing of Greek history', *MHR* 22(1): 11–22.

Volanaki-Kontoleontos, E. 1992–98. 'Μεγάρου ἐπίσκεψις I', *Horos* 10–12: 473–90.

von Ehrenheim, H. 2015. *Greek Incubation Rituals in Classical and Hellenistic Times (Kernos Supplément* 29). Liège University Press.

Wallace, R. W. 2004. 'The power to speak – and not to listen – in ancient Athens', in I. Sluiter and R. Rosen (eds.), *Free Speech in Classical Antiquity.* Leiden. Brill: 221–32.

Wallace, S. L. 1938, *Taxation in Egypt from Augustus to Diocletian.* Princeton University Press.

Waltzing, J.-P. 1895–1900. *Etude historique sur les corporations professionnelles chez les Romains: depuis les origines jusqu'à la chute de l'Empire d'Occident.* 4 vols. Brussels and Leuven. Peeters.

Warf, B., and Arias, S. 2009. 'Introduction: the reinsertion of space in the humanities and social sciences', in B. Warf and S. Arias (eds.), *The Spatial Turn: Interdisciplinary Perspectives.* New York. Routledge: 1–10.

Weinfeld, M. 1986. *The Organizational Pattern and the Penal Code of the Qumran Sect. A Comparison with Guilds and Religious Associations of the Hellenistic-Roman Period.* Göttingen. Vandenhoeck & Ruprecht/Fribourg Switzerland University Press.

Weinreich, G. 1919. *Stiftung und Kultsatzungen eines Privatheiligtums in Philadelphia in Lydien.* Heidelberg. Winter.

Whitehead, D. 1986. *The Demes of Attica 508/7 – ca 250 B.C. A Political and Social Study.* Princeton University Press.

Wiemer, H.-U. 2003. 'Käufliche Priestertümer im hellenistischen Kos', *Chiron* 33: 263–310.

Wilcken, U. 1912. *Grundzüge und Chrestomathie der Papyruskunde.* Leipzig. Teubner.

Wilhelm, A. 1902. 'Inschrift aus dem Peiraieus', *JÖAI* 5: 127–39.

1921. *Neue Beiträge zur griechischen Inschriftenkunde VI.* Vienna. Austrian Academy of Sciences.

Wilson, S. G. 1996. 'Voluntary associations: an overview', in J. S. Kloppenborg and S. G. Wilson (eds.), *Voluntary Associations in the Graeco-Roman World.* London and New York. Routledge: 1–15.

Wittenburg, A. 1990. *Il testamento di Epikteta.* Trieste. Bernardi.

Wörrle, M. 2015. 'Die ptolemäische Garnison auf der Burg von Limyra im Licht einer neuen Inschrift', in B. Beck-Brandt, S. Ladstätter and B. Yener-Marksteiner (eds.), *Turm und Tor, Siedlungsstrukturen in Lykien und benachbarten Kulturlandschaften*. Vienna. Austrian Academy of Sciences: 291–304.

Yamamoto, T., Dohi, Y., and Ishida, Y. 1988–89. *Tun-huang and Turfan Documents, Concerning Social and Economic History, vol. IV. She Associations and Related Documents*. Tokyo. The Toyo Bunko.

Yang, L. 1950. 'Buddhist monasteries and four money-raising institutions in Chinese history,' *Harvard Journal of Asiatic Studies* 13(1/2): 174–91.

Yunis, H. 2005. *Demosthenes Speeches 18 and 19*. Austin. University of Texas Press.

Zachhuber, J. 2018. 'The lost priestesses of Rhodes? Female religious offices and social standing in Hellenistic Rhodes', *Kernos* 31: 83–110.

Zevi, F. 2001. 'Iscrizioni e personaggi nel Serapeo', in R. Mar (ed.), *El santuario de Serapis en Ostia*. Tarragona. Universitat Rovira i Virgili: 171–200.

2008. 'I collegi di Ostia e le loro sedi associative tra Antonini e Severi', in C. Berrendonner, M. Cébeillac-Gervasoni and L. Lamoine (eds.), *Le quotidien municipal dans l'Occident romain*. Clermont-Ferrand. Blaise-Pascal University Press: 477–505.

Ziebarth, E. 1896. *Das griechische Vereinswesen*. Leipzig. Hirzel.

1914. *Aus dem griechischen Schulwesen. Eudemos von Milet und Verwandtes*. 2nd ed. Leipzig. Teubner.

Zimmermann, C. 2002. *Handwerkervereine im griechischen Osten des Imperium Romanum*. Mainz and Bonn. Roman-German Central Museum.

Zimmermann, K. 2016. '*Leges sacrae* – antike Vorstellungen und moderne Konzepte. Versuch einer methodischen Annäherung an eine umstrittene Textkategorie', in D. Bonanno, P. Funke and M. Haake (eds.), *Rechtliche Verfahren und religiöse Sanktionierung in der griechisch-römischen Antike*. Stuttgart. Steiner: 223–32.

Zoumbaki, S. 2019. 'Sulla's relations with the poleis of central and southern Greece in a period of transitions', in A. Eckert and A. Thein (eds.), *Sulla. Politics and Reception*. Berlin and Boston. De Gruyter: 33–53.

Subject Index

Index Locorum

1. Greek and Latin Inscriptions

2. Papyri and Scrolls

3. Greek and Latin Literary Works

4. Chinese Literary Works and Inscriptions

5. Indian Literary Works and Inscriptions

6. Syriac Texts